THE HEINLE
Picture Dictionary
LESSON PLANNER

HEINLE
CENGAGE Learning

Australia • Brazil • Japan • Korea • Mexico • Singapore • Spain • United Kingdom • United States

HEINLE
CENGAGE Learning™

The Heinle Picture Dictionary Lesson Planner
Rob Jenkins

Publisher, Adult & Academic: James W. Brown

Senior Acquisitions Editor, Adult & Academic:
Sherrise Roehr

Director of Product Development:
Anita Raducanu

Publisher, Global ELT: Christopher Wenger

Senior Development Editor: Jill Korey O'Sullivan

Development Editors: Sarah Barnicle,
Rebecca Klevberg

Editorial Assistants: Katherine Reilly,
Christine Galvin, and Lindsey Musen

Product Marketing Manager: Laura Needham

Field Marketing Manager: Donna Lee Kennedy

International Marketing Manager: Ian Martin

Director of Product Marketing: Amy Mabley

Contributing Editor: Robyn Brinks

Senior Production Editor: Maryellen E. Killeen

Senior Print Buyer: Mary Beth Hennebury

Photo Researcher: Melissa Goodrum

Photo Editor and Permissions Manager:
Sheri Blaney

Indexer: Alexandra Nicherson

Project Management, Design, and Composition:
Seven Evanston, Inc.

Cover Design: Seven Evanston, Inc.

Cover Image: © 2004 Roy Wiemann c/o
the ispot.com

Credits appear on page 262, which constitutes a
continuation of the copyright page.

ISBN-13: 978-0-8384-4413-9

ISBN-10: 0-8384-4413-X

Heinle
20 Channel Center Street
Boston, MA 02210
USA

Cengage Learning is a leading provider of customized learning solutions with office locations around the globe, including Singapore, the United Kingdom, Australia, Mexico, Brazil, and Japan. Locate your local office at
www.cengage.com/global

Cengage Learning products are represented in Canada by Nelson Education, Ltd.

Visit Heinle online at **elt.heinle.com**

Visit our corporate website at **www.cengage.com**

Printed in the United States of America
7 16 15 14 13 12

Contents

6 Housing

7 Food

8 Clothing

9 Transportation

10 Health

11 Work

12 Earth and Space

13 Animals, Plants, and Habitats

14 School Subjects

15 The Arts

16 Recreation

Acknowledgments

The publisher would like to thank the following reviewers, consultants, and participants in focus groups:

Susan Alexandre
Trimble Technical High School
Ft. Worth, TX

Lizbeth Ascencio
Dona Ana Branch
  Community College
Las Cruces, NM

Pam S. Autrey
Central Gwinnett High School
Lawrenceville, GA

JoEllen Barnett
K.E. Taylor Elementary School
Lawrenceville, GA

Linda Boice
Elk Grove Unified School District
Sacramento, CA

Chan Bostwick
Los Angeles Unified School District
Los Angeles, CA

Diana Brady-Herndon
Napa Valley Adult School
Napa, CA

Mona Brantley
Des Moines Area
  Community College
Ankeny, Iowa

Petra Callin
Child Services Center,
  Portland Public Schools
Portland, OR

David Chávez
Horizonte Instruction and
  Training Center
Salt Lake City, UT

Kathy Connelly
Ed Shands Adult School
Oakland, CA

María de Lourdes Colín Escalona
Toluca, Mexico

Sam Cucciniello
Belmont High School
Los Angeles, CA

Jennifer Daniels
Mesa County Valley School
  District 51
Grand Junction, CO

Jeff Diuglio
Boston University CELOP /
  Harvard IELP
Auburndale, MA

Dana Dusbiber
Luther Burbank High School
Sacramento, CA

Michal Eskayo
St. Augustine College
Chicago, IL

Sara Farley
Wichita High School East
Wichita, KS

Kathleen Flynn
Glendale Community College
Glendale, CA

Utzuinic Garcés
Mexico City, Mexico

Nancy Garcia
Riverbank High School
Riverbank, CA

Gerónima Garza
Cypress-Fairbanks
  Independent School District
Houston, TX

Sally Gearhart
Santa Rosa Junior College
Santa Rosa, CA

Julie Gomez-Baker
Mesa Unified School District
Mesa, AZ

Virginia Guleff
Miramar College
Escondido, CA

Katalin Gyurindak
Mt. San Antonio College
Walnut, CA

Orin Hargraves
Westminster, MD

Iordana Iordanova
Triton College
River Grove, IL

Ocean Jones
Merced High School
Merced, CA

Gemma Kang
Wonderland
Seoul, Korea

Vicki Kaplan
Adams 12 Schools
Thornton, CO

Dale R. Keith
Miami-Dade County
  Public Schools
Miami, FL

Alyson Kleiber
Stamford Public Schools
Stamford, CT

Jean Lewis
Clark County School District
Las Vegas, NV

Virginia Lezhnev
Center for Language
  Education and Development
Washington, DC

Mabel Magarinos
Orange County Public Schools
Orlando, FL

Elizabeth Minicz
William Rainey Harper College
Palatine, IL

Dianne Mortensen
John J Pershing Intermediate
  School
Brooklyn, NY

Kathryn Nelson
Wichita High School North
Wichita, KS

Andrea O'Brien
Lawrence Adult Learning Center
Lawrence, MA

Denis O'Leary
Rio del Valle Jr. High School
Oxnard, CA

Dianne Ogden
Snow College
Ephraim, UT

Bari N. Ramirez
L.V. Stockard Middle School
Dallas, TX

Nelda Rangel
Brownsville ISD Adult Ed
Brownsville, TX

David L. Red
Fairfax County Public Schools
Falls Church, VA

Eric Rosenbaum
BEGIN Managed Programs
New York, NY

Federico Salas
North Harris College—
  Community Education
Houston, TX

Claudia Sasía Pinzón
Instituto México de Puebla AC
Puebla, Mexico

Linda Sasser
Alhambra School District
San Gabriel, CA

Laurie Shapero
Miami Dade Community College
Miami, FL

Rayna Shaunfield
College of the Mainland
Texas City, TX

Carmen Siebert-Martinez
Laredo Community College
Laredo, TX

Luciana J. Soares de Souza
Britannia Juniors
Rio de Janeiro, Brazil

Susanne Stackhouse
Language Etc.
Washington, DC

Chris Lawrence Starr
Level Creek Elementary
Sewanee, GA

Betty Stone
SCALE—Somerville Center for
  Adult Learning Experience
Somerville, MA

Charlotte Sturdy
Boston, MA

Rebecca Suarez
University of Texas
El Paso, TX

Kathy Sucher
Santa Monica College
Santa Monica, CA

The Teachers of the Harvard
  Bridge Program
Harvard Bridge to Learning
  Program
Cambridge, MA

William Vang
Sacramento City Unified
  School District
Sacramento, CA

James R. Voelkel
Dibner Institute for the History of
  Science and Technology
Cambridge, MA

Wendell Webster
Houston READ Commission
Houston, TX

Colleen Weldele
Palomar College
San Marcos, CA

To the Teacher

About The Heinle Picture Dictionary

The Heinle Picture Dictionary is an invaluable vocabulary resource for students learning the English language. It presents the most essential vocabulary for beginning to intermediate students in a unique format. In contrast to conventional picture dictionaries that illustrate target words in isolation, *The Heinle Picture Dictionary* conveys word meaning through the illustration of these words within meaningful, real-world contexts. It also offers students a multitude of opportunities to see, use, hear, and practice these words in context.

The dictionary is organized into 16 thematic units. Each two-page lesson within a unit focuses on a sub-theme of the broader unit theme. So, for example, under the unit theme of *Housing*, there are lessons focusing on different styles of houses, specific rooms of a house, finding a house, household problems, household chores, etc.

The focal point of each lesson is the word list and the corresponding illustration(s) and/or photograph(s) that illustrate the words. The word lists are arranged for ease of navigation, with the words appearing in the order in which they are illustrated in the art. Singular words in the word list are preceded by an indefinite article (or the definite article, in special cases where the definite article would be more common or appropriate). The inclusion of articles is intended to help students understand when and how articles should be used with the words in the dictionary.

Each lesson includes *Words in Context, Words in Action,* and *Word Partnerships. Words in Context* is a short reading that features a selection of the words from the word list. *Words in Action* is a pair of activities that help students put the words into meaningful use. *Word Partnerships* is a selection of collocations that exposes students to high-frequency English word pairings using words from the word list.

Scientific Research Based

The Heinle Picture Dictionary was developed with research in mind. Research supports the idea that vocabulary is most effectively learned through repeated and varied exposure (Anderson, 1999) and through a strategic approach (Taylor, Graves, van den Broek, 2000). *The Heinle Picture Dictionary* provides students with not only clear illustrations to illuminate word meaning, but also numerous opportunities to encounter and use new vocabulary. The result is an approach to vocabulary learning that reinforces understanding of word meaning and helps students take ownership of new words.

The Heinle Picture Dictionary is adaptable to a variety of situations and purposes. Appropriate for both classroom and self study, *The Heinle Picture Dictionary* can be used as a stand-alone vocabulary and language learning resource or, using the array of available ancillaries, as the core of *The Heinle Picture Dictionary* program.

Word Lists

The following list includes a few ideas that can be incorporated into the class to provide practice with the vocabulary:

- **Brainstorm to gather ideas.** With the books closed, ask students to brainstorm words they think might be in the lesson you are about to begin. Then have students check to see how many items they predicted correctly.

- **Check to see what the students already know.** As a class, ask students to cover the word lists and identify pictures by numbers.

- **Introduce vocabulary.** Present each word to the students. Ask them to listen to you or the audio and repeat. Help them with pronunciation and check for comprehension.

- **Quiz students.** Ask students to point to pictures that correspond to words you call out. *Or,* ask students to point to pictures that correspond to words embedded within a sentence or a paragraph that you read aloud.

- **Have students quiz each other.** Student A covers the word list and student B asks student A to point to the correct picture. *Or,* ask students to work in pairs to define the meaning of words in the list using their own words.

- **Play Bingo.** Ask students to choose any eight words from the list and write them down on a piece of paper. Call out words to the class at random. When a student has a word on his/her list, he/she checks it off. The first student to check off every word on his/her list wins.

- **Classify.** Ask students to classify vocabulary on a chart or in a cluster diagram. Templates for many charts and diagrams are available on the *Activity Bank CD-ROM* or can be produced by the students.

- **Do a dictation.** Give students spelling tests, dictate the *Words in Context,* or dictate sentences containing vocabulary. This can also be done as a pairwork activity in which one student gives the words or sentences to another.

- **Have students create sentences/paragraphs.** Ask students to produce sentences or paragraphs using the vocabulary from the list.

- **Elicit more vocabulary.** Elicit from students additional vocabulary related to the theme of the lesson.

- **Encourage discussion.** Discuss the theme of the lesson, using the new vocabulary.

- **Provide real-life tasks.** Have students use the vocabulary in a real-life task, such as making floor plans, giving directions, giving instructions, completing forms, etc.

Words in Context

Words in Context introduces students to words from the word list in the context of a reading about the lesson topic. In addition to introducing vocabulary from the lesson in context, these readings offer a number of pedagogical possibilities. They provide interesting information that can be used to stimulate classroom discussion. The readings can also be used for classroom dictations or as models for writing.

Words in Action

The *Words in Action* section provides students with multi-skill activities to practice and reinforce the vocabulary. These activities are especially useful as an application after the students become comfortable with the new vocabulary.

Word Partnerships

The *Word Partnerships* section provides students with common high-frequency collocations using words from the word list. It may be helpful to show pictures or bring in real-life examples of the noun and adjective-based collocations, or to "perform" verb-based collocations for the class. Many of the "Word List" activities suggested above would work equally well with *Word Partnerships*.

Teaching Grammar with *The Heinle Picture Dictionary*

The scenes in *The Heinle Picture Dictionary* can be used as an effective tool for practicing grammar tenses. The following is an approach to using the dictionary to teach grammar.

Tell students to look at a scene in one of the lessons. Identify a time frame. For example, if you're teaching present continuous, tell the students to imagine that everything in the scene is happening now.

1. Identify the context—usually a story, a class discussion, or a task can work well here. Avoid correcting students at this point.

2. Reveal the objective. Let the students know the particular grammar point you will focus upon.

3. Present the structure using a simple chart. Remember to keep the context in mind.

4. Ask students to describe the picture, using the target tense. As an additional challenge, you may have students ask each other questions about the illustration.

5. Provide either written or oral practice.

6. Evaluate students' use and comprehension of the structure.

7. Provide an application that allows students to use the structure in a more independent and less guided way.

The same scene can be used over and over again to teach different tenses. The next time the scene is used to teach or review a tense, students will already be familiar with the vocabulary, so it will be easier for them to focus on the grammar.

Supplemental Materials

The Lesson Planner. The full-color *Lesson Planner* provides complete lesson plans at three different levels for each lesson in the dictionary. The levels are coded as follows:

    ★ = Beginning Low

    ★★ = Beginning

    ★★★ = Beginning High/Intermediate Low

Classes often differ in exact level, so please consider these levels only as suggestions. They are primarily given to indicate the increasing difficulty of the lessons.

The lesson plans take the instructor through each stage of a lesson, from warm-up, introduction, and presentation through to practice and application. The *Lesson Planner* includes the *Activity Bank CD-ROM,* which has additional activities for each unit. These worksheets can be downloaded and customized by the instructor.

Each of the three lesson plans provided for every lesson in *The Heinle Picture Dictionary* is designed to be used in a full class period. This planner is different from a traditional teacher's guide in that it not only gives suggestions for what to do with the student material, but it also helps you to organize your entire class experience into a proven and productive lesson plan approach. The objective-driven lesson plans propose a variety of tasks and activities that culminate in an application and often an optional project.

As you incorporate lesson plans into your instruction, you will discover how this approach ensures effective teaching and successful language learning. The lesson plan format consists of the following:

- **Warm-up and Review**—Students are given tasks or activities that will activate their prior knowledge, preparing them for the lesson.

- **Introduction**—Students are given the objective for the lesson. This is an essential step as students must know what it is they will be learning and why they will be learning it.

- **Presentation**—Teachers present new material, check student understanding, and prepare students for the practice.

- **Practice**—Students practice an activity provided by the teacher.

- **Evaluation**—The teacher checks the students' ability to do the previous practice as an indication of their readiness to perform the application.

- **Application**—Students demonstrate their ability to perform the objective of a lesson more independently, with less teacher guidance.

The HPD Workbooks. There are two HPD Workbooks, each with its own supplemental audio program. There will be one for beginning and the other for intermediate students. The full-color workbooks are correlated page by page to the dictionary. They have a variety of activities, including listening activities, to support student learning.

The HPD Interactive CD-ROM. This interactive CD-ROM provides an abundance of interactive activities to reinforce the vocabulary learned in *The Heinle Picture Dictionary.*

The HPD Audio Tapes and CDs include the readings and word lists.

We hope *The Heinle Picture Dictionary* becomes a source of engaging, meaningful language learning for your students. Please feel free to contact us at www.heinle.com with your comments and suggestions.

Welcome to
THE HEINLE PICTURE DICTIONARY

Four thousand words are presented in 16 contextualized, thematic units. Each lesson in the unit presents vocabulary through color photographs and illustrations, contextualized readings, high-frequency word patterns study, and active learning opportunities.

"Words in Context" shows how the language is actually used through accessible, contextualized readings at a high-beginning level.

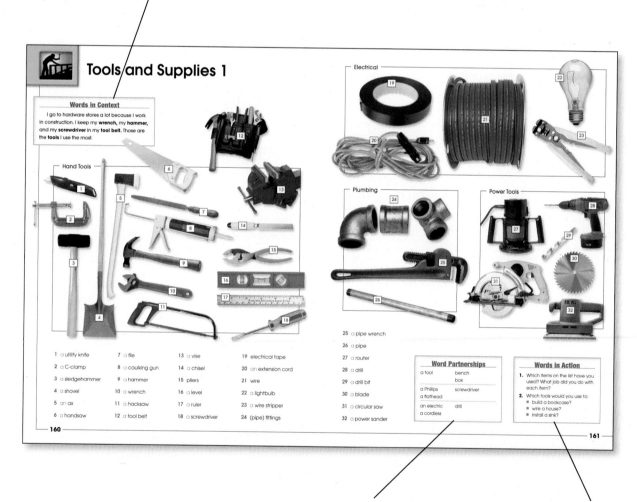

"Word Partnerships" expands students' use and understanding of high-frequency word patterns and collocations.

"Words in Action" gives critical thinking activities designed to help students put the vocabulary into meaningful use.

- The full-color **Lesson Planner** includes over 300 fully developed lesson plans that provide extensive support for the busy teacher.

  The **Lesson Planner** provides lesson plans at three levels for each lesson in the dictionary. The lessons are coded as follows:

  ★ = Beginning Low

  ★★ = Beginning

  ★★★ = Beginning High/Intermediate Low

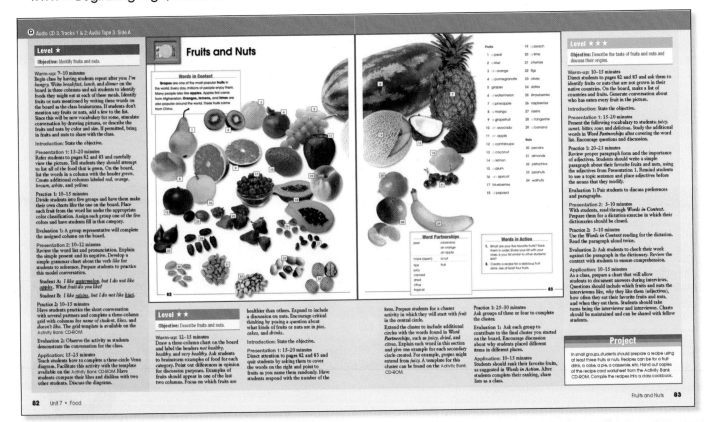

- **The Activity Bank CD-ROM** (included with the **Lesson Planner**) contains reproducible activity masters that can be customized for individual and classroom use.

- **The Heinle Picture Dictionary Workbooks,** beginning and intermediate, emphasize vocabulary and listening skills. Each workbook has its own audio program.

- **The Heinle Picture Dictionary Interactive CD-ROM** offers additional vocabulary practice through activities, games, and word webs.

- **The Heinle Picture Dictionary Transparencies** provide opportunities for group viewing of vocabulary and for class interaction.

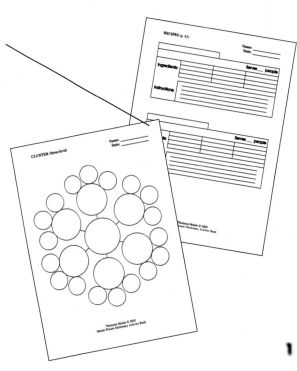

Level ★

Objective: Identify numbers associated with life skills.

Warm-up: 10–15 minutes
Before students open their books, write the school phone number on the board. Recite the phone number with them. Show how the numbers are grouped together in the United States:

(000) 000-0000

Write the address of the school on the board and explain how street numbers and the zip codes are written in the United States. Ask students to locate other numbers in the classroom. Mention that we also find numbers in games like baseball, football, soccer, and pool. Define *pool*. Ask for other examples.

Introduction: State the objective.

Presentation 1: 10–15 minutes
Ask students to open their dictionaries to **page 2**. Go over all the numbers on the pool balls (1–21). Briefly discuss the other numbers on the page. Say a number and ask students to point to that number in the dictionary. Prepare students for dictation by saying a few numbers and asking them to write the numbers on their papers.

Practice 1: 5–7 minutes
Read the phone numbers provided below as dictation. Ask students to write the numbers they hear. To begin, say each number one at a time. Add more of a challenge by sometimes saying numbers together like *23* or *14*.

(714) 555-2314
(714) 555-7654
(714) 555-6615
(714) 555-8974

Evaluation 1: Check the answers with the class.

Presentation 2: 10–15 minutes
Read *Words in Action*. Prepare students to perform this model conversation.

Student A: *What's your address?*

Student B: *My address is _____.*

Make a two-column chart on the board that students can copy. Label the first column *name* and the second *street number*. Show students how they will complete the chart by interviewing their classmates. There is a template on the Activity Bank CD-ROM to facilitate this activity.

Practice 2: 10–15 minutes
Have students talk to five other students and record the information. **Evaluation 2:** Ask for volunteers to demonstrate in front of the class.

Application: 15–25 minutes
Make a class phone directory for students who wish to participate.

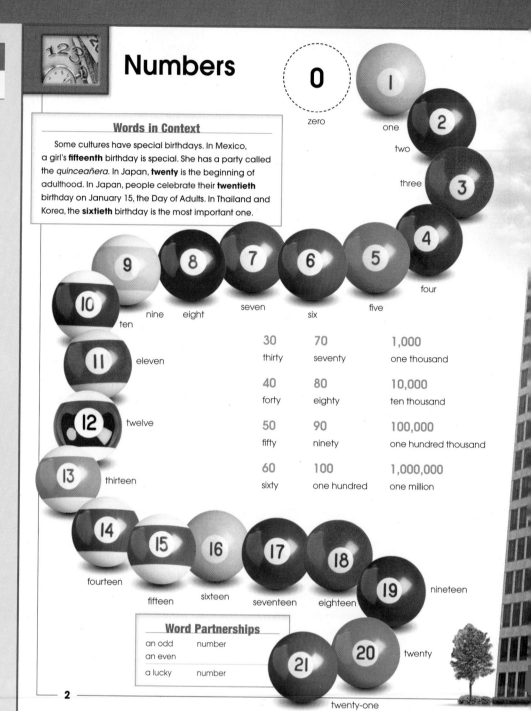

Numbers

Words in Context

Some cultures have special birthdays. In Mexico, a girl's **fifteenth** birthday is special. She has a party called the *quinceañera*. In Japan, **twenty** is the beginning of adulthood. In Japan, people celebrate their **twentieth** birthday on January 15, the Day of Adults. In Thailand and Korea, the **sixtieth** birthday is the most important one.

0 zero
1 one
2 two
3 three
4 four
5 five
6 six
7 seven
8 eight
9 nine
10 ten
11 eleven
12 twelve
13 thirteen
14 fourteen
15 fifteen
16 sixteen
17 seventeen
18 eighteen
19 nineteen
20 twenty
21 twenty-one

30 thirty	70 seventy	1,000 one thousand
40 forty	80 eighty	10,000 ten thousand
50 fifty	90 ninety	100,000 one hundred thousand
60 sixty	100 one hundred	1,000,000 one million

Word Partnerships

an odd   number
an even
a lucky   number

2

Level ★ ★

Objective: Use ordinal numbers.

Warm-up: 10–12 minutes
Write the following list on the board:
  pages in this book
  people in this school
  classrooms in this school
  cars in the parking lot
Split students into small groups and ask each group to guess how many of each there are. Discuss the answers.

Introduction: State the objective.

Presentation 1: 15–20 minutes
Ask students to open to **pages 2 and 3**. Review cardinal and ordinal numbers with students. Also present odd and even numbers from *Word Partnerships*. Work particularly with the pronunciation of the ordinal numbers on **page 3**. Help students practice by saying an ordinal number and asking them to point to it in the picture. *Note:* In many U.S. buildings, the first floor is called the *ground floor*. In this

21st	twenty-first
20th	twentieth
19th	nineteenth
18th	eighteenth
17th	seventeenth
16th	sixteenth
15th	fifteenth
14th	fourteenth
13th	thirteenth
12th	twelfth
11th	eleventh
10th	tenth
9th	ninth
8th	eighth
7th	seventh
6th	sixth
5th	fifth
4th	fourth
3rd	third
2nd	second
1st	first

Fractions

$^1/_4$ = one-quarter / a quarter

$^1/_2$ = one-half / a half

$^2/_3$ = two-thirds

$^3/_4$ = three-fourths / three quarters

Words in Action

1. Work in a group. Practice reading the following:
   - 25 minutes / 62 students / 98 pages
   - 12th birthday / 16th floor / 21st of May
2. Work with a partner. Ask and answer these questions:
   - What's your street address?
   - What's your phone number?

3

case, the next floor is called the first floor, and so on.

Practice 1: 10–15 minutes
Prepare students for dictation and then read the following:
On my twelfth birthday, I ate pizza for the second time. We went to a restaurant on First Street. The restaurant was on the eighteenth floor of a tall office building. It was a great night.

Evaluation 1: Check student work and focus on spelling of ordinal numbers.

Application: 20–30 minutes
Explain to students that the building in the picture has many large offices inside. A different company has offices on each floor. Tell students that the first floor is a lobby. Help them understand what a *lobby* is. Tell them that on the second and third floors are the offices of a major department store. Split students into small groups and ask them to identify what other kinds of offices are often in high-rise buildings. Then have them report ideas to the class.

Objective: Use ordinal numbers for dates and fractions to express needs.

Warm-up: 10–15 minutes
Talk to students briefly about the importance of dates such as birthdays and holidays in different cultures. Refer students to **page 2** and ask them to read **Words in Context**. Discuss the paragraph with the class.

Introduction: State the objective.

Presentation 1: 15–20 minutes
Ask students what time they eat their biggest meal of the day. You might mention when you eat yours. Ask students to close their dictionaries as you draw a large circle on the board and label it *a large pepperoni pizza*. Ask students how much of the pizza they can eat at one time. If students have difficulty expressing what they mean, have them draw a circle on their paper and have them fill in the amount in the circle. Refer students to **page 3**. Review fractions and their pronunciations. Revisit the previous conversation about how much pizza they can eat, but have them answer in fractions. They should also learn *a whole pizza* if they don't already know the term. Write the following on the board:

a pot of rice   *a large order of fries*
a gallon of milk   *a loaf of bread*

Practice 1: 15–20 minutes
Ask students to write down how much of each item they can eat at one time. Demonstrate how they can create a Venn diagram to compare their answers with a partner. There is a Venn diagram template available on the Activity Bank CD-ROM.

Evaluation 1: Observe the activity.

Application: 25–30 minutes
Form "family" groups. Tell students to imagine that they are a family and they have to share the food listed on the board. Ask them to determine how they will split the food based on how much they identified they could eat. In other words, what portion or fraction of the food will each family member get? Ask a few questions, such as *What happens if everyone wants a piece of pizza, but you have five people in your family? How much can each person eat?*

Project

Have students form groups and ask members to name every place they can think of where numbers are used in their daily lives. Challenge each group to identify the most places or occasions in five minutes. Their lists should include examples for each item using ordinal and cardinal numbers and fractions. Give examples: cooking: two cups flour; baseball: first base. Ask groups to write their answers on the board so everyone will have one reference list for their notes.

Level ★

Objective: Read a clock.

Warm-up: 8–10 minutes
Direct students' attention to a clock or watch. Start counting seconds. After counting 20 seconds, have students estimate the time it takes to do each of the following tasks:

walk to the classroom door and back
walk to the board and back
stand up and sit down five times

Write the tasks on the board in a column. Label a second column *seconds* and then estimate how long it will take you to do each task. Mark your guesses on the board. Then ask a student to time you and see how accurate you were. Add a third column to the board that will be used later in Presentation 2.

Introduction: State the objective.

Presentation 1: 10–15 minutes
Add the following tasks to the chart you made in the Warm-up, but change the label from *seconds* to *hours/minutes/seconds.*

brush your teeth
eat breakfast
travel (drive, walk, or ride) to class

Ask students to open to **page 4.** Review the vocabulary dealing with periods of time.

Practice 1: 7–15 minutes
Ask students to complete their own chart and instruct them to leave the third column blank. Then write the following question on the board: *How long does it take you to _____?* Have partners ask each other the question, filling in the blank with a different activity each time. Demonstrate.

Evaluation 1: Observe student exchanges.

Presentation 2: 10–15 minutes
Present and read the clocks on **page 5.** Explain that the times are referring to hours and minutes, even though those words are not used. Label the third column on the board *time.* Complete your chart with the time you perform each activity. **Note:** Since there are various ways to say the time, it might be most productive if you choose only one way to read each time: e.g., say *six-fifteen* instead of *quarter past six.*

Practice 2: 10–15 minutes
Read **Words in Action.** Ask students to complete the charts about themselves and then ask a partner the question *What time do you _____?*

Evaluation 2: Encourage volunteers to demonstrate.

Application: 15–25 minutes
Have students form groups and add new tasks to their charts after discussing ideas. Help them add more activities and complete one ordered chart based on the most popular answers.

Time

Words in Context

I usually get up at about eight o'clock. But sometimes I like to get up before **dawn.** I love the quiet of the **sunrise.** About once a **month** I sleep until **noon.** On those days, there aren't enough **hours** in the day. **Night** comes much too soon.

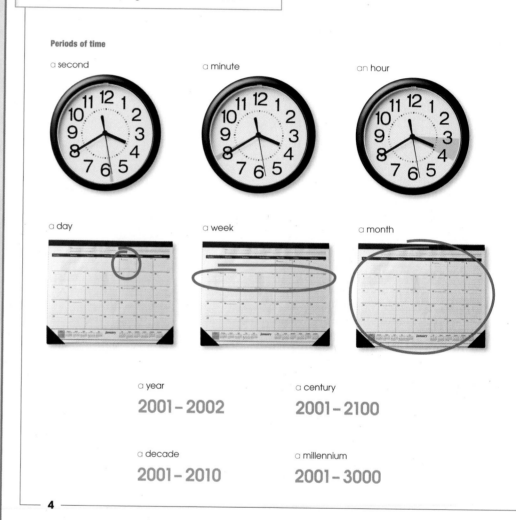

Periods of time

a second   a minute   an hour

a day   a week   a month

a year
2001–2002

a century
2001–2100

a decade
2001–2010

a millennium
2001–3000

4

Level ★ ★

Objective: Discuss daily schedules.

Warm-up: 10–12 minutes
Ask students what time class starts. Be sure to correct them if they don't use *at.* Pursue conversation with various other questions, such as *What time does class end?* and *What time do you eat breakfast?* In groups, have students discuss the times they do different things. Instruct students to open their dictionaries to **page 5** and review the clocks.

Introduction: State the objective.

Presentation 1: 15–20 minutes
Ask students to take out a piece of paper or use the planner worksheet found on the Activity Bank CD-ROM. Give students a class schedule and ask them to write their daily activities in the planner. Review their answers. Ask various questions using the new vocabulary in **Word Partnerships** and **Times of day.**

Times of day

 sunrise / dawn

 morning

 noon / midday

 afternoon

 evening

 sunset / dusk

 night

midnight

Clock times

 six o'clock

 six twenty-five /
twenty-five past six /
twenty-five after six

 six forty-five /
(a) quarter to seven /
(a) quarter of seven

 six-oh-five /
five past six /
five after six

 six-thirty /
half past six

 six fifty-five /
five to seven /
five of seven

 six fifteen /
(a) quarter past six /
(a) quarter after six

 six thirty-five /
twenty-five to seven /
twenty-five of seven

Word Partnerships	
at	ten o'clock
	night
in	the morning
	the evening
every	day
once a	week
	month
this	week
last	month
next	year
two hours	ago
five months	

Words in Action

1. What time do you usually get up? Have breakfast? Leave home in the morning? Have lunch? Go to bed?

2. What is your favorite time of day? Why? Discuss with a partner.

Objective: Describe past activities.

Warm-up: 20–40 minutes
Ask students what time they go to sleep and what time they wake up. Then ask how many hours they sleep every day. Draw a bar graph on the board illustrating the number of hours people in the classroom sleep. The vertical axis should list the number of students, and the horizontal axis should list the number of hours: *3–4 hours, 5–6 hours, 7–8 hours,* and *9–10 hours.* Discuss the bar graph after completing it as a class.

Read **Words in Context** on **page 4.** Encourage students to raise their hands if the paragraph describes them.

Introduction: State the objective.

Presentation 1: 10–20 minutes
Review all the vocabulary on **pages 4 and 5** as a class. Pay close attention to the words that would lead students to speak in the past tense. Tell students about an experience you had when you visited another country, or, if you are an immigrant, when you arrived the first time in this country. Challenge students to write down every past-tense verb they hear. Discuss the verbs. Write the following prompt on the board: *I came here _____ months (years) ago.*

Practice 1: 20–30 minutes
Ask students to write a paragraph about a time they traveled to a new place. Ask them to use at least four words from **pages 4 and 5.** If this proves difficult, consider writing your own personal paragraph on the board as a model.

Evaluation 1: Collect paragraphs or ask students to peer correct.

Application: 15–20 minutes
Ask students to share their paragraphs in small groups. After they compare and discuss their experiences, have each group select one essay to read to the rest of the class.

To start, you might ask *What do you do in the morning?* Go over all the new vocabulary on **page 5** with students. Prepare students to perform this model conversation:

Student A: *What do you do at _____ (the time)?*
Student B: *I _____.*

Develop sample answers with the proper verb tenses and supplement with other questions, such as *What do you do in the morning?*, *What do you do in the evening?*, and *What do you do every day?*

Practice 1: 15–30 minutes
Pair students and have them ask the questions of their partners and record their responses.

Evaluation 1: Ask students to give presentations about their partners. Check their subject-verb agreement.

Application: 20–25 minutes
Ask students to complete another planner page for themselves and discuss it with a partner. The planner worksheet is available on the Activity Bank CD-ROM.

Project

Split the class into groups and tell each group they are now a family. Ask them to discuss a household schedule that will work for everyone. Imagine the family has a limited amount of resources, including only one car and one person who can cook. After ample discussion time, have groups share their schedules with the rest of the class.

Level ★

Objective: Identify days and months.

Warm-up: 8–10 minutes
Begin class by writing the day and date on the board. Ask students to repeat the day and date after you. Then ask two questions to several students: *What day is it today?* and *What is the date today?* Write the two questions on the board and hand each student a copy of the calendar template found on the **Activity Bank CD-ROM**. Have each student add in the name of the current month and fill in the numbers.

Introduction: State the objective.

Presentation 1: 15–20 minutes
Instruct students to open to **page 6**. Formally explain the days of the week and the other vocabulary on this page. Draw a calendar on the board with the same days as February. As a class, fill in a few events on the calendar. Include Presidents' Day and Valentine's Day, as well as any student birthdays. Also list other special days such as Groundhog Day or events happening at the school. Students can use the calendar template on the **Activity Bank CD-ROM** to make their own calendars. If students need to review ordinal numbers, refer them to **page 3**. Quiz students upon completion of the February calendar. Ask questions, such as *What happens on the third Sunday of the month?* and *What day of the week is February 23rd?*

Practice 1: 5–10 minutes
Ask students to find a partner and quiz each other. One student will give a day and date and the other student will point to that day on the calendar.

Evaluation 1: Observe and listen to pronunciation.

Presentation 2: 10–15 minutes
Review the months found on **page 7**. Teach the pronunciation for each one. Quiz students by saying a month and asking them to point to that particular month in the dictionary. On the board, write the following question: *When were you born?* Go around the room and ask several students to share the month and day of their birth dates.

Practice 2: 10–15 minutes
Prepare students for a fun activity. Challenge them to ask each other their birth dates and form groups with others whose birth dates fall in the same month.

Evaluation 2: Evaluate how well students formed groups.

Application: 15–25 minutes
Depending on class size, create a master birth date list of all students in the classroom. Post the list on the board and encourage them to prepare birthday cards when students have birthdays during the term.

Calendar

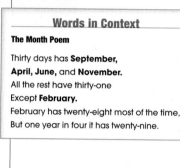

Words in Context

The Month Poem

Thirty days has **September,**
April, June, and **November.**
All the rest have thirty-one
Except **February.**
February has twenty-eight most of the time,
But one year in four it has twenty-nine.

1 date	**Days of the week**
2 yesterday	5 Monday
3 today	6 Tuesday
4 tomorrow	7 Wednesday
	8 Thursday
	9 Friday
	10 Saturday
	11 Sunday

6

Level ★★

Objective: Identify and discuss seasons.

Warm-up: 10–12 minutes
Ask students to write three special dates on a piece of paper, as suggested in **Words in Action #2**. In small groups, students should discuss their choices. Choose one student's response and provide the example *I like June 5th because it is Juan's birthday.*

Introduction: State the objective.

Presentation 1: 15–20 minutes
Read **Words in Action #1** and write some additional words about weather on the board, such as *windy, rainy, snowy, hot,* and *cold.* Create a chart on the board with four columns labeled *spring, summer, fall/autumn,* and *winter.* Ask students in which columns they would put the weather words to describe the U.S. seasons. Refer students to **pages 6 and 7** and have them read all the vocabulary silently, then aloud. Formally present the

Seasons	Months of the year	22 July
12 spring	16 January	23 August
13 summer	17 February	24 September
14 fall / autumn	18 March	25 October
15 winter	19 April	26 November
	20 May	27 December
	21 June	

Word Partnerships	
in	March
	April
	(the) summer
	(the) fall
on	Monday
	Tuesday
	March 10
	April 5

2005

16 January	17 February	18 March	19 April
S M T W T F S	S M T W T F S	S M T W T F S	S M T W T F S
. 1	. . 1 2 3 4 5	. . 1 2 3 4 5	. . . . . 1 2
2 3 4 5 6 7 8	6 7 8 9 10 11 12	6 7 8 9 10 11 12	3 4 5 6 7 8 9
9 10 11 12 13 14 15	13 14 15 16 17 18 19	13 14 15 16 17 18 19	10 11 12 13 14 15 16
16 17 18 19 20 21 22	20 21 22 23 24 25 26	20 21 22 23 24 25 26	17 18 19 20 21 22 23
23 24 25 26 27 28 29	27 28	27 28 29 30 31	24 25 26 27 28 29 30
30 31			

20 May	21 June	22 July	23 August
S M T W T F S	S M T W T F S	S M T W T F S	S M T W T F S
1 2 3 4 5 6 7	. . . 1 2 3 4	. . . . . 1 2	. 1 2 3 4 5 6
8 9 10 11 12 13 14	5 6 7 8 9 10 11	3 4 5 6 7 8 9	7 8 9 10 11 12 13
15 16 17 18 19 20 21	12 13 14 15 16 17 18	10 11 12 13 14 15 16	14 15 16 17 18 19 20
22 23 24 25 26 27 28	19 20 21 22 23 24 25	17 18 19 20 21 22 23	21 22 23 24 25 26 27
29 30 31	26 27 28 29 30	24 25 26 27 28 29 30	28 29 30 31
		31	

24 September	25 October	26 November	27 December
S M T W T F S	S M T W T F S	S M T W T F S	S M T W T F S
. . . . 1 2 3	 1	. . 1 2 3 4 5	. . . . 1 2 3
4 5 6 7 8 9 10	2 3 4 5 6 7 8	6 7 8 9 10 11 12	4 5 6 7 8 9 10
11 12 13 14 15 16 17	9 10 11 12 13 14 15	13 14 15 16 17 18 19	11 12 13 14 15 16 17
18 19 20 21 22 23 24	16 17 18 19 20 21 22	20 21 22 23 24 25 26	18 19 20 21 22 23 24
25 26 27 28 29 30	23 24 25 26 27 28 29	27 28 29 30	25 26 27 28 29 30 31
	30 31		

Words in Action

1. What's your favorite season? Month? Day? Why? Discuss with a partner.
2. What are three dates that are important to you? These can be birthdays, anniversaries, or holidays. Discuss with a partner.

— 7

Objective: Discuss a favorite season, month, or day of the week.

Warm-up: 15–20 minutes
Ask students to open their dictionaries to **page 6** and read *Words in Context*. Check comprehension by asking what is being taught in this poem. Give students five minutes to memorize it. Tell students not to worry if they don't finish memorizing. Ask for volunteers to recite the poem with their dictionaries closed.

Review all the vocabulary on **pages 6 and 7**. Quiz students on locating days of the week and each month on the planner. Remind students about when to use *in* and when to use *on*. Use the examples in *Word Partnerships*.

Introduction: State the objective.

Presentation 1: 10–20 minutes
Before class, prepare to discuss your favorites. In class, explain that you are going to speak about your favorite season, your favorite month of the year, and your favorite day of the week. Tell students you will say why they are your favorites. Encourage students to take notes, and suggest they also circle the dates on the calendars on **page 7**. Warn students that you will ask them comprehension questions to see how much they understood or wrote.

Practice 1: 20–30 minutes
Have students individually write their favorite season, month, and day of the week and why they like each. Pair students and have each practice listening and taking notes about the other. Each student will then take their notes and find a new partner. Students will use their notes to share the information about their first partner. Depending on student involvement and class time, you can continue this activity for as long as it is productive.
Evaluation 1: Observe the activity.

Application: 15–20 minutes
Upon completion of Practice 1, ask students to share what they have learned about other students with the class. On the board, create a bar graph of students' favorite seasons and determine which season is most popular in the class. Discuss who had favorite seasons in common.

Project

Provide 12 copies of the calendar template from the **Activity Bank CD-ROM**. As a class, create a calendar for the school year. Include holidays, school vacations, special events, and classmate birthdays. Post the calendar or design a class handbook/ planner that could be copied so students can each have a calendar to maintain and add to.

seasons to ensure understanding. In the chart on the board, have students determine when each season starts and ends in the United States.

Remember to guide the students, since your state may have different seasons and weather than the last place they lived.

Practice 1: 20–25 minutes
Ask students to talk to different students in the class. Direct them to ask each other which season is their favorite and why. Encourage students to take notes in a chart similar to the one created on the board.

Evaluation 1: Observe the activity and ask for reports.

Application: 15–20 minutes
Form groups. Ask students to share their favorite season, month, and day of the week with the other students in their groups. Have each group generate one chart that includes the responses of everyone in the group. Post these charts around the room.

Money and Shopping

Level ★

Objective: Count money and read prices.

Warm-up: 10–15 minutes
Begin class by showing your wallet or purse. Initiate dialog by saying *I have some money. Where should I go shopping? What do I need?* Encourage responses by saying *Should I go to the supermarket?* Create a list on the board. Start a new list on the board naming local supermarkets. Ask students where they shop. Take a vote as to the best supermarket in town. Make a class graph of the markets and how many students shop at each. Use the bar graph template from the **Activity Bank CD-ROM.**

Introduction: State the objective.

Presentation 1: 15–20 minutes
Point at your shirt or blouse and give it a price. *My shirt is $25.* Write *shirt* and *$25.00* on the board. Point to your desk. Say: *The desk is $250.50.* Identify other objects in the room and ask students to provide prices. Add each item and its price to the list on the board. The list should have at least 10 items. Include cents in several prices.

Ask students to open to **page 8.** Review the money section as a class. Practice the vocabulary until students are more confident. Select one of the items from the board and ask students which bills and coins they need to buy the item.

Practice 1: 7–15 minutes
In groups, ask students to take the remaining items from the list and identify which bills and coins they need. Tell students that there can be more than one answer.

Evaluation 1: Ask groups to report.

Presentation 2: 10–15 minutes
Read **Word Partnerships** and practice saying prices as a class. Prepare students to perform this model conversation.

> **Student A:** *How much is the _____?*
>
> **Student B:** *The _____ is _____.*

Practice 2: 5–10 minutes
Explain that you want partners to practice by inserting different items and prices from the list. Each pair should write three dialogs.

Evaluation 2: Ask volunteers to demonstrate for the class.

Application: 15–25 minutes
In groups of three, have students make a list of 10 items they have purchased at the supermarket recently. Have them perform the conversation from **Presentation 2** with the new information. Ask volunteers to share unique items someone purchased. To conclude, students should list the coins and bills they need for each item.

Words in Context

Be a smart **shopper!** Remember these things:

- Compare the **price** of the item you want in different stores.
- You can usually **return** or **exchange** items. Be sure to keep your **receipt.**
- Try to shop when there's a **sale.** You'll **save money!**

Coins

1 a penny / one cent / 1¢

2 a nickel / five cents / 5¢

3 a dime / ten cents / 10¢

4 a quarter / twenty-five cents / 25¢

5 a half dollar / fifty cents / 50¢

Bills

6 one dollar / a one-dollar bill / $1

7 five dollars / a five-dollar bill / $5

8 ten dollars / a ten-dollar bill / $10

9 twenty dollars / a twenty-dollar bill / $20

10 fifty dollars / a fifty-dollar bill / $50

11 one hundred dollars / a one hundred-dollar bill / $100

8

Level ★★

Objective: Choose payment types and make purchases.

Warm-up: 8–10 minutes
Ask students to open to **page 8.** Tell students to cover the words at the bottom of the page and say the names of each bill and coin. Then call out names of bills and have students point to them. Ask students to read **Words in Action #2** on **page 9.** Have students count how much money is on **page 8.** Review all the coins and bills on **page 8.**

Introduction: State the objective.

Presentation 1: 15–20 minutes
Make four columns on the board with the following headers: *credit card, debit card, check,* and *cash.* Explain each one. Ask students which they use the most. Many students may not have checks or cards. Discuss the pros and cons of each payment type. Review the rest of the shopping vocabulary on **page 9** with

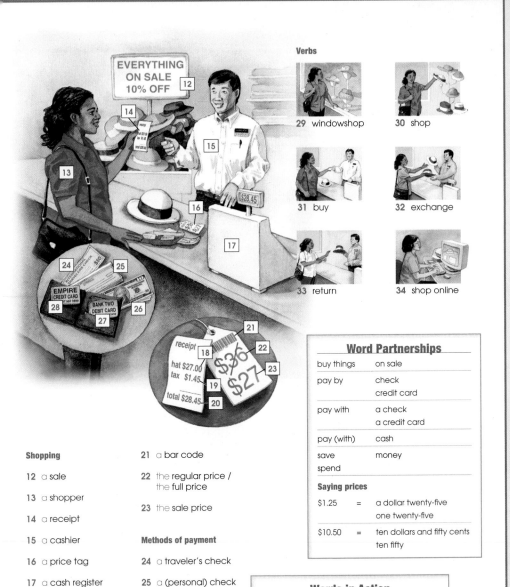

Verbs

29 windowshop
30 shop
31 buy
32 exchange
33 return
34 shop online

Shopping

12 a sale

13 a shopper

14 a receipt

15 a cashier

16 a price tag

17 a cash register

18 the price

19 the sales tax

20 the total

21 a bar code

22 the regular price / the full price

23 the sale price

Methods of payment

24 a traveler's check

25 a (personal) check

26 cash

27 a debit card

28 a credit card

Word Partnerships

buy things	on sale
pay by	check
	credit card
pay with	a check
	a credit card
pay (with)	cash
save	money
spend	

Saying prices

$1.25	=	a dollar twenty-five
		one twenty-five
$10.50	=	ten dollars and fifty cents
		ten fifty

Words in Action

1. What do you pay for with a credit card? What do you pay for with a check? What do you pay for with cash? Discuss with a partner.

2. Do you have any bills in your pocket? Which ones? Do you have any coins? Which ones?

9

Level ★

Objective: Identify colors.

Warm-up: 8–10 minutes
Before opening the dictionary, ask two volunteers to stand. Explain that when they hear a color of something they are wearing, they should sit. Encourage the rest of the students to help. Begin with a color not worn by the volunteers and ask the class if they should still be standing. After several practice examples, ask all students to participate as you say colors. Since students may not be aware of the names of many colors, help them by pointing to the color you are referring to in the dictionary.

Introduction: State the objective.

Presentation 1: 10–15 minutes
Ask students to open their dictionaries to **pages 10 and 11.** Introduce the primary colors. Ask them what happens when you combine two of the primary colors. Allow them to look at the colors in the book and to give opinions. Provide the example *Red and yellow make orange.* Consider bringing art supplies, such as markers or crayons, to class for students to use. Point to clothing and ask what color it is. Repeat this for several items. Review each color and its pronunciation.

Practice 1: 15–20 minutes
Ask students to form groups of three. Each group should look around the room and make a list of colors they can find, as suggested in **Words in Action #1.** Design a contest between groups. Each group should find as many colors and as many items for each color as possible. Set a time limit. Record answers on the board and see which group found the most colors or the most items per color. Encourage students to form a master list for their notes.

Evaluation 1: Listen to reports from students.

Presentation 2: 10–15 minutes
Prepare students to perform this model conversation.

   Student A: *What color is this?*

   Student B: *It is _____.*

Practice 2: 10–15 minutes
Ask students to walk around the room with a partner and ask questions about 10 items in the classroom. Use the short conversation to identify colors.

Evaluation 2: Observe the activity.

Application: 15–25 minutes
As a challenge, have students walk around for five minutes and ask as many classmates as possible about their favorite color. Students can then guess which is the most popular color. To conclude, take a poll and determine the most popular color.

Colors

Words in Context
Colors can make us feel different ways. **Yellow** can make us happy. **Orange** can make us feel full of energy. **Black** can make us feel sad. **Blue** can make us feel calm.

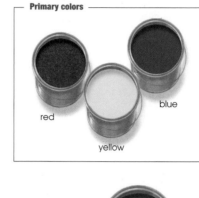

Primary colors

red   blue   yellow

1 red	7 lime green	13 gold	19 orange
2 maroon	8 teal	14 purple	20 white
3 coral	9 blue	15 violet	21 cream / ivory
4 pink	10 turquoise	16 brown	22 black
5 green	11 navy (blue)	17 beige / tan	23 gray
6 olive green	12 yellow	18 taupe	24 silver

10

Level ★★

Objective: Describe items by color.

Warm-up: 10–12 minutes
Have students do the activity suggested in **Words in Action #2.** Model the short conversation with a volunteer first to ensure that students understand the instructions.

Introduction: State the objective.

Presentation 1: 15–20 minutes
Review all the new vocabulary as a class, with an emphasis on **Word Partnerships.** As you lead the large group discussion, categorize each of the paint buckets on **pages 10 and 11** by the following words from **Word Partnerships:** *light, dark, pale, bright, cheerful, rich,* and *dull.* For example, you and the students may decide to put number 11 *(navy)* in the *dark* color category and number 15 *(violet)* in the *cheerful* color category. Inform students that there are many ways to put the words together, and that

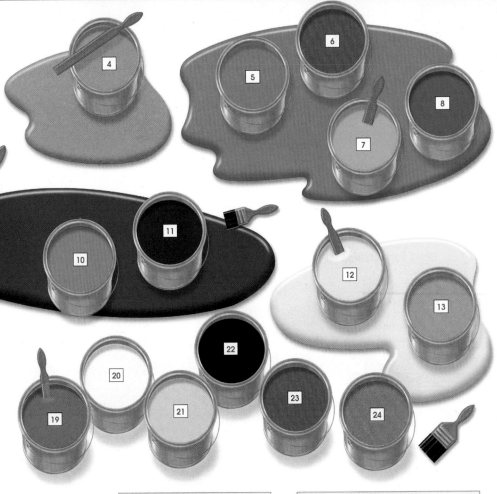

Word Partnerships

light	pink
dark	purple
pale	gray
	blue
	green
a	bright
	cheerful
	rich
	dull

(with: a ... color)

Words in Action

1. Look around the room. How many colors can you find? Make a list.
2. Work with a partner. Describe the color of one of your classmates' clothes. Your partner will guess the classmate.
   - Student A: *Someone is wearing green and blue.*
   - Student B: *It's Marcia!*

Objective: Discuss how colors make people feel.

Warm-up: 15–20 minutes
Play the color game as described in Level ★ ★, **Practice 1.** After presenting the rules explained in the two-star activity, have students choose a partner and play several rounds.

Introduction: State the objective.

Presentation 1: 10–20 minutes
Ask the class to define *cheerful*. If students don't know, explain that it means *happy*. Ask students what colors make them feel cheerful or happy. Since everyone will have different answers, encourage conversation by asking why they answered the way they did. Give the examples *I chose yellow because it makes me think about a sunny day. I like orange because my mother had a dress that color when I was a child.* Ask students how other colors, such as green and brown, make them feel. After getting some ideas, have students open their dictionaries to **page 10** and lead them in reading **Words in Context.** Discuss the paragraph.

Practice 1: 20–30 minutes
In pairs, encourage partners to discuss each color on **pages 10 and 11.** Each color should be labeled with a feeling and students can use more than one answer or repeat feelings.

Evaluation 1: Ask each pair to share and compare with another pair. After each group of four presents their findings, see if there are colors linked with feelings that the entire class can agree upon. There may not be!

Application: 30–35 minutes
Place students in groups of four and explain that they will prepare a quiz for other groups. Provide small note cards. Ask students to describe items found around the classroom by color: for example, dark gray (answer: the teacher's desk). They should include items that use the vocabulary from **Word Partnerships.** Descriptions should go on one side of the cards and answers go on the back. Students should challenge their group members to identify the items described. To add difficulty, ask students to trade cards with another group and have them look at the items first to see if they would choose the same colors.

Project

Have students design covers for personal journals. They should design journal covers using colors and images that remind them of important aspects of their lives. They can create the covers in black-and-white and then label the colors or use art supplies. Students should discuss their covers in groups, explaining why they chose particular colors.

---

some words may go in more than one category. Identify objects in the classroom by a color and category using these particular words. Seek class consensus; however, make sure students realize that other people may perceive colors differently.

Practice 1: 15–20 minutes
Teach students the rules for the color game and have them find a partner. One person says *I am thinking of something _____ (color).* After venturing a guess at the object, the second person receives

a *yes* or *no* and a *hot* or *cold* about the accuracy of the guess. This continues until the student can identify the object. Students then reverse roles.

Evaluation 1: Observe the activity.

Application: 20–25 minutes
Ask students to discuss in groups the perfect colors for a car, bedroom, kitchen, and classroom. They should also state why they think the colors would be best.

Level ★

Objective: Use prepositions of location.

Warm-up: 8–10 minutes
Initiate a conversation about pets. *Who has pets?* Provide examples of pets if necessary. Continue the group discussion by discussing pet names. Incorporate stories about your own pets and their names. At this point, ask which students have cats and how many cats they own. Pose these questions to students without pets: *Do you want one cat in your home? Do you want two cats? Do you want 17 cats?* End the discussion by asking if it is hard to own 17 cats.

Introduction: State the objective.

Presentation 1: 20–30 minutes
Ask students to open to **pages 12 and 13.** Go over each sentence as a class. Teach any new vocabulary, including *shelf/shelves, box, cats,* and *kittens.* Then write each preposition of location on the board. Practice pronunciation. Instruct students to cover the sentences in the book while you review the prepositions by asking *where is?* and *where are?* questions about the cats and kittens. Give the example *Number 1 is on top of a shelf.* Students may answer with a prepositional phrase or a complete sentence. Assist them with forms of the verb *to be.* You may choose to teach an in-depth lesson, but be sure not to lose sight of the objective.

Practice 1: 8–12 minutes
Pair students. Read **Words in Action #1** and ask students to perform the dialogs using the picture.

Evaluation 1: Observe the activity.

Presentation 2: 10–15 minutes
Refer students to **pages 10 and 11.** Have students ask partners about the colors and encourage them to use prepositions in their answers. Provide the example *Orange is next to white.*

Practice 2: 10–15 minutes
Place students in groups of four. Request six new sentences from each group; each sentence should have a different preposition.

Evaluation 2: Listen to student sentences. Have students assist their peers.

Application: 15–25 minutes
Write *There is . . .* and *There are . . .* on the board and then ask one student to read **Words in Action #2.** Instruct students to write 10 sentences about the classroom using the prepositions and the *There is/There are* sentence structure. Write model sentences on the board. Have students write their sentences on the board.

In, On, Under

Words in Context

Look around you. Can you answer these questions?

- What's **in front of** you?
- What's **behind** you?
- What do you see **above** you?
- Is there someone or something **close to** you? Who or what?

Word Partnerships

right	under
	next to
just	behind
	in front of
	to the left of
	above

12

Level ★ ★

Objective: Use prepositions of location.

Warm-up: 12–15 minutes
Ask students to describe the classroom and locations of key items. Every time a student uses a preposition of location, write it on the board. Ask questions to direct them to prepositions of location. Review the singular and plural forms of the verb *to be* briefly so sentences will contain proper grammar.

Introduction: State the objective.

Presentation 1: 20–25 minutes
Explain that prepositions of location tell where an object is. Continue to add more prepositions of location to the list on the board, including student suggestions. Instruct students to open their dictionaries to **pages 12 and 13.** Review all the prepositions and ensure all words are understood. Introduce students to the **Word Partnerships** on **page 12.** Include others students suggest.

1. This cat is **on top of** the shelves.

2. This cat is **far from** the other cats.

3. This cat is **on** a box.

4. This cat is **between** two boxes.

5. These kittens are **in / inside** a box.

6. This kitten is **outside (of)** the box.

7. This cat is jumping **off** the shelves.

8. This cat is **on the left of / to the left of** cat number 9.

9. This cat is **on the right of / to the right of** cat number 8.

10. This cat is **above / over** cat number 13.

11. This cat is **next to / beside** the shelves.

12. This cat has a ribbon **around** its neck.

13. This kitten is **below / under** cat number 10.

14. This kitten is **behind** the shelves.

15. This kitten is **near / close to** the shelves.

16. This kitten is **underneath** the shelves.

17. This cat is **in front of** the shelves.

Words in Action

1. Cover the list of words. Ask a partner questions like this:
   - *Where is cat number 10?*
2. Describe where things are in your classroom. Write ten sentences using ten different prepositions.

— **13** —

Review when to use *are* and *is*. Ask students to use the **Word Partnerships** vocabulary as well as prepositions. Prepare students to perform this model conversation.

Student A: *Excuse me. I have lost my cat. Do you know where the cat with a green bow is?*

Student B: *The cat with a green bow is on the shelf.*

Student A: *Thank you very much.*

Student B: *You are welcome.*

Practice 1: 20–25 minutes
Encourage students to practice the conversation with a partner, substituting new information from the picture for the underlined words.

Evaluation 1: Ask volunteers to demonstrate in front of the class.

Application: 8–10 minutes
Explain the activity in **Words in Context**. After finding a partner, each student should answer the questions.

Level ★ ★ ★

Objective: Use prepositions, adjectives, and action verbs to describe a scene.

Warm-up: 15–20 minutes
Refer students to **pages 12 and 13** and briefly review prepositions. Ask students to cover the sentences on **page 13** and attempt to write 10 sentences about the picture using 10 different prepositions. After five minutes, write *This cat is . . .* and *These cats are . . .* on the board. Review *this* and *these* as well as plural and singular forms of the verb *to be*. Provide time for students to correct their sentences and/or write additional sentences. Upon completion, review all sentences on **page 13**.

Introduction: State the objective.

Presentation 1: 15–20 minutes
Present the following verbs on the board: *sit, jump, land, listen, look, play, stare,* and *sneak*. To promote understanding of these words, find examples and demonstrate, but don't use the pictures in the dictionary. Inform students that although many of these verbs are used to describe cats, they can also be used to describe people. Write the following adjectives on the board: *fluffy, striped, spotted, long-haired,* and *solitary*. Be sure students understand these words, but again don't use the picture as an example.

Practice 1: 15–20 minutes
In groups, students should write five sentences to describe cats. Have them use adjectives, action verbs, and prepositions of location. Allow five minutes for a first attempt and then stop activity and provide this model: *The solitary white cat is sitting on a shelf.* Provide extra time to write additional sentences.

Evaluation 1: Ask the groups to write their sentences on the board.

Application: 18–20 minutes
Ask students to write a paragraph about the picture on **pages 12 and 13**. Proper paragraph form should be encouraged.

Project

Tell students you want them to write a letter to a friend or family member who has never seen your classroom. Each student should draw a picture of the room and include key items like the chalkboard, the teacher's desk, and the door. Students should then write 10 sentences describing the classroom, using prepositions to explain where the items are. Remind them to use the new vocabulary so their friends and family will be able to envision what the room looks like from the words they have chosen.

Level ★

Objective: Identify opposites.

Warm-up: 8–10 minutes
Begin class with the words *short* and *tall* written on the board. Define each. Choose a student to stand. Have other students stand and compare themselves to the first student. Draw two different circles on the board and label them *little* and *big*. Request assistance from the students in categorizing things around the room as little or big. They might say *The pen is little* or *The door is big*. Compile a list of these student-generated comparisons on the board.

Introduction: State the objective.

Presentation 1: 20–30 minutes
Write *opposite* on the board. Define. Have students open to **pages 14 and 15.** Guide the class through the pictures and word list. Develop other examples of opposites. For example, you might say that the classroom is full during class and empty after class when discussing *full* and *empty* (19 and 20). Promote participation by having students provide alternative examples. Ask students to cover the word list. As you recite opposites, encourage students to point to the corresponding pictures.

Practice 1: 7–10 minutes
Practice the opposites by asking pairs to continue the activity. One student will cover the words and point to a picture. The other will suggest the correct opposite vocabulary word. Have them reverse roles. Encourage them to think of more examples together.

Evaluation 1: Observe the activity.

Presentation 2: 10–15 minutes
Say a word and see if students can identify the opposite. Allow students to refer to **pages 14 and 15** for the first two, but then ask that they close the dictionary. Have students practice the opposites activity described in *Words in Action #1.*

Practice 2: 12–14 minutes
Provide students with the worksheet from the Activity Bank CD-ROM. Explain that they will match words with their opposites.

Evaluation 2: Check student answers.

Application: 15–25 minutes
In groups of four, students should look around the classroom and find 10 sets of opposites.

Opposites

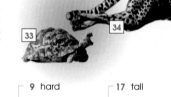

Words in Context
Opposites sometimes attract. Women with **light** hair sometimes like men with **dark** hair. Very **tall** men sometimes marry very **short** women. **Thin** people sometimes fall in love with **heavy** people.

Word Partnerships

a cold	day
a hot	drink
	room
an open	window
a closed	door
	book
a clean	car
a dirty	dish
	room
a full	cup
an empty	stomach

1 small / little	9 hard	17 tall
2 big / large	10 soft	18 short
3 strong	11 alive	19 full
4 weak	12 dead	20 empty
5 dirty	13 ugly	21 old
6 clean	14 beautiful	22 young
7 easy	15 expensive	23 heavy
8 difficult	16 cheap	24 light

14

Level ★★

Objective: Define words by stating the opposite.

Warm-up: 12–15 minutes
Write the word *opposite* on the board and ask students to give examples. Challenge students to think of as many other opposites as possible. Compile one master list on the board as students read lists.

Introduction: State the objective.

Presentation 1: 25–30 minutes
Pose the question *What does ugly mean?* Accept any correct answers. Explain that words can be defined by giving opposites. Provide and write on the board the example *Ugly is the opposite of beautiful.* Ask students to open to **pages 14 and 15.** As a whole class, discuss the vocabulary. Guide students to respond in sentences similar to the model on the board.

On the blackboard:
$$1 + 1 = 2$$
$$f(x) = \frac{20x}{\sqrt{x^2 + 12}}$$

25	fat / heavy	33	slow
26	thin	34	fast
27	rich	35	loud / noisy
28	poor	36	quiet
29	hot	37	open
30	cold	38	closed / shut
31	new	39	man
32	old	40	woman

Words in Action

1. Work in pairs. Say one of the words on the list. Your partner will say the opposite.
2. Describe things that are the same or different about two people you know. Use words from the list.
   - *Leo and Ali are strong.*
   - *I'm tall. My brother is short.*

15

Objective: Write a paragraph.

Warm-up: 20–30 minutes
Begin by looking at **pages 14 and 15.** Review opposites and address any questions about the vocabulary. Have students write a sentence for every item in **Word Partnerships** and check their work. Offer an example, such as *I like a cold drink on a hot day.*

Introduction: State the objective.

Presentation 1: 10–20 minutes
Read **Words in Context** as a class. Review the vocabulary, check for understanding, and ask for opinions regarding the paragraph. Present a brief lecture on paragraph format, including how to indent, use margins, and develop a topic sentence. Explain that students will write a paragraph stating their opinions about **Words in Context** and tell them they should use complete sentences.

Practice 1: 20–30 minutes
Provide a general title: *What I Think About Opposites.* Ask each student to include a topic sentence and two or three supporting sentences. Teach students phrases that may be used to voice an opinion.

Evaluation 1: Have students peer edit and rewrite their work.

Application: 15–20 minutes
Depending on class size, divide students into groups of four. Students then share their paragraphs and have a discussion with classmates.

Prepare students to perform this model conversation.

Student A: *What does ugly mean?*

Student B: *Ugly is the opposite of beautiful. These are pictures of ugly and beautiful.* (Student B points to pictures 13 and 14 in the book.)

Practice 1: 10–15 minutes
Ask students to practice the conversation with a partner, substituting new vocabulary from **pages 14 and 15** each time. Instruct students to reverse roles after three practice dialogs.

Evaluation 1: Ask volunteers to demonstrate in front of the class.

Application: 15–18 minutes
In pairs, have students make descriptions as suggested in **Words in Action #2.** Initiate the activity by telling students to think about their families and friends. Using examples of people they know will make this activity easier and more fun, but avoid discussing other students' physical appearances.

Project

Create flashcard sets. Have scrap paper cut into 3-by-5-inch pieces. Students should write each of the vocabulary words on a card with the opposite on the flip side. Include all words from **pages 14 and 15.** Upon completion, have each student add five sets of opposites not included in the dictionary. Compile that list on the board so students can add those to the study set of opposite flashcards.

The Telephone

Level ★

Objective: Identify phone vocabulary.

Warm-up: 8–10 minutes
Read *Words in Action #1.* Prepare students to perform this model conversation.

> **Student A:** *Excuse me, what is your area code and phone number?*
>
> **Student B:** *My area code and phone number is (___) ___ - ___. or I am sorry. That is personal.*

Students should practice with two partners and perform both roles. Initiate a group conversation by asking for feedback from students. If students need additional review on numbers, refer to **pages 2 and 3.**

Introduction: State the objective.

Presentation 1: 20–30 minutes
Ask for comments about what to do in emergencies. Act out a scene where you witness an accident and run to a pay phone. Write *911* on the board. Discuss. Write *411* on the board and discuss directory assistance. Ask students how much it costs to make a local call and lead a conversation about *local* and *pay phones.* Direct attention to **pages 16 and 17.** Study the words in a whole-class setting. Draw a five-column chart on the board and label the columns *phone, assistance, payment, numbers or locations,* and *other.* Write *pay phone* in the phone column.

Practice 1: 10–15 minutes
Assign students to groups of three. Ask each group to place the words from the list into the best category in the chart.

Evaluation 1: Review the words as a class.

Presentation 2: 10–15 minutes
Review the vocabulary thoroughly and teach the rules for Bingo. Have students make a list of any eight objects from dictionary **pages 16 and 17.** There are Bingo cards set up in the worksheet folder on the **Activity Bank CD-ROM** for a more formal game. Play a practice round to ensure all students understand the rules. Use one of the vocabulary words in a sentence read to the class. Every student who has that vocabulary word listed should cross it off. Continue until there is a winner.

Practice 2: 7–10 minutes
Play Bingo.

Evaluation 2: Observe the activity. Reward the winner(s).

Application: 15–25 minutes
Read *Words in Action #2.* Ask students to make a bar graph that displays how many times a month their classmates make local, long distance, and international phone calls. There is a template for this graph on the **Activity Bank CD-ROM.**

Words in Context

Do you want to make a **long-distance phone call** in the U.S.? **Pick up** the **receiver** and **dial** 1 + the **area code** + the **phone number.** Do you need **directory assistance?** You can dial **411.** Remember, there are four **time zones** in the U.S. When it is 9:00 P.M. in Los Angeles, it's midnight in New York!

1 a pay phone

2 a receiver

3 a calling card / a phone card

4 a coin

5 911 / emergency assistance

6 411 / information / directory assistance

7 a coin return

8 a telephone book / a phone book

9 a local call

10 a long-distance call

11 an international call

12 time zones

13 a caller

14 a phone jack

15 a cord

16 a headset

17 an operator

18 an answering machine

19 a cordless phone

20 a cell phone / a mobile phone

21 an antenna

22 an area code

23 a telephone number / a phone number

16

Level ★★

Objective: Communicate with an operator.

Warm-up: 20–30 minutes
Present the idea of a class phone book. Begin by having students exchange phone numbers with three other students. Each group should then send a representative to other groups to share and add to their lists. Students should list names in alphabetical order. If students don't want to give their number, they should remain *unlisted* or students can give fictitious numbers.

Introduction: State the objective.

Presentation 1: 15–20 minutes
Ask students to open their dictionaries to **pages 16 and 17.** Review the vocabulary as a class. Quiz students by asking them to close their dictionaries and acting out the verbs. Students should respond with a verb for each action. Review the verbs in *Word Partnerships.* Prepare students to perform the following conversation.

Dialing...
1-805-
555-9788
OK   Cancel

Verbs

24 pick up the phone

25 dial a number

26 hear the phone ring

27 answer the phone

28 have a conversation

29 hang up the phone

Word Partnerships

make	an international call
	a long-distance call
	a local call
call	directory assistance
	911
look up	a phone number
telephone	company
	service
	bill

Words in Action

1. What is your area code and phone number?
2. How often do you make local, long-distance, and international calls? Who do you call? Why? Discuss with a partner.

— **17** —

Operator: *Directory assistance. What city and state?*

Caller: *Los Angeles, California, please.*

Operator: *Thank you. Name, please.*

Caller: *Jose Valenzuela.*

Operator: *The number is: area code (213)555-7421.*

or

Operator: *Sorry, the number is unlisted.*

Caller: *Thank you.*

Practice 1: 15–10 minutes
Ask students to practice the conversation. Tell the callers to do their role without looking at the conversation on the board.

Evaluation 1: Ask volunteers to demonstrate in front of the class.

Application: 5–10 minutes
Ask students to use the student directory created in the Warm-up to perform the conversation by inserting different student information each time.

Objective: Discuss phone habits.

Warm-up: 20–30 minutes
Prepare pairs to write a conversation between a caller and an operator. Read **Word Partnerships** on **page 17** and ask that phrases be used in the dialog.

Introduction: State the objective.

Presentation 1: 20–30 minutes
Review the vocabulary on **pages 16 and 17** and answer any questions. Conduct a survey and see how many students have cell phones, cordless phones, answering machines, and/or calling cards. Read *Words in Context* aloud and discuss. Focus special attention on time zones. Create a list of questions on the board and encourage student participation.

1. *How often do you make local calls?*
2. *How often do you make long-distance calls?*
3. *How often do you make international calls?*
4. *Whom do you call?*
5. *What time zones do you call in the U.S.?*
6. *Do you answer the phone at home or do you let the answering machine answer?*

Students should prepare a conversation grid where they can take notes after speaking to their classmates. A grid is available on the **Activity Bank CD-ROM**. Teach students certain phrases to make this exchange a conversation and not an interview. You might include colloquialisms such as *How about you?*, *That is interesting.*, *Not me, I . . .*, and *Me too.*

Practice 1: 20–30 minutes
Ask students to discuss their phone habits with a partner. Encourage note-taking. After three minutes, ring a bell and have students speak to a new partner about the partner they just finished speaking with. Ring the bell and switch partners as time allows.

Evaluation 1: Ask students to share information about students they spoke with for the class and complete a grid on the board.

Application: 15–20 minutes
Review Venn diagrams. Demonstrate by presenting a Venn on the board with the information from the Evaluation. Have partners compare their phone habits and draw a Venn diagram to illustrate. A template is available on the **Activity Bank CD-ROM**.

Project

Ask students to make personal phone directories, including the instructor's contact information and information about other students. A worksheet is available on the **Activity Bank CD-ROM**.

Classroom

Verbs

31 cheat on a test   **32** fail a test

Words in Context

What does the ideal **classroom** look like? Some experts think that a classroom should look friendly. It should have comfortable **seats** and **desks**. It should have a large **bookshelf** with many **books**. It should also have bright **posters** and **bulletin boards** to show **students'** work.

Word Partnerships

go to	the board
write on	
erase	
a high school	student
a college	
an international	
a graduate	
a hard / difficult	test / exam
an easy	
a midterm	
a final	

18

Level ★

Objective: Identify classroom vocabulary.

Warm-up: 7–10 minutes
Begin class by asking about the physical aspects of the classroom: *Where is a board?* Allow time for student response (orally or by pointing to the object). Continue this activity with other items in the room: *book, pencil, pen,* and *desk.* As you lead the class, use the article *a* when identifying singular items.

Introduction: State the objective.

Presentation 1: 15–20 minutes
To evaluate what students already know, instruct them to open to **pages 18 and 19** and cover the word list. Explain that you will say the name of an item in the classroom. As students hear the word, they will point to the corresponding picture in the dictionary. Additionally, have them call out the item number. For example, when you say *a book,* they should find the book, point to it, and say *number 11.*

Upon completion, tell students to uncover the word list. Promote correct pronunciation by reading the words aloud and having the students repeat. Include the articles while reading the list.

Ask students to look at **page 18** and point to the alphabet. Write the alphabet across the board and review the pronunciation and formation of each letter. Say *notebook.* Ask: *Who knows the first letter?* When volunteers respond *n,* ask one volunteer to write *notebook* on the board under the letter, while another volunteer assists by spelling the word. Demonstrate. Continue with more items in the picture and vary the choice of student volunteers.

Practice 1: 10–15 minutes
Once students have grasped the idea, request that they write the alphabet in their notebooks. Students should transcribe the words from their dictionary on their charts.
Evaluation 1: Ask individuals to write the words on the board under the alphabet.

Presentation 2: 5–7 minutes
Prepare the students to perform this model conversation.

  Student A: *Where is the <u>clock</u>?*

  Student B: *The <u>clock</u> is here.* (The student points to the object in the picture.)

Practice 2: 10–15 minutes
Explain that students should practice the short conversation with a partner and substitute other vocabulary words for the underlined words.
Evaluation 2: Observe the activity.

Application: 15–25 minutes
Challenge the group to perform the conversation again but with their books closed. To end the session, solicit volunteers to physically walk to the items in the classroom.

Level ★ ★

Objective: Identify teacher and student classroom activities.

Warm-up: 8–10 minutes
Lead students in a labeling activity. If possible, supply small cards and tape. Call for volunteers to label different items in the room. If supplies are limited, read **Words in Action** on **page 19** and request that small groups make lists of classroom items. After labeling and listing, ask students to open to the word list on **page 19**. Identify any words they may have missed. Allow time to label the items and correct spelling.

Introduction: State the objective.

Presentation 1: 15–20 minutes
As a group, brainstorm about things students do in a classroom. Refer to the picture on **pages 18 and 19.** Make a cluster on the board. A cluster template can be found on the **Activity Bank CD-ROM.** Mark the center circle *classroom activities.* Begin labeling the secondary

33 study for a test

34 take a test

35 pass a test

1 the alphabet	14 a (white)board
2 a teacher	15 a marker
3 chalk	16 an overhead projector
4 a (blackboard) eraser	17 a table
5 a homework assignment	18 a workbook
6 a (black)board	19 a pen
7 a bulletin board	20 a pencil
8 a flag	21 a desk
9 a globe	22 an eraser
10 a bookshelf	23 a poster
11 a book	24 a cassette player / a tape recorder
12 a map	25 a student
13 a clock	26 a chair / a seat
	27 a notebook
	28 a grade
	29 a test / an exam
	30 a textbook

Words in Action

1. Work with a group. Make a list of everything in your classroom. Which group has the longest list?

2. Cover the word list. Find one word in the picture that starts with each of the following letters: a, b, c, d, e, f, g, h.

19

Objective: Use *should* to discuss an ideal classroom.

Warm-up: 15–20 minutes
Divide students into groups of three or four and allow time for the group to discuss and study the picture on **pages 18 and 19**. Ask each group member to write two sentences about the picture. Prepare groups for dictation. Within groups, students should read their sentences while their group members take dictation. Members should check answers when all have finished.

Introduction: State the objective.

Presentation 1: 15–20 minutes
Request students close their books and lead them in a discussion about a good classroom. Ask what items are needed for a perfect classroom. Teach the modal *should*. Depending on class level, you may wish to create a chart on the board with other modals (*could, must,* etc.). Practice using *should* for the ideas offered to create the perfect classroom.

Practice 1: 15–20 minutes
Extend the discussion by inquiring what is needed to learn English. Have partners or small groups develop lists. Jump-start the ideas by suggesting *books, teachers,* and *study time.* After several minutes, students should read **Words in Context** and include on their group lists any new ideas the reading inspires.

Evaluation 1: Have groups assign a spokesperson to share what they discussed.

Application: 15–20 minutes
Ask students to compare their ideal classroom to the classroom depicted on **pages 18 and 19**. This can be done by using a Johari Squares chart. A template for this chart is found on the **Activity Bank CD-ROM**.

level of circles with verbs such as *study, teach, read, write, take,* or *listen.* Elicit other ideas from students. Direct attention to the pictures that depict verbs associated with test taking and **Word Partnerships.** If there is room, add these verbs to the cluster. Extend the cluster to another set of circles with direct objects (*read: a test, a book, a board, the alphabet,* etc.). Demonstrate how to make sentences by using the circles in the cluster.

Practice 1: 25–30 minutes
Pose a challenge. *Which group can write the most sentences?* Sentences should

pertain to the picture and include words from the list. Restrict time to 10 or 15 minutes.

Evaluation 1: Ask volunteers from groups to write their sentences on the board and review the sentences as a class.

Application: 12–15 minutes
Review the imperative with students by presenting a few commands, such as *Point to a desk, please,* or *Please write your name on the board.* Ask each student to walk around with a partner asking and following simple commands.

Project

Assign groups. Tell students to imagine they are *builders.* A school needs a new building, and each classroom should be perfect. Students should draw a layout of a perfect classroom and label the key parts. For lower levels, have students create a picture of the classroom as it is now and make changes where appropriate. Give class presentations to pick the winning *design.*

Level ★

Objective: Identify classroom activities.

Warm-up: 8–10 minutes
Have everyone stand. Write *stand up* on the board. Ask students to raise their hands. Write *raise your hand* on the board. Last, tell students to sit. Explain that students can now give you instructions. Begin with volunteers and allow several students to give you classroom commands. Write the verbs on the board.

Introduction: State the objective.

Presentation 1: 10–15 minutes
Turn to **pages 20 and 21**. Pantomime several activities and see if students can identify your actions by looking in the dictionary. For items 22–29, use the board to draw examples. Divide the class into groups of four or five students and split the vocabulary so that each group has an equal number of words. Depending on class size, one group might have slightly fewer. For example, if you have six groups, five groups will get five words and one group will get four.

Practice 1: 20–30 minutes
Groups should develop ways to act out the provided words. Let students know that no speaking is allowed when they present their "act." Make sure all students participate by having every student take responsibility for one vocabulary word and become the class "expert." Each student should present his or her action. After practicing within groups, students will pantomime for the class. Allow other students to respond when they've determined the word.

Evaluation 1: Observe the activity.

Presentation 2: 2–5 minutes
Prepare students to perform this model conversation.

   Student A: *Stand up.*

   Student B: (Student B stands.)

Practice 2: 8–10 minutes
Present two examples with volunteers, and then allow time for students to quiz each other by doing the exchange from the presentation. Instruct them to substitute different verbs from the vocabulary, as suggested in *Words in Action #1*.

Evaluation 2: Observe the activity.

Application: 15–25 minutes
Read *Words in Action #2*. Create a list identifying what actions are most often done in class. Inquire what student favorites are.

Listen, Read, Write

Words in Context

People learn languages in different ways. Some students like to **listen** to the language. Others like to **write** lists of words. Others like to **read** a lot or **talk** with a group and **discuss** their ideas. What about you? How do you learn languages best?

1 raise your hand

2 hand in your paper

3 collect the papers

4 copy the sentence

5 exchange papers

6 write your name

7 read

8 look up a word (in the dictionary)

9 close your book

10 open your book

11 discuss your ideas

12 listen

13 spell your name

14 take a break

15 sit down

16 go to the board

17 erase the board

20

Level ★ ★

Objective: Develop classroom rules.

Warm-up: 10–15 minutes
Before opening the dictionaries, ask small groups to identify and list as many classroom activities as possible. Suggest *listening, speaking, reading,* and *writing* as starting ideas and list these on the board. *What other activities can be added to the list?* Allow the groups to mingle and share answers; a representative from each group can take notes. Discuss each group's words as a class.

Introduction: State the objective.

Presentation 1: 15–20 minutes
Ask students to open to **pages 20 and 21** and to compare the word list to the one they created. Provide time for students to identify words they didn't think of and embellish their lists. Review the list as a class. Read *Word Partnerships* carefully and demonstrate as needed. Request

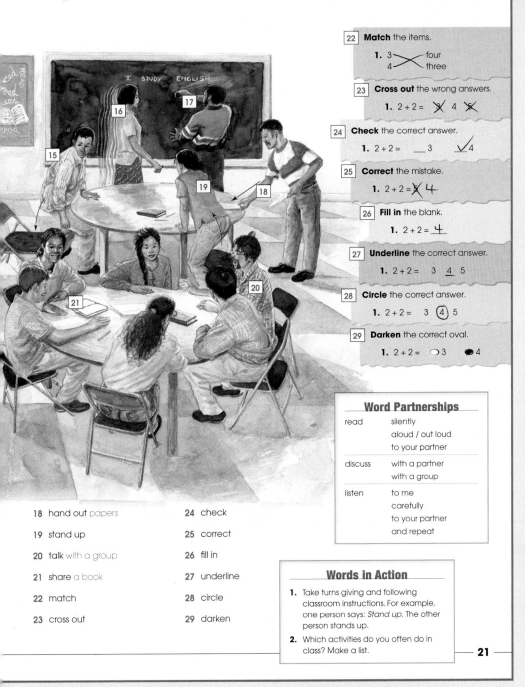

22 Match the items.

1. 3 —— four
   4 —— three

23 Cross out the wrong answers.

1. 2 + 2 = ✗ 4 ✗

24 Check the correct answer.

1. 2 + 2 = ___ 3 ✓ 4

25 Correct the mistake.

1. 2 + 2 = ✗ 4

26 Fill in the blank.

1. 2 + 2 = 4

27 Underline the correct answer.

1. 2 + 2 = 3 <u>4</u> 5

28 Circle the correct answer.

1. 2 + 2 = 3 ④ 5

29 Darken the correct oval.

1. 2 + 2 = ○3 ●4

18	hand out papers	24	check
19	stand up	25	correct
20	talk with a group	26	fill in
21	share a book	27	underline
22	match	28	circle
23	cross out	29	darken

Word Partnerships

read	silently
	aloud / out loud
	to your partner
discuss	with a partner
	with a group
listen	to me
	carefully
	to your partner
	and repeat

Words in Action

1. Take turns giving and following classroom instructions. For example, one person says: *Stand up.* The other person stands up.

2. Which activities do you often do in class? Make a list.

— **21**

Objective: Discuss good techniques to learn English.

Warm-up: 15–20 minutes
Begin with **pages 20 and 21.** Challenge students to identify what each number in the picture is describing. Request that students cover the word list as they quiz one another. After finishing, allow students to uncover the words and see how well they did. Answer any questions.

Introduction: State the objective.

Presentation 1: 10–20 minutes
With the dictionaries closed, ask students if they can help create a list of ways to learn English. *What are the best ways to learn?* Encourage students to maintain a list of the five most important things they can do to learn English faster and better. Discuss the ideas as a class and write those ideas on the board. Ask students to open to **page 20** and read *Words in Context.* Discuss the reading and then try to narrow the master list down to the four most important ways to learn English. Encourage the entire class to agree on the four ways that all will try to practice. Number the ways 1 to 4.

Practice 1: 15–20 minutes
Ask students to secretly write down the number of their favorite way to learn English. Assign each corner of the room a number correlated to the four ways agreed upon. Write the numbers or ideas on paper and tape those to the wall in each corner. Direct students to go to the corner that they think is the best for them. With the others in their corner, students should discuss details about how they try to improve their English. Provide leading questions, such as *How much do you study or practice outside of class?* and *Where do you study or practice?* After ample discussion time, have students select a different corner and discuss another way to study.

Evaluation 1: Ask for a group report.

Application: 15–20 minutes
Teach students about goals and objectives. Explain that you'd like them to write study goals and include details about time, books, and study techniques. Share the individual reports.

that students suggest things NOT to do in class. Guide the discussion by asking if it is a good idea to talk while the teacher is talking. This is a good opportunity to clarify class rules. Review the simple present tense and create a chart on the board using verbs from these pages.

Practice 1: 15–20 minutes
Ask students to write simple present sentences about **pages 20 and 21.** In order for students to practice both, ask them to write four sentences in the affirmative and four in the negative.

Evaluation 1: Transcribe student examples on the board and review as a class.

Application: 20–25 minutes
Explain the concept of class rules. Review the imperative form of the verb in the affirmative and in the negative. Develop a list of classroom rules. If the class is large, divide into smaller groups. There is a class rules worksheet on the **Activity Bank CD-ROM** that can facilitate this activity.

Project

As a class, design a class management chart. Describe activities that students can participate in to help the teacher. Students should be able to explain how the ideas will maintain a systematic and organized classroom. There is worksheet on classroom management to facilitate this activity on the **Activity Bank CD-ROM.**

Level ★

Objective: Identify school vocabulary.

Warm-up: 8–10 minutes
As you direct attention around the classroom, point out key classroom items. If necessary, review the vocabulary on **pages 18 and 19**. Draw two columns on the board with the headers *same* and *different*. Title your chart *Two Classrooms*. To clarify the concept, present examples of the dictionary's classroom items that are the same as or different from your classroom's items. Write these into the chart. Ask students for more ideas. Expand the conversation by asking students if they have classes in other schools or rooms. Help students get started by posing the questions *What is the same about the two rooms/schools?* and *What is different about the two rooms/schools?* or complete **Words in Action #2**.

Introduction: State the objective.

Presentation 1: 10–15 minutes
Present the vocabulary and picture on **pages 22 and 23**. Spend some time adjusting student pronunciation by asking each student to pronounce several words.

Practice 1: 8–10 minutes
Review the grammatical differences between *what/who* and *he/she/it*. Prepare students to perform this model conversation.

  Student A: *What (Who) is this?*

  Student B: *It (He/She) is _____.*

Create a grammar chart on the board to help students sort people from things. Try some conversations where students ask and the instructor responds.

Evaluation 1: Focus on correct pronunciation.

Presentation 2: 8–10 minutes
Start a cluster diagram on the board. Note that a cluster template is also available on the **Activity Bank CD-ROM**. The school cluster is composed of three principle circles: *people*, *places*, and *things*. Demonstrate by placing *principal* in the *people* circle and *classroom* in the *places* circle.

Practice 2: 10–15 minutes
Allow time for students to complete the cluster with items 3–27.

Evaluation 2: Ask for input and complete the cluster you started on the board with the correct answers.

Application: 20–30 minutes
Draw another two-column chart on the board. As a class, identify things the school *has* and things it *doesn't have*. Then ask students to copy the same in their notebooks and add to the list. A two-column template is available on the **Activity Bank CD-ROM** to assist with this activity.

School

Words in Context

In the U.S., a **principal** manages the school. **Guidance counselors** help students plan their **schedules**. Students take home **report cards** a few times a year, and parents must sign them. Many students participate in **extracurricular activities** such as **drama clubs** or **sports**.

Word Partnerships

elementary	school
middle	
high	
join	a team
	a club

Level ★ ★

Objective: Identify school activities.

Warm-up: 10–15 minutes
Initiate a discussion about why people go to school. Suggest a few ideas such as *to learn English* and *to get a good job*. Keep a master list of students' reasons on the board.

Introduction: State the objective.

Presentation 1: 15–20 minutes
Have students open to **page 23** but cover the picture and focus attention on the word list. Compile a list of words students don't know and teach these in depth. As you progress, take each new word and begin your explanation in question format: *What does* <u>lounge</u> *mean?* Once all vocabulary is understood, identify things people <u>can</u> do in school. Place *learn English* on the list.

Practice 1: 15–20 minutes
Divide students into groups of four and

1 a coach

2 a team

3 a language lab

4 a gym

5 bleachers

6 a cafeteria

7 a (school) library

8 a school nurse

9 a teachers' lounge

10 a restroom /
a bathroom

11 a water fountain

12 a school bus

13 a loudspeaker

14 a locker

15 a backpack

16 a principal

17 a guidance
counselor

18 an auditorium

19 a graduation

20 a classroom

21 sports

22 Spanish club

23 drama club

24 a report card

25 a (student) schedule

26 a permission slip

27 an absence note

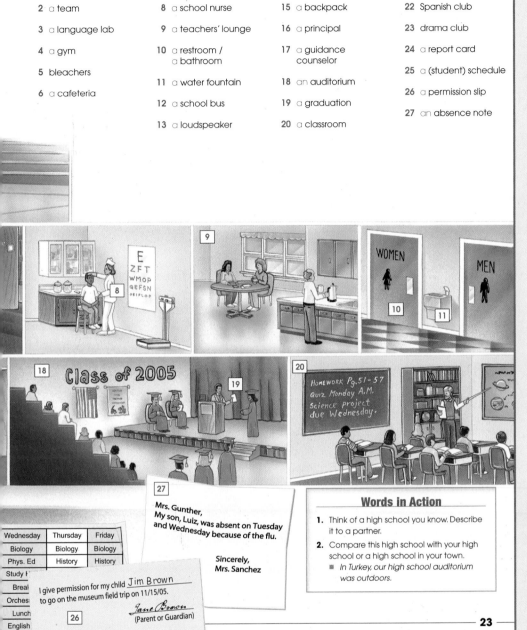

27 Mrs. Gunther,
My son, Luiz, was absent on Tuesday and Wednesday because of the flu.

Sincerely,
Mrs. Sanchez

Wednesday	Thursday	Friday
Biology	Biology	Biology
Phys. Ed	History	History
Study H		
Breal		
Orches		
Lunch		
English		
Algebr		

I give permission for my child Jim Brown
to go on the museum field trip on 11/15/05.

Jane Brown
26 (Parent or Guardian)

Words in Action

1. Think of a high school you know. Describe it to a partner.

2. Compare this high school with your high school or a high school in your town.
   - *In Turkey, our high school auditorium was outdoors.*

— 23

have them identify their own lists of new words. Have them also read and practice complete sentences using the vocabulary introduced in **Word Partnerships**. Incorporate writing skills by asking students to write several complete sentences. Present an example sentence that includes *You can . . . at school.* Encourage correct grammar as they expand their sentences into a full paragraph that you begin on the board. *There are many things you can do at our school. You can study English in a*

classroom. You can talk to a counselor. You can also . . .

Evaluation 1: Ask groups to read their paragraphs to the class.

Application: 20–25 minutes
Formally teach the use of *like*. Students should complete an individual paragraph about what they like to do at school. Offer the topic sentence *There are many things I like to do at school. I like to . . .*

Computers

Level ★

Objective: Discuss computer costs and parts.

Warm-up: 5–7 minutes
Show students an envelope and tell them you need to send it a great distance. Pose several specific scenarios: California to New York, United States to China, and England to Greece. Accept student ideas about how long it would take your envelope to arrive. Write *e-mail* on the board. Take a poll to see who has an e-mail account. Draw two computers on the board and somehow convey distance between them—possibly by putting them on opposite sides of a circle (the world). Compare how long it would take to send an e-mail from one computer to the other. Discuss *Are computers important today?*, *Can computers help you learn English?*, and *Do you have a computer in your home?*

Introduction: State the objective.

Presentation 1: 8–10 minutes
Formally study the vocabulary on **pages 24 and 25** of the dictionary. Provide an opportunity for each student to pronounce every word. *Note:* For students who have no experience with computers, some of the vocabulary won't be as meaningful. If possible, provide these students with the opportunity to see and work on a real computer.

Practice 1: 8–10 minutes
Students should quiz a partner by pointing to an item and asking *What is this?* If there are computers in the room, or a computer lab, use these computers to illustrate vocabulary examples.

Evaluation 1: Observe the activity. Assist as needed.

Presentation 2: 15–20 minutes
Write *machines* on the board. With student participation, create a list of the machines in the picture on **pages 24–25**. In a second column, decide on a cost for each machine. Prepare students to perform this model conversation.

> **Customer:** *Excuse me, how much is this laptop?*
>
> **Salesperson:** *The laptop is _____.*
>
> **Customer:** *That is a good price. I will buy it!*

Practice 2: 8–10 minutes

Request that students practice the conversation with five other students and insert new information from the board for each type of machine.

Evaluation 2: Ask for volunteers to demonstrate for the class.

Application: 20–30 minutes
Read sample newspaper advertisements. Students should use items from the dictionary and prices they create to design their own newspaper advertisement for a computer store.

Words in Context

Computers keep getting smaller and faster. Scientists built the first computer in the 1940s. It was the size of a large room. In the 1970s, stores began to sell **desktop computers.** Then, in the 1990s, small **laptops** appeared. Now tiny **handheld computers** are popular.

Verbs

30 be online

31 enter your password

32 select text

33 click

34 scan

35 print (out)

24

Level ★★

Objective: Read Internet and e-mail addresses.

Warm-up: 20–30 minutes
Make a technology cluster map on the board using the template on the Activity Bank CD-ROM as a guide. In the secondary circles write *machines, verbs, connected to computers,* and *on the computer.* Help students understand each category by filling in one circle with an item from the word list and **Word Partnerships** list. The category *on the computer* includes items like the *cursor* and *scroll bar.*

Introduction: State the objective.

Presentation 1: 15–20 minutes
Answer any questions thoroughly as you review **pages 24 and 25.** Review the Internet symbols in **Word Partnerships** carefully and discuss the addresses found in **Words in Action #2.** Allow sufficient time for students to use the Internet, if available. Prepare students for dictation.

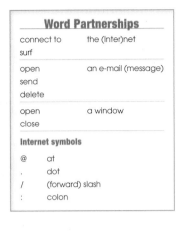

1. a CD-ROM
2. a disk
3. a window
4. a toolbar
5. a folder
6. a cursor
7. a file
8. a (drop down) menu
9. icons
10. a scroll bar
11. a cable
12. a power strip
13. a projector
14. a scanner
15. a printer

16. a PDA / a handheld (computer)
17. a desktop (computer)
18. a key
19. a monitor
20. a screen
21. a keyboard
22. an e-mail (message)
23. a laptop (computer) / a notebook (computer)
24. trackpad / a touchpad
25. software / a (computer) program
26. a mouse pad
27. a mouse
28. a CD-ROM drive
29. the (Inter)net / the (World Wide) Web

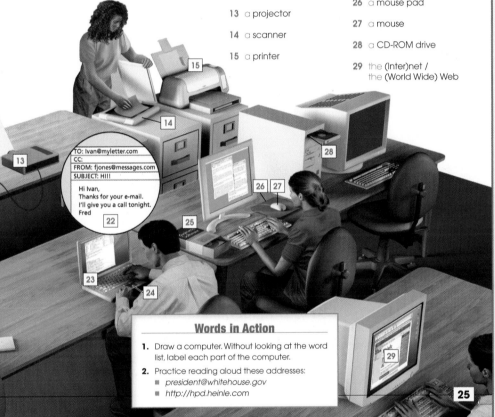

TO: Ivan@myletter.com
CC:
FROM: fjones@messages.com
SUBJECT: HI!!

Hi Ivan,
Thanks for your e-mail.
I'll give you a call tonight.
Fred

Words in Action

1. Draw a computer. Without looking at the word list, label each part of the computer.
2. Practice reading aloud these addresses:
   - president@whitehouse.gov
   - http://hpd.heinle.com

Practice 1: 15–20 minutes
Dictate a few sample e-mail and Web site addresses. Worksheets for this exercise are available on the Activity Bank CD-ROM. Note that the worksheets will allow students to dictate to each other. Dictate e-mail or Web site addresses that you have checked in advance of the lesson. Web sites change frequently and it's best to avoid "surprises."

Evaluation 1: Ask students to peer check their work.

Application: 15–20 minutes
If you have computers available, ask students to research helpful English Internet sites that you provide, or teach them to obtain an e-mail account if they don't have one. Discuss *favorites*. If there are no computers or Internet access, supply addresses to several Web sites from businesses in your area. Use those that will be familiar and include the local newspaper. Challenge students to guess whose address it is. After discussion, have students create a personal e-mail address book.

Objective: Write instructions.

Warm-up: 15–20 minutes
Read *Words in Context* on **page 24** as a class. Discuss the bold-faced words and ensure all students understand. Hold a class discussion about the question *Can computers get any smaller?*

Introduction: State the objective.

Presentation 1: 10–20 minutes
Ask students if they have e-mail and why they believe e-mail is good or bad. Create a chart with two columns on the board. Label the columns *advantages* and *disadvantages*. If it proves difficult for students to think of disadvantages, help by suggesting *spam* or *junk mail*.

Review all the vocabulary on **pages 24 and 25.** Clarify any words the students struggle with. If you have access to the Internet in your facility, consider leading the rest of this lesson on the computers. Begin by discussing turning computers on and off. Find out which students know how to perform basic tasks and group them with students who have less experience with technology.

Practice 1: 15–20 minutes
Inquire how many students are familiar with instruction manuals. Present a scenario that you have never seen a computer before and need step-by-step instructions on how to turn a computer on and off. When sentences are written, ask students to compare their instructions. Request that several volunteers write the instructions on the board.

Evaluation 1: Compare the instructions. *Note:* If too few students have enough technology experience, consider dictating instructions.

Application: 10–15 minutes
Challenge students to commit the instructions to memory and practice giving the instructions to one another. If possible, ask students to go to a library or school computer lab and practice turning the computers on and off. Have them identify parts of the computer that they studied in class. Have students draw and label the parts of a computer to become more familiar with the terms.

Project

Ask students to design a Web site about themselves. Ask what they would include. Each should develop an address. For example, suggest www.jcarlos.com (Web site was available for purchase at the time of publishing). For a more group-oriented e-mail, arrange pen pals. Have students exchange e-mail addresses and have them write once a week to practice vocabulary and writing.

Objective: Identify family relationships.

Warm-up: 10–15 minutes
Generate conversation by asking students how many brothers and sisters they have and how many people live in their homes. Take a class poll and make a bar graph describing the students and the size of their families. A bar-graph template is available on the **Activity Bank CD-ROM**.

Introduction: State the objective.

Presentation 1: 15–20 minutes
Ask students to close their dictionaries while you draw a simple family tree on the board. Label with names of your parents, your sisters and brothers, and your children, nieces, and nephews. Question the class to determine how many relationship words they know. Have students begin a list of vocabulary in their notebooks. Ask students to open to **pages 26 and 27** but to cover the word list on **page 27**. See if they can match each word on the board to a numbered picture in the dictionary. Have them write the number of the picture next to the word in their notebooks. Uncover the word list in the dictionary and check answers.

Practice 1: 20–30 minutes
In small groups, ask students to count all the brothers, sisters, parents, children, grandparents, grandchildren, cousins, etc. from the family tree in the dictionary. Suggest students begin a brief family tree of their own and provide an example on the board.

Evaluation 1: Review the results.

Presentation 2: 10–15 minutes
Explain the use of the possessive *s* and give the students the following example on the board: *My brother's name is Omar.* Prepare students to perform this brief conversation, and emphasize pronunciation of the possessive *s*.

   Student A: *What is your <u>brother's</u> name?*

   Student B: *Omar*

Practice 2: 8–10 minutes
Ask students to practice the conversation with a partner. Explain that they should replace the underlined word with other words from the list, such as *brother's*, *sister's*, and *mother's*. Ask them to record their answers. Use the template on the **Activity Bank CD-ROM** or tell students they can make their own grid to record their answers.
Evaluation 2: Volunteers demonstrate for the class.

Application: 20–30 minutes
Ask students to write each vocabulary word on a flashcard and write the name of a family member by each word. In small groups, students should share their flashcards by saying sentences such as *My sister's name is _____.*

Family

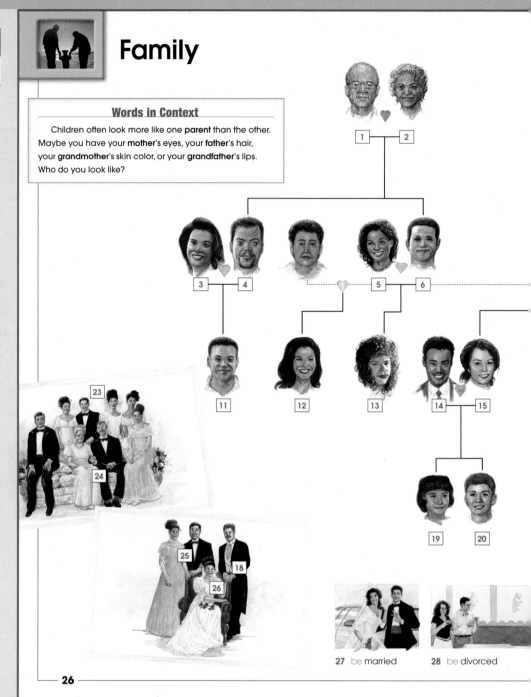

Words in Context
Children often look more like one **parent** than the other. Maybe you have your **mother**'s eyes, your **father**'s hair, your **grandmother**'s skin color, or your **grandfather**'s lips. Who do you look like?

27 be married   28 be divorced

26

Objective: Describe family relationships.

Warm-up: 15–20 minutes
Ask students to list the numbers 1–26 on a piece of paper. They may open their dictionaries but ask them to cover the word list on **page 27**. Help students understand that the family-chart vocabulary references the picture. Without looking at the words, have students write the relationship the framed woman has with each numbered picture. Then check the answers.

Introduction: State the objective.

Presentation 1: 15–20 minutes
Go over **Word Partnerships**. Begin a class discussion by asking which students have younger or older brothers and how many they have. Refer to the pictures on **pages 26 and 27**. Identify brothers and sisters on the board with the students' input. Write the model on the board. Show how to perform this model conversation.

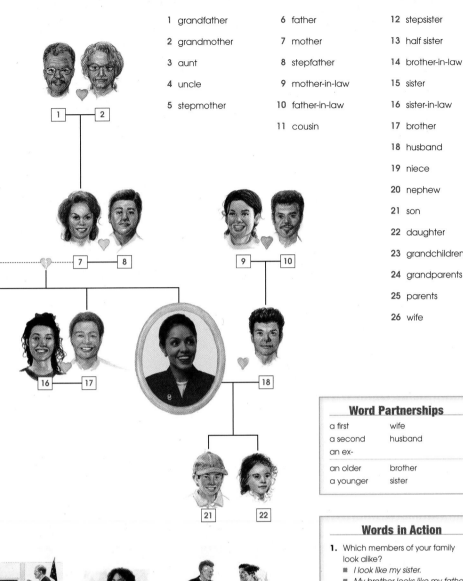

1 grandfather	6 father	12 stepsister
2 grandmother	7 mother	13 half sister
3 aunt	8 stepfather	14 brother-in-law
4 uncle	9 mother-in-law	15 sister
5 stepmother	10 father-in-law	16 sister-in-law
	11 cousin	17 brother
		18 husband
		19 niece
		20 nephew
		21 son
		22 daughter
		23 grandchildren
		24 grandparents
		25 parents
		26 wife

Word Partnerships

a first	wife
a second	husband
an ex-	
an older	brother
a younger	sister

Words in Action

1. Which members of your family look alike?
   - *I look like my sister.*
   - *My brother looks like my father.*
2. Draw a family tree or bring pictures to class. Tell a partner about your family.

29 be a single mother   30 be remarried

— 27 —

Show how to substitute information.

Student A: *Who do you think is younger, 4 or 6?*

Student B: *I think 4 is younger and 6 is older. Who is 4?*

Student A: *He is an uncle.*

Practice 1: 15–20 minutes
Ask students to practice the conversation with a partner, replacing items that are underlined with other numbers from the picture.

Evaluation 1: Ask volunteers to demonstrate in front of the class.

Application: 15–20 minutes
Ask each student to draw a family tree, as suggested in *Words in Action #2*. Then, encourage discussion in small groups by having students describe their family using *older* and *younger* in their descriptions.

Warm-up: 10–15 minutes
Ask students to open their dictionaries and look at the photographs on **pages 26 and 27.** Have each student find a partner and discuss the relationships in the family tree.

Introduction: State the objective.

Presentation 1: 10–20 minutes
Review the possessive *s* and possessive adjectives and make sure all students understand. Examine the small pictures on the two pages as a class to check for questions about the vocabulary. Read *Words in Context* with students and ask them if they have any family members that look alike or similar to each other. Continue the conversation by asking for specific examples. Write the following short paragraph on the board as a model.

> *My family members look like each other. For example, my father has a big nose. My brother looks like my father. He also has a big nose. My mother has beautiful long black hair, and so does my sister. My mother's eyes are brown. I have brown eyes and so do my sisters and my brothers. All my brothers and my sisters look like my mother or my father.*

Read the paragraph with the students.

Practice 1: 20–25 minutes
Ask students to make lists of distinguishable traits that members of their family have. There is a worksheet on the **Activity Bank CD-ROM** that can assist students' practice.

Evaluation 1: Go over the lists.

Application: 20–30 minutes
Using the sample paragraph and the information the students listed in Practice 1, ask students to write their own paragraphs. They may use the topic and conclusion sentences from the model or write their own.

Project

In small groups, students should choose one member to supply family information. The others will create a tree in the same format as the one in the dictionary with the selected student as the central figure. Ask students to draw pictures or look for pictures in magazines to represent individuals. Present the work to the class. Alternate project activities include having students research a famous family on the Internet **or** having students bring in photographs to enhance their family trees.

Level ★

Objective: Use verbs to discuss raising children.

Warm-up: 7–10 minutes
Generate classroom discussion by asking who has children and if it is easy or hard to take care of children. Continue by making a list of what people need to do to take care of children. Since students may have little vocabulary with which to describe this, ask them to act out anything they might think of and then write on the board what they are showing. Help them understand by pantomiming spoon-feeding a baby.

Introduction: State the objective.

Presentation 1: 15–20 minutes
Have students close their dictionaries. Explain that you are going to pantomime several actions. See if students can identify them. Encourage them to call out words when they think of them. Write the words on the board. Ask students to open to **pages 28 and 29.** Cover all the vocabulary with the students. Create a pantomime that is acceptable to students for each action. Incorporate the words from *Word Partnerships* as well.

Practice 1: 10–15 minutes
Review the word list. Have students form groups of four or five and quiz each other by pantomiming actions from the list.

Evaluation 1: Observe the activity.

Presentation 2: 8–10 minutes
Prepare students to play Bingo. Ask them to list eight verbs related to raising a child and use the Bingo card template available on the Activity Bank CD-ROM. As an alternate activity, have students use the Bingo worksheets from the Activity Bank CD-ROM.

Practice 2: 10–15 minutes
Play Bingo with the students. Read different actions in random order from the verbs they provided. Every time you say one of the items the students have listed, they check it off. The first student to check off all items is the winner. To make it more challenging, you might ask them to cover the words on **page 29.**

Evaluation 2: Check for accuracy during the game.

Application: 20–30 minutes
Have members of small groups make a list of the five actions an adult should do to take care of children. Report to the class.

Raising a Child

Words in Context

Everyone loves to **hold** and **rock** a baby. But it takes time and energy to **love, protect,** and **encourage** children. It also costs a lot of money to **raise** them. The average family in the U.S. spends $160,000 to raise a child to the age of 18!

28

Level ★ ★

Objective: Discuss ways to care for children.

Warm-up: 10–15 minutes
Ask if students have children or younger siblings at home. Have students look on **pages 26 and 27** and read *Words in Action #2.* In groups, follow the instructions. Be prepared to teach ranking so they understand the assignment.

Introduction: State the objective.

Presentation 1: 20–30 minutes
Go over the complete vocabulary list. Make sure students understand all words and phrases well. Study several, if not all, of the situations in the pictures. Create sample sentences, such as *In 14, the mother is protecting her child from a dog, In 17, the mother is praising her child for the picture,* and *In 20, the father is reading a book to his son.* Write these sentences on the board. Define direct object and indirect object. Help

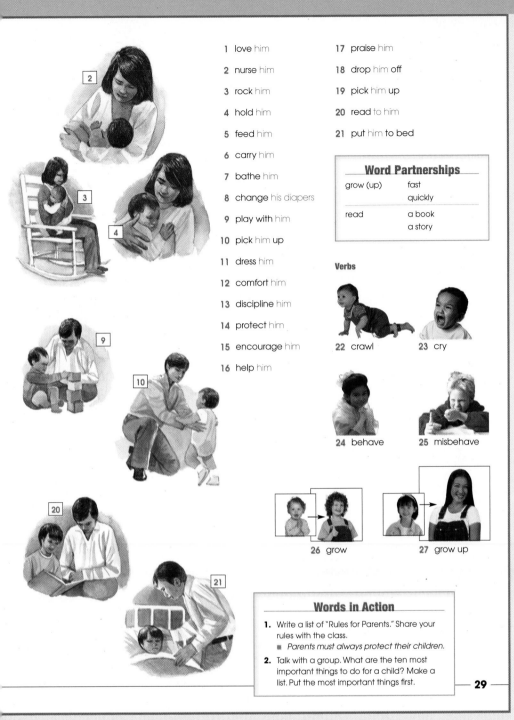

1 love him
2 nurse him
3 rock him
4 hold him
5 feed him
6 carry him
7 bathe him
8 change his diapers
9 play with him
10 pick him up
11 dress him
12 comfort him
13 discipline him
14 protect him
15 encourage him
16 help him

17 praise him
18 drop him off
19 pick him up
20 read to him
21 put him to bed

Word Partnerships

grow (up)	fast
	quickly
read	a book
	a story

Verbs

22 crawl
23 cry
24 behave
25 misbehave
26 grow
27 grow up

Words in Action

1. Write a list of "Rules for Parents." Share your rules with the class.
   ■ *Parents must always protect their children.*
2. Talk with a group. What are the ten most important things to do for a child? Make a list. Put the most important things first.

Objective: Discuss raising children properly.

Warm-up: 10–15 minutes
Have students form discussion groups and talk about how much they believe it costs to raise a child from birth to age 18. Expand the conversation by asking them to make a list of items needed to raise children.

Introduction: State the objective.

Presentation 1: 15–20 minutes
Ask students to open their dictionaries to **page 29** and closely study the vocabulary. If students see words that need to be included, encourage them to add to their lists. Ask students to identify items that might cost money. For example, reading a book to a child might require buying a book. Read *Words in Context* with students. Ask students if it is important to raise children with more discipline or more encouragement.

Practice 1: 15–20 minutes
Have students regroup and identify problems that could result if children are raised without discipline or encouragement. When students have thought of as many problems as they can, ask representatives to go to other groups and bring back other ideas.

Evaluation 1: As a class, make a master list on the board.

Application: 20–30 minutes
Based on the master list, ask the groups to establish a list of "Rules for Parents" as suggested in *Words in Context*. Group leaders can share results with the class.

students understand the placement of the direct object and the indirect object and practice inserting objects into sentences.

Practice 1: 8–10 minutes
Ask students to quiz one another by choosing a numbered picture and asking a partner to give a sentence describing the picture. Partners should switch roles so each creates three sentences. Expand this into a writing activity by having students choose their favorite pictures and write sentences.

Evaluation 1: Ask volunteers to read their sentences for the class or write them on the board.

Application: 20–30 minutes
Ask the groups to rank all the actions identified on the page about raising children (1–21) in order of importance.

Project

After forming small groups, have students list items that babies need. Start the discussion by suggesting *diapers* and *baby food.* Supply newspaper advertisements and store flyers for students to use. Have students create a budget to buy baby supplies. Encourage conversation about how much caring for a baby costs and what a year's worth of diapers might cost.

Level ★

Objective: Identify life events.

Warm-up: 15–20 minutes
Write *future* on the board. Under the word, write actions such as *get married, have children,* and *complete school.* See how much students know by asking them to describe by pantomiming. Add a question mark by each word. Then ask individuals who are single *Do you want to get married in the future? Do you want to have children?* Ask any other students with children or partners *Do you want to finish school?* Write *When?* on the board. Ask students to write the year, and perhaps the month, they hope to accomplish items on the list.

Introduction: State the objective.

Presentation 1: 20–30 minutes
Encourage students to think about time as you draw a line across the board with a dot in the middle. Label the dot *present* and add *past* and *future* to the ends. Discuss each item on **pages 30 and 31.** Be sure students understand each one. Work on pronunciation as necessary. Quiz them briefly by saying a word and asking them to point to the corresponding picture in their dictionaries. Draw a three-column chart on the board and label the columns *past, present,* and *future.* Complete the chart with events from your life. There is a template available on the **Activity Bank CD-ROM.**

Practice 1: 10–15 minutes
Ask students to draw their own chart. Ask students to put items they have already done, are doing, or will do in the appropriate columns.
Evaluation 1: Encourage students to share their charts with the class.

Presentation 2: 10–15 minutes
Review **Word Partnerships.** Write *Do you want to . . . ?* on the board. Explain the grammatical use of *want to.* You may choose to create a grammar chart on the board to help students understand. Explain that all the words in the list and **Word Partnerships** are verbs. Prepare students to perform this model conversation.

Student A: *In the future, do you want to buy a house?*
Student B: *Yes I do.* **OR** *No I don't.*

Practice 2: 8–10 minutes
Ask students to practice the conversation and then replace the underlined phrase with others from the word list or **Word Partnerships.**
Evaluation 2: Ask for volunteers to demonstrate in front of the class.

Application: 20–30 minutes
Ask students to write their three most important life events, as suggested in **Words in Action #2.** Ask students to share their answers with the class.

Life Events

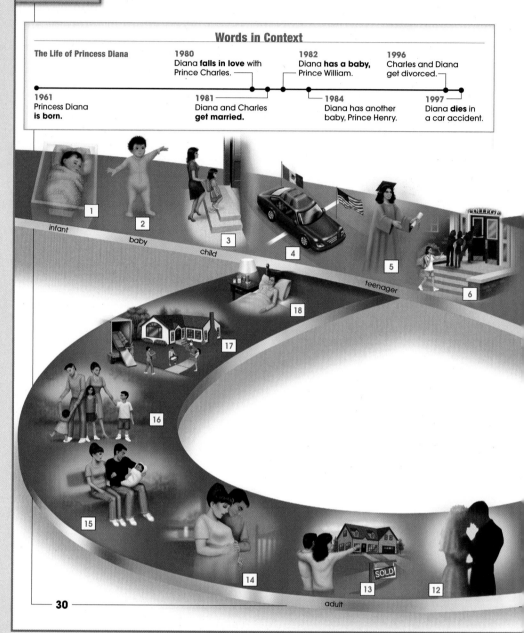

Words in Context

The Life of Princess Diana

1980 Diana **falls in love** with Prince Charles.

1982 Diana **has a baby,** Prince William.

1996 Charles and Diana get divorced.

1961 Princess Diana **is born.**

1981 Diana and Charles **get married.**

1984 Diana has another baby, Prince Henry.

1997 Diana **dies** in a car accident.

infant
baby
child
teenager
adult

Level ★ ★

Objective: Discuss life events in the past.

Warm-up: 10–15 minutes
Ask students to think about what the most important life events are to them. Direct them to open to **pages 30 and 31.** In small groups, members should discuss life events and decide on the three most important events, as suggested in **Words in Action #2.** The groups should report results to the class.

Introduction: State the objective.

Presentation 1: 20–30 minutes
Lecture on all the verbs on the two pages. Help students understand each item and answer any questions they may have. Ask students if they know who *Princess Diana* was. See how much they know without looking in their dictionaries. Ask students to read **Words in Context** silently and ask them comprehension questions using the simple past tense. Teach students vocabulary that might help them discuss

1	be born	9	date	17	move
2	learn to walk	10	fall in love	18	get sick
3	start school	11	get engaged	19	take a vacation
4	immigrate	12	get married	20	celebrate a birthday
5	graduate from high school	13	buy a house	21	become a grandparent
6	go to college	14	be pregnant	22	retire
7	rent an apartment	15	have a baby	23	travel
8	get a job	16	raise a family	24	die / pass away

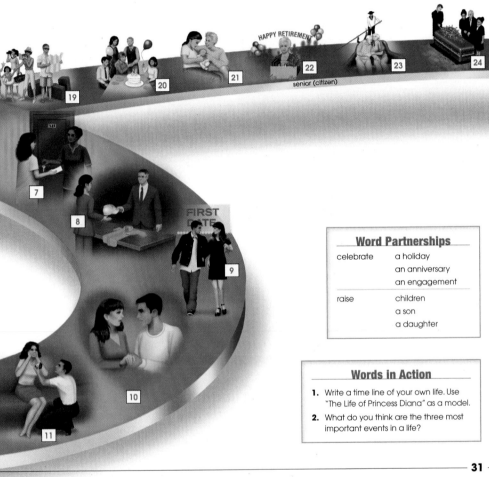

Word Partnerships

celebrate	a holiday
	an anniversary
	an engagement
raise	children
	a son
	a daughter

Words in Action

1. Write a time line of your own life. Use "The Life of Princess Diana" as a model.
2. What do you think are the three most important events in a life?

31

---

the time line. Write your list on the board and include terms such as *after that, during this time,* and *before that.*

Practice 1: 15–20 minutes
Ask pairs to discuss Diana's life, interjecting the new vocabulary where they think events might have happened. Make sure they use the simple past tense appropriately.

Evaluation 1: Observe the activity.

Application: 15–20 minutes
Have students orally list past events in their lives. Then, they can interview each other about their lists and take notes. If students are interested, create paragraphs from notes for all students to read.

Objective: Discuss past, present, and future events and goals.

Warm-up: 15–20 minutes
Make a list of several events, such as *be born, learn to walk,* and *immigrate.* Write them on the board and ask students to copy them. Include some things students have obviously done. Ask students to write the date they finished each action next to each word or phrase. Then ask them to share the dates in pairs or with the class.

Introduction: State the objective.

Presentation 1: 15–20 minutes
Ask students to turn to **pages 30 and 31.** Study the vocabulary and make sure they understand each item. Write the word *goal* on the board and ask the students if they have any *dreams* or *goals* for the future. Inquire about planned dates for their goals. Use *will* to describe what students plan to do and encourage them to use proper grammar in their sentences. Formally teach the use of *will.* Then draw a cluster diagram on the board for your own goals. The central circle should be labeled *my goals.* Extend the circle to three smaller circles and label them: *past goals, present goals, future goals.*

Write sentences about these goals. Demonstrate how it is possible to use the present continuous for things you are doing now, the simple past for goals you completed, and the future, using *will,* for things you still need to complete.

Practice 1: 15–20 minutes
Ask students to make their own goals cluster. There is a cluster template on the Activity Bank CD-ROM or students can create their own clusters. Ask students to write sentences describing the cluster. After finding a partner, students should read their sentences orally and then share their written sentences.

Evaluation 1: Ask volunteers to write their sentences on the board.

Application: 15–20 minutes
Have students write a three-paragraph essay from their sentences based on the cluster they created. They should entitle this essay *My Goals.*

Project

Ask students to make their own personal time lines, including events in the past and planned events for the future. Then ask them to share their time lines with the class. Students can copy the formatting of Diana's time line or use the time line worksheet available on the Activity Bank CD-ROM.

Face and Hair

Level ★

Objective: Identify facial features and hairstyles.

Warm-up: 8–10 minutes
Begin class with all students standing. Issue "sitting" instructions by hair color until all students have taken seats. Students with *blond* hair should sit, followed by students with *red* hair, *brown* hair, *gray* or *white* hair, and finally *black* hair. Assist students who may not understand when to sit. Repeat the activity with hair types. Students stand until they hear the word that describes their hair: *curly, long, short,* or *straight.* Write the words on the board as they are called. Again, assist students who may not understand when to sit by drawing on the board.

Introduction: State the objective.

Presentation 1: 15–20 minutes
Lead a quick corners activity. Assign one of the following characteristics to each corner of the room: *curly, straight, wavy, no hair* or whatever characteristics the students' hair have. Instruct students to go to the corner that best describes their hair. Have one representative from each group say to the class *We have _____ hair.* After students return to their seats, direct them to **pages 32 and 33** to review the word list. As a class, name each person illustrated in the pictures and have students write names above or below each picture. Prepare students to perform the following conversation.

> **Student A:** *What is Beverly's hair like?*
>
> **Student B:** *Her hair is black and wavy.*

Practice 1: 10–15 minutes
Pair students and have them practice the conversation about six pictures. They should take turns being Student A and B.
Evaluation 1: Ask volunteers to demonstrate in front of the class.

Presentation 2: 10–15 minutes
Teach *have* in the simple present. Use the previously named pictures in the book. Ask questions, such as *Who has a mole?* Practice this with a few other characteristics in preparation for the Practice.

Practice 2: 8–10 minutes
Ask pairs to practice the same questions and answers from Practice 1, using different words from the word list. Challenge students by asking them to cover the word list and just look at the pictures.
Evaluation 2: Ask for volunteers to demonstrate in front of the class.

Application: 20–30 minutes
Have each student copy the word list onto a piece of paper. For each name, students should pick a classmate, family member, or famous person as an example of this facial or hair characteristic. Then ask each group to share the names with the class.

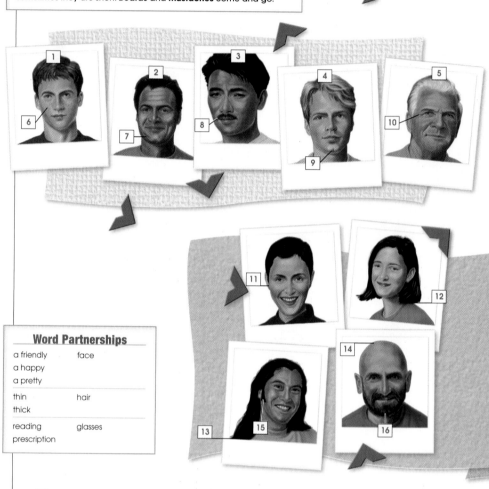

Words in Context

The way people wear their hair changes often. One year, **long hair** is the fashion for women. The next year, it is **short hair**. Sometimes **curly hair** is popular. But then soon everyone wants **straight hair**. Men's fashions change too. Sometimes **sideburns** are long and sometimes they are short. **Beards** and **mustaches** come and go.

Word Partnerships

a friendly	face
a happy	
a pretty	
thin	hair
thick	
reading	glasses
prescription	

32

Level ★ ★

Objective: Describe people.

Warm-up: 8–10 minutes
Form small groups. A group of three is ideal, if class size permits. With dictionaries closed, ask each group to draw a table with three columns labeled *hairstyle, hair color,* and *facial features.* Teach students what *facial features* are by writing *wrinkle* in the chart on the board and draw an example. Students should attempt to fill in words in each of the columns. Add new vocabulary if students inquire about other features.

Introduction: State the objective.

Presentation 1: 18–20 minutes
Ask students to open to **pages 32 and 33** and present the vocabulary to them. Allow time for students to add any words they haven't written in their three-column tables. Review *have* in the simple present. Prepare students to do Practice 1 by describing one student and then having students describe you.

1 red hair
2 brown hair
3 black hair
4 blond hair
5 gray hair
6 freckles
7 a scar
8 a mustache
9 a dimple
10 a wrinkle
11 short hair
12 shoulder-length hair
13 long hair
14 bald
15 sideburns

16 a beard
17 straight hair
18 curly hair
19 wavy hair
20 pierced ears
21 braids
22 a bun
23 bangs
24 a ponytail
25 cornrows
26 pigtails
27 a mole
28 glasses

Words in Action

1. Compare yourself with a partner.
   - *We both have short hair.*
   - *I have freckles. Alex doesn't.*
2. Work with a partner. Take turns describing the face of someone you know. The other person will draw the face.

— 33 —

Level ★ ★ ★

Objective: Discuss and write about popular things.

Warm-up: 11–13 minutes
Create a cluster activity, brainstorming with students to fill it in. Make the primary circle *describing people.* The secondary circles might include *hair, body,* and *face.* Let the discussion develop but make sure that *face* and *hair* are included.

Introduction: State the objective.

Presentation 1: 15–20 minutes
Focus attention on reviewing and/or learning one word at a time from **pages 32 and 33.** As a class, add any new words to the cluster. Choose several individual pictures from the spread and ask students to offer complete descriptions. Review **Word Partnerships.** Lead a discussion about what makes a friendly face look friendly. Write *popular style* on the board. Initiate conversation by discussing popular styles. Read **Words in Context.**

Practice 1: 18–20 minutes
Prepare small groups for a roundtable paragraph-writing activity. Write the topic sentence *Today, popular hairstyles are important for some people, but what is popular? Popular is . . .* on the board. Instruct one student in each group to write a sentence to follow the topic sentence. Students pass the paper around, with each adding a new sentence. Final paragraphs can be peer edited after each member has contributed. Offer transition words to help students expand their ideas. Further expand the paragraphs by passing the papers to other groups.

Evaluation 1: Ask groups to read their paragraphs to the class.

Application: 18–20 minutes
Suggest two topics for individual student paragraphs: *Describe your facial features* OR *Discuss the styles you think are popular.* Allow enough time for students to construct a well-developed, grammatically correct paragraph.

Practice 1: 15–20 minutes
Initiate the activity in **Words in Action #2.** For ease, allow students to see the person they are describing. Provide colored pencils or markers. Another approach is to supply magazine pictures to describe. Extend the activity into a writing practice by having students write sentences or a paragraph about their magazine picture. For an alternative activity, Student A could describe the individuals on **pages 32 and 33** and Student B could point when he or she knows the correct picture.
Evaluation 1: Observe the activity.

Application: 20–22 minutes
Pair students by level and perform the activity described in **Words in Action #1.** This activity can also be effectively done in a Johari Squares chart in which students fill in the information:

Student A only	Student B only
Both Students A and B	Not Student A or B

A Johari Squares template is available on the Activity Bank CD-ROM.

Project

Provide magazines or ask students to bring pictures of their family and friends to create a personal picture dictionary. Challenge them to find a picture to represent every word on **page 33.** Increase the difficulty by allowing them to use only seven pictures for all the vocabulary words. Have students share results.

Daily Activities

Level ★

Objective: Discuss daily activities.

Warm-up: 10–15 minutes
Write the following phrases on the board: *eat breakfast, eat lunch,* and *eat dinner.* Begin a discussion about what time students eat each meal on an average day. If necessary, review time vocabulary on **pages 4 and 5.** Expand the class conversation by asking what time people perform other daily activities.

Introduction: State the objective.

Presentation 1: 15–20 minutes
Write *verbs* on the board and see if students can call out examples. Supply the first verb *eat,* and begin a list on the board. Initiate a pantomime of other words students probably know such as *run* and *walk.* Refer to **pages 34 and 35.** Study each action as a class to ensure everyone understands and can properly pronounce each vocabulary word.

Practice 1: 10–15 minutes
Begin an independent activity. Students should look over the word list and compile a list of things they do in the course of a day. Students can make a separate list of the dictionary actions they <u>do not</u> perform each day. When finished, students should put the events in time order and indicate a time each task on their lists takes place.

Evaluation 1: Inquire how many actions are on students' "do not do" lists. Extend conversation by comparing what actions are listed and why each is not performed.

Presentation 2: 10–15 minutes
Have students select five actions they do daily from the list. To aid students, choose five from your own list. Prepare the class for a visual dictation.

Practice 2: 10–15 minutes
Execute a dictation for the group by acting out your five items and having students write the actions from the word list based on what they see. Invite students to portray words from their lists. If the class is large, divide into smaller groups.

Evaluation 2: Ask students to peer check their dictation.

Application: 8–10 minutes
Prepare students to perform this model conversation based on their schedules in Practice 1.

Student A: *What time do you <u>eat breakfast</u>?*

Student B: *I <u>eat breakfast</u> at <u>7:00 in the morning</u>.*
OR
Student B: *I do not <u>eat breakfast</u>.*

Words in Context

José and I have two children and we both work. Our lives are busy. I usually **wake up** early. I **go** to work at 6:00 A.M. I'm a clerk at a market. José wakes the kids up and **takes** them to school. I go home at noon and **have** lunch. Then José goes to work. I **do** the housework and **make** dinner. The children **go** to bed before José returns at 10:00 P.M. The next day we **get up** and do it all again!

1 wake up	19 eat dinner / **have** dinner
2 get up	20 take a walk
3 brush your teeth	21 do housework
4 take a shower	22 take a bath
5 comb your hair	23 go to bed
6 shave	24 sleep
7 put on makeup	25 watch television
8 get dressed	
9 eat breakfast / have breakfast	
10 take your child to school	
11 go to work	
12 take a coffee break	
13 eat lunch / have lunch	
14 go home	
15 take a nap	
16 exercise / work out	
17 do homework	
18 make dinner	

Words in Action

1. Take turns asking and answering questions about the picture.
   - Student A: *What does the family do in the morning?*
   - Student B: *They wake up, get dressed, and eat breakfast.*
2. Tell your partner about your typical morning.
   - *I wake up at 9:00. First I brush my teeth and then I take a shower.*

— 34 —

Level ★ ★

Objective: Describe a typical day.

Warm-up: 12–15 minutes
Before directing students to the dictionary, ask them to write their daily schedule and share it with students sitting near them. Provide students with your own example. Encourage them to specify as many actions as possible. Next, propose a contest to see who finishes the most actions before 9:00 in the morning (A.M.). Limit the contest to five minutes of writing.

Introduction: State the objective.

Presentation 1: 18–20 minutes
Open to **pages 34 and 35.** Discuss each action as a class. Prepare students to do the activity suggested in *Words in Action #1.* As an alternative activity, students should try to change each verb in this activity from present to past tense.

Objective: Write a paragraph about a daily schedule.

Warm-up: 12–15 minutes
Initiate a large-group discussion about what makes life busy. Pose the questions *Who has a busy life?* and *What would you do if you had more time?* Launch a conversation circle. Students should arrange themselves in two circles, one inside and one outside, with the same number of students in each. Explain that you would like students to talk to their partner in the other circle for one minute about their daily routine. When they hear a signal, the other partner should take over. When the signal sounds twice, the circles should rotate by two students and students should work with their new partners. Repeat this activity three or four times.

Introduction: State the objective.

Presentation 1: 18–20 minutes
Refer students to **pages 34 and 35** of the dictionary and review the word list as a class. Read the word list aloud or play the audio, and then ask students to call out any words that are new to them. Create a master list on the board and discuss these new words in depth. Invite students to participate in developing definitions. Structure the lesson to allow time for students to write sentences with the new words.

Practice 1: 12–15 minutes
Have students close their dictionaries and make suggestions on how to prepare for dictation. Use *Words in Context* as the text, reading it once at normal speed, once slowly, and then once again at normal speed.

Evaluation 1: Ask students to peer check each other's work without the dictionary. Examine problems together to understand what students misunderstood in the dictation.

Application: 20–25 minutes
Ask students to write a paragraph about their own schedules, using the paragraph in *Words in Context* as a model.

Example:

Student A: *What <u>did</u> the family do in the morning?*

Student B: *They <u>woke</u> up, <u>got</u> dressed, and <u>ate</u> breakfast.*

Practice 1: 12–15 minutes
After pairing students, provide time for students to complete the conversation suggested in *Words in Action #1.* Have students trade roles and describe at least six pictures.

Evaluation 1: Ask for volunteers to demonstrate for the class.

Application: 18–20 minutes
Deliver a review lecture on transition words, such as *first, next, second, after that,* and *finally.* Allow time for students to complete the *Words in Action #2* activity aloud using these words. If students complete this activity with ease, extend the activity by discussing other times of the day or a specific past day of the week.

Ask students to complete a planner for the current week. Tell students to include actions from the list and the day or time they do each item. Encourage students to add other actions not included on the pages. Share schedules with others or conduct formal presentations. A planner template is included on the **Activity Bank CD-ROM.**

Walk, Jump, Run

Level ★

Objective: Identify common action verbs.

Warm-up: 15–20 minutes
Write *transportation* on the board. Invite students to talk about the transportation they take to get to school. Be prepared to suggest answers, such as *take the bus, walk, drive,* or *ride a bicycle*. Write complete sentences on the board as students respond. *I walk to school every day.* Supply each student with a small card so they can write a sentence about how they get to school: *I . . .* Tell them NOT to write their names. Next, solicit volunteers to tell the class what activities they like to do. Place the samples on the board: *I like to walk with my husband.* Request that students add a sentence to their card stating one thing that they *like* to do. Before collecting the student sentences, remind them that their names should not be on the cards. Pass the papers out randomly and ask students to find the owner of the paper they were assigned. Students walk around and read the sentences to students until they find the writer. *Note:* Students at this level shouldn't be expected to write perfect sentences, so don't focus on grammar or overcorrect unless the meaning is unclear.

Introduction: State the objective.

Presentation 1: 15–20 minutes
Open to **pages 36 and 37** and discuss each action as a class. Offer a thorough explanation of verbs, if necessary. Spend time focusing on pronunciation. Have students suggest a person or object that performs each action. Use the illustrations.

Practice 1: 8–10 minutes
Pair students and have partners quiz each other. With the word lists covered, students take turns calling out an action while the other points to the corresponding picture.
Evaluation 1: Observe the activity.

Presentation 2: 8–10 minutes
Prepare students to participate in **Words in Action #2.** Explain the idea of pantomiming and then act out a few actions in front of the class.

Practice 2: 8–10 minutes
Ask students to practice a few pantomimes with their partner from Practice 1. Bring the class together and open the floor to student volunteers. Consider structuring this activity as a team event and work through all the actions on these pages.
Evaluation 2: Judge students' responses.

Application: 8–10 minutes
Ask students to make a list of five things they do every day, as suggested in **Words in Action #1.** Have students write on a half sheet of paper. Again, ask that no names be used. Read the lists and ask students to identify the correct classmate.

Words in Context

I live in Los Angeles. What a busy place it is! I often **run** because I am always late. I have to **get on** the bus at 8:00 in order to arrive at work by 9:00. There is a lot of traffic. It is probably faster to **walk.** But I study English while I **ride** the bus. I am learning a lot!

36

Level ★★

Objective: Describe actions using the present continuous.

Warm-up: 10–15 minutes
Explain and then play the game Simon Says. Give directions and have students act them out only if you say *Simon says* first. Students who jump when you say *Jump!* must leave the game. Instead, they should wait for you to say *Simon says,*

"Jump!" Use action words from **pages 36 and 37.**

Introduction: State the objective.

Presentation 1: 18–20 minutes
Refer students to **page 37** and review each word. Pay special attention to **Word Partnerships.** Teach the present continuous in detail and present a grammar chart to help promote understanding. Show students how to describe the picture, using the present continuous and an object to follow. Write *What is he doing?* on the board. Then ask

1	fly	7	fall	13	walk	19	go down	24	jump
2	leave	8	slip	14	get off	20	go up	25	push
3	enter / go in	9	jog	15	stand up	21	crawl	26	ride
4	march	10	cross	16	sit (down)	22	kneel	27	pull
5	get out (of)	11	run	17	follow	23	squat		
6	get in	12	get on	18	lead				

Word Partnerships

fall	off
jump	down
	over
get in	a car
get out of	a taxi
get on	a train
get off	a bus
ride	a bicycle / a bike
	a motorcycle
	a horse
cross	the street

Words in Action

1. What five things do you do every day? Use words from the list.
2. Take turns acting out some of the verbs on the list. The other students will guess what you are doing.

37

Warm-up: 10–12 minutes
Read **Words in Context** aloud as a class. Focus on the sentence *But I study English while I ride the bus.* Start a conversation about doing two or three things at the same time. Define *multitasking.* Continue the conversation by asking what students consider to be the pros and cons of *multitasking.*

Introduction: State the objective.

Presentation 1: 18–20 minutes
Tell students to close their dictionaries and state that the vocabulary lesson is about everyday action verbs. Divide students into groups of four and request that each group compile a list of all actions they consider daily activities that would be necessary to list in a picture dictionary. Group members should select a representative to travel to other groups to collect more actions. When completed, students should open to **pages 36 and 37** and add any missing actions to their group list. Discuss each of the vocabulary words as a class and make sure definitions and pronunciations are clear. Begin a conversation about exercising regularly. Decide as a class whether walking to school could be considered exercise.

Practice 1: 12–15 minutes
Reconvene student groups. Have students separately list the words that are related to exercise. All members of the group need to agree on these. When all concur, have members decide which exercise is most effective in gaining good physical health. Again, all must agree; list words in order from the most helpful to the least.

Evaluation 1: Ask the groups to share lists.

Application: 20–25 minutes
Ask students to individually determine how much time they exercise a week, based on their prior discussions and lists. Request itemized lists of exercises and times. As a class, develop a bar graph describing what types of exercises students prefer or how much each member of the class exercises. A template of the bar graph is available on the Activity Bank CD-ROM.

the question about the numbered pictures on **pages 36 and 37**. Use every picture and make sure that the answers include the correct action, as well as proper use of the present continuous and an object.

Practice 1: 12–15 minutes
Place students in small groups in order for them to ask each other questions about the pictures. Encourage responses in the present continuous. Ask each group to discuss at least 15 of the people in the illustration. **Evaluation 1:** Ask questions orally and have students attempt a written

answer. Check the answers as a class by having volunteers write their present continuous sentences on the board.

Application: 20–30 minutes
Take a 10-minute field trip around the school, inside and/or outside. Instruct students to bring notebooks and record each action they see. Suggest they will see *walking* and *sitting.* Upon returning to class, allow time to write complete sentences using the present continuous. Include a sharing period to compare sentences.

Project

Ask students to find pictures in magazines that display human activities. Schedule a day for students to bring their selection to class and create their own picture dictionary page by labeling the actions. Actions found in books may be photocopied. Compile all the pictures together to create a personalized class dictionary. Answer questions about new action word vocabulary.

Audio CD 2, Tracks 7 & 8; Audio Tape 2, Side A

Level ★

Objective: Describe feelings.

Warm-up: 8–10 minutes
Introduce the common phrase *How are you?* and generate responses. Most students will answer *Fine*. Write *fine* on the board and ask for its meaning or synonyms. If nothing is suggested by students, write *OK* or *happy* on the board. Expand the discussion by asking for the opposite of *happy*. Students will likely offer *sad* as an answer, but if not, add it to the board. Write a few sentences on the board, including *I am sad* and *I am happy*. Practice pronunciation by having students repeat. Now, when asked *How are you?*, have students' answers include *happy* or *sad*. Encourage complete sentences.

Introduction: State the objective.

Presentation 1: 15–20 minutes
Write the following list on the board: *happy*, *nervous*, and *comfortable*. If students are unsure of the meaning, pantomime the action. Have students tell you the opposites. Put the correct answers on the board as they are called out. Next, refer to **pages 38 and 39** and help students use the pictures and words to find feelings and their opposites. Formally review the word list. Then, cover the word lists and quiz students by saying a feeling. Students should identify the picture by its number.

Practice 1: 15–20 minutes
Ask students to cover the whole word list at the top of the page. Use the worksheet available on the **Activity Bank CD-ROM** that has one to three letters of each feeling word identified. Without referring to the word list, students should match the pictures and numbers on the worksheet. Then they should write the corresponding vocabulary word.

Evaluation 1: Observe as students work on this task in pairs and then peer correct using the word list.

Presentation 2: 8–10 minutes
Teach the verb *to be*. Consider creating a grammar chart on the board to facilitate this instruction. Show students how they can use the words in the list with a form of *be* to describe how someone feels. Write the following on the board.

　Student A: *How does she feel today?*

　Student B: *She is thirsty.*

Practice 2: 8–10 minutes
Referring to the pictures, ask students to practice the exchange with a partner. Encourage proper use of *he/she*.

Application: 8–10 minutes
Ask a few students *Words in Action #1*. Students ask three additional students how they feel.

Feelings

Words in Context
People cry when they feel **sad** or **homesick**. Sometimes they also cry when they are **happy, angry,** or **scared**. People laugh when they are happy. Sometimes they also laugh when they are **nervous** about something.

1　proud
2　happy
3　angry
4　interested
5　calm

6　nervous
7　embarrassed
8　in love
9　full
10　hungry

38　Unit 4 • People

Level ★ ★

Objective: Describe how people feel and why.

Warm-up: 15–20 minutes
Introduce the common phrase *How are you?* and write responses on the board. In groups, students can discuss responses to the question. Conduct a competition to see which group can think of the most responses.

Introduction: State the objective.

Presentation 1: 15–20 minutes
Open to **pages 38 and 39** and study each adjective as a class. Point attention to the picture depicting *angry*. Inquire for possible reasons for the man's anger. Teach the use and punctuation of *because* in a sentence. Make sure students understand that *because* is followed with a subject and a verb but that a comma is never used. Use the board to display students' reasons for the man's anger in complete sentences using *because*: *The*

11 thirsty	16 homesick	20 excited	24 comfortable	
12 frustrated	17 lonely	21 sad	25 uncomfortable	
13 bored	18 confused	22 surprised		
14 sick / ill	19 afraid / scared	23 tired		
15 worried				

Word Partnerships

angry	about
confused	
embarrassed	
happy	
afraid	of
proud	
tired	
frustrated	by
confused	

Words in Action

1. How do you feel right now? Use one or more words from the list.
2. Find a picture of a person in a magazine or newspaper. How do you think the person feels?
   - *She is not smiling. She looks bored or angry. Maybe she is in pain.*

— 39

Objective: Tell a story.

Warm-up: 12–15 minutes
Write *cry* and *laugh* on the board and start a conversation about why or when people laugh or cry. Steer students toward thinking about the feeling words without opening their dictionaries. When a sizeable list is on the board, direct students to open their dictionaries and read *Words in Context* silently. Call for student opinions of agreement or disagreement.

Introduction: State the objective.

Presentation 1: 15–20 minutes
As a class, discuss each vocabulary word and include examples of when or why people might feel each emotion. Open the floor for additional words that could be included in the list. Point attention to the picture of people eating. Divide students into groups of four and have each group develop ideas for a story. Consider what happened to the characters before they arrived at the restaurant and predict what will happen when they leave. Share answers. Encourage use of the vocabulary, including the *Word Partnerships* where appropriate.

Practice 1: 12–15 minutes
Mix the groups and allow each group to pick another scene from the pages and write a story in the same sharing fashion. The first student should write the topic sentence, with each member adding a new sentence. Tell students to think about what happened to the characters prior to the action in the picture and what will happen after. Pass the story around the circle at least twice so each group has a paragraph of eight sentences. Accept any reasonable sentences and scenario. Students can peer correct for grammar and tense.

Evaluation 1: Ask a group representative to read the story to the class.

Application: 22–25 minutes
Maintain the same groups. This time, members should choose another picture with a role for each of them as a character. Next, they should develop a conversation and act it out for the class as their character. Encourage students to think of names for their characters.

Project

Explain that facial expressions can often let someone know how people feel. Draw a happy face on the board for *happy*. Erase the smile and replace it with a frown. Tell students this now represents *sad*. See how many other faces students can draw. Extend into a pantomime activity with students using their own facial expressions.

man is angry because . . . Read **Word Partnerships** as a class and show how an object follows the preposition. Extend the sentence with the partnerships.

Practice 1: 15–20 minutes
Form groups of three to write sentences about the pictures. Ask that all responses include a feeling word and answer the question *Why?* with *because* in the sentences. Ask each group to write as many sentences as they can in 10 minutes.

Evaluation 1: Ask for a volunteer to

write a few sentences on the board. Allow time for comparison, but make sure all feeling words (1–25) and the **Word Partnerships** are covered.

Application: 15–20 minutes
Supply pictures from the daily paper or magazines or online news sources. Give each student a picture. Students should attempt **Words in Action #2**. Again, allow time for comparison. Students enjoy comparing their different answers and reading other students' interpretations.

Wave, Greet, Smile

Level ★

Objective: Identify greeting words.

Warm-up: 8–10 minutes
Show students different ways to greet others in the United States. Teach the proper, acceptable way to shake hands and review *How are you?* Move around the room and shake hands with each student, making sure your handshake is firm and you maintain eye contact. Stage a mock social party or business meeting and ask students to practice this greeting with other partygoers or business people.

Introduction: State the objective.

Presentation 1: 15–20 minutes
Before referring students to the dictionary, pantomime several actions, such as *hug, smile, kiss,* and *shake hands.* Encourage students to raise their hands and call out the words when they recognize the action. Open to **pages 40 and 41.** Challenge students to find the corresponding number and word for your pantomimes. Define each word and open the class to discussion. Divide students into small groups and assign each group an equal number of vocabulary words. Students will create an effective pantomime for each assigned word.

Practice 1: 15–20 minutes
Prepare the class for a game in which each group will pantomime to the other groups to see if students can identify the words. Have each member of the group act out at least one word. Additionally, within groups, have students select one expert who can perform the group's three to five words. The expert can later perform these words again for the class or travel to the other groups to teach the words.

Evaluation 1: Observe the activity.

Presentation 2: 8–10 minutes
Begin a discussion about how often certain activities happen. Suggest activities from the word list on **page 40** but also incorporate student ideas. Elicit answers that range anywhere from once a month to three times a day. Examples: *I dance with my friends three times a month* or *I hug my daughter every day.*

Practice 2: 8–10 minutes
Return students to their groups from Practice 1 and have them write the words (1–24) in order, from *all the time* to *one time a year.*

Evaluation 2: Compare student lists.

Application: 8–10 minutes
Individually, students should reevaluate the group lists and put all the words in these categories according to their own personal lives: *every day, once a week, once a month, once a year.*

Words in Context

Ways to **greet** people differ from country to country. In the U.S., people often **shake hands** when they first meet. In Japan, people frequently **bow** to each other. In Chile, women often **hug** and **kiss** each other.

1 argue	9 apologize	17 hug
2 greet	10 compliment	18 smile
3 visit	11 agree	19 help
4 shake hands	12 disagree	20 wave
5 touch	13 comfort	21 kiss
6 have a conversation	14 bow	22 dance
7 give a gift	15 introduce	23 invite
8 write a letter	16 call	24 congratulate

40

Level ★★

Objective: Use interaction words in conversation.

Warm-up: 10–15 minutes
Read *Words in Action #1.* Give every student a chance to respond and discuss their answers as a class. Maintain a record on the board. Do all students from the same country agree about greetings? Maybe not!

Introduction: State the objective.

Presentation 1: 15–20 minutes
Direct students to **pages 40 and 41** but ask them to cover the word list. Form small groups. Each group should number their papers 1–24 and attempt to identify the action depicted in each picture. Review each word with students until clearly understood. Include *Word Partnerships* phrases. Create a short conversation with the class about meeting some friends at the mall or at school. Write the conversation on the board. Try

Word Partnerships

agree	with
dance	
argue	
apologize	to
bow	
wave	

Words in Action

1. How do men and women in your culture greet someone new? How do they greet good friends? Family members?

2. Write five sentences about your best friend. Use words from the list.

— 41

Warm-up: 12–15 minutes
Ask all students to say a sentence about their best friend. Students should include their best friend's name and how long the friendship has lasted. Briefly remind students of the components of a complete sentence and ask them to complete *Words in Action #2* using proper sentence structure and punctuation.

Introduction: State the objective.

Presentation 1: 15–20 minutes
Ask students to open to **pages 40 and 41.** As a class, discuss each word's definition. Formulate a brainstorming session, including which greetings are acceptable and unacceptable in other countries. Write students' ideas on the board. Classify the words into the following categories: *greetings, friendly exchanges, loving exchanges, unfriendly exchanges,* and *professional exchanges.* **Note:** Words can be classified in more than one category. Allow time to discuss differences of opinion. Utilize the Cluster Map Level 3 template available on the Activity Bank CD-ROM. Prepare students for dictation by teaching phrases that come before the subject in sentences and proper comma usage.

Practice 1: 15–18 minutes
For the dictation, use the *Words in Context* content. Repeat several times if necessary. For more advanced classes, add extra sentences about interaction, using the vocabulary prior to the dictation.

Evaluation 1: Ask students to peer edit for spelling and punctuation, particularly commas.

Application: 20–25 minutes
Using *Words in Context* as a guide, have students write their own paragraphs about when and why people smile. Again, encourage checks for proper grammar and punctuation.

to use as many words in the list and write at least six conversation lines.

Practice 1: 15–20 minutes
Pair students and ask them to add six more lines to the conversation. Have them add at least six additional words from the list or *Word Partnerships.* Offer practice time for partners to read the dialogs. Move through the groups to correct pronunciation and help students converse naturally.

Evaluation 1: Ask the pairs to share their conversations with the class.

Application: 20–30 minutes
Combine pairs into groups of four. Tell students they have the opportunity to write a *skit* about a new situation. Define *skit* as a short drama. In each skit, students should use as many words from the list as possible. Develop a friendly competition to see which group can use the most words. After ample time, have students perform their skits for the other groups.

Project

Encourage students to bring their dictionaries to a public place (a mall, the library, a city street) and see how many of the actions they can observe in one hour outside of the school. Students might also want to observe greetings by characters on English-speaking TV shows. When students bring their lists to class, share the results and focus on when and where these greetings were observed. Students should record the action, time, and place on piece of paper to share with others.

Level ★

Objective: Complete a personal information form.

Warm-up: 8–10 minutes
Refer to **pages 6 and 7** and review calendar information as a class. Write *What is your birth date?* on the board. Explain to students that they will ask four classmates for birth dates. Teach strategies and ways to report the information. Write *Nguyen's birth date is January 13th.* Students should orally report what they recorded. *Note:* Inform students to only inquire about the month and the day because asking for the birth year can be a culturally sensitive question. Create a simple two-column grid as a sample for recording the information.

Introduction: State the objective.

Presentation 1: 15–20 minutes
Before providing page references, write *school application* on the board and determine if any students know the definition. Provide a copy of your school's application form or obtain samples from local schools. Many can be found on the Internet. Study the pieces of information needed. Make sure the basic components, such as *name*, *address*, and *phone number* are included. Give examples of last names, middle names, and middle initials. Direct student attention to **pages 42 and 43.** Review the personal information form as a class and briefly discuss the many different documents.

Practice 1: 15–20 minutes
In small groups, with the word list document names covered, have students first guess the names of all 13 documents; then check their answers. Demonstrate one or two examples. Next, distribute the documents form from the **Activity Bank CD-ROM** and have students check the boxes for information each form supplies. Review as a class.

Evaluation 1: Check answers as a class.

Presentation 2: 2–5 minutes
Provide copies of the registration form worksheet from the **Activity Bank CD-ROM**. Review essential vocabulary. Students should not fill this in now.

Practice 2: 10–15 minutes
Allocate time for students to attempt putting Susan Hong's personal information on their form. Guide them to the answers by pointing out the pictures of the Permanent Resident card and the driver's license. Let students know they will leave blank spaces for unavailable information. Offer help as needed.

Evaluation 2: Observe the activity.

Application: 10–15 minutes
Print another registration form and have students use their own personal information.

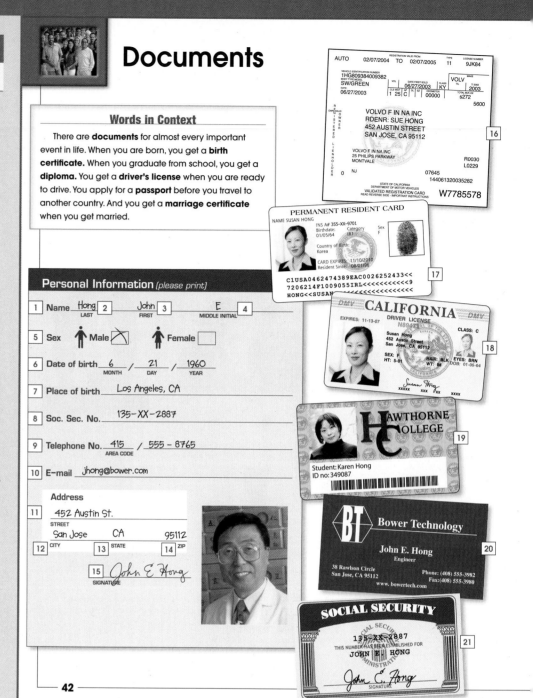

Documents

Words in Context

There are **documents** for almost every important event in life. When you are born, you get a **birth certificate.** When you graduate from school, you get a **diploma.** You get a **driver's license** when you are ready to drive. You apply for a **passport** before you travel to another country. And you get a **marriage certificate** when you get married.

Personal Information *(please print)*

1 Name: Hong 2 John 3 E 4
  LAST FIRST MIDDLE INITIAL

5 Sex ♂ Male ☒ ♀ Female ☐

6 Date of birth 6 / 21 / 1960
  MONTH DAY YEAR

7 Place of birth Los Angeles, CA

8 Soc. Sec. No. 135-XX-2887

9 Telephone No. 415 / 555-8765
  AREA CODE

10 E-mail jhong@bower.com

Address
11 452 Austin St.
  STREET
  San Jose CA 95112
12 CITY 13 STATE 14 ZIP

15 John E Hong
  SIGNATURE

42

Level ★★

Objective: Complete a registration form for a classmate.

Warm-up: 10–15 minutes
Write *documents* on the board and ask students for examples. Brainstorm as a class and then ask students to classify the documents in a cluster activity. Provide the center circle and label it *documents.* Develop the secondary circles if students need assistance. Label the secondary circles *education, travel, personal*

information, and *permission*. Refer students to **pages 42 and 43** and attempt to fill in a third level of circles from the secondary circles, using the word list. A template for this activity is on the **Activity Bank CD-ROM.**

Introduction: State the objective.

Presentation 1: 15–20 minutes
Review the vocabulary as a class. Talk briefly about question formation. Prompt students to think of questions they might ask if they were helping someone complete a registration or personal information

A (registration) form

1. name
2. last name / surname / family name
3. first name
4. middle initial
5. sex / gender
6. date of birth
7. place of birth
8. Social Security number
9. telephone number
10. e-mail address
11. street address
12. city
13. state
14. zip code
15. signature

Documents

16. a vehicle registration card
17. a Resident Alien card / a green card
18. a driver's license
19. a student ID
20. a business card
21. a Social Security card
22. a passport
23. a visa
24. a birth certificate
25. a marriage certificate
26. a Certificate of Naturalization
27. a college degree
28. a high school diploma

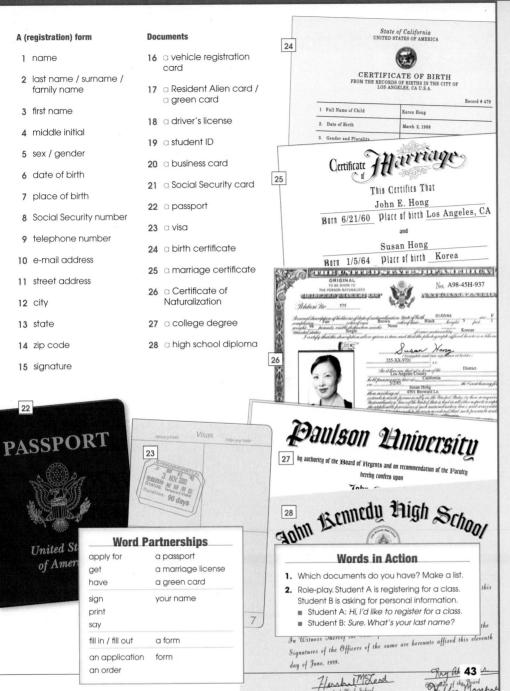

State of California
UNITED STATES OF AMERICA

CERTIFICATE OF BIRTH
FROM THE RECORDS OF BIRTHS IN THE CITY OF
LOS ANGELES, CA U.S.A.

Record # 479

1. Full Name of Child — Karen Hong
2. Date of Birth — March 2, 1988
3. Gender and Plurality

Certificate of Marriage

This Certifies That

John E. Hong
Born 6/21/60 Place of birth Los Angeles, CA

and

Susan Hong
Born 1/5/64 Place of birth Korea

No. A98-45H-937

Susan Hong
355-XX-9701

Paulson University

by authority of the Board of Regents and on recommendation of the Faculty
hereby confers upon

John Kennedy High School

Word Partnerships

apply for	a passport
get	a marriage license
have	a green card
sign	your name
print	
say	
fill in / fill out	a form
an application	form
an order	

Words in Action

1. Which documents do you have? Make a list.
2. Role-play. Student A is registering for a class. Student B is asking for personal information.
   - Student A: *Hi, I'd like to register for a class.*
   - Student B: *Sure. What's your last name?*

---

form. Create a grammar table to illustrate question formation using *what*. Elicit samples by writing questions about numbers 1–3 on the word list.

Practice 1: 15–20 minutes
Assign question writing for the remaining vocabulary on the list. **Evaluation 1:** Read students' work as you walk around the room. Have students with excellent examples write their questions on the board. Choose students to answer the questions to ensure comprehension.

Application: 20–25 minutes
Have students number a piece of paper 1–15 to indicate the information from the word list. Have students interview each other about each item using the role-play activity suggested in *Words in Action #2*. Use the personal information registration form on the **Activity Bank CD-ROM** if desired. Recommend that students make up answers for the spaces about information used for identity confirmation such as birth date and social security number.

Level ★ ★ ★

Objective: Read documents.

Warm-up: 12–15 minutes
Request that students make lists of all the important life documents they can think of, as suggested in *Words in Action #1*. Ask students not to reference the dictionary yet. Call for answers and create a master list on the board. Direct students to open their dictionaries to **page 42** and read *Words in Context* silently. Answer any questions before reviewing the word list. Add any new documents that are mentioned during discussion of the word list.

Introduction: State the objective.

Presentation 1: 10–20 minutes
Prior to class time, compile a list of questions about Susan Hong. Prepare students for an oral quiz about Susan. Note student comprehension and timing as students search for the information in the dictionary. Answers must be based on the information found on the two-page spread. Develop some questions and encourage student answers to incorporate verbs included in *Word Partnerships*. If students are advanced enough, ask a challenging question.

Practice 1: 20–25 minutes
In groups of four, ask students to compile all the information about Susan Hong in time or chronological order. See which group can find the most information. Warn students to carefully peruse every available document. When all groups are satisfied, have each present its list. Compile a master list on the board so all students will have the same, complete information.
Evaluation 1: Clarify that students have collected all relevant information.

Application: 18–20 minutes
Individually, have students take the itemized list about Susan and write their own personal information next to each item. If Susan has information that does not pertain to them, teach students the use of *N/A* (or *not applicable*) and *private*. It is important that although students may hold back some information, they should have most personal numerical information memorized in case a figure of authority asks for it.

Project

Ask students to accumulate all the important documents they have at home and to identify them by making a list and bringing the list to class to share. Have students report on how they keep documents safe and remind them that essential documents should all be kept together in a fire-safe, locked box and the key should be where family members can always find it.

Level ★

Objective: Identify nationalities.

Warm-up: 10–15 minutes
Involve all students by going around the room and having them tell which city or region or country they are from. After the brief survey, students should attempt to fill in the chart. Encourage them to move about and ask classmates for information in order to complete the grid about everyone in class. Prepare students to perform this model conversation.

Student A: *Where are you from?*

Student B: *I am from Chile.*

Name	City/Region/Country

Introduction: State the objective.

Presentation 1: 15–20 minutes
Write *Brazil, United States,* and *Mexico* on the board. Next to *Brazil* add *Brazilian.* Have students provide answers for the other nationalities. Instruct students to open to **pages 44 and 45** and introduce the word list. Develop spelling strategies, such as simply adding an *"n"* to the country name in a few cases. Develop other categories to help students see spelling consistencies. After some study, quiz the class by saying a country and having students respond with the nationality. Begin with the countries on the map, but keep the word list covered.

Practice 1: 15–20 minutes
Pair students for a quizzing session, as suggested in *Words in Action #1.*

Evaluation 1: Observe the activity.

Presentation 2: 2–5 minutes
Provide students with a nationality and ask what color the flag is for that country. Prepare students to perform this model conversation.

Student A: *What colors are the Canadian flag?*

Student B: *The Canadian flag's colors are red and white.*

Practice 2: 10–15 minutes
With a partner students should practice the conversation and substitute different nationalities and flag colors. Demonstrate and review **pages 10 and 11** on colors.

Evaluation 2: Review answers and proper pronunciation.

Application: 10–15 minutes
Ask students to make a list of places they would like to visit. Next to each country, have them write the nationality.

Nationalities

Words in Context

Women from many different countries have been in space. In 1963 Valentina Tereshkova, a **Russian** woman, was the first woman in space. Sally Ride was the first **American** woman in space. Chiaki Mukai was the first **Japanese** woman in space. A **French** woman, a **Canadian** woman, and an **English** woman have also been in space.

1 Canadian
2 American
3 Mexican
4 Venezuelan
5 Colombian
6 Peruvian
7 Brazilian
8 Chilean
9 Argentine / Argentinean
10 British
11 German
12 French
13 Spanish
14 Italian
15 Greek
16 Turkish
17 Iranian
18 Egyptian
19 Saudi Arabian
20 Nigerian
21 Russian
22 Indian
23 Chinese
24 Korean
25 Japanese
26 Thai
27 Vietnamese
28 Filipino
29 Malaysian
30 Australian

44

Level ★ ★

Objective: Read a map.

Warm-up: 12–15 minutes
Prepare students to interview each other with the question from *Words in Action #2.* Make a two-column chart with students' names and nationalities. Upon completion, allow time for comparing spelling.

Introduction: State the objective.

Presentation 1: 18–20 minutes
Refer students to **pages 44 and 45** and thoroughly review the vocabulary list and country names. Specify a country and see if they can identify where it is. Responses should include: *North America, South America, Asia, Europe, Middle East,* or *Africa.* Prepare students to perform this conversation.

Student A: *Excuse me, what nationality are you?*

Student B: *I am Japanese.*

Words in Action

1. With a partner, practice matching countries and nationalities. One person will say a country. The other will say the nationality. Take turns.
   - Student A: *Brazil*
   - Student B: *Brazilian*

2. Do you have classmates or friends from other countries? Make a list of their nationalities.

Student A: *Where is Japan?*

Student B: *It is in Asia.*

Practice 1: 15–20 minutes
If students are from the same country, practice the conversation by having students choose to be a different nationality each time.

Evaluation 1: Ask for volunteers to demonstrate for the class.

Application: 15–20 minutes
Have students create a grid as illustrated. Ask that each student interview eight classmates and complete the grid. Compile one log for the entire class on the board. See the example below.

Name	Country	Location	Nationality
Yuko	Japan	Asia	Japanese

Objective: Learn geographic location of countries.

Warm-up: 12–15 minutes
Have a volunteer student read **Words in Context** aloud while everyone else follows along, or play the audio. Generate a class discussion about other famous women around the world and what countries these women represent. List their names, nationalities, and countries on the board. Add a column to name the category each woman is famous for. Think of categories such as *science*, *sports*, *entertainment*, and *business*.

Introduction: State the objective.

Presentation 1: 15–20 minutes
Ask students to look at dictionary **pages 44 and 45** and discuss the different countries and their locations on the map. Supply an atlas or a globe for additional maps. Practice the pronunciation of each country's name and nationality by noting the importance of stress in pronunciation. Briefly quiz students by saying a country and seeing how fast they can find it on the map and name the continent. Further challenge them by adding new countries. Say *I am from Vietnam*. Students respond: *You are Vietnamese*. For an alternative challenge, have students list all 30 countries on the map and alphabetize them in a certain amount of time. Repeat this activity but shorten the time limit.

Practice 1: 15–20 minutes
Provide copies of the nationality chase worksheet available on the **Activity Bank CD-ROM**. With the random country list on the worksheet, have students compete to see who can write the correct country number next to each country name. The chase should begin with open dictionaries. Discover who can finish first with the most correct answers. Try again with the word list covered, shortening the time limit and lengthening the list of names given each time.

Evaluation 1: Allow time for all students to finish. Observe the results and note who needs more review.

Application: 18–20 minutes
Ask students to learn about people from a different country. Ask them to interview other students, present information to the class, and make a map of that country. If the class is from one country, have students choose another country they know nothing about to research.

Project

Let all students choose a country they would like to visit. Provide maps, tour books, and encyclopedias. Allow class and library time for research on selected countries. Each student may draw a map marked with bordering countries, city names, and a picture of the nation's flag. Present the drawings to the class.

Level ★

Objective: Locate places in the community using prepositions of location.

Warm-up: 10–15 minutes
Write *park* on the board. Identify a park in the community near the school. Draw a map detailing a path between the park and school on the board. Ask students to help complete the map of the local area by adding additional streets. Add familiar landmarks, buildings, and intersections and include any that the students suggest.

Introduction: State the objective.

Presentation 1: 15–20 minutes
Ask students to open to dictionary **pages 46 and 47.** Thoroughly review each word on the list. Encourage questions and discussion. Determine understanding of the vocabulary by asking students for examples from the surrounding community. For example, when discussing *motel,* begin a list of local motels and hotels that students call out. If possible, add an example of each place to the map drawn in the Warm-up. Prepare students to perform this conversation using the dictionary or the map.

Student A: *Where is the motel?*

Student B: *The motel is there.* (B points.)

Practice 1: 7–10 minutes
Pair students who do not usually sit next to each other. Have them practice the above exchange six times—three times in each role. Explain that the underlined word should be replaced in each exchange.
Evaluation 1: Observe the activity.

Presentation 2: 15–20 minutes
Review prepositions of location on **pages 12 and 13** and compile a comprehensive list of more, including *next to, between, around the corner from, on the corner,* and *across from.* During the conversation, ask students where places are and encourage use of prepositions. Prepare students to practice and perform this conversation.

Student A: *Where is the motel?*

Student B: *The motel is across from the mosque.*

Practice 2: 7–10 minutes
After choosing new partners, students should practice the exchange and replace the underlined words with new vocabulary and correct prepositions.
Evaluation 2: Listen for correct use of prepositions.

Application: 10–15 minutes
Group students for a community map drawing exercise. Request inclusion of places listed in the word list. Remind students that they can use the map drawn on the board as a starting point. It might be wise to divide up your city or town.

Places Around Town

Words in Context

I come from Concon, a small town in Chile. There's a **church**, a **gas station**, a **school**, and a soccer **stadium**. There is no **mall**, no **hospital**, no **library**, and no **movie theater**. Concon is beautiful. There are **parks** in the town and beaches nearby. Sometimes I get homesick for my little town.

Level ★ ★

Objective: Give and follow directions.

Warm-up: 10–12 minutes
List common prepositions of location from **pages 12 and 13** on the board. Review briefly with the class. Ask students to turn to **page 47** and complete *Words in Action #1.*

Introduction: State the objective.

Presentation 1: 18–20 minutes
Discuss each word from the list at length.

Then request names of local places to match the vocabulary. Present **Word Partnerships** and discuss examples of these in the community. Have students copy vocabulary with names of local places to create a local directory. Next, as a class, create street names for those on the picture. Label the streets from left to right as *1st, 2nd, 3rd,* and *4th.* Label the streets from bottom to top as *Broadway, Central,* and *Main.* Feel free to use local street names. Some students may not want to write in their dictionaries to label the streets.

1 a factory	11 a theater	21 a parking garage
2 a stadium	12 a movie theater	22 a high-rise (building)
3 a mall	13 a church	23 a car dealership
4 a motel	14 a post office	24 a sidewalk
5 a mosque	15 an office building	25 a corner
6 a school	16 a fire station	26 an intersection
7 a synagogue	17 a city hall / a town hall	27 a street
8 a hospital	18 a library	28 a park
9 a college	19 a courthouse	
10 a police station	20 a gas station	

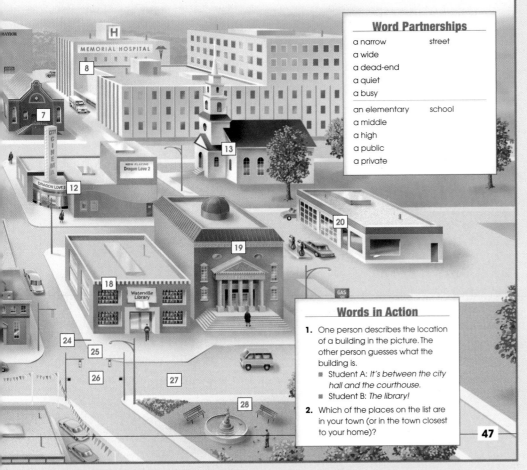

Word Partnerships

a narrow	street
a wide	
a dead-end	
a quiet	
a busy	
an elementary	school
a middle	
a high	
a public	
a private	

Words in Action

1. One person describes the location of a building in the picture. The other person guesses what the building is.
   - Student A: *It's between the city hall and the courthouse.*
   - Student B: *The library!*
2. Which of the places on the list are in your town (or in the town closest to your home)?

47

Pick a central point like the courthouse. Teach students how to give directions and review words such as *turn, go straight, left, right,* and *stop.* Quiz students by giving directions to specific locations from a central point. Have students perform this conversation.

Student A: *Excuse me. I am lost. Can you help me?*
Student B: *Sure. Where do you need to go?*
Student A: *Can you tell me where the motel is?*
Student B: *Yes, go straight on Broadway and turn right on 1st. Go down 1st Street. Go left on Main Street. The motel is on the right.*

Practice 1: 12–15 minutes
Students practice the conversation and change the locations and directions.
Evaluation 1: Select pairs to demonstrate new conversations.

Application: 20–22 minutes
Bring in a local or regional map with which to practice directions. Then have students discuss good weekend drives or walks and places of interest.

Objective: Write a paragraph about the city.

Warm-up: 12–15 minutes
Divide students into groups of three or four. Request that each group create a list of important places in the community, such as *library* and *post office.* Help students get started by writing a few ideas on the board. Invite groups to a friendly competition in which they try to think of the most community places. Ask representatives from each group to write all the places they came up with on the board. Decide the winner by eliminating duplicates. Create a master list of places around town for the class to use.

Introduction: State the objective.

Presentation 1: 15–20 minutes
Formally teach the whole word list and **Word Partnerships** on **page 47.** Note the items students didn't think of in the Warm-up and add those to the master list. At this point, encourage any other ideas students have for the master list. As a class, discuss **Words in Action #2.** On the board, show students how to make a Venn diagram. Use the Activity Bank CD-ROM template for this. As a group, create a diagram that compares the town in "Places Around Town" with the local community. Take time to review writing rules and paragraph form, including margins and indenting.

Practice 1: 10–12 minutes
Ask that students close their dictionaries and prepare for dictation. Use the paragraph in **Words in Context.** Read once at a moderate pace, once slowly, and a third time at a moderate pace. Invite questions about the paragraph.

Evaluation 1: Ask students to peer correct.

Application: 25–30 minutes
Generate a discussion about what places people consider important in the community. Write some of the student ideas on the board. Using the paragraph in **Words in Context** as a model, students should write their own paragraphs about the places that are most important to them and their families.

Project

Ask students to draw a map of a neighboring community or of the community where they grew up. Guide them to begin by listing landmarks, buildings, and street names. Maps can be presented to the class when completed. Post the maps to encourage student discussion and feedback.

Level ★

Objective: Identify types of stores.

Warm-up: 10–15 minutes
Write *shopping* on the board and ask students where they go if they are hungry. Although most students will give answers such as the market or grocery store, accept answers such as local store names and restaurants. Write all answers on the board. Add a new phase to the conversation by writing *clothing* on the board and listing student-suggested store types and names. Do not erase these master lists.

Introduction: State the objective.

Presentation 1: 15–20 minutes
Add the following categories to the board: *school supplies, books,* and *electronics.* To define these terms, point to or draw items of each type that can be purchased. Using the *clothing* master list as a guide, ask three volunteers to put student answers for these three new categories on the board. Refer to **pages 48 and 49.** Discuss each vocabulary word from the list and assist in comprehension and correct pronunciation. Lead the class in an identification activity. Separate retail stores from service-oriented ones. Explain that store numbers 11–13, 15–17, and 23 are all buildings where service is bought and sold rather than products.

Practice 1: 15–20 minutes
In groups, have students list the retail stores on a piece of paper and ask them to think of two products to sell at each place. Permit students to look at other pages of the dictionary or to ask you for specific words. Take this opportunity to review previous dictionary lessons.

Evaluation 1: Check answers and ask students to report.

Presentation 2: 10–15 minutes
Prepare students to perform this model conversation.

　Student A: *Excuse me, where can I buy shoes?*

　Student B: *You can buy shoes at a shoe store. There is a shoe store in the mall.*

　Student A: *Thank you.*

Practice 2: 10–15 minutes
Pairs should practice the conversation, using different stores and items from the master lists on the board and the group lists from Practice 1.
Evaluation 2: Observe pairs during practice.

Application: 10–15 minutes
Ask students to continue the previous conversation using the names of stores instead of store types. For example, student B would say *You can buy shoes at Bill's Boot Outlet.*

Shops and Stores

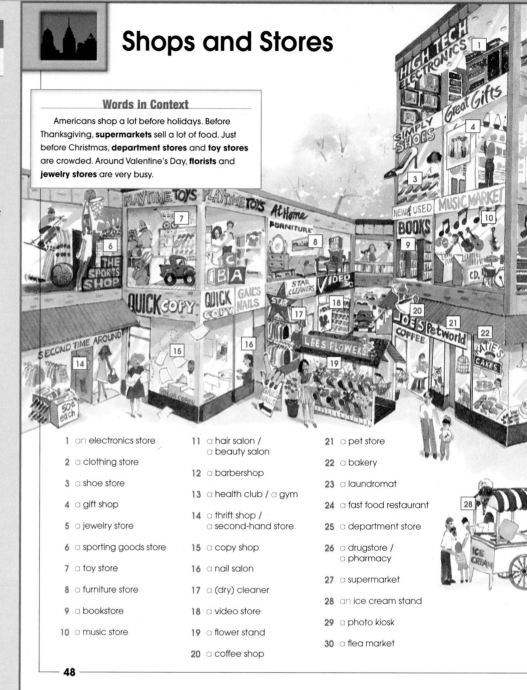

Words in Context

Americans shop a lot before holidays. Before Thanksgiving, **supermarkets** sell a lot of food. Just before Christmas, **department stores** and **toy stores** are crowded. Around Valentine's Day, **florists** and **jewelry stores** are very busy.

1　an electronics store
2　a clothing store
3　a shoe store
4　a gift shop
5　a jewelry store
6　a sporting goods store
7　a toy store
8　a furniture store
9　a bookstore
10　a music store

11　a hair salon / a beauty salon
12　a barbershop
13　a health club / a gym
14　a thrift shop / a second-hand store
15　a copy shop
16　a nail salon
17　a (dry) cleaner
18　a video store
19　a flower stand
20　a coffee shop

21　a pet store
22　a bakery
23　a laundromat
24　a fast food restaurant
25　a department store
26　a drugstore / a pharmacy
27　a supermarket
28　an ice cream stand
29　a photo kiosk
30　a flea market

48

Level ★ ★

Objective: Use prepositions of location to identify store locations.

Warm-up: 14–16 minutes
Students open to **pages 48 and 49** but cover the word list. Read *Words in Action #1* aloud. Tell students to complete this task in pairs, using prepositions of location to explain to their partners where the store is. They can describe and name the location of two possible places to buy each thing.

Introduction: State the objective.

Presentation 1: 18–20 minutes
Students should follow along as you review all vocabulary from **pages 48 and 49,** including *Word Partnerships.* Ask students to tell you where stores are in the picture. As students use prepositions of location, write them on the board. Maintain the conversation until the list includes *next to, around the corner,*

Word Partnerships

shop at	a bookstore
work at	a jewelry store
manage	a music store
own	a bakery

Words in Action

1. You need bread, dog food, aspirin, a swimsuit, and a CD. Which stores will you go to?
2. What three stores in the picture do you most like to go to? Why? Tell a partner.

49

Objective: Discuss business and make business decisions.

Warm-up: 12–15 minutes
Instruct students to open to **pages 48 and 49** while you lead a discussion about a few of the locations pictured. Ask students if they would visit this mall if it existed. Continue the discussion by asking for pros and cons of the pictured mall. Arrange students in small groups and prepare them to have a roundtable conversation using *Words in Action #2*.

Introduction: State the objective.

Presentation 1: 15–20 minutes
Review each word from the list as a class and answer any questions. Begin a new conversation about what time of year stores are the busiest or do the best business in your area. Guide the conversation so the following words are included: *busy, profitable, slow,* and *in debt*. Read *Words in Context* aloud and request opinions on which stores students would like to own or manage and why. Add whatever business vocabulary might be needed, such as *loan* and *capital*.

Practice 1: 12–15 minutes
Have students gather in their small groups and identify five businesses that would be most profitable to own. All students in the group should agree before their final list is announced to the other groups. Students should have sound rationale for their choices and seek consensus on all points.

Evaluation 1: Groups present and explain choices.

Application: 20–25 minutes
Within the same groups, students should narrow their list to one store. Consensus is required. Have students discuss what would be needed to start such a business, including merchandise, equipment, and personnel. During the activity, students should name their place of business. Use the worksheet for starting a business available on the Activity Bank CD-ROM for this activity.

under, over, between, and *on the corner.* Briefly quiz the class by offering an item or product in the picture and asking students to identify its location. For example, you might say *It is in the barbershop.* The students might respond *a barber, a man,* or *a chair.* Accept only the item you want students to identify as correct. Ask students to write down any 10 items from the picture and list them on a piece of paper.

Practice 1: 10–12 minutes
Pair students for a quizzing activity.

Partners will do the same as you did in the presentation but will use their own lists.

Evaluation 1: Let students quiz you with their words while you guess the store.

Application: 18–20 minutes
Ask students to make a list of stores in their neighborhoods. They should write sentences with prepositions of location to describe where the stores are located in relation to their homes or to the school.

Provide a list of local businesses from the surrounding community, some common and some harder to identify. Request that students attempt to list items sold by each establishment. Higher levels can find the locations and design brochures or flyers for the businesses.

Bank

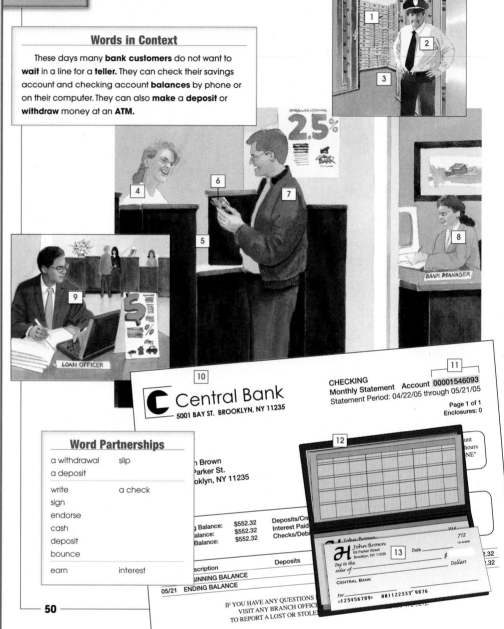

Words in Context

These days many **bank customers** do not want to **wait** in a line for a **teller**. They can check their savings account and checking account **balances** by phone or on their computer. They can also **make** a **deposit** or **withdraw** money at an **ATM**.

Word Partnerships

a withdrawal	slip
a deposit	
write	a check
sign	
endorse	
cash	
deposit	
bounce	
earn	interest

50

Level ★

Objective: Identify bank vocabulary.

Warm-up: 10–15 minutes
Ask students what they do with the money they earn. Some students might be too intimidated to use a bank. Convey the importance of using a bank and the different functions of a bank. Ask students to identify banks in the community and make a list. Have students describe the locations.

Introduction: State the objective.

Presentation 1: 15–20 minutes
Ask students to open to **pages 50 and 51.** Teach each vocabulary word formally before creating a five-column chart on the board. Label the columns *people in a bank, items in a bank, personal items, document,* and *other.* Begin with the first five items in the word list and generate students' help to place them in the correct columns.

Practice 1: 15–20 minutes
Divide students into groups of five to complete the table with the words from the word list.
Evaluation 1: Have a representative from each group fill in one of the five categories on the board. Allow some overlap.

Presentation 2: 10–15 minutes
Write *teller* on the board and ask students which words from the list a teller or customer might say. Generate answers such as *cash, money order, deposit, withdrawal, (your) balance, need a money order,* and *make a deposit/withdrawal.* Prepare students to perform this model conversation.

> **Teller:** *Can I help you?*
> **Customer:** *Yes, I need a money order.*
> **Teller:** *How much?*
> **Customer:** *Fifty dollars, please.*

Practice 2: 10–15 minutes
Pair students for practice and encourage them to substitute needs and amounts.
Evaluation 2: Listen for accuracy during student practice and assist as needed.

Application: 10–15 minutes
Have students make goals. Write the following list on the board or use the Activity Bank CD-ROM worksheet and check off what they do at the bank. Encourage students to attempt at least one of these activities at their local bank.
• Find a bank.
• Open an account.
• Get a money order.
• Deposit cash or a check.
• Withdraw money.
• Talk to a teller, a loan officer, or a bank manager.
• Write a check.
• Get or use an ATM card.

Level ★ ★

Objective: Describe how to use an ATM.

Warm-up: 10–12 minutes
Prepare students to answer the questions in *Words in Action #1* on **page 51** and share their answers with a group.

Introduction: State the objective.

Presentation 1: 18–20 minutes
Direct students to a complete review of all word list vocabulary, including *Word*

Partnerships. Instruct students to cover the word list and identify items as you call out the number of a picture. Next, tell students to close their dictionaries. Pantomime using an ATM. Perform the steps until students correctly guess what you are doing. When they correctly identify each step, write the verb on the board. Have students open to **page 51** for review.

Practice 1: 8–10 minutes
Assign students to small groups. Students

1 a safe-deposit box / a safety-deposit box

2 a security guard

3 a vault

4 a teller

5 a teller window

6 cash / money

7 a customer

8 a bank manager

9 a loan officer

10 a (monthly) statement

11 a checking account number

12 a checkbook

13 a check

14 a (savings account) passbook

15 interest

16 a deposit

17 a withdrawal

18 a balance

19 a money order

20 an ATM

21 a drive-up window

22 an ATM card / a bankcard

Verbs

23 wait in line

24 insert your ATM card

25 enter your PIN

26 withdraw cash

27 make a deposit

28 remove your card

SAVINGS ACCOUNT (14)

NOTE	% INTEREST	+ DEPOSITS	- WITHDRAWALS	BALANCE
Open account		$500.00		$500.00
Textbooks			$75.00	$425.00
Interest	$3.21			$428.21
Birthday gift from Mom		$25.00		$453.21
Interest	$3.68			$456.99

POSTAL MONEY ORDER (19)

Words in Action

1. When was the last time you went to the bank? What did you do there? What part of the bank did you go to? Who did you speak to?

2. Work with a partner. One person says the steps to using an ATM. The other acts out the steps.

— 51

---

should attempt to write instructions for using an ATM without using the dictionary.

Evaluation 1: Peer check answers with information given in the dictionary.

Presentation 2: 6–8 minutes
Review each step for using an ATM. Challenge students to recite the instructions for using one without looking at the sentences they wrote.

Practice 2: 8–10 minutes
Students can practice describing how to

use an ATM without referring to the dictionary. Prepare students to follow the suggestion in *Words in Action #2.*

Evaluation 1: Pairs should verify answers in the dictionary. Choose a couple of pairs to perform for the class.

Application: 10–15 minutes
Students should describe four places to locate an ATM in the community. Compile a master list on the board. Discuss ATM functions other than withdrawing cash and making a deposit.

Level ★ ★ ★

Objective: Balance a checkbook.

Warm-up: 12–15 minutes
Read *Words in Context* aloud and divide students into groups for discussion. Encourage students to discuss their personal banking experiences. After ample time, include the whole class in a discussion about different ways to use a bank.

Introduction: State the objective.

Presentation 1: 15–20 minutes
Challenge students to draw the interior of a bank. Instruct students to close their dictionaries and base their drawing on a local bank. Label the picture with as many bank-related words as possible. When complete, direct students to open to **pages 50 and 51** and add any words from the list that may have been forgotten. Allow time for students to share their drawings to ensure comprehension of the vocabulary. Identify useful bank-related terms that are excluded from the word list and review. Next, focus attention on the passbook and draw a ledger on the board similar to the one in the dictionary. Let students know that a checkbook ledger is similar. Hand out copies of the sample ledger worksheet from the Activity Bank CD-ROM. Describe the transactions each column represents and review the past tense. Provide the following information and show students how to add appropriate sequential check numbers.

July 1 Beginning Balance: $1,406.75

July 2 Groceries: $312.15

July 2 Payroll Deposit: $615.50

July 2 Shoes for Less: $33.57

July 5 Cash Withdrawal ATM: $100

Practice 1: 13–15 minutes
Students should complete the ledger with the above information and use the past tense to describe all the transactions to a partner.

Evaluation 1: Choose volunteers to describe the transactions to the class.

Application: 20–25 minutes
Ask students to create a family checkbook ledger in groups of three to four. Students may start with $1,000 in the checkbook and include purchases made at five different businesses found on **pages 48 and 49**. Upon completion, have groups describe their transactions to each other.

Project

Arrange groups and have each write a conversation between a bank teller or manager and a customer. Conversations should include two or three transactions. Students can perform role-plays for the rest of the class.

Level ★

Objective: Address an envelope.

Warm-up: 10–15 minutes
Draw an envelope on the board. Tell students that if they want to write a letter to you, it can be sent to your work address. Illustrate how the envelope should be addressed with your name and school address. Make a list of mailing address parts, including *first and last name, street address, city, state,* and *zip code.* Discuss why each piece of this information is necessary to mail a letter. Encourage volunteers to come to the board and draw a line from the words in the list to the actual item on the envelope. Create a fictitious return address and identify the sections in the same fashion.

Introduction: State the objective.

Presentation 1: 20–30 minutes
Ask students how many visits they make to the post office in a month and have them describe these visits. Discuss why some people never go to a post office. Follow up with a bar graph of the results. Utilize the bar graph template available on the Activity Bank CD-ROM.

Refer students to **pages 52 and 53** of the dictionary. Present each item from the list and make sure students pronounce each item correctly. Initiate an oral quiz in which students cover the word list. Say one vocabulary word at a time from the list. When students recognize the word, they should point to the picture, state its number, and then pronounce the word.

Practice 1: 15–20 minutes
Set aside time for students to quiz each other. Student A covers the words and looks for the picture corresponding to the word that Student B says. Students should reverse roles several times.
Evaluation 1: Observe the activity.

Presentation 2: 10–15 minutes
Review the parts of an envelope to ensure comprehension. Write fictitious envelope information in random order on the board. For example, write and say: *90217, 4599 Spring Hill Road, Dr. Peter Crane, Winfield, CA.* Have students put them in order. More practice for addressing an envelope is available on the Activity Bank CD-ROM. Blank envelope forms are also available on the same worksheet. Before practicing, supply actual envelopes or sample envelope forms printed from the Activity Bank CD-ROM.

Practice 2: 10–12 minutes
Have students complete at least one envelope with given information.

Application: 8–10 minutes
Ask students to address an envelope from their homes to you at school. Discuss mailing prices.

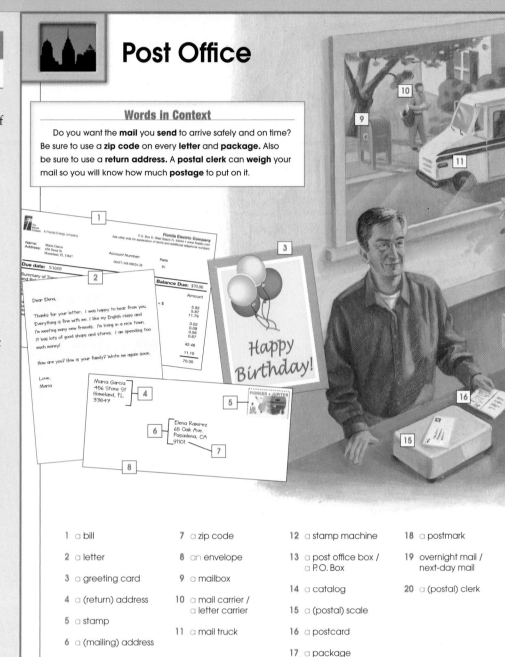

Post Office

Words in Context

Do you want the **mail** you **send** to arrive safely and on time? Be sure to use a **zip code** on every **letter** and **package**. Also be sure to use a **return address**. A **postal clerk** can **weigh** your mail so you will know how much **postage** to put on it.

1 a bill	7 a zip code	12 a stamp machine	18 a postmark
2 a letter	8 an envelope	13 a post office box / a P.O. Box	19 overnight mail / next-day mail
3 a greeting card	9 a mailbox	14 a catalog	20 a (postal) clerk
4 a (return) address	10 a mail carrier / a letter carrier	15 a (postal) scale	
5 a stamp	11 a mail truck	16 a postcard	
6 a (mailing) address		17 a package	

52

Level ★ ★

Objective: Use post office vocabulary.

Warm-up: 13–15 minutes
Read *Words in Action #1* aloud and have students close their dictionaries. Allow time for students to converse in small groups and then lead a whole-class discussion comparing answers.

Introduction: State the objective.

Presentation 1: 18–20 minutes
Instruct students to open to **pages 52 and 53** and follow along as you present the vocabulary from the list and from *Word Partnerships.* Determine understanding by asking students to participate in a word association activity. Give clues to a vocabulary word. For example, you might say *book of* or *sheet of* and students must think of a word that can be associated with it. In this case, the answer you are seeking is *stamps.* Or, provide definitions such as *a small, short letter sent in the mail without an*

Verbs

21 address

22 weigh

23 put a stamp on

24 mail / send

Tomorrow.

Word Partnerships

a business	letter
a personal	
a love	
a first class	stamp
a book of	stamps
a sheet of	
a roll of	
a postage-paid	envelope
a self-addressed stamped	

Words in Action

1. What kinds of mail do you send? What kinds do you get? What is your favorite kind of mail to receive? What is your least favorite? Discuss with a group.

2. Describe your last visit to the post office. What did you do? Who did you talk to? What did you see? Tell your partner.

---

envelope. The answer would be *postcard.* Further the activity by offering sentences with missing words, such as *I need to send this letter so they get it tomorrow. I need to send this by ____ mail!* The answer is *overnight.* As you dictate sentences, ask volunteers to write them on the board so that the class can review the vocabulary in context.

Practice 1: 18–20 minutes
Permit students to refer to **pages 52 and 53.** Individually, students should identify any new words on the word list and in **Word Partnerships.** Ask students to write

sentences for each new word. Teach writing strategies so students use the words in context and so other students are able to determine the vocabulary word if it is left blank in the sentence.
Evaluation 1: Have students write sentences on the board, leaving the vocabulary word as a blank. Other students should guess the missing word.

Application: 12–15 minutes
Assign pairs to participate in **Words in Action #2.** Allow time for pairs to share answers with other pairs.

Objective: Write and send a letter.

Warm-up: 13–15 minutes
Give students a dictation using the paragraph from **Words in Context.** Depending on student level, read the paragraph two or three times. Students can open their dictionaries to **page 52** to check for accuracy and to correct errors.

Introduction: State the objective.

Presentation 1: 15–20 minutes
Present each item carefully and answer questions as you progress through the word list. Generate discussion about the students' experiences at the post office (**Words in Action #2**). Compare stories and create a list of actions other than mailing letters that can take place at a post office. Let students know about passport services, phone cards, and post office boxes. Focus attention on the letter pictured in the spread and have students dictate it to you so you can write it on the board. Formally present the form of the letter. Show students where they might add a date. Discuss friendly and formal letter styles and formats.

Practice 1: 12–15 minutes
Ask students to close their books and discuss the features of the letter in a small group. Each group should attempt to reproduce the letter from memory. Note: This is a difficult task, so allow sufficient time. Tell students that you are not seeking perfection but just the general idea. Inform them that their goal is not to capture the exact words but to learn the correct format. Explain that although you do not want the exact words, you do expect well-constructed sentences.

Evaluation 1: Groups may share their letters with the class.

Application: 20–22 minutes
Review parts of a sentence and provide well-written examples. Discuss the reasons people write letters. Offer sufficient time for students to write a letter to a friend, a family member, or a business. Solicit ideas for letter topics and list those on the board. Students can select from those ideas or use one of their own ideas.

Project

Students should reflect on what they hope to accomplish by attending class. Invite students to write you a letter, properly addressed, about their hopes and goals for this English class. Offer an incentive, such as a letter in return, if students correctly address, stamp, and mail letters to you after they leave the classroom.

Level ★

Objective: Identify library vocabulary.

Warm-up: 10–15 minutes
Ask students to hold up any books, including this dictionary. Write *title* on the board and begin a list of the titles. Enhance the conversation by discussing, for example, *softcover* versus *hardcover*. Guide the conversation to include places to find books; elicit such answers as bookstore and library. Write *library* on the board.

Introduction: State the objective.

Presentation 1: 18–20 minutes
Do not permit students to open their dictionaries at this point. Take a survey to determine how many students 1) have been in a library where English is the principle language, 2) have a current library card, 3) know where the library nearest to the school is, and 4) have ever borrowed a book from a library. Provide copies of the sample library card application worksheet from the **Activity Bank CD-ROM.** After they complete the form, have students exchange applications and discuss the required information. Refer students to **pages 54 and 55.** As the vocabulary is difficult, choose to study only the vocabulary that is most pertinent and write those words on the board. Write *Things to Read* on the board. Prepare students to do Practice 1 by listing one or two words that can fall into the *Things to Read* category. Expand the activity by incorporating the adjectives in **Word Partnerships.**

Practice 1: 8–15 minutes
Ask students what they like to read. Have groups of three or four add more words to the *Things to Read* category from **pages 54 and 55.**

Evaluation 1: Request oral reports from each group.

Presentation 2: 10–15 minutes
Review each vocabulary word. Prepare students to perform this model conversation.

  Student A: *Excuse me. Where is the _____?*

  Student B: *The _____ is here.* (Student B points.)

Practice 2: 8–10 minutes
Partners should practice the conversation using different vocabulary from the list. Encourage the pairs to try the conversation with the list covered.
Evaluation 2: Observe the activity.

Application: 8–10 minutes
As a class, create a checklist of items that are on **pages 54 and 55.** Name an item and have students check whether they use the item every day, one time a week, one time a month, or one time a year.

Library

Words in Context

Libraries can change people's lives. In 1953, **author** Frank McCourt arrived in New York City from Ireland. One day a man told Frank to go to a library. So Frank did. He got a **library card, checked out** a **book,** and fell in love with reading. All of the reading he did at the library helped Frank McCourt become a successful **writer.** Now people can read his **autobiography** in 30 different languages!

Verbs

26 look for a book

27 check out books

Level ★ ★

Objective: Discuss library verbs.

Warm-up: 10–12 minutes
What do your students read? How many types of books can the students list? Accept all answers but realize the list might be limited. Allow ample time for brainstorming. If students need help getting started, write *children's books* on the board. To expand the list, introduce **Word Partnerships** on **page 55** and encourage students to look over **pages 54 and 55.**

Introduction: State the objective.

Presentation 1: 15–20 minutes
Review the word list in its entirety. Offer class time to add new vocabulary to the lists started in the Warm-up. Direct attention to **Words in Action #2.** Lead a class discussion using these questions. Next, give a short oral quiz covering the vocabulary. Ask students to hide their word list. Instruct them to point to the corresponding picture when you say a

28 read

29 return books

1 the periodical section
2 a magazine
3 a microfilm machine
4 the reading room
5 the reference desk
6 an online catalog / a computerized catalog
7 the fiction section
8 the nonfiction section
9 a dictionary
10 an encyclopedia
11 a librarian
12 a library card
13 a hardcover (book)

14 a paperback (book)
15 an atlas
16 the circulation desk / the checkout desk
17 a newspaper
18 a headline
19 a title
20 a novel
21 an author / a writer
22 a cookbook
23 a biography
24 an autobiography
25 a picture book

Fiction
7

Nonfiction
8

Reference

Children's Section

Fishy, Fish, Fish
25

Gandhi's Life 23

My Life by Abraham Lincoln 24

Word Partnerships

a library	book
a good	book
a boring	writer
a detective	novel
a romance	
a science-fiction	
a historical	

Words in Action

1. Imagine you will spend an afternoon in this library. What will you do?
2. Discuss the following questions with a group:
   - What is your favorite book?
   - What is your favorite magazine?
   - What is your favorite newspaper?

— 55 —

Objective: Write about libraries.

Warm-up: 10–15 minutes
Put students in groups of three or four. Tell them to imagine they are doing research about the city and they need to list appropriate library activities. Encourage critical thinking by leading them to include actions, such as *talk to the librarian* and *read a magazine*. Ask groups to share ideas with the class.

Introduction: State the objective.

Presentation 1: 15–20 minutes
Ask students to open to **pages 54 and 55** and formally discuss each vocabulary word. Answer questions as needed. Begin a conversation about students' library experiences. Compile a list of other places in the community on the board, including the *library*. Refer to **pages 46 and 47** and review. Have students rate the items on the word list from most helpful to least important for research. Allow sufficient time for students to poll each other and compare answers. Read *Words in Context* together and ask them how a library can change a life.

Practice 1: 15–20 minutes
Regroup students in threes or fours. Group members should discuss what they consider to be the most important parts of a library and the most important things that can be done in a library. Create one list for each group. The lists should have the most important items listed first.

Evaluation 1: Groups will report by writing their lists on the board. Compare the lists and discuss why certain actions were rated higher than others.

Application: 20–30 minutes
Review rules for writing a summary. Invite students to write one to three paragraphs from the following prompt: *Why are libraries important and how do they benefit people?*

Project

Prepare students to go to a local library. If possible, each student should get a library card or show that they already have one. Have those who don't have a card fill out a library card application in advance. Students should also list topics or questions they would research if they were to spend two hours in the library. Give students a choice of research prompts if they struggle with ideas. Arrange a trip to a library during class time. Notify the librarian in advance so a short orientation can be prepared specific to your students' interests. If students are parents, include the children's section. If students plan to continue with their education, show them the reference section. For instructors in non-English-speaking countries, try the English section of your local library or an English bookstore.

word. Include the verbs (numbers 27–30). Use pantomimes for emphasis. Write the following sentence on the board: *You can check out books from the library.* Teach the following verbs: *find, check out, read, study, look up,* and *give.* Include student suggestions and make an inclusive verb list on the board.

Practice 1: 15–20 minutes
After reviewing proper sentence structure (subject-verb-object), students should write 5–10 sentences with the vocabulary on the new verb list.

Evaluation 1: Check quickly and have each student write his or her best sentence on the board. Discuss the model sentences.

Application: 20–30 minutes
Ask students to imagine they are spending an afternoon at the library, as suggested in *Words in Action #1.* Request that their sentences be in chronological order, so their first sentences should describe what they would do first. Have students turn the sentences into paragraphs and share the paragraphs with a partner.

Level ★

Objective: Identify daycare vocabulary.

Warm-up: 8–10 minutes
Pose the discussion topic *children*. Encourage students who are parents to talk about their children's caregivers. Involve others by asking who has been a babysitter or childcare worker. Generate a brainstorming session about what babies need. Make a list on the board with students.

Introduction: State the objective.

Presentation 1: 15–20 minutes
Focus on students who offered stories about children in daycare centers and encourage more details about their experiences. Students should open to **pages 56 and 57.** Present the words from the word list. Make sure they understand the definitions and pronounce each word correctly. Create a cluster on the board. Label the center circle *daycare center.* The secondary circles should include *furniture, people, supplies,* and *other.* Work with students to begin filling in the tertiary circles. The cluster template on the Activity Bank CD-ROM can facilitate this activity.

Practice 1: 15–20 minutes
Assign students to small groups. Set a goal for each group to complete the cluster using every word in the list.

Evaluation 1: Groups will report their cluster answers.

Presentation 2: 10–15 minutes
Review the words in as much detail as necessary. This is an ideal time to revisit the dictionary unit on colors on **pages 10 and 11.** Help students identify items in the secondary circles by color. For example, the playpen falls in the furniture circle and is green and blue. Model the statement *I am thinking of furniture that is green and blue.* Write the sentence on the board and prepare students to say and write similar sentences about the daycare center.

Practice 2: 8–10 minutes
Pair students who do not normally work together. They should quiz each other by using the phrases modeled after the example on the board but substituting other words and colors.

Evaluation 2: Choose strong student sentences to be read for the class.

Application: 8–10 minutes
Divide students into groups and ask a student who is a parent or familiar with childcare to lead the discussion. Tell students to answer the question posed in *Words in Action #1.* Share answers after adequate time has passed.

Daycare Center

Words in Context

Parents should look for the following things at a **daycare center:**

*   Are the children busy and happy?
*   Do the **childcare workers** take good care of the children?
*   Is there a special room for **newborns**?
*   Are the **high chairs, potty chairs,** and **changing tables** clean?

Word Partnerships

a cute	baby
a newborn	
baby	food
a clean	diaper
a dirty	
change	a diaper
play with	toys
put away	
share	

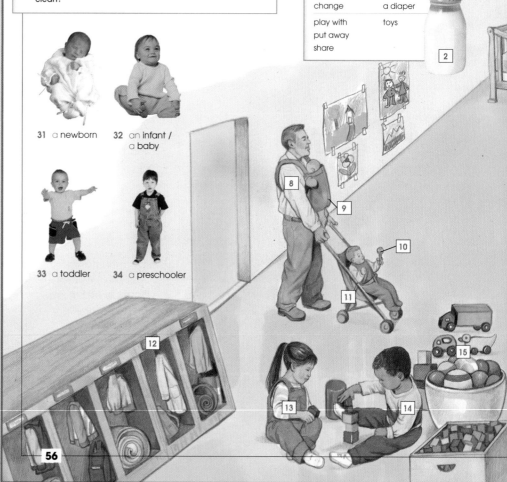

31 a newborn
32 an infant / a baby
33 a toddler
34 a preschooler

56

Level ★ ★

Objective: Describe a daycare center.

Warm-up: 8–10 minutes
Assign students to groups and prepare them to address the situation in **Words in Action #2.** Give students time and opportunity to negotiate. Have each group report their answers to the class.

Introduction: State the objective.

Presentation 1: 15–20 minutes
Direct students to open to **pages 56 and 57** and present the word list thoroughly. Give special attention to **Word Partnerships.** Test student knowledge by randomly reading a word and asking students to either say the number of the picture that illustrates it or provide a verb that might be associated with the word. Work as a class to develop a verb to accompany each of the 31 words (including *to be, to have,* and action verbs).

1 a nipple	8 a parent	16 a bib	24 (baby) wipes
2 a bottle	9 a baby carrier	17 a childcare worker	25 a pacifier
3 a crib	10 a rattle	18 a high chair	26 a changing table
4 a playpen	11 a stroller	19 formula	27 a (disposable) diaper
5 a rest mat	12 a cubby	20 a potty chair	28 training pants
6 a baby swing	13 a girl	21 a diaper pail	29 a (cloth) diaper
7 a teething ring	14 a boy	22 (baby) powder	30 a diaper pin
	15 toys	23 (baby) lotion	

Words in Action

1. Which are the 10 most important items for a newborn? Discuss and make a list with a group.

2. Imagine you have a one-year-old baby. You are taking a trip on an airplane. Which items will you take?

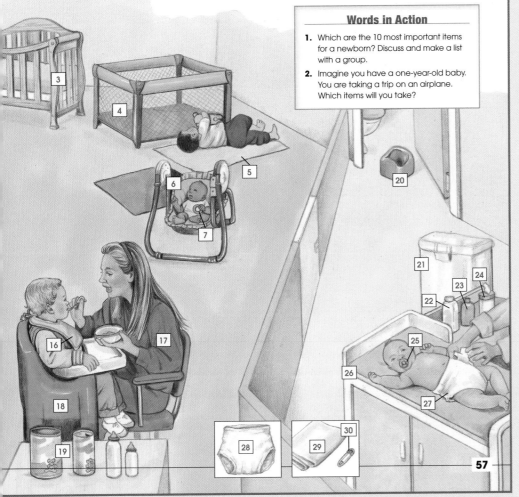

57

Objective: Discuss daycare center responsibilities.

Warm-up: 15–30 minutes
Solicit the students who are parents to assist discussion groups. Read *Words in Action #2* and allow sufficient time for groups to compile a list. After completion, a volunteer from each group can write group lists on the board for class comparison and discussion. Teach students how to complete a Venn diagram and hand out the Venn diagram template from the Activity Bank CD-ROM. Compare group responses in a large Venn diagram on the board, filled in by volunteers. Allow time for students to place their answers in their own diagrams.

Introduction: State the objective.

Presentation 1: 15–20 minutes
Instruct students to open their dictionaries to **pages 56 and 57** and follow along as the class studies each item carefully. Answer questions about the vocabulary. Encourage questions and discussion about students' experiences with babies, and open a discussion about daycare centers. Read *Words in Context* aloud and discuss why each of those questions is important when looking for a daycare center. Encourage students with relevant experience to share their knowledge with the class.

Practice 1: 15–20 minutes
Place students in brainstorming groups to make a list of responsibilities that a manager at a daycare center might have. Offer a few general suggestions for the students to build on, such as *scheduling, hiring, cleaning,* and *supplying equipment*.

Evaluation 1: Listen to presentations by each group.

Application: 20–30 minutes
Assign students to groups of three or four. Each group should create a "to do" list as if they manage a daycare facility. They should provide a list of jobs for employees and include times when each task should be done. Remind students to carefully consider the children's needs. Challenge students to use as many of the 31 words from the word list as possible.

Practice 1: 15–20 minutes
Divide the class into groups and assign each an equal number of words from the list. Participants should write one sentence for each of their words. Ask that each sentence imply the meaning of the word.

Evaluation 1: Each student writes one group sentence on the board, replacing the vocabulary word with a blank line. The rest of the class will guess which word is appropriate for the sentence.

Application: 22–30 minutes
Groups should imagine they are going to open a new daycare center in town. They are to come up with a plan, including where it will be, how much space they will need, how many children they will take, who they will hire (e.g., nurse, janitor, teachers), how it will be designed, and what supplies they will need. Remind students to carefully consider the children's ages and needs. Each daycare center should be named, and groups can describe their plans to the class.

Assign two groups to present skits. The first group should prepare a list of questions every parent should ask when investigating a daycare center. Build on the questions started in *Words in Context*. The second group should write a list of questions a manager would ask a prospective daycare center employee. Both groups should then prepare dialogs that can be presented to the class.

Level ★

Objective: Identify city vocabulary.

Warm-up: 8–10 minutes
Begin a conversation about the local community by asking students what important main or cross streets are near the center of their town or city. Write *cross streets* on the board and show by example what the phrase means. Extend the activity by asking what buildings are located at particular cross streets in the local community. Start with the location of the school and continue the list on the board.

Introduction: State the objective.

Presentation 1: 18–20 minutes
Tell students to use **pages 58 and 59** for reference as you draw a picture of the intersection closest to the school. Call for student suggestions to add details, including many of the vocabulary words. Describe, draw, or otherwise illustrate as many of the words that are found both in the dictionary and near the school. Use this guide to determine how much students already know. Allow students to draw their own map of an intersection in town or near their homes and add applicable words. Formally present **pages 58 and 59** and concentrate on the pronunciation of the vocabulary. Quiz students about locations and encourage them to avoid looking at the word list. Model pronunciation and provide a written example of this conversation on the board.

> **Student A:** *Where is the <u>newsstand</u>?*
>
> **Student B:** *The <u>newsstand</u> is here.* (Student B points.)

Help students practice the exchange in pairs.

Practice 1: 8–10 minutes
Offer time for pairs to practice the exchange. Ask students to review the word list, reverse roles several times, and substitute as many vocabulary words as possible.

Evaluation 1: Observe the activity.

Presentation 2: 8–10 minutes
Exhibit a four-column chart on the board and label the columns *places, streets, people,* and *other*. Complete the *people* column by eliciting *pedestrian, tourist,* and *street musician* from the students.

Practice 2: 10–12 minutes
Divide the class into three groups. Hand out the four-column table template on the Activity Bank CD-ROM.

Evaluation 2: Check student answers after a representative from each group fills in one of the columns on the board's master chart.

Application: 8–10 minutes
Request that students do the activity suggested in *Words in Action #1.*

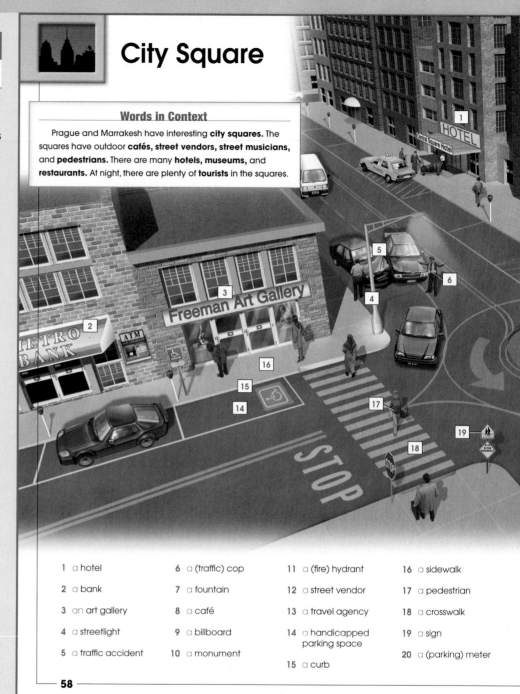

City Square

Words in Context

Prague and Marrakesh have interesting **city squares.** The squares have outdoor **cafés, street vendors, street musicians,** and **pedestrians.** There are many **hotels, museums,** and **restaurants.** At night, there are plenty of **tourists** in the squares.

1 a hotel	6 a (traffic) cop	11 a (fire) hydrant	16 a sidewalk
2 a bank	7 a fountain	12 a street vendor	17 a pedestrian
3 an art gallery	8 a café	13 a travel agency	18 a crosswalk
4 a streetlight	9 a billboard	14 a handicapped parking space	19 a sign
5 a traffic accident	10 a monument	15 a curb	20 a (parking) meter

58

Level ★ ★

Objective: Use prepositions of location to describe a scene.

Warm-up: 12–15 minutes
Have students look at **pages 58 and 59** while you read *Words in Action # 1.* In groups, students compile a list of ideas. Each group chooses a representative to share ideas with other groups. Allow time for groups to report and write key vocabulary on the board.

Introduction: State the objective.

Presentation 1: 18–20 minutes
Focus attention on **pages 58 and 59** and discuss each vocabulary item carefully. Give special attention to *Word Partnerships.* Thoroughly review the function of prepositions and list prepositions of location. Identify items in the spread by using the prepositions. State *Where is the statue?* Help students understand that an appropriate response would be *The statue is in front of the museum.* Guide the class through other questions and examples.

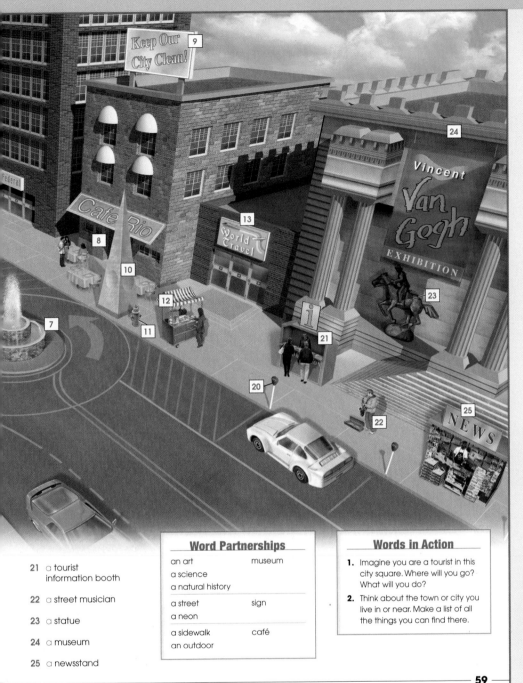

Keep Our City Clean! 9

Cafe Rio

World Travel

Vincent *Van Gogh* EXHIBITION

NEWS

21 a tourist
      information booth

22 a street musician

23 a statue

24 a museum

25 a newsstand

Word Partnerships	
an art	museum
a science	
a natural history	
a street	sign
a neon	
a sidewalk	café
an outdoor	

Words in Action

1. Imagine you are a tourist in this city square. Where will you go? What will you do?

2. Think about the town or city you live in or near. Make a list of all the things you can find there.

Objective: Write a paragraph about a popular area in the community.

Warm-up: 15–30 minutes
Individuals should make a list of places and things that might be found in a tourist area of a city. Prepare to have a few specific sites selected if students struggle with choosing a place. Extend the activity by asking students to interview four other students in class and add one new item to their lists from each student they talk to. Discuss answers or observations the students found unique.

Introduction: State the objective.

Presentation 1: 15–20 minutes
Review each word in the list and develop a definition with students. Encourage questions and discussion. Select a student to read *Words in Context* for the class and discuss the boldfaced words and theme. Begin a class discussion about areas in your community or city that might be similar to those described in the paragraph or the picture. Boost the conversation by mentioning famous local places to visit near the city center.

Practice 1: 15–20 minutes
Provide examples of adjectives and remind students of the function of an adjective. Ask students to make a list of items from the center of the community. For each item, students should think of two adjectives that could be included in a paragraph about that locale. Offer sample sentences and have students write complete sentences utilizing items and adjectives from their lists.

Evaluation 1: Request that students write their sentences on the board.

Application: 20–30 minutes
After reminding students about topic sentences and proper paragraph form, ask students to write a topic sentence and to develop their sentences about the local area into a grammatically sound paragraph describing a central section of their community.

Practice 1: 12–15 minutes
Have students develop and write a few questions individually. After ample writing time, pair students and exchange questions so students will have the opportunity to answer questions using prepositions of location.

Evaluation 1: Circle the classroom and identify well-written questions. Have volunteers write those on the board for a class quiz. Correct all sentences as a group.

Application: 18–20 minutes
Instruct students to select a community intersection. Students should take time to describe stores and points of interest located at their chosen intersection. Pair students and allow each to describe their intersection using prepositions of location. Students should make corrections together. Stage a game in which students read their descriptions and see who can guess which local intersection is being described.

Have students imagine they work for a travel agency. Their boss has requested that they design a brochure inviting tourists to a city of interest. Allow students to choose the city they wish to highlight. If possible, supply brochures, maps, and books about the local area or surrounding cities for students to use as reference (or try Internet sites for tourists). If this isn't possible, have students describe the City Square illustrations on **pages 58 and 59.** Provide students with the city brochure worksheet from the **Activity Bank CD-ROM.**

Crime and Justice

Level ★

Objective: Identify crimes.

Warm-up: 10–15 minutes
Seek a volunteer who has a purse or backpack and pretend to steal it. When students correctly guess the crime, solicit feedback about why theft is wrong. Write the word *crime* on the board and ask students to identify other crimes you pantomime. Since student vocabulary may be limited, accept any close answers. Remain sensitive to student emotions during this vocabulary work since some students may have experienced a serious crime.

Introduction: State the objective.

Presentation 1: 15–20 minutes
Write the word *safe* on the board and ask students if they feel safe in their communities. Draw a horizontal line on the board indicating a continuum of safety. On the left side of the line write *safe* and on the right side write *unsafe*. Ask students where certain communities or neighborhoods would be placed on the spectrum. Refer students to the word list on **pages 60 and 61**. Review the words as a class and focus attention on the crimes numbered 1–14. Prepare students to perform this model conversation.

> **Student A:** *What is this crime?* (Student A points to picture.)
>
> **Student B:** *That crime is <u>drunk driving</u>.*

Practice 1: 8–10 minutes
Encourage students to form pairs and quiz each other using the exchange and substituting new vocabulary. Student A covers the words and points to a picture. Student B inserts the name of the corresponding crime. Students should reverse roles.
Evaluation 1: Observe the activity.

Presentation 2: 10–15 minutes
Draw a vertical line on the board. At the top, write *most serious crime* and at the bottom, write *least serious crime*. As a class, decide on the most serious crime (probably murder) and write it at the top of the line and the least serious crime and add it to the bottom. Remind students that although some crimes are less serious, no crime is acceptable.

Practice 2: 10–15 minutes
Read **Words in Action #2** and review crimes 1–14. In groups, students should rate the other crimes and place them on the spectrum.
Evaluation 2: Compare answers after each group has had the chance to put their spectrum on the board.

Application: 8–10 minutes
Have the groups list the four most common crimes in their neighborhoods and report to the class, as suggested in **Words in Action #1**. If time allows, you might ask students why these crimes are more common than others in their neighborhoods.

Words in Context

Iceland has very little **crime**. There are only four **prisons**, and many of the **prisoners** are part-time! There are usually only one or two **murders** a year, and crimes like **armed robbery** are extremely rare. There are sometimes **muggings** in the capital city of Reykjavík, but Iceland is still one of the safest countries in the world.

— 60 —

Level ★ ★

Objective: Describe crimes.

Warm-up: 10–12 minutes
Before students open the dictionary, read *Words in Action #1* aloud and assign students to small groups. Ask students to list the most common crimes in their communities. Ask if their neighborhood is *safe* or *unsafe*.

Introduction: State the objective.

Presentation 1: 18–20 minutes
Begin a master list on the board of all the crimes the students thought of in the Warm-up. Study **pages 60 and 61** and review all **Word Partnerships**. Add any crimes from the word list to the master list. Initiate a conversation about having reported or witnessed a crime. Take time to describe each scene as depicted in the dictionary. For example, the students might describe number 6 as *The woman in yellow is drinking and driving*.

1 auto theft

2 bribery

3 burglary

4 theft

5 drug dealing

6 drunk driving

7 arson

8 graffiti

9 mugging

10 murder

11 shoplifting

12 vandalism

13 gang violence

14 armed robbery

15 an arrest

16 a victim

17 a witness

18 a criminal

19 handcuffs

20 a police officer

21 a trial

22 a jury

23 a judge

24 a lawyer / an attorney

25 a courtroom

26 a jail / a prison

27 a prisoner

Word Partnerships

a fair	trial
a speedy	
commit	a crime
witness	
report	
go to	prison
spend time in	
get out of	

Words in Action

1. Talk with a group. Which crimes are most common in your community?

2. Put the crimes in a list from the least serious crime to the most serious crime. Discuss your list with a partner.

— **61**

Objective: Write about a crime.

Warm-up: 20–30 minutes
Challenge students to think of as many crimes as they can. Brainstorm as a class. Make sure that everyone is familiar with dialing 911 or the local emergency number for help. Ask small groups to prepare a skit in which a person witnesses and reports a crime, clearly asking authorities for help.

Introduction: State the objective.

Presentation 1: 15–20 minutes
Ask students to open their dictionaries to **pages 60 and 61**. Discuss each item carefully until students have no more questions. Generate a discussion about students' experiences with crime by mentioning a personal or family experience with crime. Due to the sensitive nature of this discussion, do not insist that everyone participate. Have students choose the city they consider the safest in the world. Accept all answers as nominations. See if the class can decide on one winner. Have the class list the reasons why they think this place is so safe. Why are some communities safer than others? Go over the reasons. Read **Words in Context** aloud and discuss.

Practice 1: 15–20 minutes
Have students check off 10 words that are not familiar to them. They should incorporate the words into sentences. Remind them that the context of the sentence is very important.

Evaluation 1: Put well-crafted sentences on the board but leave the vocabulary word blank. Quiz the class to fill in the blanks.

Application: 20–30 minutes
Assign students to "round robin" writing groups and inform them that they will write a *short, fictitious story* about a crime, using as many words as possible from the list. To accomplish this task, one student in the group writes a sentence and passes the paper to the next. Each student adds a sentence and at least one vocabulary word to the story. Set a time limit. Hold a storytelling contest upon completion and award points. The points are determined by dividing the number of word list words used by the total number of sentences. Recognize the group with the most points.

Project

Determine students' knowledge about how to report a crime by asking leading questions. Students should investigate ways to prevent crime in their neighborhoods by reading public safety pamphlets, looking on the Internet, or talking with a police officer or security guard. Students should write, design, and publish a public safety poster or brochure for other students in your program. There is a worksheet to facilitate this activity on the **Activity Bank CD-ROM.**

Practice 1: 12–15 minutes
Teach students how to give verbal clues and prepare them to quiz each other using those clues. Student A will describe the scene and Student B will identify it by giving the vocabulary word from the word list.

> **Student A:** *This scene has 12 people in a courtroom.*
>
> **Student B:** *A jury.*

Ask pairs to create five verbal clues and challenge them to write a quiz for the entire class.

Evaluation 1: Students will read verbal clues to the entire class and determine who gets the answers correct.

Application: 20–25 minutes
Place students in small groups and tell them to pretend they are a jury. The jury must decide how much time in jail should be allotted for each of the 14 crimes studied. All jury members must agree. If jail time is not an appropriate punishment, the jury can offer other suggestions. Compare and discuss answers.

Types of Homes

Level ★

Objective: Identify types of homes.

Warm-up: 12–15 minutes
Launch a discussion about where students live. Accept any answers, including cities, streets, and neighborhoods, but eventually guide the conversation to include types of homes. Draw a picture of your own home—whether it is a *house*, an *apartment*, or a *condominium*. Ask students to open their dictionaries and look at **page 63**. Briefly discuss the *urban, suburban, town,* and *rural* pictures. Poll the class on which types of places students were born. If the class includes enough diversity, create a bar graph, using the template available on the Activity Bank CD-ROM.

Introduction: State the objective.

Presentation 1: 15–20 minutes
Introduce the vocabulary from the word list. Evaluate comprehension by reading a word and having students point to the correct picture while covering the word list. Follow up by having students choose eight words from the list and write them on a piece of paper, or use the Bingo cards from the Activity Bank CD-ROM.

Practice 1: 8–10 minutes
Play Bingo by giving words in a random order. When students have a word on their lists, they cross it off. The first student with all words crossed off wins.

Evaluation 1: Observe the activity.

Presentation 2: 10–15 minutes
Pass out small cards, each with a type of home written on it. Do not use *house*. Plan so each type occurs on at least two cards. The words will serve as a prompt for the following exchange:

Student A: *Where do you live?*

Student B: *I live in (city/town name).*

Student A: *Do you live in a house?*

Student B: *No, I live in a (word on the card).*

Student A: *I live in a (word on the card).*

Practice 2: 8–10 minutes
Ask students to perform the exchange with several classmates. You may set a limit on time or the number of conversations. Consider adding a stipulation, such as students must keep practicing until they find someone with the same card—then they sit down.

Evaluation 2: Ask several pairs to read for the class.

Application: 8–10 minutes
Add a new twist to the exchange. Students should practice with five different students but replace words with their personal information. Have them prepare a grid and record the information, or hand out the template from the Activity Bank CD-ROM.

Words in Context

Do you live in a **house**, an **apartment**, or a **condo**? There are many other kinds of homes, too. For example, some people in the Sahara Desert live in **tents**. Some people in the U.S. live in **mobile homes**. And some people near the North Pole live in **igloos**.

Word Partnerships

live in	a house
	an apartment
	a dorm
live on	a houseboat
	a ranch

62

Level ★★

Objective: Describe homes.

Warm-up: 10–12 minutes
Read *Words in Action #1* to students and generate small conversation groups to discuss. Allow adequate time.

Introduction: State the objective.

Presentation 1: 20–25 minutes
Brainstorm types of housing in the world as a class. Alert students that their goal is to guess as many types as possible. You might have them do this in groups and report to the class. When students finish, shift attention to **pages 62 and 63** and review all vocabulary with them, including *Word Partnerships*. Compile a list on the board including student suggestions not in the dictionary. As a class, discuss where some types of homes might be found in the world. Review the form and function of an adjective and offer adjective examples so students can describe the pictured homes. They may need words like *small, large, long, tall,*

1 a house

2 a tent

3 a cottage

4 a (log) cabin

5 a chalet

6 a duplex / a two-family house

7 a mobile home

8 a farmhouse

9 an apartment

10 a condominium / a condo

11 a villa

12 a townhouse

13 a houseboat

14 a palace

15 an igloo

16 a ranch

17 a retirement home

18 a dormitory / a dorm

19 a castle

20 the city / an urban area

21 the suburbs

22 a small town

23 the country / a rural area

Words in Action

1. What kinds of homes have you lived in or stayed in? Tell your class.

2. You can stay in three of these homes. Which three will you choose? Why?

63

Objective: Make and defend decisions.

Warm-up: 8–10 minutes
Have students open to **page 63** and follow along as you read the question posed in *Words in Action #2*. Have students address the question in groups of three before sharing answers with the class.

Introduction: State the objective.

Presentation 1: 15–20 minutes
Go over the word list carefully and answer questions. Encourage discussion about student experiences. Read *Words in Context* with students and discuss. Introduce a sharing activity permitting all students to state where they would prefer to live and why. Expand by asking where they would not want to live and why. Begin by asking *Would you like to live in an igloo?*

Practice 1: 20–30 minutes
Ask students to make a list of the best places to live using the word list. Individually, they should rank all 19 words, with number 1 being their top choice. Assign groups of four to streamline their lists so that all members of the group can agree on one list as much as possible. Students should discuss why they like or dislike certain homes and defend their choices.

Evaluation 1: Ask group representatives to write the lists on the board and explain any disagreements. Acknowledging disagreements, attempt to merge the group lists into one final list as a class.

Application: 20–30 minutes
Create a ballot of the five most popular homes and take a final class poll to identify where students would prefer to live. Create a bar graph before grouping students with the same answers together. Have the groups combine reasons for why their choice is best. For example, the *house* group should list reasons that a house is the best and might suggest that it is quieter. The *apartment* group could say that apartments are cheaper.

---

flat, and *unusual*. Describe two homes and have students identify them by number and name.

Practice 1: 15–20 minutes
Pair students for a quizzing exercise. Students should take turns choosing a picture to describe and, using adjectives, describe it so their partners can correctly identify it. Have students exchange roles four times. Ask students to then choose their two favorite pictures and use several adjectives to describe them. Circle the room and have the pairs quiz you with descriptions.

Evaluation 1: Solicit volunteers to demonstrate by quizzing the class.

Application: 15–20 minutes
Have students describe their own homes in detail. They should discuss why they chose a certain housing type and describe homes around theirs. Groups should then go through the entire word list and decide why people choose each type of home. Groups write five sentences to share. To aid this activity, provide examples of well-known people. For example, you can mention that *Queen Elizabeth lives in a palace in London.*

Ask students to research what types of housing different countries and different cultures have. Make materials available or plan a trip to a library so students can use encyclopedias and the Internet. Challenge students to determine why specific types of housing are more popular than others in certain cities or countries.

Finding a Place to Live

Level ★

Objective: Understand the renting or buying process.

Warm-up: 15–20 minutes
Build on the conversation about where students live. Lead students to say their city or town's name. Write types of homes on the board, including *house, apartment, condominium,* and *mobile home.* Take a class poll to determine where people in the class live and make a bar graph on the board by utilizing the template on the Activity Bank CD-ROM.

Introduction: State the objective.

Presentation 1: 15–20 minutes
Ask students how to find a new home. Accept any reasonable answers, including *newspapers, friends,* and *rental or real estate agents.* Ask students to open their dictionaries to **page 64** and present the word list. Make sure students can pronounce each item well. Explain that the bold word in each phrase is a verb. As a class, pantomime several actions and decide on the best pantomime for each verb. Increase the students' comfort levels with the new vocabulary by calling out words and having students pantomime the responses. Study the entire phrases so that when you say the nouns students will be able to respond with the verbs. For example, you might say *a van or truck* and students respond with *load a van or truck.*

Practice 1: 8–15 minutes
Pair students for a quizzing exercise. Student A will give verbs or nouns from the phrases and Student B will state the complete phrase. Have students reverse roles and close their dictionaries.

Evaluation 1: Observe the activity and choose several students to perform for the class.

Presentation 2: 10–15 minutes
Go over each of the words and phrases on **pages 64 and 65,** including *Word Partnerships.* Make comparisons and find similarities between the two processes. Prepare students for a listening activity in which they will listen to a phrase from the word list on **page 65** and identify the picture.

Practice 2: 8–10 minutes
With their partners, students should rely on listening skills. Student A covers the word list and Student B gives a phrase. Student A responds with the number of the picture and repeats the phrase.

Evaluation 2: Observe the activity.

Application: 8–10 minutes
Take a class poll to determine which students own a house and which rent an apartment. Discuss any other answers.

Words in Context

Are you **looking for** an apartment? It isn't always easy. Read the classified ads in newspapers and talk to your friends. **Make** appointments to see a lot of apartments. Before you **sign** a lease, talk to the landlord. **Ask** questions like these:

- How much is the security deposit?
- When is the rent due?
- When can I **move in**?

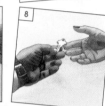

Renting an Apartment

1 **look for** an apartment

2 **make** an appointment (with the landlord)

3 **meet** the landlord

4 **see** the apartment

5 **ask** questions

6 **sign** the lease

7 **pay** a security deposit

8 **get** the key

9 **pack**

10 **load** a van or truck

11 **unpack**

12 **arrange** the furniture

13 **decorate** the apartment

14 **pay** the rent

15 **meet** the neighbors

64

Level ★ ★

Objective: Use the imperative to describe a process.

Warm-up: 12–15 minutes
Tell students that you are going to act out the process of renting an apartment. Ask them to watch you pantomime process described in the word list and write every verb that they see. Tell them that their goal is 15 verbs.

Introduction: State the objective.

Presentation 1: 20–25 minutes
Instruct students to open their dictionaries to **page 64** and check their answers. Study the vocabulary carefully. As a class, compare the verbs given with the verbs they wrote. Teach the imperative form. Explain the concept in a chart on the board. Write a few imperative sentences describing how to rent an apartment with *First, look for an apartment.* Offer several transitional words and phrases, such as *first, next, finally, after that,* and *the second step is.* Review correct paragraph format.

Buying a House

16 call a realtor

17 look at houses

18 make a decision

19 make an offer

20 negotiate the price

21 inspect the house

22 apply for a loan

23 make a down payment

24 sign the loan documents

25 move in

26 make the (house) payment

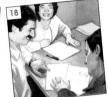

Word Partnerships

look for	an apartment	in the classified ads
		online
		with a realtor
pay	the rent	early
		late
		on time

Words in Action

1. Work in pairs. Cover the words. Say what's happening in one of the pictures. Your partner will find and point to this picture. Take turns.

2. Have you rented an apartment or bought a house? Tell your group what steps you took.

Practice 1: 8–10 minutes
Prime students for a vocabulary memory game. Have them cover the word lists and provide five minutes for students to study pictures 1–26. Read *Words in Action #1* aloud and have pairs participate in quizzing each other. Students should take turns describing actions from the dictionary while the partners point to the correct picture and state the phrase.

Evaluation 1: As a class, write each step of the house-buying proccess and decide if any are more or less important.

Application: 20–30 minutes
Review transition words and paragraph format with students. Then, have them put the steps of either renting an apartment or buying a house in a paragraph, using transition words throughout. Encourage critical thinking. Tell students that they need only include steps they deem necessary. Depending on the students' level, this can be an individual or partner activity. Read student samples and discuss why some students left certain steps out, while others did not.

Objective: Explain the process of buying a house or renting an apartment.

Warm-up: 15–30 minutes
Each student should attempt to write about the process of renting an apartment. Get them started by giving them the first step: *look for an apartment.* Tell them that there are 14 more steps. You may choose to simplify this activity by having students complete the worksheet on the Activity Bank CD-ROM about renting an apartment. It lists the phrases and leaves the verbs as blanks. Students fill in the verbs, using the word bank on the sheet. Check answers.

Introduction: State the objective.

Presentation 1: 15–20 minutes
Ask students to open to **pages 64 and 65** and follow along as each word is covered. Encourage students to ask questions. Launch questions about the students' experiences and open up discussions about renting an apartment or buying a house. List the pros and cons to renting and buying. Read *Words in Context* with students and discuss it. Open the floor to other questions students may have about moving into a new home.

Practice 1: 15–20 minutes
Ask students to rewrite the paragraph in *Words in Context* and substitute the terminology for buying a house. This should be done as an individual activity so each student has a slightly different paragraph with different bulleted questions.

Evaluation 1: Assign groups to compare paragraphs.

Application: 20–30 minutes
Prior to class, type the list of phrases about renting an apartment and buying a house. Cut them into strips and shuffle them, keeping apartment and house steps separate. Split the class into two sections. Hand the set of strips about buying a house to one group and the set about renting an apartment to the other. Challenge them to put the strips in order from memory. Then, have each group write a script that exemplifies part of the process of renting an apartment or buying a home. The spectator group guesses which step or steps are being performed.

Project

Assign groups of four or five students to design a guide to renting an apartment or to buying a house. Each group can decide. There is a worksheet to facilitate this activity on the Activity Bank CD-ROM. Students are welcome to use the dictionary phrases and steps for this purpose, but should write in complete sentences and include their unique points of view and experiences. Consider supplying art materials and real estate/rental catalogs for this activity.

Apartment Building

Level ★

Objective: Identify apartment vocabulary.

Warm-up: 15–20 minutes
Begin a discussion about bedrooms and ask students how many bedrooms they have at home. Prepare students to perform this model conversation.

Student A: *Where do you live?*

Student B: *I live in Ventura.*

Student A: *How many bedrooms does your home have?*

Student B: *My home has three bedrooms.*

Students should gather information from five classmates and record it on a grid or table from the Activity Bank CD-ROM.

Introduction: State the objective.

Presentation 1: 15–20 minutes
Build on the earlier conversation and determine how many students live in an apartment or have lived in one in the past. Elicit details about the apartments, such as the number of bedrooms and bathrooms, number of residents in the unit and in the building, and if there is a garage. Refer students to **pages 66 and 67**. Study each word with students and match the phrases in **Word Partnerships** with floors in a common building in the community, such as a school, library, town hall, or recreation center.

Practice 1: 8–15 minutes
Have students look at each floor in the apartment building and write at least one sentence about it.
Evaluation 1: Ask students to peer correct the spelling.

Presentation 2: 10–15 minutes
Prepare students to perform this model conversation. Student B's word list is covered.

Student A: *Where is the air conditioner?*

Student B: *The air conditioner is here.* (Student B points)

Practice 2: 8–10 minutes
Encourage students to practice and substitute other words from the list.
Evaluation 2: Observe the activity.

Application: 8–10 minutes
Have students perform this model conversation and insert personal information.

Student A: *Do you have a deadbolt?*

Student B: *Yes I do.* **OR** *No I don't.*

Replace the underlined words with *an elevator, a balcony,* and *a laundry room.* Students should record the information on the student information grid template provided on the Activity Bank CD-ROM.

Words in Context

I'm the **superintendent** of an **apartment building** in Los Angeles. We have 30 **unfurnished apartments.** Most of these are **studios.** We have a **laundry room** in the **basement.** There's no **doorman,** but I watch everyone who comes in the **lobby.** I take good care of my building.

66

Level ★ ★

Objective: Ask questions about apartments.

Warm-up: 12–15 minutes
Have students form groups of three and describe their homes. To help, offer a few suggestions on the board to guide their conversation, such as *number of bedrooms, number of bathrooms, yard, patio, balcony, large or small,* and *number of floors.*

Introduction: State the objective.

Presentation 1: 18–20 minutes
Direct students to **pages 66 and 67** and introduce vocabulary. Inform them that many questions should be asked when looking for an apartment. Brainstorm a list of questions as a class, and post it on the board. Read *Words in Action #1* aloud and prepare students to practice.

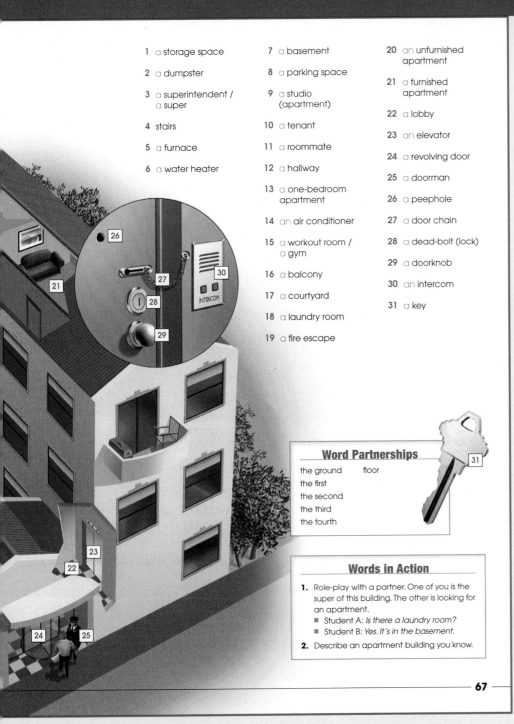

1 a storage space

2 a dumpster

3 a superintendent / a super

4 stairs

5 a furnace

6 a water heater

7 a basement

8 a parking space

9 a studio (apartment)

10 a tenant

11 a roommate

12 a hallway

13 a one-bedroom apartment

14 an air conditioner

15 a workout room / a gym

16 a balcony

17 a courtyard

18 a laundry room

19 a fire escape

20 an unfurnished apartment

21 a furnished apartment

22 a lobby

23 an elevator

24 a revolving door

25 a doorman

26 a peephole

27 a door chain

28 a dead-bolt (lock)

29 a doorknob

30 an intercom

31 a key

Word Partnerships

the ground   floor
the first
the second
the third
the fourth

Words in Action

1. Role-play with a partner. One of you is the super of this building. The other is looking for an apartment.
   - Student A: *Is there a laundry room?*
   - Student B: *Yes. It's in the basement.*
2. Describe an apartment building you know.

Objective: Write a paragraph about a local apartment complex.

Warm-up: 10–15 minutes
Read **Words in Action #2** aloud. Brainstorm as a class a list of apartment characteristics. Students should offer ideas about their own apartment complexes.

Introduction: State the objective.

Presentation 1: 15–20 minutes
Peruse the picture on **pages 66 and 67.** As the words are presented, add any new words to the list started on the board. Include **Word Partnerships.** Put students in two groups and have them quiz each other briefly on spelling. Stage a spelling bee in which one member of each team walks to the board. They attempt to spell the word quickly and correctly. Whoever spells the word correctly should also state the definition. All dictionaries should be closed for this activity.

Practice 1: 15–20 minutes
Prepare students to take dictation. Use the text provided in **Words in Context.** Offer to read the paragraph twice, if necessary.

Evaluation 1: Solicit volunteers to write sections on the board. Allow students to peer correct the spelling.

Application: 20–30 minutes
Using the paragraph in **Words in Context** as a model, students should imagine that they are a manager or superintendent of a local apartment complex and write a similar paragraph, using different vocabulary words. Encourage them to add adjectives to enliven the paragraph.

Practice 1: 10–15 minutes
To accomplish the role-play activity, place students in two lines facing one another. Students speak to the classmates located directly across from them and role-play until the preset time limit expires. Shift one line down by one person, and have the last person move to the front of the line. Restart the role-play. Repeat this activity until students have mastered the vocabulary and pronunciation.

Evaluation 1: Observe the activity.

Application: 20–30 minutes
Tell students this is a chance for them to create the ideal apartment. Individually, students should list all the things that would be necessary in an apartment if they were looking to rent one for their family. Each student should make a second list of all the items they would want in addition. Compare lists. Students should write 10 questions for the landlord about the items they listed.

Project

Place students in groups of four. Have them write a "Welcome to your new apartment" pamphlet for new residents of the apartment building on **pages 66 and 67.** Recommend all the positive features of the apartment building, but also mention the safety features and how to use them. Give warnings about locks, the doorman, the peephole, and the intercom to keep everyone in the building safe.

House and Garden

Words in Context

Different cultures have different kinds of **houses**. North American houses often have **yards** with **lawns**. People cook on their **grills** and relax on a **patio**, **porch**, or **deck**. Some Arab and Mexican houses have courtyards. Even **windows** are different from place to place. In France, windows open like **doors**. In Greece and North Africa, windows are painted blue.

Level ★

Objective: Identify home and garden vocabulary.

Warm-up: 10–15 minutes
In small groups, students should brainstorm a list of words associated with homes and houses. Draw a picture of a house to get students thinking. As groups report, transfer responses to the board. Allow several more minutes of brainstorming as a class and add any reasonable answers to the list.

Introduction: State the objective.

Presentation 1: 15–20 minutes
Refer students to dictionary **pages 68 and 69.** Gather responses as students answer if this home is anything like their homes. Expand the conversation by calling for similarities and differences. Study each word from the word list as a class and encourage questions and discussion as you progress. Explain what alphabetical order means. Give students two words and see who can tell you which is first in alphabetical order.

Practice 1: 8–15 minutes
Challenge students to put all the words in alphabetical order as fast as they can. Allow them to work with partners but let them know that they will not be evaluated simply on time. Words must be in the correct order and be spelled correctly.

Evaluation 1: The group to finish first with all words in the correct order writes the answer on the board and wins the friendly competition. Supply some sort of award.

Presentation 2: 12–15 minutes
Draw a three-column chart on the board. Label the columns *living things*, *parts of a house*, and *equipment*. Explain what each label means and categorize three vocabulary words: one example for each classification. Answer questions and review definitions as necessary.

Practice 2: 8–10 minutes
Divide the class into three groups to complete the chart. After sufficient time, assign one category to each group and ask them to double-check those answers. When they're certain they are correct, have them fill that column in on the board for the other groups.

Evaluation 2: Go over the chart.

Application: 8–10 minutes
Tell students to focus on their own homes. They should compile a list of items from the word list that they have either in their own homes or in homes they are familiar with. Suggest making the list two columns: one for items they have, and the other for items they don't have. Allow time for comparison and discussion.

Level ★ ★

Objective: Compare homes.

Warm-up: 12–15 minutes
Read *Words in Action #1* and prepare students to complete this activity with their classmates.

Introduction: State the objective.

Presentation 1: 20–22 minutes
Before referring to the dictionaries, draw on the board a house with a yard. Label any parts of the house that students already know. Have students open to **pages 68 and 69** and follow along as you cover each item in the word list. Ask them to make comparisons between that home and either their own home or that of someone they know. Teach them comparison words such as *bigger than* and *smaller than*. Show students how to use a Venn diagram to compare items from the house on the board to items from the one in the picture. Use the Venn diagram template on the **Activity Bank CD-ROM.**

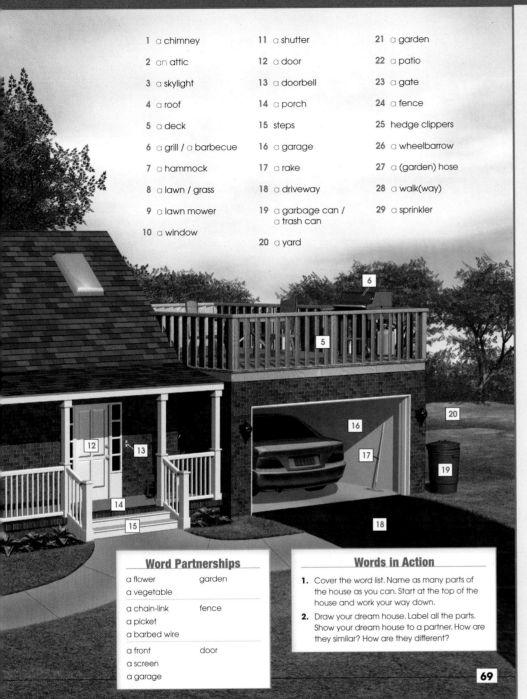

1 a chimney	11 a shutter	21 a garden
2 an attic	12 a door	22 a patio
3 a skylight	13 a doorbell	23 a gate
4 a roof	14 a porch	24 a fence
5 a deck	15 steps	25 hedge clippers
6 a grill / a barbecue	16 a garage	26 a wheelbarrow
7 a hammock	17 a rake	27 a (garden) hose
8 a lawn / grass	18 a driveway	28 a walk(way)
9 a lawn mower	19 a garbage can / a trash can	29 a sprinkler
10 a window	20 a yard	

Word Partnerships

a flower	garden
a vegetable	
a chain-link	fence
a picket	
a barbed wire	
a front	door
a screen	
a garage	

Words in Action

1. Cover the word list. Name as many parts of the house as you can. Start at the top of the house and work your way down.

2. Draw your dream house. Label all the parts. Show your dream house to a partner. How are they similar? How are they different?

69

Level ★ ★ ★

Objective: Write a paragraph about houses in other cultures.

Warm-up: 20–30 minutes
Before turning to the pages in the dictionary, tell students that the dictionary pages are titled *House and Garden*. Students should develop a picture and label it according to what they expect to see. Have students compare the imagined dictionary pages with classmates.

Introduction: State the objective.

Presentation 1: 15–20 minutes
Instruct students to open their dictionaries to **pages 68 and 69** and follow along as words are defined. Include *Word Partnerships* as part of this presentation. Ask students if there are any other words they might add to the list. Open a discussion about what culture or what country is best represented by the home in the picture. Students should explain their answers. Extend by asking if they believe that the home in the picture could be in any country. Read *Words in Context* with students and continue discussing the topic.

Practice 1: 15–20 minutes
Ask students to find a partner from a different country. Have them conduct interviews in which students ask about homes in their partners' countries. Each student should write six sentences describing homes his or her partner's country. If students are all from the same country, choose different areas or cities within that country.

Evaluation 1: Every student should write one sentence on the board and ask classmates to guess the country in question and correct any spelling errors.

Application: 20–30 minutes
Each student should write a paragraph about homes that are different from the one pictured using the sentences they created and additional ones they write. You might supply them with the following prompt as a topic sentence:

Homes in _____ are different from ones in the United States.

Practice 1: 12–15 minutes
Pair students to complete the Venn diagram comparing the house on the board to the one in the dictionary. Students should use comparison vocabulary to describe the similarities and differences and write in complete sentences.

Evaluation 1: Check the Venn diagrams for accuracy and compare results.

Application: 20–22 minutes
Students should create another Venn diagram comparing their current home to the house pictured in the dictionary. Give students time to begin by drawing a picture of their house and listing details before attempting to place the details in a Venn diagram. Encourage them to ask for peer correction and ideas. Alternatively, students can compare current homes to homes they lived in previously, either in this country or different ones.

Project

Read *Words in Action #2* and ask students to respond and prepare a short presentation for the class. Encourage students to illustrate their dream homes with pictures from magazines or their own artwork.

Kitchen and Dining Area

Level ★

Objective: Identify kitchen and dining room vocabulary.

Warm-up: 8–15 minutes
Pantomime making a cake. Solicit guesses about what action it is. Be prepared for simple answers such as *cake*. Include actions such as turning on the oven, taking eggs from a refrigerator, cracking the eggs in a bowl, mixing flour and other ingredients, pouring the mixture into a pan, putting the cake in an oven, waiting, opening the oven, cutting the cake, offering pieces to students, and eating. Repeat the pantomime and ask students to identify nouns and verbs associated with your actions. List their responses on the board. If permitted, bring in a cake to share with the class.

Introduction: State the objective.

Presentation 1: 12–15 minutes
Ask students if they have a big or a small kitchen and discuss. Determine how many words students know by pantomiming the use of kitchen items. Write each correct answer on the board. Direct students to **pages 70 and 71**. Review each word as a class and take time to teach proper pronunciation when you discuss the definitions.

Practice 1: 8–10 minutes
Pair students for practice. Students should identify vocabulary by giving their partners words from the list. Partners should respond by pointing to the correct objects and repeating the words. Challenge students to try this activity with the word list covered. Make sure students reverse roles.

Evaluation 1: Observe the activity.

Presentation 2: 15–20 minutes
Draw a cluster diagram on the board or use the template available on the **Activity Bank CD-ROM**. Label the inner circle *kitchen/dining room* and the secondary circles *furniture, appliances, dinnerware, other*. Define each category and prepare students to complete the cluster. Provide one example of each category from the word list.

Practice 2: 10–15 minutes
Explain that students should complete the cluster with the remaining words from the list. Divide students into groups of three. Prepare students for reporting, with each student reporting a different category.

Evaluation 2: Listen to group reports.

Application: 8–10 minutes
In the same groups, have students perform *Words in Action #2*. Compare answers.

Words in Context

Before 1900, few **kitchens** had electricity. People used **candles** for light. There were no **refrigerators**, no **ovens**, no **dishwashers**, and no **blenders**. There were no faucets, either. To wash **dishes**, people had to get water from outdoors and heat it over a fire.

1	a microwave (oven)	21	a stool
2	a cabinet	22	a chair
3	dishes	23	a plate
4	a shelf	24	a bowl
5	a counter(top)	25	a glass
6	a stove	26	a placemat
7	a (tea) kettle	27	silverware
8	an oven	28	a candle
9	a potholder	29	a teapot
10	a coffeemaker	30	a mug
11	a spice rack	31	a napkin
12	a blender	32	a table
13	a toaster		
14	a dishwasher		
15	a sink		
16	a drying rack / a dish rack		
17	a garbage disposal		
18	a dish towel		
19	a freezer		
20	a refrigerator		

Word Partnerships

a dining room	table
a kitchen	chair
an electric	stove
a gas	
load	the dishwasher
start / turn on	
empty	

70

Level ★ ★

Objective: Use kitchen and dining room vocabulary in conversation.

Warm-up: 8–10 minutes
Refer students to **pages 70 and 71**. Read *Words in Action #1* and divide the class into groups of three. Have each group list the most important things in the picture. Group members need to agree on 10 items and then rank them. The first item on the list should be the most important.

Introduction: State the objective.

Presentation 1: 15–20 minutes
Review the word list in its entirety and include *Word Partnerships* in your presentation. Have students cover the word list and then quiz students on the vocabulary. As you read the vocabulary, students should respond by identifying the correct item by its number. If students struggle, pantomime as you speak. When students have a thorough understanding, they should return to their Warm-up groups.

Objective: Write instructions for kitchen appliances.

Warm-up: 10–15 minutes
Ask students to read *Words in Context* on **page 70** silently and then find a partner. Pairs should summarize the paragraph. Set a goal of condensing the paragraph into one sentence. Request that students change partners, compare sentences, and create ones. Repeat a third time. By this time, students should be able to complete the exercise without using the dictionary. Lead a class discussion comparing sentences.

Introduction: State the objective.

Presentation 1: 15–20 minutes
Guide attention to **pages 70 and 71**. Formally present the words in the list, ensuring a clear understanding of each. Encourage questions and discussion as you progress. Focus on *garbage disposal* and ascertain how many students know how to use this appliance. Tell students to imagine that you do not know how to use a garbage disposal and ask them to explain the process to you. As they offer instructions, pantomime and write them on the board. Teach the grammatical use of imperatives and rewrite the instructions on the board appropriately. Correct any errors in grammar or directions. Answer key: *1) Add food items to the disposal, avoiding items that may cause problems, 2) Turn on the cold water, 3) Turn on the disposal switch, 4) Wait, 5) Turn off the disposal switch, 6) Turn off the water.* Ask the class what items might cause disposal problems, such as corncobs and meat bones).

Practice 1: 15–20 minutes
Assign groups of three or four a few objects from the dictionary's kitchen. You might want to have items written on small cards and have students pick two from the stack. Have each group write instructions without naming the item.

Evaluation 1: Determine accuracy during presentations; see how many students can identify items from the instructions.

Application: 20–30 minutes
Have students work on another appliance from the kitchen. They can choose another card from your stack, an appliance from the dictionary's kitchen, or an item from their own kitchens.

Words in Action

1. What do you think are the ten most important things in this kitchen? Why?
2. Work with a group. What things do all of you have in your kitchen? Make a list.

71

Practice 1: 30–40 minutes
In their groups, students should work together to develop a role-play. Have each skit include a minimum of eight words from the list. Encourage students to work together and develop a situation that happens in a kitchen. Each group will perform its skit for the other groups.

Evaluation 1: Observe the activity. The group that uses the most kitchen and dining area words is the winner. Award kitchen-related prizes.

Application: 20–30 minutes
Give students a copy of the Venn diagram available on the **Activity Bank CD-ROM**. Teach students how to use the Venn diagram to compare their kitchen at home to the one in the dictionary and to another student's. Illustrate a three-circle Venn diagram on the board with the intersecting circles representing the student's kitchen, the picture, and a fellow student's kitchen. Ask students to compare diagrams when complete.

Project

Simulate a situation in which students are interior designers and must improve the dictionary's kitchen. Each student should examine the picture and determine ways to remodel or improve it. Hand out copies of the graph paper available on the **Activity Bank CD-ROM**.

Level ★

Objective: Identify living room vocabulary and use prepositions of location.

Warm-up: 12–15 minutes
Draw a floor plan of your home on the board. Label the rooms. Explain floor plans and discuss your model in depth. Ask students to illustrate their homes in a similar manner and label the rooms and furniture.

Introduction: State the objective.

Presentation 1: 10–15 minutes
Ask students to open their dictionaries to **pages 72 and 73**. Study each word from the list as a class. Test students' comprehension by randomly calling out words from the list and having students point to the corresponding item in the picture. Start a four-column table. Label the columns *things you sit or walk on*, *things that hang*, *things in or on the wall*, and *other*. Define each of the categories and supply one example for each column.

Practice 1: 10–15 minutes
Assign students to groups of three. Students should complete the table using all the words on the list. Discuss the answers. If desired, utilize the cluster diagram template available on the Activity Bank CD-ROM and ask students to classify the words into new categories they create.

Evaluation 1: Ask groups to report.

Presentation 2: 8–10 minutes
Teach students the following prepositions: *in, on, next to, in back of, in front of, over,* and *under*. Create sentences using items in the dictionary's living room. Prepare students to perform this model conversation.

   Student A: *Where is the end table?*

   Student B: *The end table is next to the sofa.*

Practice 2: 8–10 minutes
Ask students to perform the exchange. Tell partners that each should play both roles three times. Each time, different vocabulary should be used. Offer variety by challenging students to add a question to the exchange as outlined.

   Student A: *It is next to the sofa. What is it?*

   Student B: *It is the end table.*

Evaluation 2: Ensure proper use of prepositions.

Application: 12–15 minutes
Focus student attention on the living rooms of their floor plans. Students should add more details and label them properly. They may want to enlarge the living room plan on a new piece of paper.

Living Room

Words in Context

Some people like lots of furniture in their living rooms—a **sofa**, a **love seat**, a **coffee table**, chairs, a **wall unit**, and several **lamps**. Others like just a rug and a couple of **easy chairs**. In the Middle East, people often sit on **cushions** or low **benches** instead of chairs. And in some Asian countries, people sit on the **floor**.

1 a bench	9 a (throw) pillow	17 a ceiling	25 a thermostat
2 a cushion	10 a window seat	18 a smoke detector	26 a mantel
3 an armchair / an easy chair	11 a love seat	19 blinds	27 a fireplace
4 an end table	12 a coffee table	20 a curtain	28 a fire screen
5 a lamp	13 an ottoman	21 a wall	29 a house plant
6 a lampshade	14 the floor	22 a bookcase	30 a fire
7 a wall unit	15 a curtain rod	23 a vent	31 a rocking chair
8 a sofa / a couch	16 a (ceiling) fan	24 a (light) switch	32 an outlet

72

Level ★★

Objective: Discuss furniture costs.

Warm-up: 8–10 minutes
In small groups, students should attempt to list as many pieces of furniture as they can for a living room, kitchen, and dining room. Compare group answers.

Introduction: State the objective.

Presentation 1: 15–20 minutes
Refer students to **pages 72 and 73**. Present each word from the word list and include **Word Partnerships**. Offer the scenario that their own living rooms are empty and students have a chance to buy everything in the illustrated room. As a class, determine a price for a *ceiling fan*. Write *ceiling fan* on the board and the price the class agrees upon.

Word Partnerships

a floor	lamp
a table	
a desk	
sit	in an armchair
	in a rocking chair
	on a sofa
	on the floor
	on a cushion

Words in Action

1. How is your living room similar to this one? How is it different? Discuss with a partner.
   - *I have a fireplace like the one in the picture.*
   - *My sofa is bigger than the one in the picture.*
2. Draw your perfect living room. Label all the items in the drawing.

73

Objective: Use comparatives to discuss similarities and differences.

Warm-up: 20–30 minutes
Ask students to think about their own living rooms. Let them imagine they are rich and can have anything they want in their rooms. Students should design and label the perfect living room, as suggested in *Words in Action #2.* Allow time for presentations of students' ideas and drawings.

Introduction: State the objective.

Presentation 1: 15–20 minutes
Direct students to **pages 72 and 73.** Discuss each item on the list as a large group. Offer students the chance to add to their designs from the Warm-up as they see items or learn vocabulary they hadn't included. Be sure students understand each item and encourage questions and discussion. Read *Words in Context* aloud and discuss living rooms from other countries. Teach students the following vocabulary: *similar to, different than, bigger than, smaller than, taller than, shorter than, wider than, narrower than, darker than,* and *lighter than.* Use examples as often as possible.

Practice 1: 8–10 minutes
Prepare students for a circle conversation. Place students in two groups with the first group creating a small circle and the second group forming their circle around them. You must have the same number of students in both circles. The people in the inside circle face out and the people in the outside circle face in so that each student has a partner. If your classroom does not have enough space, this activity can be done in lines. The students should discuss *Words in Action #1* with their partners, comparing their living rooms to the dictionary's living room. After a few minutes, rotate the inside circle so students can discuss the topic with a new partner.
Evaluation 1: Observe the activity.

Application: 20–30 minutes
Students should write 10 sentences comparing their own living rooms to the one in the picture.

Project

In small groups, students create their own furniture stores. They should decide what style of furniture the store might include. For example, it might have sophisticated or cheap furniture, furniture for sports fans, for families, for young people, or for older people. Then, have students create an inventory list by naming each piece and determine market prices. Students may also create a floor plan of the store. Encourage creativity by having students describe or draw the furniture. Allow time for presentations.

Practice 1: 20–30 minutes
After students return to their groups from the Warm-up, have each group assign prices to all the items in the word list. When finished, each group should submit a total dollar amount.

Evaluation 1: Ask groups to share their work with the class and compare the totals.

Application: 20–30 minutes
Supply newspaper advertisements and catalogs for living room items. Students should compare their own living rooms to the one in the book and the one they would like to have. After looking through the advertisements, students should design a new living room and determine a cost estimate.

Level ★

Objective: Identify bedroom and bathroom vocabulary.

Warm-up: 12–15 minutes
Draw a floor plan of your home on the board and label the rooms. Quickly review the kitchen, dining room, and living room vocabulary from **pages 70 to 73.** Write *kitchen, dining room, living room, bedroom,* and *bathroom* in a column on the board. Write *eat, wash hair, talk to friends, cook,* and *sleep* in another column. See that students understand these words and phrases. Match the actions to the proper rooms.

Introduction: State the objective.

Presentation 1: 12–15 minutes
Direct students to open to **pages 74 and 75.** Present each word from the word list. As you move through the list, have students point to the corresponding picture. When complete, pronounce words randomly and call on students to respond with either *bathroom* or *bedroom.* Focus on clear student pronunciation.

Practice 1: 8–10 minutes
Ask students to cover the word list. Have a master set of flash cards created with each word from the word list. Shuffle the cards and hold one up at a time. Students should point to the correct item and say the word aloud. Clarify pronunciation. Students can find a partner and continue to quiz each other.

Evaluation 1: Evaluate accuracy and pronunciation.

Presentation 2: 8–10 minutes
Teach students the following prepositions: *in, on, next to, in back of, in front of, over,* and *under,* giving examples from **pages 74 and 75.** Prepare students to perform this model conversation:

Student A: *Where is the dresser?*

Student B: *The dresser is next to the bed.*

Student A: *The dresser is next to what?*

Student B: *It is next to the bed.*

Teach students how to use correct stress and intonation when asking for clarification. Read the dialog several times, using correct inflection.

Practice 2: 8–10 minutes

Students should practice the exchange described while substituting vocabulary and prepositions.

Evaluation 2: Ask volunteers to demonstrate.

Application: 12–15 minutes
Repeat the activity but challenge students to say and write sentences describing their own homes.

Bedroom and Bathroom

Words in Context

Feng shui is a Chinese art. It suggests ways to make homes healthy and happy. For a calm **bedroom,** your **bed** should not face a door. Your **bedspread** should not touch the floor. In the **bathroom,** the **toilet** should not face the door. You should have many **mirrors.** Mirrors bring happiness.

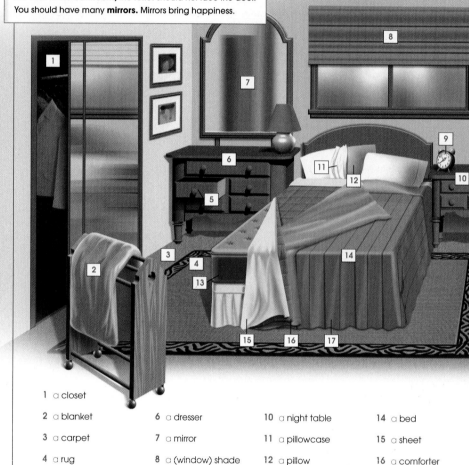

1 a closet			
2 a blanket	6 a dresser	10 a night table	14 a bed
3 a carpet	7 a mirror	11 a pillowcase	15 a sheet
4 a rug	8 a (window) shade	12 a pillow	16 a comforter
5 a drawer	9 an alarm clock	13 a mattress	17 a bedspread

74

Level ★ ★

Objective: Describe a bedroom and a bathroom.

Warm-up: 8–10 minutes
As a class, briefly view **pages 74 and 75** and read **Words in Action #2.** Allow time for students to discuss the questions.

Introduction: State the objective.

Presentation 1: 15–20 minutes
Formally present each word from the list and include the adjectives in **Word Partnerships.** Demonstrate how students can describe different items in the dictionary's bedroom illustration. For example, you may say *The twin bed is small.* Review word order and provide examples of the two acceptable locations for adjectives. Working as a class, generate a list of adjectives that could be used to describe the items in the picture. Have students practice this conversation.

18 a shower	22 a (bath)tub	26 a towel	30 a toilet brush
19 a shower curtain	23 a plunger	27 a faucet	31 a wastebasket
20 a drain	24 toilet paper / toilet tissue	28 a sink	
21 a medicine cabinet	25 a toilet	29 a washcloth	

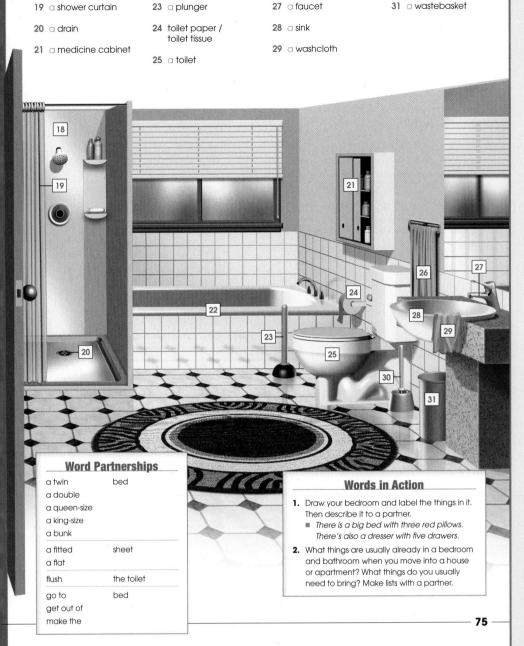

Word Partnerships

a twin	bed
a double	
a queen-size	
a king-size	
a bunk	
a fitted	sheet
a flat	
flush	the toilet
go to	bed
get out of	
make the	

Words in Action

1. Draw your bedroom and label the things in it. Then describe it to a partner.
   - *There is a big bed with three red pillows. There's also a dresser with five drawers.*
2. What things are usually already in a bedroom and bathroom when you move into a house or apartment? What things do you usually need to bring? Make lists with a partner.

— 75

Level ★ ★ ★

Objective: Use conditional verb forms.

Warm-up: 10–15 minutes
Explain what a *morning routine* is and give an example. In small groups, students should discuss what they do in the morning to get ready for work or for school. Remind students to only include actions that take place every morning. Discuss the difference between routine actions and those that are exceptions. List a few ideas on the board.

Introduction: State the objective.

Presentation 1: 20–30 minutes
Ask students to open to **pages 74 and 75** and follow as you present each word. Read **Words in Context** with students and talk about *feng shui.* Solicit adjectives from students about how they feel in their homes. If needed, offer suggestions such as *warm, comfortable,* and *happy.* Continue the conversation by asking if the rooms in the school are inviting according to *feng shui.* **Suggestion:** Prior to class, research *feng shui* on the Internet. A wealth of information is available and it is a popular topic with students. Present additional information at this point in your lecture. Introduce the conditional grammar concept. Focus on *would* and how it can be used to describe what people would do if they were to follow *feng shui.*

Practice 1: 10–12 minutes
Allot class time for students to draw pictures of their own bedrooms and bathrooms. Supply graph paper from the Activity Bank CD-ROM to facilitate their drawings. Divide students into conversation groups to discuss how and why they would change the rooms if they were following *feng shui.*
Evaluation 1: Observe the activity.

Application: 20–30 minutes
Students should write a paragraph about how they feel in their home. Develop the paragraphs to include how their homes could be better if they had the time or money to change them. Encourage the use of *would* and provide example sentences.

Student A: *Can you describe the bed?*

Student B: *Yes, it is a twin bed. It is very comfortable.*

Practice 1: 20–30 minutes
Pair students and allow time for the pairs to practice the exchange several times. Students should play both roles and substitute new words and adjectives each time. Expand the activity by having students rewrite the conversation by describing their own bedrooms or bathrooms. Write this model conversation on the board.

Student A: *Can you describe your bathroom?*

Student B: *My bathroom is very small and blue. It has a small shower.*

Evaluation 1: Observe the activity.

Application: 20–30 minutes
Read **Words in Action #1** and allow students time to draw diagrams and write about their bedrooms and bathrooms. Students can write detailed descriptions and share their sentences with the class.

Project

Before class, write the names of famous living people on small cards along with pictures and/or descriptions of them. Divide students into groups and have them imagine they are architects. Each group gets two cards and should choose for which famous person they would like to design a new house. They should draw a floor plan and include appropriate furniture. Have the house include a kitchen, dining room, bathroom(s), bedroom(s), living room, and garage. Any other rooms or features can be added (suggest yards, patios, pools). Encourage creativity. Allow time for the groups to present their finished products.

Household Problems

Level ★

Objective: Identify household items and problems.

Warm-up: 10–15 minutes
Write the following chant on the board. Define key vocabulary before practicing the chant as a class.

What do we do? What do we do?
Our sink is clogged. What do we do?
Call the plumber. She knows what to do.
Our power is out. What do we do?
Call the electrician. He knows what to do.
Our lock is jammed. What do we do?
Call the locksmith. She knows what to do.
What do we do? What do we do?

Divide the class into three groups. Group 1 chants lines 2, 4, and 6; Group 2 chants lines 3, 5, and 7; and Group 3 chants *What do we do?* continuously.

Introduction: State the objective.

Presentation 1: 15–20 minutes
Ask students to open to **pages 76 and 77.** Choose two students to read *Words in Context* aloud. Explain each word from the list. Encourage questions and discussion. Manage a class exercise in which you say a vocabulary word and the students point to the corresponding picture.

Practice 1: 8–15 minutes
Explain that you'd like students to find partners and quiz each other. Student A says a word and Student B points to it. After 5 minutes, ask students to cover the words to make it more challenging.

Evaluation 1: Observe the activity.

Presentation 2: 10–15 minutes
Write *jobs/occupations* on the board. Help students understand the definition. Ask students to call out the vocabulary words that are names for workers. Write the answers in a column on the board. Promote a second round by asking which words are *actions* and *tools* used by workers. Write those answers in columns to the right, but do not list correct answers directly across from the workers they match. Draw a line from one action to one worker. Explain that this is a matching activity.

Practice 2: 10–12 minutes
Assign the matching activity to small groups. Supply copies of the two-column table template available on the **Activity Bank CD-ROM** to facilitate this activity.

Evaluation 2: Check group work for accuracy.

Application: 8–10 minutes
Encourage students to list the household problems that they have experienced. Assign groups to discuss their specific house problems.

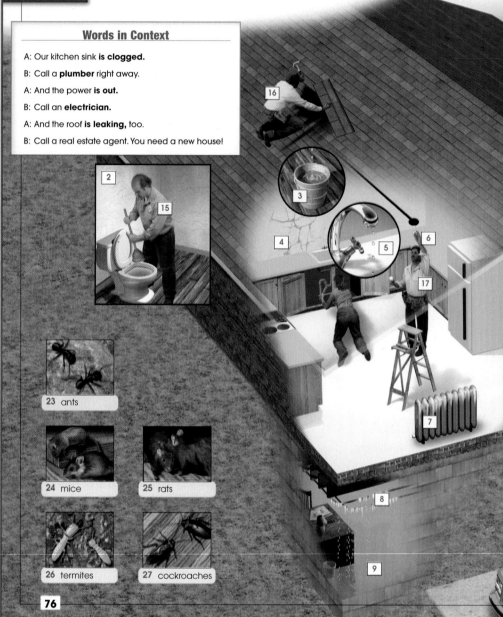

Words in Context

A: Our kitchen sink **is clogged.**

B: Call a **plumber** right away.

A: And the power **is out.**

B: Call an **electrician.**

A: And the roof **is leaking,** too.

B: Call a real estate agent. You need a new house!

23 ants
24 mice
25 rats
26 termites
27 cockroaches

76

Level ★ ★

Objective: Describe household problems and ask for help.

Warm-up: 12–15 minutes
Begin by reading *Words in Action #1.* Divide the class into sharing groups and allow time for discussion.

Introduction: State the objective.

Presentation 1: 17–20 minutes
Share the discussions from the Warm-up.

Present each vocabulary item on **pages 76 and 77,** including *Word Partnerships.* Specify which words are *workers* and list those on the board. Formulate a discussion about students who can do the same repairs as each worker. Compile a list of student responses on the board by student names and the professions they have had experience with, such as *Armando: locksmith.* Read the conversation provided in *Words in Action #2.* Add two more lines to the conversation:

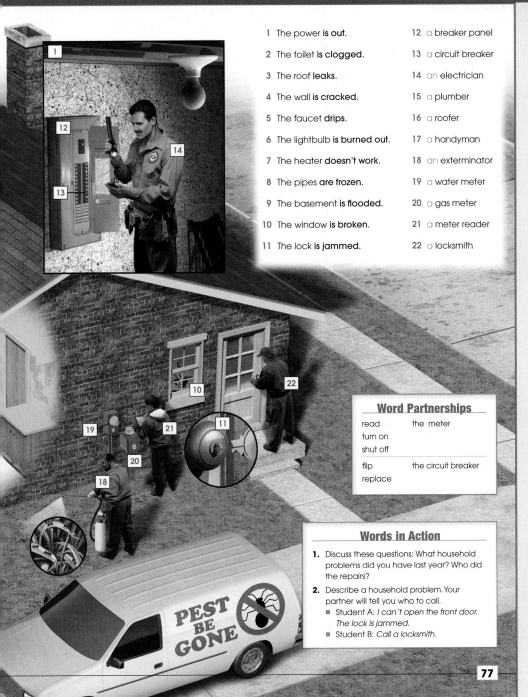

1 The power **is out**.
2 The toilet **is clogged**.
3 The roof **leaks**.
4 The wall **is cracked**.
5 The faucet **drips**.
6 The lightbulb **is burned out**.
7 The heater **doesn't work**.
8 The pipes **are frozen**.
9 The basement **is flooded**.
10 The window **is broken**.
11 The lock **is jammed**.

12 a breaker panel
13 a circuit breaker
14 an electrician
15 a plumber
16 a roofer
17 a handyman
18 an exterminator
19 a water meter
20 a gas meter
21 a meter reader
22 a locksmith

Word Partnerships

read   the meter
turn on
shut off

flip   the circuit breaker
replace

Words in Action

1. Discuss these questions: What household problems did you have last year? Who did the repairs?
2. Describe a household problem. Your partner will tell you who to call.
    - Student A: *I can't open the front door. The lock is jammed.*
    - Student B: *Call a locksmith.*

77

Objective: Write a letter of complaint.

Warm-up: 20–30 minutes
Before class begins, display the words in random or alphabetical order on the board. Tell students to open their dictionaries to **pages 76 and 77** and immediately cover the word list. Their assignment is to identify each numbered picture in the dictionary with the proper word or phrase listed on the board. Check answers as a class.

Introduction: State the objective.

Presentation 1: 15–20 minutes
Define a *complaint*. Discuss things that people complain about. Formally lecture on the sections of a business letter. Revisit the conversation about household problems by asking which problems need a complaint letter. Decide as a class why the other situations do not need a complaint letter. Hand out copies of the complaint letter available on the Activity Bank CD-ROM.

Practice 1: 15–20 minutes
Prepare the class for a dictation exercise. Use the Cloze exercise complaint letter available on the Activity Bank CD-ROM for the dictation. Depending on the level of your students, a worksheet is available with only portions of the letter left blank. Read the letter twice if necessary.

Evaluation 1: Solicit volunteers to write sections of the letter on the board. Students can help correct any errors.

Application: 20–30 minutes
Share an instance in which you had to write a complaint letter about something that happened in your household. Encourage all students to share real-life examples. Have students write letters to their landlords or a company about problems they may have or have had in the past. Make sure letters contain the proper sections.

Student A: *Do you know a <u>locksmith</u>?*

Student B: *Yes, <u>Armando</u> in our class is a <u>locksmith</u>.*

If no students have had any experience, they can respond <u>*No, look in the yellow pages*</u>. Prepare students to perform the conversation and substitute professions and problems as appropriate.

Practice 1: 12–15 minutes
Students should practice the conversation in pairs. Have everyone switch roles three times.

Evaluation 1: Ask volunteers to demonstrate.

Application: 20–22 minutes
Have students write household problems they have experienced on small cards. Remind them NOT to write their names. Collect the cards and randomly pass them back out. Tell students to write which worker they should call and any ideas they have about how to fix the problem. Share answers before allowing students to mingle and find the owner of the card. Have them ask, for example, *Does your roof leak? Is your window broken?*

Project

Divide students into seven small groups and assign each a profession from the list (numbers 14–18, 21, 22). Supply copies of phone books so each group can create a list of local professionals who can be called to fix household problems. Compile the seven lists into one class directory.

Household Chores

Level ★

Objective: Identify household chores.

Warm-up: 10–15 minutes
Pantomime four different chores illustrated in the dictionary. As you act, encourage students to guess the word. When students respond correctly, write the answers on the board. Allow sufficient time for answers. Be sure to include pantomimes for *make a bed, wash the dishes, sweep the floor,* and *wash a car.* Reverse the order and say *cook dinner* while you write it on the board. Choose a student to pantomime the phrase. If time permits, have other students act out more chores.

Introduction: State the objective.

Presentation 1: 15–20 minutes
Ask students to open their dictionaries to **pages 78 and 79.** Study each word from the list. Prepare students for a timed quiz, allowing 30 seconds for students to write down the corresponding numbered picture when you say a word. Challenge them to attempt this quiz with the word list covered. Remind students of the pantomimes you did in the Warm-up and add pantomimes for **Word Partnerships.** Divide the class into groups of four or five. Give each group an equal share of the words from the word list.

Practice 1: 8–15 minutes
Members will develop pantomimes for the words their groups have been assigned. Every student should accept responsibility for becoming an expert on a particular word. Offer time for students to develop a pantomime for their words and practice with their groups. With dictionaries closed, students will stand individually and perform a pantomime.
Evaluation 1: Judge understanding by how many correct student responses follow from the pantomimes.

Presentation 2: 8–10 minutes
Draw a table on the board with columns labeled *kitchen, bedroom, bathroom, living room,* and *yard.* Help students categorize *clean the sink* from the word list under *bathroom* and *kitchen.* Remind them that some answers will fall under only one classification; others can be placed in two or more categories. Students can take notes on the five-column table template available on the Activity Bank CD-ROM.

Practice 2: 12–15 minutes
Groups should complete the table with all vocabulary from the word list. Students should not compare answers with the other groups.
Evaluation 2: Stage a comparison discussion and let groups state how many items they put in each column. Discuss the reasons for each categorization.

Application: 8–10 minutes
Keep students in groups for **Words in Action #1.**

Words in Context

In many houses, men and women share **household chores.** For example, in some houses women **do** the cooking, and men **wash** the dishes. Sometimes women **do** the laundry, and men **fold** the clothes. Sometimes women **weed** the garden, and men **rake** the leaves. What chores do you do in your family?

78

Level ★ ★

Objective: Describe household chores using gerunds.

Warm-up: 10–12 minutes
As a class, develop a list of actions students perform in the classroom every day. Items might include *opening books, writing, reading, listening,* and *speaking.* Include classroom management actions that teachers ask students to do, such as *passing out papers* and *helping others.*

Introduction: State the objective.

Presentation 1: 20–25 minutes
Write *chores* on the board and ask students for the definition. Help them understand that chores are tasks people do regularly around the home. Shift focus from classroom tasks to those done in the home. Refer students to **pages 78 and 79.** Review each chore.
Teach students how adding *-ing* to the end of the base form of a verb can create a noun called a *gerund.* First, give several examples in sentences to ensure understanding. For example, write *I like*

1 **make** the bed

2 **change** the sheets

3 **do** the laundry

4 **sweep** the floor

5 **fold** the clothes

6 **pay** the bills

7 **vacuum** the carpet

8 **dust**

9 **polish** the furniture

10 **clean** the sink

11 **scrub** the toilet

12 **mop** the floor

13 **empty** the wastebasket

14 **shake out** the rug

15 **weed** the garden

16 **wash** the car

17 **mow** the lawn /
mow the grass

18 **water** the lawn

19 **take out** the trash /
put out the trash

20 **rake** the leaves

21 **do** the dishes /
wash the dishes

22 **cook / do** the cooking

23 **dry** the dishes

24 **put away** the dishes

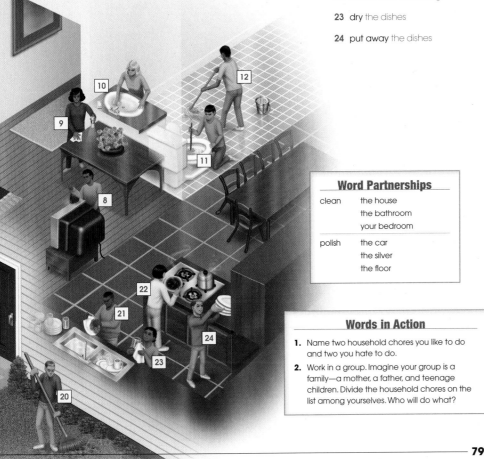

Word Partnerships

clean	the house
	the bathroom
	your bedroom
polish	the car
	the silver
	the floor

Words in Action

1. Name two household chores you like to do and two you hate to do.

2. Work in a group. Imagine your group is a family—a mother, a father, and teenage children. Divide the household chores on the list among yourselves. Who will do what?

— 79 —

Objective: Write a paragraph about household chores.

Warm-up: 20–30 minutes
Review the definition of *chores* and solicit examples from the class. Request that students write the names of their family members or roommates on a piece of paper. Under each name, students should write all the chores that each member does around the house. Give them an example by writing some information about your family.

Introduction: State the objective.

Presentation 1: 15–20 minutes
Direct students to **pages 78 and 79** in their dictionaries and discuss each item on the list. Make sure students understand each word before proceeding. Ask a student to read *Words in Context* aloud and ask if there are different gender roles in the students' homes. Are they happy in their roles? Ask if there are certain chores that only men or only women do in different countries or within different cultures. Allow ample time for discussion.

Practice 1: 15–20 minutes
Explain that well-written paragraphs address the five W's: *who, what, where, when,* and *why*. Ask students to outline a paragraph about household chores and answer these questions about several tasks on the word list: *What is the chore?, Who does the chore?, Where does that person do the chore?, When does the person do the chore?,* and *Why does that person do it?* Ask that students also take note of the frequency of the chores: *How often does that person do the chore?* Have students record their personal household chore schedules on the **Activity Bank CD-ROM** chores duty roster worksheet.

Evaluation 1: Share worksheets in pairs or groups.

Application: 20–30 minutes
Using the notes compiled in Practice 1, students should convert their charts into paragraphs that address the five W's. Each paragraph should contain at least three tasks from the word list. Have a few volunteers share their paragraphs with the class.

Project

Have students form "family units." If possible, divide students into groups of four, so that the group will be representative of a mother, father, and two teenage children—other family groupings are fine. Complete the activity described in **Words in Action #2.** Enhance the project by having students consider the frequency of chores. Print out the chores duty roster worksheet and calendar template from the **Activity Bank CD-ROM** to schedule chores. Students may want to rotate chores week to week. Have students use the calendar template to decide on monthly chores.

playing soccer on the board. Tell students that *playing soccer* is a noun.

Give a sentence in which the direct object becomes the subject. For example, write *Playing soccer is fun.* Discuss how *playing soccer* continues to be a noun. Provide similar examples with gerunds and use verbs from the word list. For example, write *I like cooking* and *Cooking is difficult.* Make a three-column chart labeled *chores I like to do, chores I don't mind doing,* and *chores I hate to do.* Use the template on the Activity Bank CD-ROM.

Practice 1: 12–15 minutes
Students fill in the table, listing the chores by categories to describe their feelings. Encourage them to use gerunds and provide more examples as needed.
Evaluation 1: Compare answers.

Application: 18–20 minutes
Students complete Johari Squares with a partner. The squares include: *chores I like to do, chores my partner likes to do, chores my partner and I don't like to do,* and *chores my partner and I like to do.* The Activity Bank CD-ROM has a template for this activity.

Cleaning Supplies

Level ★

Objective: Identify and locate cleaning supplies.

Warm-up: 10–15 minutes
Write *recycle* on the board. Explain this concept by pantomiming opening and drinking an imaginary soda and throwing the aluminum can in the trash. Use real props for better effect. Place a bag or bin labeled *recycling* nearby. Act as if you did a terrible thing: pull the can out of the trash and put it in the bag. When you are convinced students understand the concept, begin a discussion about what things can be recycled. As a class, make a list on the board.

Introduction: State the objective.

Presentation 1: 18–20 minutes
Write *to clean* on the board. Define and ensure all students understand the meaning. Initiate conversation about what needs to be cleaned in the students' homes. Compile a list of student ideas on the board. Instruct students to open their dictionaries to **pages 80 and 81.** Study each word from the word list as a class. Quiz students by having them point to items when you say the vocabulary word. Review singular and plural grammar functions. Students should identify the four items in the list that are plural. Write *Where is the _____?* and *Where are the _____?* on the board. Examine the grammatical differences between the singular and plural questions. Allow time for practice.

Practice 1: 8–10 minutes
Pair students for peer quizzing. Students should ask each other where items are in the picture. Monitor student dialogs to make sure all students use the plural where appropriate.

Evaluation 1: Solicit volunteers to demonstrate.

Presentation 2: 8–10 minutes
Write *Where are the paper towels? They are on the top shelf.* Teach students *first* and *second shelf, under the bottom shelf, to the right of,* and *to the left of.* Review prepositions of location and encourage students to use others as appropriate. Give pairs additional practice with item locations.

Practice 2: 8–10 minutes
Read the sentences from Presentation 2 as a model conversation. Pairs should perform the exchange but insert new vocabulary each time. Recommend that each pair reverse roles three times.

Evaluation 2: Listen to the dialogs.

Application: 10–12 minutes
Ask all students to scan the word list and make a list of items they have in their homes along with the primary uses of each item and the location of each item in their homes. Next, have students make a list of the cleaning supplies they don't have.

Words in Context

Do you want to wash a window? Follow these steps:

- Put on **rubber gloves.**
- Mix a gallon of warm water with a little ammonia.
- Put the liquid on the window with a clean **sponge.**
- Pull a **squeegee** across the window.
- Wipe the squeegee with a **rag** or a **paper towel** and repeat.

1 a feather duster
2 a dustpan
3 a vacuum cleaner bag
4 vacuum cleaner attachments
5 a vacuum (cleaner)
6 a squeegee
7 paper towels
8 trash bags
9 furniture polish
10 a dust cloth
11 glass cleaner
12 dishwasher detergent
13 dish soap / dishwashing liquid
14 a scouring pad
15 bug spray / insect spray
16 a bucket / a pail

17 a rag
18 rubber gloves
19 cleanser
20 a scrub brush
21 a sponge
22 a flyswatter
23 a stepladder
24 a mousetrap
25 a recycling bin
26 a mop
27 a dust mop
28 a broom

Word Partnerships

heavy-duty	trash bags
20-gallon	
plastic	
a sponge	mop
a string	
a floor	
a push	broom
a kitchen	

80

Level ★ ★

Objective: Give instructions for household supplies.

Warm-up: 12–15 minutes
Form groups of three or four. Have groups list everything members would do that would require protective gloves. Suggest a few activities to get them started: *hospital tasks, cleaning chores, garbage pick-up,* and *construction work.* Permit time for group reports. Then, have them review **pages 78 and 79** to extend the list.

Introduction: State the objective.

Presentation 1: 18–20 minutes
Ask students to turn to **pages 80 and 81.** Study the vocabulary in the word list as a class and include **Word Partnerships.** Choose a strong reader to read **Words in Context** aloud. Point out the imperative verb forms at the beginning of each sentence. Write the following verbs: *mix, ring out, rinse,* and *mop* on the board. Make sure students understand the

Objective: Create a test for other students.

Warm-up: 10–12 minutes
Prepare students to perform the activity suggested in *Words in Action #1.* Encourage a thorough list and allow time for individuals to share their lists with others. Place some of the more innovative answers on the board and discuss them as a class.

Introduction: State the objective.

Presentation 1: 12–15 minutes
Have students open their dictionaries to **pages 80 and 81** and discuss each item on the list. Encourage questions and discussion to ensure understanding of each definition. Start a conversation about uses for *scouring pads.* Accept any reasonable answers. See if students can provide a detailed definition. Help as necessary. If they say a scouring pad is for scrubbing a sink, verify their answer by saying *A scouring pad is a household cleaning supply used to scrub sinks.*

Practice 1: 18–20 minutes
Split the class into three groups. Assign each group eight words from the list. Group members should write definitions for their eight words, as modeled in the presentation. Continue this activity by having each group create a test for other students. At the top of the written test, they should give the following instructions: *Read the sentence and identify the cleaning supply.* Using the example given in the presentation, they would write as one of their test items: *This is a cleaning supply used to scrub sinks.*

Evaluation 1: Have group members take turns reading test questions aloud. Students from responding groups should raise a hand when they know the answer. After several hands are up, call on someone to respond.

Application: 20–30 minutes
Challenge students to think of five more cleaning supply items in their homes that are not included in the dictionary. Create a test for classmates using these items. Collect the tests and compile them into one test to be given to students during the next class period.

Words in Action

1. Name cleaning supplies you use often. What do you use each item for?
2. You need to clean your living room, your bathroom, and your kitchen. Which cleaning items will you use for each room?

meaning of each word. Then, write these nouns on the board: *bucket, soap,* and *mop.*

Practice 1: 10–15 minutes
Place students in new groups of three and have them write instructions on how to mop a floor. Ask students to utilize the words on the board. Encourage them to pantomime the action as they think of words to describe the action. Remind everyone to take one step at a time and imagine that they are writing instructions for people who have never mopped a floor before.

Evaluation 1: One group member should read the instructions aloud while another pantomimes the steps. Repeat for each group.

Application: 20–25 minutes
Compile a master list of everything that requires cleaning in a bathroom and have groups write instructions for each job. Combine the best instructions from each group and compile them into an instruction book for new students of English. Have students use the words in the word list as well as new words.

Project

Ask students to form groups of four and answer the question detailed in ***Words in Action #2.*** Have students post answers. For more detailed projects, have students mention specific appliances and furniture found on **pages 70 through 75.**

Fruits and Nuts

Level ★

Objective: Identify fruits and nuts.

Warm-up: 7–10 minutes
Begin class by having students repeat after you: *I'm hungry.* Write *breakfast, lunch,* and *dinner* on the board in three columns and ask students to identify foods they might eat at each of these meals. Identify fruits or nuts mentioned by writing these words on the board as the class brainstorms. If students don't mention any fruits or nuts, add a few to the list. Since this will be new vocabulary for some, stimulate conversation by drawing pictures, or describe the fruits and nuts by color and size. If permitted, bring in fruits and nuts to share with the class.

Introduction: State the objective.

Presentation 1: 15–20 minutes
Refer students to **pages 82 and 83** and carefully view the picture. Tell students they should attempt to list all of the food that is green. On the board, list the words in a column with the header *green.* Create additional columns labeled *red, orange, brown, white,* and *yellow.*

Practice 1: 10–15 minutes
Divide students into five groups and have them make their own charts like the one on the board. Place each fruit from the word list under the appropriate color classification. Assign each group one of the five colors and have students fill in that category.

Evaluation 1: A group representative will complete the assigned column on the board.

Presentation 2: 10–12 minutes
Review the word list and pronunciation. Explain the simple present and its negative. Develop a simple grammar chart about the verb *like* for students to reference. Prepare students to practice this model conversation.

> **Student A:** *I like <u>watermelon</u>, but I do not like <u>apples</u>. What fruit do you like?*
>
> **Student B:** *I like <u>raisins</u>, but I do not like <u>kiwi</u>.*

Practice 2: 10–15 minutes
Have students practice the short conversation with several partners and complete a three-column grid with columns for *name of student, likes,* and *doesn't like.* The grid template is available on the Activity Bank CD-ROM.

Evaluation 2: Observe the activity as students demonstrate the conversation for the class.

Application: 15–25 minutes
Teach students how to complete a three-circle Venn diagram. Facilitate this activity with the template available on the Activity Bank CD-ROM. Have students compare their likes and dislikes with two other students. Discuss the diagrams.

Words in Context

Grapes are one of the most popular **fruits** in the world. Every day, millions of people enjoy them. Many people also like **apples.** Apples first came from Afghanistan. **Oranges, lemons,** and **limes** are also popular around the world. These fruits came from China.

82

Level ★ ★

Objective: Describe fruits and nuts.

Warm-up: 12–15 minutes
Draw a three-column chart on the board and label the headers *not healthy, healthy,* and *very healthy.* Ask students to brainstorm examples of food for each category. Point out differences in opinion for discussion purposes. Examples of fruits should appear in one of the last two columns. Focus on which fruits are healthier than others. Expand to include a discussion on nuts. Encourage critical thinking by posing a question about what kinds of fruits or nuts are in *pies, cakes,* and *drinks.*

Introduction: State the objective.

Presentation 1: 15–20 minutes
Direct attention to **pages 82 and 83** and quiz students by asking them to cover the words on the right and point to fruits as you name them randomly. Have students respond with the number of the

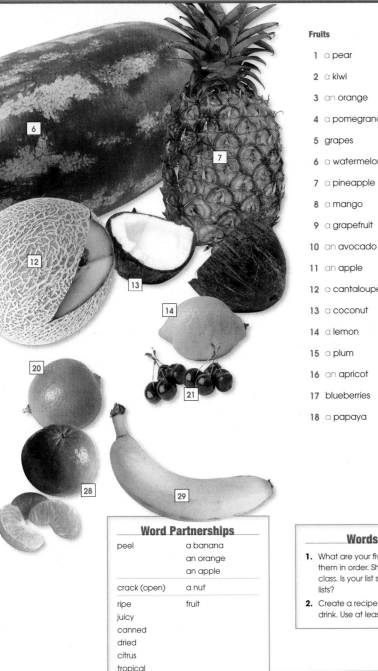

Fruits

1. a pear
2. a kiwi
3. an orange
4. a pomegranate
5. grapes
6. a watermelon
7. a pineapple
8. a mango
9. a grapefruit
10. an avocado
11. an apple
12. a cantaloupe
13. a coconut
14. a lemon
15. a plum
16. an apricot
17. blueberries
18. a papaya
19. a peach
20. a lime
21. cherries
22. figs
23. olives
24. dates
25. strawberries
26. raspberries
27. raisins
28. a tangerine
29. a banana

Nuts

30. pecans
31. almonds
32. pistachios
33. peanuts
34. walnuts

Word Partnerships

peel	a banana
	an orange
	an apple
crack (open)	a nut
ripe	fruit
juicy	
canned	
dried	
citrus	
tropical	

Words in Action

1. What are your five favorite fruits? Rank them in order. Share your list with your class. Is your list similar to other students' lists?

2. Create a recipe for a delicious fruit drink. Use at least four fruits.

Objective: Describe the taste of fruits and nuts and discuss their origins.

Warm-up: 10–15 minutes
Direct students to **pages 82 and 83** and ask them to identify fruits or nuts that are not grown in their native countries. On the board, make a list of countries and fruits. Generate conversation about who has eaten every fruit in the picture.

Introduction: State the objective.

Presentation 1: 15–20 minutes
Present the following vocabulary to students: *juicy, sweet, bitter, sour,* and *delicious.* Study the additional words in **Word Partnerships** after covering the word list. Encourage questions and discussion.

Practice 1: 20–25 minutes
Review proper paragraph form and the importance of adjectives. Students should write a simple paragraph about their favorite fruits and nuts, using the adjectives from Presentation 1. Remind students to use a topic sentence and place adjectives before the nouns that they modify.

Evaluation 1: Pair students to discuss preferences and paragraphs.

Presentation 2: 5–10 minutes
With students, read through **Words in Context.** Prepare them for a dictation exercise in which their dictionaries should be closed.

Practice 2: 5–10 minutes
Use the **Words in Context** reading for the dictation. Read the paragraph aloud twice.

Evaluation 2: Ask students to check their work against the paragraph in the dictionary. Review the context with students to ensure comprehension.

Application: 10–15 minutes
As a class, prepare a chart that will allow students to document answers during interviews. Questions should include which fruits and nuts the interviewees like, why they like them (adjectives), how often they eat their favorite fruits and nuts, and when they eat them. Students should take turns being the interviewer and interviewee. Charts should be maintained and can be shared with fellow students.

item. Prepare students for a cluster activity in which they will start with *fruit* in the central circle.

Extend the cluster to include additional circles with the words found in **Word Partnerships,** such as *juicy, dried,* and *citrus.* Explain each word in this section and give one example for each secondary circle created. For example, *grapes* might extend from *juicy.* A template for this cluster can be found on the **Activity Bank CD-ROM.**

Practice 1: 25–30 minutes
Ask groups of three or four to complete the cluster.

Evaluation 1: Ask each group to contribute to the final cluster you started on the board. Encourage discussion about why students placed different items in different places.

Application: 10–15 minutes
Students should rank their favorite fruits, as suggested in **Words in Action.** After students complete their ranking, share lists as a class.

Project

In small groups, students should prepare a recipe using at least three fruits or nuts. Recipes can be for a fruit drink, a cake, a pie, a casserole, etc. Hand out copies of the recipe card worksheet from the **Activity Bank CD-ROM.** Compile the recipes into a class cookbook.

Objective: Identify vegetables.

Warm-up: 10–15 minutes
Write *salad* on the board. In groups, students should list items they would include in a salad. Since students won't necessarily know the vocabulary, encourage them to ask one another. Accept any reasonable answers, including fruit items from **pages 82 and 83**. Remind students to review the previous unit. Also accept food items in the students' languages or in pictures if students do not know the vocabulary. Start by writing the word *lettuce* on the board. Groups should read their lists aloud.

Introduction: State the objective.

Presentation 1: 15–20 minutes
Focus attention on **pages 84 and 85**. Begin discussing which vegetables are liked and disliked. Pass out small cards and have students write three favorite vegetables on the cards. Students should not write their names on the cards. Practice this conversation.

Student A: *What vegetables do you like?*

Student B: *I like _____. What vegetables do you like?*

Student A: *I like _____. Is this your card?*

Student B: *Yes/No. Is this your card?*

Student A: *Yes/No.*

Practice 1: 10–15 minutes
Collect and shuffle the cards before handing them out. Students should repeat the conversation with classmates until they find the person who wrote the card they are holding.

Evaluation 1: Have volunteers demonstrate.

Presentation 2: 10–12 minutes
Review the word list in depth. Make sure students take the opportunity to pronounce each word. Write *My favorite vegetable is _____. I eat it _____ times per _____ (week, month)* on the board. Initiate a corners activity in which students choose their favorite vegetable from the list and note its number. Then assign each corner of the room a section of the word list: 1–8, 9–16, 17–24, and 25–32. Students go to the corners with their numbers and discuss their favorites.

Practice 2: 10–15 minutes
After they are grouped, students tell the others what their favorite vegetable is and how often they eat it, according to the model on the board.

Evaluation 2: Observe the activity and discuss.

Application: 7–10 minutes
Allow time for students to write the sentences modeled on the board in Presentation 2 with their own vegetable of preference.

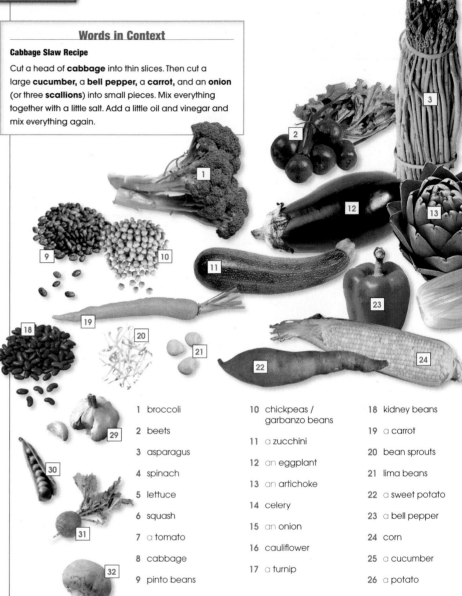

Vegetables

Words in Context

Cabbage Slaw Recipe

Cut a head of **cabbage** into thin slices. Then cut a large **cucumber**, a **bell pepper**, a **carrot**, and an **onion** (or three **scallions**) into small pieces. Mix everything together with a little salt. Add a little oil and vinegar and mix everything again.

1 broccoli	10 chickpeas / garbanzo beans	18 kidney beans
2 beets	11 a zucchini	19 a carrot
3 asparagus	12 an eggplant	20 bean sprouts
4 spinach	13 an artichoke	21 lima beans
5 lettuce	14 celery	22 a sweet potato
6 squash	15 an onion	23 a bell pepper
7 a tomato	16 cauliflower	24 corn
8 cabbage	17 a turnip	25 a cucumber
9 pinto beans		26 a potato

84

Objective: Understand vegetable quantities.

Warm-up: 12–15 minutes
Open the dictionary to **pages 84 and 85**. Pair students to discuss the questions posed in *Words in Action #2* and complete the four squares of the Johari Squares template found on the Activity Bank CD-ROM. Title the squares *I like and my partner doesn't like, My partner likes and I don't like, We both like,* and *We both don't like.*

Introduction: State the objective.

Presentation 1: 15–20 minutes
Open the dictionary to **pages 84 and 85**. Quiz students by having them cover the words on the right and point to the appropriate vegetable as you say its name. Explain count and noncount nouns and present *Word Partnerships*. Explain how certain vegetables are counted. Discuss the articles *a* and *an* found on the word list. With students' help, make a list on

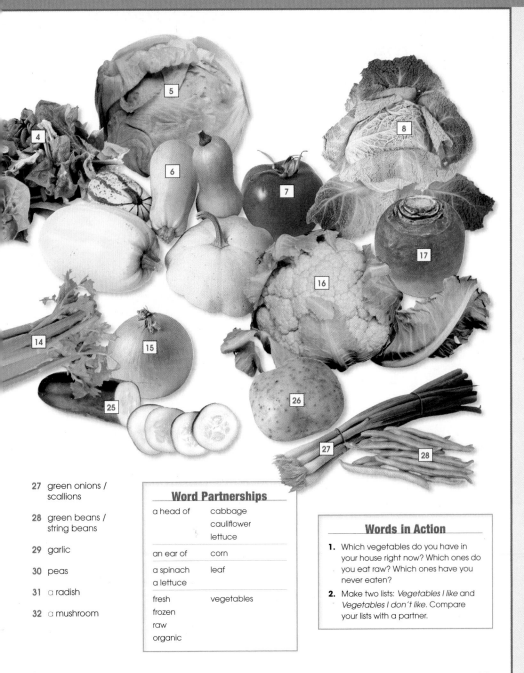

27 green onions / scallions

28 green beans / string beans

29 garlic

30 peas

31 a radish

32 a mushroom

Word Partnerships

a head of	cabbage
	cauliflower
	lettuce
an ear of	corn
a spinach	leaf
a lettuce	
fresh	vegetables
frozen	
raw	
organic	

Words in Action

1. Which vegetables do you have in your house right now? Which ones do you eat raw? Which ones have you never eaten?

2. Make two lists: *Vegetables I like* and *Vegetables I don't like.* Compare your lists with a partner.

Objective: Read and write recipes.

Warm-up: 20–30 minutes
Tell students that they will participate in a discussion about *vegetables*. In groups, students should make a list of the vegetables they think might be included on **pages 84 and 85**. After ample time, students should send representatives to different groups to increase their lists and to check spelling. Allow 10 minutes to complete this exchange and then ask groups to count the number of items on their lists. Students should present their groups' vegetables and write them on the board.

Introduction: State the objective.

Presentation 1: 10–20 minutes
Thoroughly present the word list on **pages 84 and 85**. Compare the list with the one on the board and define any new vocabulary. As a class, read **Words in Context**. Then ask students if they cook and if they use vegetables. Find out who the "chefs" are in the classroom. Organize groups of four or five students, with the chefs as group leaders. Chefs should lead a brainstorming session with their groups to develop ideas for meals that can be prepared with vegetables. Review the verbs used in **Words in Context**. Discuss additional words students could use in a vegetable recipe, such as *herbs* and *spices*.

Practice 1: 15–25 minutes
In their groups, students should write a recipe for a dish that includes several vegetables. Ask them to include different vegetables from the word list while thinking creatively.

Evaluation 1: Observe the activity.

Application: 15–20 minutes
Rearrange groups so students can share their recipes with their new groups via dictation. Students should read their recipes while others take notes. Upon completion, ask students to discuss which recipes they would like to try. Compile the recipes and add them to the class cookbook started in the previous lesson on fruits and nuts.

the board of all the vegetables generally considered noncount.

To the right of each word, place the vocabulary that can identify quantity, such as an *ear* of corn or a *stalk* of celery. Develop a complete list for students to reference.

Practice 1: 25–30 minutes
Spur creative thinking by having students imagine they are throwing a dinner party for 20 people. They should plan on serving a large salad and make a grocery list that includes the items they need and

their quantities. Students should present their salads to the class and describe them.

Evaluation 1: Check for accuracy of vegetable quantities and of count and noncount words.

Application: 15–17 minutes
Place students in small groups and read **Words in Action #1** as a class. Allow sufficient time for students to discuss and expand by having students discuss the following question: *How much (how many) do you have?*

Project

Assign a vegetable from the list to each student or have them choose. Students should bring in a sample of their vegetable—raw or cooked—and others can identify and then taste each one. Before class, find level-appropriate reference materials on vegetables, and allow students to use them in class. Each student should prepare a presentation in which they describe where the vegetable is grown, how it is cultivated, how much it costs, and how consumers use it. Use statistical material presented to create pie charts or bar graphs on templates from the **Activity Bank CD-ROM**.

Meat, Poultry, and Seafood

Level ★

Objective: Identify meat, poultry, and seafood while using the negative simple present.

Warm-up: 10–15 minutes
Write *meat, poultry,* and *seafood* on the board and briefly discuss what these words mean, first by giving examples of each category. Develop a clear definition for each classification. Take a class poll to determine which of the three types of food students prefer, or if there are any students who don't eat meat. Make a bar graph on the board or use the template available on the Activity Bank CD-ROM. Show sensitivity toward vegetarians in class.

Introduction: State the objective.

Presentation 1: 15–20 minutes
Ask students to open their dictionaries to **pages 86 and 87.** Present each item formally and practice the vocabulary by using it in sentences. Collect responses to the question *Which items does your family eat?* Expand the discussion by finding out where students shop for food. Write the market names on the board. Illustrate a cluster diagram and hand out a copy of the template from the Activity Bank CD-ROM.

Practice 1: 10–15 minutes
Assign small groups to complete two clusters, *meat* and *seafood,* using the information in the dictionary.

Evaluation 1: With student input, display correct clusters on the board.

Presentation 2: 10–12 minutes
Teach the simple present—positive and negative—with adverbs. Illustrate the grammar concept in a diagram on the board. Use examples with *eat* as the verb, as in *I don't eat <u>chicken</u>, I never eat <u>chicken</u>, Sometimes I eat <u>chicken</u>,* and *I always eat <u>chicken</u>.* Go over the words of frequency carefully to be sure students understand. Specify further if necessary. For example, *"Never" means zero times* and *"Sometimes" is different for everyone but could mean two times a month.*

Practice 2: 10–15 minutes
Provide time for small groups to discuss the frequency words and define what each means to them in terms of eating meat. Open the floor for discussion of differences in eating habits.

Evaluation 2: Observe the activity.

Application: 7–10 minutes
Students should make a list of the meats, seafood, and poultry they have eaten in the past week. Use the calendar worksheet on the Activity Bank CD-ROM. Allow time for comparison.

Words in Context

Fish and **shellfish** are healthy foods. They contain very little fat. The Koreans and the Japanese eat a lot of **seafood. Clams, oysters, shrimp,** and **tuna** are favorite foods in these countries. However, Americans love **meat.** The average American eats 27 pounds (12.3 kilograms) of **ground beef** a year—mostly in hamburgers.

86

Level ★ ★

Objective: Discuss prices.

Warm-up: 10–12 minutes
Write *barbeque* on the board and define. Extend the discussion by encouraging students to tell the class if they have ever had a barbeque outdoors and what they cooked. Make a list on the board, including fruits and vegetables. Read *Words in Action* #2 and allow time for students to discuss.

Introduction: State the objective.

Presentation 1: 18–20 minutes
Present and discuss all the words from the word list. Make sure students understand what each item means. As a class, complete *Words in Action #1.* Create a bar graph but limit answers to three to five items. Hand out copies of the bar graph template available on the Activity Bank CD-ROM to facilitate this activity. Begin a discussion about the costs of certain items.

1	lamb chops	11	roast beef	22	cod
2	leg of lamb	12	liver	23	swordfish
3	pork chops	13	veal cutlets	24	salmon
4	ham	14	lobster	25	trout
5	salami	15	oysters	26	tuna
6	sausages	16	clams	27	thighs
7	pork roast	17	mussels	28	wings
8	ground beef	18	crab	29	breasts
9	ribs	19	scallops	30	turkey
10	steak	20	shrimp	31	chicken
		21	filet of sole	32	duck
				33	drumsticks / legs

SEAFOOD

SHELLFISH

FISH

SHELLFISH

FISH

SHELLFISH

FISH

Word Partnerships

raw	fish
fresh	
frozen	
grilled	
fatty	meat
lean	
a rare	steak
a medium	
a well-done	

Words in Action

1. Pick your favorite items from the meat, poultry, and seafood sections. Compare your favorites with a partner.

2. Imagine you are having a barbecue. What meat, poultry, and seafood will you buy?

87

Objective: Discuss food preparation and health.

Warm-up: 20–30 minutes
Define *healthy* and take a poll about which is healthiest: *meat, seafood,* or *poultry.* Define the categories if necessary. Read **Words in Context** aloud and discuss. In groups, students should talk about what they eat from each of the three categories. Write some student answers on the board.

Introduction: State the objective.

Presentation 1: 15–20 minutes
As a class, define each word from the word list on **pages 86 and 87.** Encourage classroom discussion and questions. Extend your lecture by discussing food preparation, including **Word Partnerships** and words such as *broil, deep-fry, stir-fry, simmer,* and *roast.*

Practice 1: 20–25 minutes
Divide students into groups of four to discuss the best ways to eat and prepare food. As part of their conversation, they should decide which foods and preparation methods are healthiest. Have groups imagine that they are the owners of the Always Healthy Restaurant. Their task is to create an exciting menu for their restaurant. For each item on the menu, they should explain what is in it and how it will be prepared.

Evaluation 1: Have students present their menu to the class.

Application: 10–30 minutes
Groups of four should prepare a role-play in which they are restaurant employees of the Always Healthy Restaurant. Give the scenario that they are sitting around a conference table discussing the menu. Students should create a dialogue that is 16 sentences in length so that each student is responsible for reading four sentences. Schedule time for performances.

Practice 1: 20–30 minutes
Divide students into groups and have them imagine they are opening a local grocery store. Their task is to name the store and prepare a price list of 15 different items from the illustration. Remind them that in order to be profitable, they should choose the 15 items they feel would sell the best. Representatives can write their choices on the board for comparison. Initiate a discussion about why some groups selected items that others didn't and why all groups selected some items.

Evaluation 1: Encourage correct pronunciation and spelling.

Application: 12–15 minutes
In the same groups, the "store owners" should prepare an advertisement for the local newspaper about their 15 items. Supply flyers and brochures from local stores and newspapers for students to refer to. Allow them to choose certain items to be on sale and give free reign as to design. Display advertisements.

Project

Ask students to design a butcher shop. They should draw a picture of the displays and price each item individually. Ask students to add types of meat that they may enjoy eating that might not be included on these dictionary pages. Discuss different *cuts* of meat, poultry, and fish and why the special cuts of meat or types of fish can make prices differ. Continue the activity by requesting that students create an advertisement for their butcher shop. Supply advertisements from local grocery stores and butchers so students work with authentic prices.

Inside the Refrigerator

Level ★

Objective: Identify items in a refrigerator.

Warm-up: 10–15 minutes
Write *cold things to drink* on the board and brainstorm a list as a class.

Introduction: State the objective.

Presentation 1: 20–30 minutes
Ask students to open their dictionaries to **pages 88 and 89.** Go over each item out loud and practice the vocabulary. Initiate a conversation by having students name the foods they have in their refrigerators at home, starting with drinks. Try to figure out, by a show of hands, which is the most popular refrigerator item. Start a second brainstorming period to develop a list of items students would never have in their refrigerators at home. Define the following phrases as you write them on the board: *on the top shelf of the refrigerator, on the middle shelf, on the bottom shelf, in the drawer, in the door,* and *in the freezer.* Quiz students for a few minutes on each phrase by asking where items in the dictionary's refrigerator/freezer are. Write the following exchange on the board:

Student A: *Where are the eggs?*

Student B: *The eggs are in the door.*

Student A: *Where is the mayonnaise?*

Student B: *The mayonnaise is on the top shelf.*

Teach the grammar rules for *are* and *is* and provide examples of plural and singular nouns.

Practice 1: 8–10 minutes
Pair students to practice the model conversation and perform the exchange, substituting appropriate words and changing roles each time.
Evaluation 1: Observe the activity.

Presentation 2: 10–15 minutes
Prepare students to do a focused listening activity by writing the following numbers in their books. Write the following key on the board: *freezer = 1, top shelf = 2, middle shelf = 3, bottom shelf = 4, drawers = 5, door = 6.* Have students study the refrigerator illustration for a few minutes.

Practice 2: 6–8 minutes
Ask students to close their dictionaries. Randomly call out food items from different sections and have students hold up the number of fingers that will tell you in which section the item is located. Students remain silent. Have them practice this activity with a partner, with one student looking in the dictionary. The responding student can answer aloud. For example, *Is it in the door?*
Evaluation 2: Observe the activity. Note problems.

Application: 7–10 minutes
Read **Words in Action #2** and have students share their dinner menus.

Words in Context

Do you want a well-organized **refrigerator**? Here are some suggestions. Keep fruit and vegetables in the drawers. Put **milk, apple juice,** and **orange juice** in the door rack. **Eggs** are safe in the egg container in the door. Always keep raw meat, poultry, and fish on the bottom shelf. **Ice cream** and **frozen vegetables** stay frozen in the freezer.

1 frozen vegetables
2 frozen waffles
3 ice cream
4 ice tray
5 soda
6 margarine
7 mayonnaise
8 sour cream
9 iced tea
10 pickles
11 tofu
12 yogurt
13 syrup
14 cream
15 bottled water
16 cake
17 jam
18 salad
19 (salad) dressing
20 bacon
21 cold cuts
22 (cheddar) cheese
23 butter
24 (Swiss) cheese
25 eggs
26 milk
27 orange juice
28 apple juice

Word Partnerships

fruit	salad
potato	
pasta	
scrambled	eggs
fried	
hard-boiled	
poached	
mozzarella	cheese
Parmesan	
cottage	

88

Level ★ ★

Objective: Discuss healthy food choices.

Warm-up: 13–15 minutes
Get students thinking by requesting that they make a list of food items they currently have in their refrigerators. Divide students into conversation groups to compare and contrast.

Introduction: State the objective.

Presentation 1: 12–15 minutes
Direct students to **pages 88 and 89.** Define the words from the word list as a class. Make sure students understand each definition. Plan an identification activity in which students identify items in the refrigerator that they consider very healthy. Begin a master list by drawing a table on the board with three columns labeled *very healthy, less healthy,* and *not healthy.*

89

Words in Action

1. Think about the foods in the refrigerator. Make three lists: *Very healthy, Less healthy,* and *Not healthy.* Discuss your list with a partner.

2. Plan your dinner tonight using the food in this refrigerator.

Objective: Write a "how-to" paragraph.

Warm-up: 20–30 minutes
Hand out copies of the refrigerator worksheet from the Activity Bank CD-ROM. Point out that each refrigerator has three shelves, ample door space, and two drawers. Discuss similarities and differences between students' refrigerators at home. Allow time for students to fill this refrigerator with vocabulary words as they would fill their home refrigerator with food. Encourage them to list as many items as they can think of in the appropriate places on the worksheet (example: ice cream in the freezer).

Introduction: State the objective.

Presentation 1: 7–10 minutes
Study the word list on **pages 88 and 89.** Read *Words in Context* as a class and focus on the bold-faced words. Go around the room and ask students if they organize their refrigerators differently at home and if they agree with the advice in the reading.

Practice 1: 15–25 minutes
Divide students into small groups and give the task of adding at least 15 more items to the word list. Accept any reasonable answers. When their lists are complete, have group members place each of their new items in the best place on their refrigerator worksheets. Further the topic by asking groups to determine how long each item will stay fresh in the refrigerator. Teach the use of *should.*

Evaluation 1: Groups should compare their results with other groups.

Application: 20–30 minutes
Review proper paragraph form and the components of a good topic sentence. Students should write a short "how-to" paper informing people of the best way to organize their refrigerators and when to dispose of items that might be too old. Recommend that students use *should* in the paragraphs to give advice. They may incorporate *Words in Context* if they include their own pieces of advice as well.

Practice 1: 15–18 minutes
Divide students into three evenly sized groups to discuss the different columns in relation to the new vocabulary. Each group should complete the table. Assign each group one of the three categories and send a representative to the board to fill in that column.

Evaluation 1: Compare answers and reasons. Discuss disagreements about the healthiness of certain items. Correct spelling.

Application: 20–25 minutes
Generate a classroom discussion about the Olympics and athletes. Poll the class to see who exercises regularly. Students should imagine that they are Olympic athletes. Before continuing, ask students which Olympic sport they would like to participate in. Group students by similar sports and have the groups compile lists of food and drink items that would be in their refrigerators for health and training purposes.

Project

Read **Word Partnerships** as a class and discuss the different types of salads, eggs, and cheese. Bring samples to class if possible. See how many students know how to prepare the salad and egg varieties. Have them choose one of the three salads or four egg dishes and attempt to write directions for its preparation. Supply recipes from a cookbook so students can check their answers.

Level ★

Objective: Express food preferences and design a menu.

Warm-up: 10–15 minutes
Write *fast food* on the board and start a conversation about well known fast-food restaurants. Write responses on the board, and then create a list of fast foods. The list might include *hot dogs, fries,* and fast food from other cultures (e.g., *crepes*). Take a poll to discover if students prefer hot dogs, garden burgers, or hamburgers. Draw a pie chart to show results.

Introduction: State the objective.

Presentation 1: 20–30 minutes
Direct students to **pages 90 and 91**. Go over the vocabulary and practice it in context. Take a second poll to determine student preferences among Italian, American, Asian, or Mexican foods. Write *I want Italian food today* on the board. Explain that this is an answer to the common question *Where do you want to eat?* Prepare students to perform this dialog.

Student A: *Where do you want to eat?*

Student B: *I want Italian food today.*

Student A: *OK, let's eat at Little Italy!*

Student B: *Great. I want pizza.*

Practice 1: 8–10 minutes
Pair students for practice and have them substitute vocabulary for the underlined words.
Evaluation 1: Encourage volunteers to demonstrate.

Presentation 2: 10–15 minutes
Explain that prices can be read as *seven ninety-five* or *seven dollars and ninety-five cents.* Students should use both dollars and cents or neither. Give examples. Write the following dialog on the board.
Student A: *Can I help you?*
Student B: *Yes, I would like vegetable fried rice, but without onions.*
Student A: *Anything else?*
Student B: *No, that's it. How much is it?*
Student A: *Five dollars and fifty cents.*

Define *without*, and make sure students understand the conversation.

Practice 2: 10–15 minutes
Have pairs imagine they are at the take-out counter at a local restaurant and one student is the cashier. Practice the dialog above, switching roles and substituting food items and prices.
Evaluation 2: Observe the activity.

Application: 10–12 minutes
In groups, students should create a menu with prices for at least one restaurant in the dictionary. Hand out copies of the menu worksheet from the Activity Bank CD-ROM. Have groups present their menus to the class and ask students which item is their favorite.

Food to Go

Words in Context

Do you eat at the **food court**? Health experts have some advice for you. Don't order a **hot dog** and **french fries.** Order a salad instead. Don't have a **hamburger.** Have **beans** and **rice** instead. And finally, don't order **coffee** or soda. Have water or juice.

1 pizza	7 french fries	13 a straw
2 lasagna	8 a hot dog	14 a muffin
3 spaghetti	9 a baked potato	15 a doughnut
4 a hamburger	10 a sandwich	16 ketchup
5 a bagel	11 coffee	17 mustard
6 fish and chips	12 tea	18 chopsticks

90

Level ★ ★

Objective: Order at a fast-food restaurant.

Warm-up: 12–30 minutes
Individually, students should develop a four-column table with these headers: *Italian food, American food, Asian food,* and *Mexican food.* Use the Activity Bank CD-ROM template to facilitate this activity. Recognize that many students might not know items to place in each column. Allow extra time for students to

move around to solicit information from classmates (or, if time allows, research in the library or computer lab). Create a master list on the board compiled from student input.

Introduction: State the objective.

Presentation 1: 12–15 minutes
Go over each of the words from the word list on **pages 90 and 91** as a class. Review each item, including phrases in **Word Partnerships.** Review the dialog in **Words in Action #2** and prepare students

Word Partnerships

sticky	rice
steamed	
fried	
black	beans
pinto	
refried	
a slice of	pizza
a piece of	
a small	
a medium	
a large	

19 rice

20 stir-fried vegetables

21 chicken teriyaki

22 an egg roll

23 sushi

24 soy sauce

25 a burrito

26 a taco

27 salsa

28 beans

29 a tortilla

Words in Action

1. Which take-out foods do you like? Which ones don't you like?

2. Work with a partner. Role-play ordering food at one of the places in the picture.
   - Student A: *Can I help you?*
   - Student B: *Yes, I'd like two egg rolls.*
   - Student A: *Do you want something to drink?*
   - Student B: *Yes. Coffee, please.*

Level ★ ★ ★

Objective: Describe fast-food items in detail.

Warm-up: 15–20 minutes
Focus attention on **pages 90 and 91.** Place students in small groups to complete a table with two columns with the headers *healthy* and *not as healthy.* Allow time for reports. Make a final table on the board with input from each group. Read *Words in Context* and see if student responses are the same as the ideas found in the paragraph. Make note of agreements and disagreements.

Introduction: State the objective.

Presentation 1: 7–10 minutes
Explain the word list on **pages 90 and 91.** As a class, make a list of foods, such as *pizza, tacos,* and *stir-fried vegetables.* Call for student input to collect adjectives to describe the items, such as *hot, messy, crispy, oily, soft,* and *spicy.* Expand the discussion to include ingredients or varieties and think of adjectives to describe them. For example, discuss the varieties of beans or rice from *Word Partnerships.*

Practice 1: 18–25 minutes
Pair students and have them write a dialog for the fast-food restaurant of their choosing, beginning with *What is (are) _____?* Each pair should write 10 lines. After ample practice time, each pair can read its dialog to another pair. Listeners should comment on the dialogs and give advice for improvement.

Evaluation 1: Pairs demonstrate for the class.

Application: 20–30 minutes
In groups of four, students should create a *press release* for a new healthful restaurant they are opening. Explain what a press release is. Students should explain where the restaurant will be, what hours it will be open, and how it is different from all the other restaurants in town. It should give sample menu items with prices and explain how they are prepared. Also, students should mention what the atmosphere is like: romantic, casual, comfortable, sophisticated, eccentric, etc.

---

for practice. On the board, write the additional Student A lines *Anything else?, Would you like . . . ?, How about . . . ?* and the Student B closing *No, thanks!*

Give partners the task of preparing four more questions to add to the conversation.

Practice 1: 22–25 minutes
Pairs should create a menu for one of the dictionary's restaurants. Give students a copy of the menu worksheet from the Activity Bank CD-ROM. Ask students to form groups of four by finding another

pair who chose the same restaurant. With their menus, students can practice the conversation—including the additional four questions—and create several dialogs.

Evaluation 1: Observe the activity.

Application: 15–20 minutes
Read *Words in Action #1.* During the conversation, students should complete a Johari Squares chart using the template available on the Activity Bank CD-ROM. Squares include *foods only I like, foods only my partner likes, foods both of us like,* and *foods both of us don't like.*

Project

Bring menus from local fast-food restaurants or find them on the Internet and print out. Have students choose the items they like best from each menu and design a new menu for a new fast-food restaurant. Include categories such as *appetizers, salads,* and *drinks.* Every item should have an appropriate price. Students should also consider what types of employees would be necessary to staff the restaurant, where the restaurant would be, and what food items need to be stocked in the kitchen.

Cooking

Level ★

Objective: Identify verbs associated with cooking.

Warm-up: 10–15 minutes
Pantomime making a common meal, such as omelets. Choose something students will be familiar with, either because it is local or well known. Repeat until students identify the meal. Perform the pantomime again but allow time for students to identify each step. Students should determine the verb for each step, as in *break* the eggs. As students call out verbs, write them on the board. If necessary, students can look at **pages 92 and 93** for ideas.

Introduction: State the objective.

Presentation 1: 20–30 minutes
Ask students to open their dictionaries to **pages 92 and 93.** Pronounce each recipe name and practice the vocabulary in *Shish Kebab Recipe* by using the words in sentences. Develop a pantomime for all verbs in the *shish kebab* recipe. Practice these actions with students.

Practice 1: 20–30 minutes
Divide the class into four groups—one for each recipe. Do not assign the *shish kebab* recipe but instead let students use it as a model. Write recipe names on slips of paper and have groups select a slip without looking. Groups should not share which recipe they were given. Ask students to create pantomimes for each of the verbs in their recipe.

Evaluation 1: Have groups perform their pantomimes while the other groups determine which recipe it represents and call out the verb represented. Even if the other groups guess the recipe early on, have students finish the pantomime.

Presentation 2: 10–15 minutes
Read *Words in Action #1.* Allow discussion time for students to answer which dictionary recipe is their favorite and what, in general, are their favorite ingredients.

Practice 2: 15–20 minutes
Pair students for a quizzing activity. Students should use the pantomimes developed for the different action verbs to quiz their partners. Challenge each pair to think of other ways to pantomime the verbs and practice these.

Evaluation 2: Stage a charades game in which students can act out their new pantomimes for others to guess.

Application: 7–10 minutes
Go around the room and have students state their favorite recipe from home. They should write the verbs associated with making it and then share them with a small group. Allow brief first-language use if students need to use verbs other than those in the dictionary.

Shish Kebab Recipe

1 **Measure** 1/4 cup of olive oil.

2 **Dice** 1 tablespoon of garlic.

3 **Whisk** the oil and garlic with a little lemon juice.

4 **Add** 1 pound of lamb cubes.

5 **Marinate** overnight in the refrigerator.

6 **Grill** the kebabs for 5 minutes on each side.

Breakfast Burrito Recipe

7 **Scramble** 2 eggs in a bowl.

8 **Fry** the eggs.

9 **Broil** 2 slices of bacon.

10 **Steam** a cup of broccoli.

11 **Grate** 1/4 cup of cheese.

12 **Fold** everything into a tortilla.

13 **Microwave** for 30 seconds.

Roast Chicken with Potatoes Recipe

14 **Season** the chicken with garlic and rosemary.

15 **Roast** at 350°F (175°C). (20 minutes per pound)

16 **Baste** frequently with pan juices.

17 **Boil** the potatoes.

° = degrees

92

Level ★ ★

Objective: Describe ingredients in a recipe.

Warm-up: 12–15 minutes
Have each student make a list of meals they like. Have students read lists to the class. Write names of meals on the board.

Introduction: State the objective.

Presentation 1: 15–20 minutes
Refer students to the recipes on **pages 92 and 93.** As you present each word from the word list and **Word Partnerships,** make sure students understand. Read *Words in Action #1* and allow time for sharing answers. Teach measurements and the associated verbs carefully. As a class, make a list of all the ingredients and another list of all the verbs for the *shish kebab* recipe. Place this master list in a column on the board.

Pea Soup Recipe

18 **Slice** 1 large onion.

19 **Sauté** the onion in oil.

20 **Stir** the onion and 1 pound of split peas into 2 quarts of water.

21 **Simmer** for 2 hours.

22 **Peel** 4 large carrots.

23 **Chop** the carrots and add to the soup.

24 **Cook** for 30 minutes more.

25 **Puree** the soup in a blender.

Candy Pecans Recipe

26 **Grease** a cookie sheet.

27 **Beat** 1 egg white.

28 **Sift** 1/2 cup of sugar with 2 teaspoons of cinnamon.

29 **Mix** 3 cups of pecans and the sugar and cinnamon into the egg white.

30 **Spread** the mix on a cookie sheet.

31 **Bake** at 250°F (120°C).

Word Partnerships

bake	bread
	a cake
steam	vegetables
chop	
cook	
peel	potatoes
boil	

Words in Action

1. Which recipe looks the best to you? Why?
2. Write down your favorite recipe. Put your recipe together with your classmates' recipes to make a class cookbook.

— 93 —

Objective: Describe recipes.

Warm-up: 10–15 minutes
Focus students' attention on **pages 92 and 93** in their dictionaries. After they read and decide which recipe they like best, take a poll and make a bar graph of recipes by popularity. Group students by their favorite recipes. Groups should then decide how they might change the recipe to make it better.

Introduction: State the objective.

Presentation 1: 7–10 minutes
Play the audio recording for **pages 92 and 93.** As a class, make a list of all the utensils, appliances, and ingredients necessary to complete the recipe. For each appliance, students should identify the proper verb. Include all the items from the dictionary.

Practice 1: 25–40 minutes
Prepare students to simulate a television cooking show. In groups, one or two students become "television chefs." After selecting one dictionary recipe, students should develop a script that uses pantomimes for each action and a dialog using the names of utensils and appliances. Encourage them to be creative. Ask that the dialog sufficiently describe the recipe and ask that additional words and phrases be included. Encourage the use of transition words, such as *first, next, then,* and *finally.*

Evaluation 1: Groups can present scripts to the class.

Application: 20–30 minutes
Ask students to think of their favorite recipe and write down instructions for preparation. Have them tell the recipe to a classmate. When sharing, students should give the recipe, identifying utensils and appliances as they progress. Hand out the recipe worksheet from **page 83** on the Activity Bank CD-ROM.

Practice 1: 18–20 minutes
Have students complete a table in which each ingredient is a header. Under each ingredient, students should write the verbs from the recipe that might work with it. For example, under *chicken* they might write *fry, marinate,* and *broil.*

Evaluation 1: Let students fill the chart on the board.

Application: 20–30 minutes
In groups, students should create a new recipe using the ingredients and the verbs on the board. To extend this activity, ask students to write the recipe on a small card or on the blank recipe card from the **page 83** lesson worksheet on the Activity Bank CD-ROM. Instruct them not to list the name of the finished product. Each group should make one copy for each of the other groups. Distribute copies to the groups and have a guessing match to see how many recipes they can figure out.

Project

Ask students to think of a recipe originating in a country different from their own. Allow sufficient time for research in the library, computer lab, or at home to compile lists of ingredients, equipment, and preparation steps. Students should write their chosen recipe on the worksheet from **page 83** on the Activity Bank CD-ROM and be able to explain all the vocabulary. Compile the recipes into a class cookbook and copy it for everyone.

Level ★

Objective: Identify cooking equipment.

Warm-up: 10–15 minutes
In small groups, students should make a list of rooms in their home. Review instructions for clustering and ask students to complete a cluster diagram that identifies two things in each room, including the kitchen. Depending on the level of the students, you may wish to write a word bank on the board. Use the Activity Bank CD-ROM cluster worksheet. In this exercise, the center circle is *home*. The secondary circles are rooms, and the tertiary circles are items in the rooms. Groups can share their words, and a complete list should be written on the board.

Introduction: State the objective.

Presentation 1: 20–30 minutes
Have students open their dictionaries to **pages 94 and 95.** Go over each item as a class and practice vocabulary by developing sentences using the new words. Read *Words in Context* aloud to students. Encourage questions and discussion. Say items from the list in a random order and ask students to point to the items as you mention them.

Practice 1: 20–30 minutes
Pair students to continue the quizzing activity. After they have practiced sufficiently, ask them to cover the list and identify objects by number. Student A says the number and Student B says the word.

Evaluation 1: Observe the activity.

Presentation 2: 10–15 minutes
Advance the activity by having students identify food items that could be associated with *a cutting board, knives,* and *a frying pan.* For example, the class might come up with *carrots, steak,* and *eggs,* respectively. Take advantage of this opportunity to revisit other lessons in this unit, allowing students to use words from previous pages. Accept any reasonable answers.

Practice 2: 15–20 minutes
Divide the class into groups of three and give each group numbers from the word list. Students should find food items that relate to their words.

Evaluation 2: Stage a game. Groups present their list of foods and ask their classmates to identify the new vocabulary word. For example, *eggs, flour,* and *sugar* might suggest *mixing bowl.* Discuss answers.

Application: 7–10 minutes
Allow ample time for students to read and complete *Words in Action #1.* Share answers as a class.

Cooking Equipment

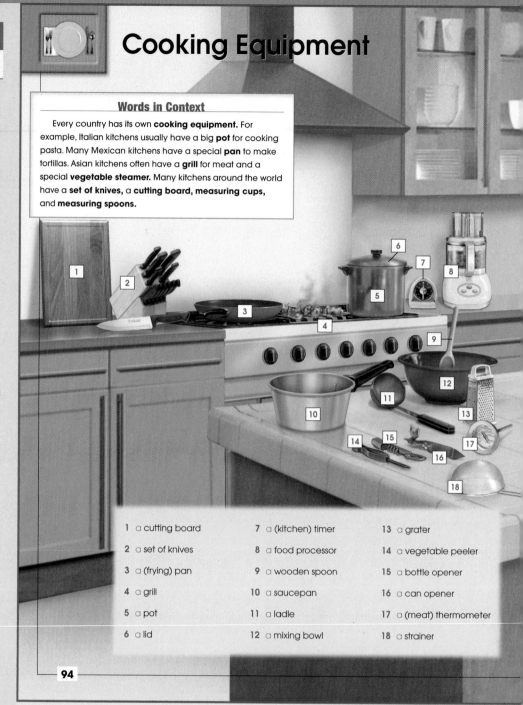

Words in Context

Every country has its own **cooking equipment.** For example, Italian kitchens usually have a big **pot** for cooking pasta. Many Mexican kitchens have a special **pan** to make tortillas. Asian kitchens often have a **grill** for meat and a special **vegetable steamer.** Many kitchens around the world have a **set of knives,** a **cutting board, measuring cups,** and **measuring spoons.**

1 a cutting board	7 a (kitchen) timer	13 a grater
2 a set of knives	8 a food processor	14 a vegetable peeler
3 a (frying) pan	9 a wooden spoon	15 a bottle opener
4 a grill	10 a saucepan	16 a can opener
5 a pot	11 a ladle	17 a (meat) thermometer
6 a lid	12 a mixing bowl	18 a strainer

94

Level ★★

Objective: Describe locations and uses of cooking equipment.

Warm-up: 15–20 minutes
Remind students about the recipes covered in previous lessons and have everyone think of their favorite home recipes. Offer time for students to make a list of the utensils, cooking equipment, and food items they would need to make the recipe. Students will read their lists without saying what the dish is and ask their classmates to guess the recipe.

Introduction: State the objective.

Presentation 1: 15–20 minutes
Present the word list on **pages 94 and 95.** Make sure all words are clearly understood before continuing with *Word Partnerships.* As a class, review prepositions of location and practice identifying the location of certain items. Review other vocabulary associated with the dictionary's kitchen, including *countertop, cabinet, shelf, stovetop, sink,*

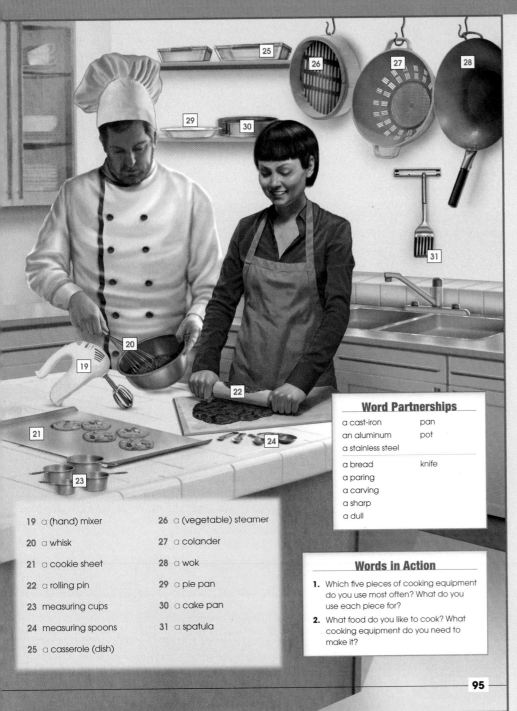

19	a (hand) mixer	26	a (vegetable) steamer
20	a whisk	27	a colander
21	a cookie sheet	28	a wok
22	a rolling pin	29	a pie pan
23	measuring cups	30	a cake pan
24	measuring spoons	31	a spatula
25	a casserole (dish)		

Word Partnerships

a cast-iron	pan
an aluminum	pot
a stainless steel	

a bread	knife
a paring	
a carving	
a sharp	
a dull	

Words in Action

1. Which five pieces of cooking equipment do you use most often? What do you use each piece for?
2. What food do you like to cook? What cooking equipment do you need to make it?

Level ★ ★ ★

Objective: Prepare a quiz to help other students.

Warm-up: 10–15 minutes
Read *Words in Action #2* to the class. After all students announce their favorite meal, have them find a partner and explain how to make it. Allow use of pantomimes for words students don't know. Move about the room and assist as needed.

Introduction: State the objective.

Presentation 1: 15–20 minutes
Study the word list on **pages 94 and 95.** Explain to students that they will create a test for beginning students. Write an example question on the board. Explain the different types of test questions, including matching, multiple choice, true/false, and fill-in-the-blank. Create examples of each and why test-taking is an important part of the educational experience. A multiple-choice question can be similar to *This is something people use in the kitchen to cut meat. a) a timer b) a ladle c) a knife.* Pictures may be substituted as answers instead of words.

Practice 1: 25–40 minutes
In groups, students should design tests for beginning students. Requirements include 2 matching questions, 5 true/false, 5 fill-in-the-blank, and 10 multiple-choice questions with an answer key on a separate page.

Evaluation 1: Each group can write three of their multiple-choice questions on the board to see if other students can answer correctly. Open a forum to discuss how some questions can be improved.

Application: 15–20 minutes
Groups should exchange tests from the Practice. After tests are completed, they can be given back to the original group to be scored. Consider copying the tests and using them for a future review. Let students try to challenge you by writing the most difficult questions possible and giving the test to you.

and *island.* Prepare students to perform the following conversation.

Student A: *Excuse me, where is the grater?*

Student B: *The grater is on the island. Why do you need it?*

Student A: *I need to grate cheese for pizza.*

Practice 1: 10–15 minutes
Pair students and ask them to practice the conversation by substituting a different piece of equipment and its

appropriate location and use.

Evaluation 1: Have each pair perform twice. Check accuracy of pronunciation. Students may need assistance with verb choices.

Application: 20–30 minutes
Have each pair join another. Ask the groups to prepare a skit in which they use a minimum of eight words from the word list. They may be creative with the situation and "prepare" any foods they like. Encourage creativity while focusing on using the words in context.

Project

Place students in groups of four and let them imagine they are interior designers. They have been hired to design a new kitchen for a big house. Students need to draw a diagram for the kitchen and mark all the places where appliances and items from the word list would be stored. Encourage them to think of other items that would be included in the ideal kitchen and add these to their diagrams. Allow time for presentations. Students might want to cut out pictures from magazines for their kitchen displays.

Measurements and Containers

Level ★

Objective: Identify containers.

Warm-up: 10–15 minutes
Begin a conversation about where students buy food. Ask: *Where does the food from markets come from?* Provide a brief definition of *market*. In groups, students should make a list of foods they might buy in a market. Assign each group one of the following categories: *fruits, vegetables, drinks, breads* and *pastries*. A representative from each group should put the group list on the board.

Introduction: State the objective.

Presentation 1: 15–20 minutes
Have students open their dictionaries to **pages 96 and 97**. Go over each item as a class and practice vocabulary by using the words in sentences. Say random container names and ask students to identify the numbered pictures.

Practice 1: 10–15 minutes
Divide students into groups of three to continue the quizzing exercise. Tell them they have three minutes to practice. After the set time, increase the difficulty by having students cover the word list.

Evaluation 1: Observe the activity and help with pronunciation.

Presentation 2: 8–10 minutes
Make a table on the board with two columns. Label the headers *measurements* and *containers*. With the class, put two items from the dictionary into each column. For each container, challenge students to think of another item that could be found in that type of container. For each measurement, ask students to think of an item that is measured by that quantity. For example, when *a tube of hand cream* is placed in column 1, students can write *tube of toothpaste* as the alternate form. For a *gallon,* students can write *milk.*

Practice 2: 10–15 minutes
Students should attempt to complete the table with all the words available on **pages 96 and 97,** as well as provide extra examples.

Evaluation 2: Ask groups to report to the class.

Application: 7–10 minutes
Mention that students should think about their own kitchens. Read *Words in Action #2* and have students name containers and their uses. Place students in groups for a comparison discussion.

Words in Context

At a farmer's market, you can see a **pile** of ripe tomatoes, smell a warm **loaf** of bread, buy a **jar** of honey, and find a **bunch** of fresh carrots. You can meet the farmers who grow your food and vendors who sell **bars** of homemade soap and **bouquets** of fresh flowers.

Abbreviations		
tsp.	=	teaspoon
TBS.	=	tablespoon
c.	=	cup
oz.	=	ounce
qt.	=	quart
pt.	=	pint
gal.	=	gallon
lb.	=	pound
g.	=	gram
kg.	=	kilogram
l.	=	liter

4 qt.	=	1 gal.
3 tsp.	=	1 TBS.
1 qt.	=	.94 l.
1 oz.	=	28 g.
1 lb.	=	.45 kg.

96

Level ★★

Objective: Identify quantities and shop.

Warm-up: 10–15 minutes
Define *farmers' market* and discuss a local example, giving students directions and the schedule. Read *Words in Action #1*. Pair students to develop an answer. They should think of at least five items before sharing answers with another pair.

Introduction: State the objective.

Presentation 1: 10–15 minutes
Discuss the vocabulary on **pages 96 and 97** as a class. Make sure students understand each item, and include the phrases from *Word Partnerships*. Have students suggest other foods for the partnerships. Gather student opinions about what they think a box of strawberries should cost. Keep the conversation moving by developing costs for a few other items from the word list. Extend the conversation to discuss measurements. For example, ask *How*

1 a pint
2 a cup
3 an ounce
4 a teaspoon
5 a tablespoon
6 a bouquet of flowers
7 a bottle of olive oil
8 a bar of soap
9 a tube of hand cream
10 a carton of orange juice
11 a tray of pastries
12 a pot of coffee

13 a cup of coffee
14 a pitcher of lemonade
15 a piece of cake
16 a loaf of bread
17 a liter of water
18 a quart of milk
19 a pound of cherries
20 a box of strawberries
21 a gallon of cider
22 a bag of potatoes
23 a carton of eggs
24 a jar of honey

25 a container of yogurt
26 a six-pack of soda
27 a can of soda
28 a pile of tomatoes
29 a bunch of carrots
30 a crate of melons
31 a basket of apples

Word Partnerships

a can of	soup
	tuna
a box of	cereal
	pasta
	cookies
a cup of	tea
	sugar
	flour
a piece of	pie
	bread

Words in Action

1. Imagine you are shopping at a farmer's market. What will you buy? Why?
2. Name five containers you have at home. Tell what is in each container.

---

much cider is in the container in the picture? or *How are liquids generally measured?* If needed, review count and noncount nouns.

Practice 1: 15–20 minutes
Place students in groups of four and have them make a list of all the items, assigning prices to each of them. All group members should agree on a price. When complete, compare answers as a group and discuss the differences.

Evaluation 1: As a class, decide which group has the cheapest prices and discuss

which local markets are most cost-effective.

Application: 30–40 minutes
In the same groups of four, students should imagine that they are a family preparing to stock their new kitchen. Groups should create a role-play in which they go shopping at the farmers' market. Ask students to use 10 measurements and 15 containers in their dialogs. Allow time for student performances at the end of class.

Objective: Write a story.

Warm-up: 10–15 minutes
Review **pages 90–95** and see if students can remember some of the favorite recipes discussed. Write a few on the board. Have students choose one and discuss what ingredients are included. Focus the discussion on measurements. Guide students to discuss words such as *ounces* and *tablespoons*.

Introduction: State the objective.

Presentation 1: 15–20 minutes
Read the word list on **pages 96 and 97** out loud or play the audio so students will understand and produce the correct pronunciation. Make sure students understand each word. Expand the list with students' help either by thinking of other containers to include or other products that come in the containers listed (e.g., a pound of tomatoes). Ask a volunteer to read **Words in Context** and lead a group discussion about students' experiences with farmers' markets or similar open markets. Focus attention on what the people in the picture would say to a customer and/or a vendor.

Practice 1: 15–20 minutes
Divide students into groups of four to perform a roundtable writing activity. Each person should write a sentence about the picture, skipping lines on the page. Set time limits so that students stay on track. When time is up, students exchange papers, read the first sentence, and add a new one. The stories should rotate through the four members twice so each group has four eight-sentence stories. At that point, groups should exchange their stories with another group.

Evaluation 1: Each student should read the story he or she started to the class.

Application: 30–40 minutes
Discuss the stories students just wrote. Students should review the stories as a whole and check that they didn't stray from the picture. Then ask students to go back and include additional container and measurement vocabulary. After the review, have students write individual stories about a time when they went to an open-air or farmers' market. Tell students that you will check for use of lesson vocabulary and overall focus of the paragraph. If students have trouble remembering specific experiences, they may create a fictional story.

Project

In groups, students should imagine that they own a farmers' market that caters to 500 customers a day. Have them think of what types and quantities of food they should have on hand. Encourage the use of container and measurement vocabulary.

Supermarket

Level ★

Objective: Identify supermarket vocabulary.

Warm-up: 12–15 minutes
Challenge students to make a list of all the fruits and vegetables they can without opening their dictionaries. Write *produce* on the board. Tell students that when they go to a supermarket, they find fruits and vegetables in the produce section.

Introduction: State the objective.

Presentation 1: 15–20 minutes
Refer students to dictionary **pages 98 and 99.** Go over each item as a class and practice vocabulary by discussing examples of aisles and sections from well-known supermarkets. Draw a table on the board with six columns labeled *on the left wall, on the back wall, on the right wall, in the front, in aisle 1,* and *in aisle 2.* As a class, place one example supermarket section or area vocabulary word from the picture in each of the six columns.

Practice 1: 10–15 minutes
Individually, students should attempt to categorize all the vocabulary in the list. Combine students into groups of three or four and ask them to compare answers and complete the table. Students can discuss similarities and differences between the dictionary's supermarket and a local supermarket.

Evaluation 1: Listen to group reports.

Presentation 2: 8–10 minutes
Prepare students to perform this model conversation.

   Student A: *Excuse me, where is the pet food?*

   Student B: *The pet food is in aisle 1.*

   Student A: *Thank you.*

Provide a second example.

Practice 2: 8–10 minutes
Pair students to practice the conversation and substitute vocabulary. Remind them to switch roles.

Evaluation 2: Observe the activity.

Application: 7–10 minutes
Ask students what they do to prepare for a trip to the supermarket. Put students in groups of four and tell them to imagine they are a family. What do they need to buy for a family dinner tonight? Students should decide what food they want to prepare, develop a grocery list, and then create a plan for buying items in the dictionary supermarket. The plan can be either a list or a paragraph, and should include the order of areas to visit and which items will be picked up from each area.

Words in Context

The first **supermarket** opened in France in the early 1900s. Before that, people bought **groceries** like **produce, dairy products,** and **canned goods** in small shops and markets. Now there are supermarkets in every country of the world. Besides food, you can find **household cleaners, paper products,** and **pet food** in most supermarkets.

Level ★ ★

Objective: Express needs at the supermarket.

Warm-up: 10–15 minutes
Present **Words in Action #1** and place students in small groups for conversation. Students can share their first purchases with the class.

Introduction: State the objective.

Presentation 1: 10–15 minutes
Define each of the words from the word list and the phrases in **Word Partnerships** on **pages 98 and 99.** Practice vocabulary by writing simple sentences. Write this conversation:

Cashier: *Hello, did you find everything you need?*

Customer: *I didn't find the cottage cheese.*

Cashier: *I'm sorry. We're out. We will have more in tomorrow.*

Customer: *OK, thanks. How much is the total today?*

Cashier: *That will be $76.43.*

1 produce
2 meats and poultry
3 dairy products
4 frozen foods
5 bakery
6 a deli counter
7 a scale

8 paper products
9 household cleaners
10 pet food
11 beverages
12 canned goods
13 an aisle
14 a paper bag
15 a checkout counter
16 a cash register
17 a shopping cart
18 a bagger

19 a barcode scanner
20 a plastic bag
21 a cashier / a checker
22 groceries
23 a shopper
24 a shopping basket

Snacks

25 a candy bar
26 pretzels
27 (potato) chips
28 popcorn

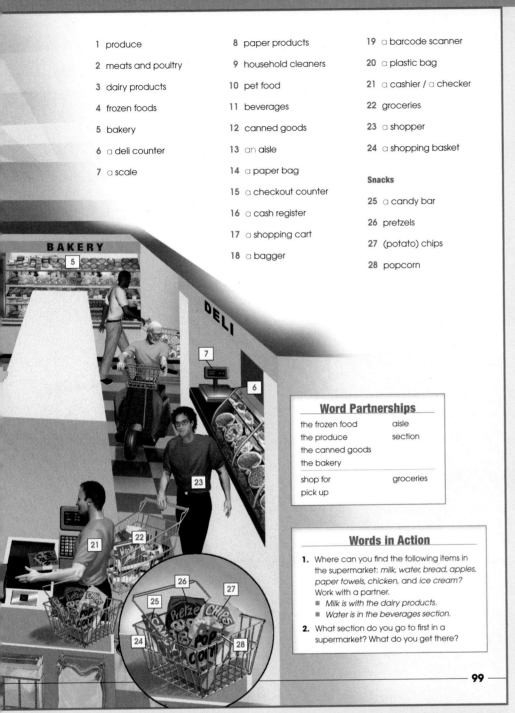

Word Partnerships

the frozen food	aisle
the produce	section
the canned goods	
the bakery	
shop for	groceries
pick up	

Words in Action

1. Where can you find the following items in the supermarket: *milk, water, bread, apples, paper towels, chicken,* and *ice cream*? Work with a partner.
   - *Milk is with the dairy products.*
   - *Water is in the beverages section.*
2. What section do you go to first in a supermarket? What do you get there?

99

Practice 1: 15–20 minutes
Ask students to write conversations about one of the following situations:

1. A shopper goes to the checkout with many items. The total is $45.65. The customer has $43.00.
2. A child breaks a bottle of juice in aisle 3. What should the father do?
3. A customer in line at checkout forgot to buy eggs. This customer is next in line for checkout.

Evaluation 1: Ask for volunteers to demonstrate in front of the class. Check for proper verb usage.

Application: 30–40 minutes
Students should think of questions they have about the local supermarket. Write out the questions. See if other students can answer them or if more research needs to be done either at the supermarket or in the library. Consider having students call the supermarket from class to get answers. Discuss the answers.

Warm-up: 10–15 minutes
Students should read **Words in Context** in small groups. When finished, have students close their dictionaries. Group members should state a fact they learned from the paragraph. As a class, students should compare differences in supermarkets in other countries.

Introduction: State the objective.

Presentation 1: 15–20 minutes
Go over the word list on **pages 98 and 99.** Describe a favorite supermarket using this vocabulary. As a class, students should expand the word list by thinking of types of items they buy from the grocery store. Add new ideas to the board. Discuss important sections that are found in their local supermarkets. Next ask students to identify where they might find bargains at the supermarkets. Introduce *coupons* and supply samples from local newspapers. Expand the discussion by calling for other money-saving ideas. Generate thoughts about *buying in bulk.* Provide an example of a location where students can buy in bulk *(wholesale clubs, cooperatives)* and see who believes they can save money shopping this way.

Practice 1: 10–15 minutes
In small groups, students should write down as many ways as they can to save money shopping for food. Each list should begin with *coupons* and *buying in bulk.* Answers may include *sale, discount,* and *rebate.* Groups can discuss what things they do to save money and compile a group list. Encourage them to talk about how much money they spend on food per week/month as individuals or for their families.

Evaluation 1: Observe the activity and supply vocabulary as needed.

Application: 30–40 minutes
Groups should share their list of cost-saving techniques with the class. A master list should be written on the board. As a class, design an instructional booklet to teach others how to save money when grocery shopping. Edit, copy, and distribute to the class.

Project

Encourage students to imagine they are managing a local supermarket. Students should design what they consider to be a perfect market. Rationales should be provided for placement of each section of the market. Compare and contrast the created supermarket to the dictionary's picture and local markets.

Restaurant

Level ★

Objective: Identify restaurant vocabulary.

Warm-up: 10–15 minutes
Tell students that you are very hungry and need to eat right after class but that you don't have time to go home. Ask for solutions. When students suggest stopping at a restaurant, allow them to give specific examples. Write *expensive restaurant, moderate restaurant,* and *cheap restaurant* on the board. Explain *moderate.* In groups, students should think of as many restaurants as possible to fit into the three categories. Compare answers.

Introduction: State the objective.

Presentation 1: 15–20 minutes
Have students open their dictionaries to **pages 100 and 101.** Discuss each word as a class and practice vocabulary by using the words in sentences. Call out items and ask students to point to the correct pictures.

Practice 1: 10–15 minutes
Pair students to continue the quizzing exercise. Student A will name an item and Student B will point to the object. After three minutes, have students reverse roles. After another three minutes, challenge pairs to cover the list while quizzing each other.

Evaluation 1: Observe the activity.

Presentation 2: 8–10 minutes
Write the following sentences on the board: *1. It is on the table next to the spoon. 2. It is a special chair for children. 3. It is where you can find a variety of salad items. 4. He or she is a person who takes your order and brings food. 5. It covers the table. 6. It holds flowers. 7. It is the food you eat after the main course. 8. It is food you eat before the main course. 9. It is what you look at to choose what to eat. 10. At the end of a meal, it shows the prices of everything you ate.*

Practice 2: 15–20 minutes
Although this may be difficult, ask students to guess what each sentence refers to. Have them work with a partner or small group. Tell students they should guess the correct words based on the words they know. To extend this activity, students can use new sentences to quiz one another about the vocabulary.

Evaluation 2: Go over the answers as a class.

Application: 7–10 minutes
Read **Words in Action #1.** Show students how to use a Venn diagram to complete this task. For a second task, have students work with partners and complete Venn diagrams comparing their favorite restaurants. Utilize the Venn diagram template available on the **Activity Bank CD-ROM.**

Words in Context

The first **restaurant** opened in Paris in 1765. The only thing on the **menu** was soup. There were no **appetizers** and no **desserts.** Restaurants have changed a lot since then. Now you can eat at a Chinese restaurant in Moscow or a Mexican restaurant in Beijing. The biggest restaurant in the world is the Royal Dragon in Bangkok. The dining room seats 5,000 **diners.** The **servers** wear roller skates!

100

Level ★ ★

Objective: Make complaints about service.

Warm-up: 10–15 minutes
Discuss favorite foods with students. Read **Words in Action #2** and allow time for discussion. Explain terms as needed.

Introduction: State the objective.

Presentation 1: 20–30 minutes
Study the words on **pages 100 and 101** and make sure students comprehend the words, including the **Word Partnerships.** Ask students to imagine that each person in the picture is talking. As a class, write a few things they might be saying. Next, write these scenarios on the board for discussion and request student opinions for handling each circumstance:
1. Imagine that you are at the restaurant and there is a fly in your soup. 2. Imagine that the bill or check has food on it you didn't order or the total is wrong. 3. Imagine that a server spilled the food on your table. 4. Imagine that the server

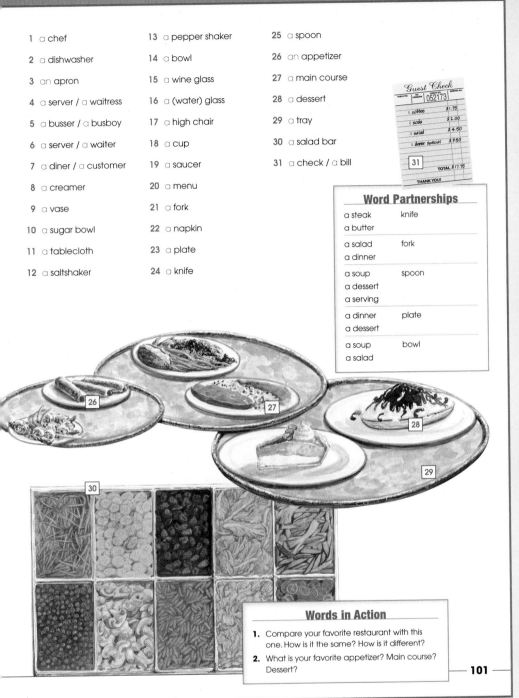

1 a chef
2 a dishwasher
3 an apron
4 a server / a waitress
5 a busser / a busboy
6 a server / a waiter
7 a diner / a customer
8 a creamer
9 a vase
10 a sugar bowl
11 a tablecloth
12 a saltshaker

13 a pepper shaker
14 a bowl
15 a wine glass
16 a (water) glass
17 a high chair
18 a cup
19 a saucer
20 a menu
21 a fork
22 a napkin
23 a plate
24 a knife

25 a spoon
26 an appetizer
27 a main course
28 a dessert
29 a tray
30 a salad bar
31 a check / a bill

Guest Check
052173
1 coffee	$1.75
1 soda	$2.00
1 salad	$4.50
1 diner special	$9.50

31

TOTAL $17.75

THANK YOU!

Word Partnerships

a steak a butter	knife
a salad a dinner	fork
a soup a dessert a serving	spoon
a dinner a dessert	plate
a soup a salad	bowl

Words in Action

1. Compare your favorite restaurant with this one. How is it the same? How is it different?
2. What is your favorite appetizer? Main course? Dessert?

101

Objective: Write a paragraph.

Warm-up: 10–15 minutes
Have students read **Words in Context** in a group. Groups should briefly discuss restaurants in their native countries or local communities that serve international food. Students should discuss the different types of foods they have experienced in restaurants they have visited in other parts of the world or country. Write a list of international cuisines represented.

Introduction: State the objective.

Presentation 1: 18–20 minutes
Present the word list on **pages 100 and 101.** Make sure students understand each word before attempting to expand the list. Write a master list of additional vocabulary on the board. Explain why terms like *busser* and *server* are slowly replacing *busboy* and *waiter/waitress.* Find out if any students have worked in those positions and expand on their experiences. See if any students have ever had a bad experience as an employee or as a customer in a restaurant and ask for specifics. Write a list of things that can go wrong in a restaurant and different points of view (server vs. customer) about those things.

Practice 1: 12–15 minutes
Prepare students to complete a round robin writing activity. Divide students into evenly sized groups and have them select a secretary who will take notes about what is discussed. The other students in the group take turns saying a sentence about the picture, expanding on what the previous student said, as if writing a story. Choose a topic from the presentation. Set a time limit. Group members help the secretary transform the notes into complete sentences to form a coherent paragraph.

Evaluation 1: Ask the secretaries to read the stories to the class.

Application: 15–20 minutes
Students should choose one memorable restaurant experience. It should be a true story, but the experience can be positive or negative. Allow time for students to write down as much as they can remember about the experience and then share their stories with a small group.

gave you the wrong order.
5. Imagine that the food is cold.
6. Imagine that you have to wait one hour for your order.

Practice 1: 15–20 minutes
Divide students into four to six groups and assign one scenario to each. Students should determine a solution for each issue and write a conversation they might have in order to handle the situation. Conversations should contain a speaking role for each group member and vocabulary from the list.

Evaluation 1: Observe group performances.

Application: 30–40 minutes
Lead a class discussion about problems students have encountered at restaurants. Discuss where and when each experience happened and how the student resolved the problem. Create a list of the worst local restaurants according to the students. Reasons may include poor service, not enough food for the money, dirty, or bad food. Then have students create a list of the best local restaurants.

Project

Have students in groups imagine they are restaurant owners and answer these questions: *What is the name of your restaurant? Where is your restaurant? How many employees do you have? What are your hours?* Students should create a menu. There is a worksheet to facilitate this activity on the **Activity Bank CD-ROM.**

Order, Eat, Pay

Level ★

Objective: Identify restaurant phrases.

Warm-up: 7–10 minutes
Go around the room and ask each student what his or her favorite restaurant is. Circle the room again and ask which restaurants students eat at often. Accept all answers. Consider comparing fast-food restaurants to more formal restaurants. Write the word *restaurant* on the board and make a list of what foods students like to eat at their top choices.

Introduction: State the objective.

Presentation 1: 15–20 minutes
Refer students to dictionary **pages 102 and 103.** Go over each item as a class and practice vocabulary by stating which restaurants from the student-created list would use those verbs. Start a table on the board and label the columns *customer, server, busser,* and *other.* As a class, place one example verb from the word list under the person who performs that action at a restaurant. Provide copies of the four-column table template from the Activity Bank CD-ROM to facilitate this activity.

Practice 1: 20–30 minutes
In small groups, students should complete the table with the remaining words from the word list. Remind students that some words might fall into more than one category. Provide an example of a restaurant where one person might have to perform several roles.

Evaluation 1: Have groups report. Discuss actions when there is more than one answer about who does the restaurant task.

Presentation 2: 8–10 minutes
Prepare students for an oral quiz. Say a few phrases from the word list and ask students to identify who in the picture might be doing it. If students do well, use the verbs in complete sentences. Provide adequate time so students will understand and be able to quiz a partner with complete sentences.

Practice 2: 7–10 minutes
Pair students by similar level and have them quiz each other. Students should attempt to do this without referring to the word list. Have students write additional statements and ask them to quiz their classmates.

Evaluation 2: Observe the activity and assist.

Application: 7–10 minutes
Read *Words in Action #1.* Inform students that they should tell three other students their answers. Students should write down their five actions in complete sentences. Share the sentences in small groups.

Words in Context

I'm a waitress. I **wait on** lots of customers every night. Some customers are difficult. They **order** things that aren't on the menu. They **spill** their drinks. One customer left and didn't **pay** the check! But most customers are great. Some of them **compliment** me and **leave** a big tip. They're my favorite customers!

1 make a reservation
2 pour water
3 light a candle
4 carry a tray
5 set the table
6 wait on someone
7 look at the menu
8 butter the bread
9 spill a drink
10 order
11 take an order
12 drink
13 compliment someone
14 refill the glass
15 eat
16 serve a meal
17 ask for the check
18 signal the server
19 share a dessert
20 offer a doggie bag
21 thank the server
22 wipe the table
23 leave a tip
24 pay the check
25 clear the table / bus the table

— 102 —

Level ★ ★

Objective: Use proper restaurant terminology.

Warm-up: 20–30 minutes
In groups, students should develop a menu for a restaurant they want to open in the city. Review important stages of a meal from **pages 100 and 101.**

Introduction: State the objective.

Presentation 1: 10–15 minutes
Present each of the words from the word list on **pages 102 and 103** in lecture format. Make sure students understand the definitions before directing attention to *Word Partnerships.* Read *Words in Action #2* and stage a game of charades. Students should identify each verb phrase being pantomimed. Repeat the activity with dictionaries first opened then closed. Prepare students to write sentences people might say in a restaurant. Examples include *Please wipe*

I'd like . . . 10

11

8

9

13

Very good!

14

12

15

16

Check please.

17

18

19

20

21 Thank you.

22

24

23

25

Word Partnerships

eat	out
order	breakfast
	lunch
	dinner
	supper
	a meal
	a snack

Words in Action

1. Think about the last time you ate out. Tell your class about five things you did at the restaurant.

2. Work with a partner. Act out a verb from the word list. Your partner will guess what you are doing. Take turns.

103

Objective: Write a paragraph.

Warm-up: 15–20 minutes
Have students focus on actions they have seen in a restaurant by customers, servers, and others. Individually, students create a list of every verb they can think of. When finished, students should draw a line below their last word. Allow a five-minute sharing time for students to walk around the room and add new words below the line. They may only get two additional words from any one student. Students should maintain a log of which classmates supplied them with their additional restaurant verbs.

Introduction: State the objective.

Presentation 1: 15–20 minutes
Define the vocabulary on **pages 102 and 103.** Make sure students understand each word and can use it in context. Write a sentence using one of the verbs in a contextually related sentence. Explain that it is possible to determine meanings from the situation in the sentence. Challenge students to give you complete sentences using many of the words. Encourage them to use the words in context.

Practice 1: 10–20 minutes
Prepare students for dictation. Instruct them to close their dictionaries and write down the words they hear. Read **Words in Context.** Repeat the dictation as necessary.

Evaluation 1: Students can self-check their dictation by opening their dictionaries. Find out which words were challenging to students.

Application: 20–25 minutes
Review what is needed to write a complete sentence and give examples of a subject and verb. Write a few complete sentences using the words in the word list. Lecture on the parts of a paragraph: topic sentence, supportive body, and concluding sentence. Ask students to write a paragraph about a visit to a restaurant. It can be real or fictional but must contain vocabulary from the lesson. All sentences must be complete.

down the table and *May I pour you some more water?*

Practice 1: 15–20 minutes
In groups of six, students should write 12 sentences that could be said in a restaurant. They should include two sentences that might be said by a customer, two sentences by a server, and two sentences by a busser. Students should select the six best sentences. Groups should send representatives to other groups for sharing and add two more sentences to each category.

Evaluation 1: Choose the best examples from each group and write them on the board. Correct errors as a class.

Application: 30–40 minutes
In groups of three, students should create a skit in which one student is the server, one is the customer, and one is the busser. Students can draw on the sentences they wrote in the Practice. If students struggle at the beginning, give suggestions of situations. Make sure all students have a speaking part.

Project

Inform students that restaurants must pass inspection to stay in business. Lead a discussion about what types of things restaurants must do to remain in business. In groups, have students create a list of DOs and DON'Ts for restaurant staff. Encourage students who have worked in restaurants to talk about restaurant problems. Make a list of cleaning responsibilities for restaurant employees.

Level ★

Objective: Identify clothing items.

Warm-up: 10–15 minutes
Take time to describe your own clothing. Then, introduce an identification game. Explain that you are thinking of someone and describe the clothing this person is wearing. Students will need to look around the class and guess the name of the person you are describing. Provide an example: *I am thinking of someone who is wearing black sneakers, blue jeans, and a white T-shirt.* After the student is correctly identified, have that student stand and restate the clothing description, adding details if desired. Provide assistance if necessary.

Introduction: State the objective.

Presentation 1: 15–20 minutes
Refer students to **pages 104 and 105.** Present each item to the class and practice vocabulary by finding a student wearing each item named. Generate a discussion about what types of clothing students like to wear and what they are required to wear for work. Read *Words in Action #1.*

Practice 1: 8–10 minutes
Read *Words in Action #1* as a class. Ensure students understand the task and provide time for them to complete the activity suggested.

Evaluation 1: Observe the activity.

Presentation 2: 10–15 minutes
As a class, give names to each individual in the page spread. Consider assigning each person a number and writing their names by their numbers on the board for reference. Lead a game similar to the one done in the Warm-up. Referring to a person in the page spread, say *I am thinking of someone who is wearing a red blouse and a black skirt.* Students should answer with the person's assigned name. Discuss why answers are correct or incorrect.

Practice 2: 10–12 minutes
Pairs of students should continue the game in the dictionary. After a set time limit, have students write descriptions about three classmates. Collect and read the sentences students have written. Students should guess which classmate the descriptions were written about. Write on the board any items of clothing that are not included in the dictionary. Guide a discussion about clothing from different countries and write new vocabulary on the board.

Evaluation 2: Observe the activity.

Application: 7–10 minutes
Read *Words in Action #2* aloud and give students time to complete it with a partner or a small group.

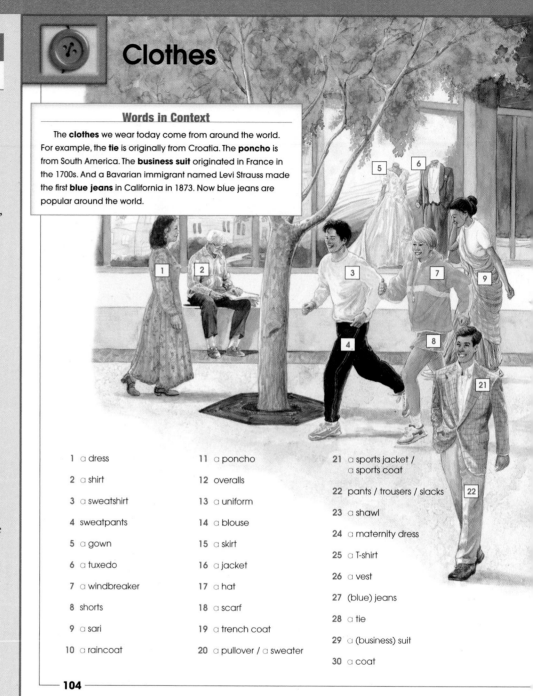

Clothes

Words in Context

The **clothes** we wear today come from around the world. For example, the **tie** is originally from Croatia. The **poncho** is from South America. The **business suit** originated in France in the 1700s. And a Bavarian immigrant named Levi Strauss made the first **blue jeans** in California in 1873. Now blue jeans are popular around the world.

1 a dress
2 a shirt
3 a sweatshirt
4 sweatpants
5 a gown
6 a tuxedo
7 a windbreaker
8 shorts
9 a sari
10 a raincoat

11 a poncho
12 overalls
13 a uniform
14 a blouse
15 a skirt
16 a jacket
17 a hat
18 a scarf
19 a trench coat
20 a pullover / a sweater

21 a sports jacket / a sports coat
22 pants / trousers / slacks
23 a shawl
24 a maternity dress
25 a T-shirt
26 a vest
27 (blue) jeans
28 a tie
29 (business) suit
30 a coat

104

Level ★ ★

Objective: Describe clothing.

Warm-up: 12–15 minutes
In groups, students should make a list of every item of clothing they see people wearing around the room. Groups should send one member to the board to write their words. To make sure all items are represented but not repeated, consider giving each group a different assignment. For example, one group could handle women's clothing, and another men's clothing.

Introduction: State the objective.

Presentation 1: 15–20 minutes
Go over the word list on **pages 104 and 105** as a class. Discuss varieties of clothing and bring *Word Partnerships* into the presentation. Remind students of the form and function of an adjective. Lecture briefly on adjectives and adjective order before nouns. Create a table on the board with examples. Include sizes, colors, and patterns (such

Word Partnerships

a leather	jacket
a down	coat
a winter	
a cowboy	hat
a sun	
a straw	
a silk	blouse
	tie

Words in Action

1. Work with a partner. One person says a kind of clothing. The other person points to the clothing in the picture. Take turns.

2. Choose three or four people in your class. Say what each person is wearing.

---

as stripes). Make sure students know to use *a* with singular nouns. Prepare students to perform the following model conversation:

Student A: *Excuse me. I am looking for a friend.*

Student B: *What was <u>she</u> wearing?*

Student A: *A black shirt and brown pants.*

Student B: *Yes, I saw <u>her ten</u> minutes ago. She went that way.*

Student A: Thanks.

Practice 1: 15–20 minutes
Students should practice the dialog by imagining that the "friend" is someone in the picture. Have students reverse roles and substitute vocabulary.
Evaluation 1: Observe the activity.

Application: 20–25 minutes
Give each student a small card on which to write sentences describing what they are wearing. They should be as descriptive as possible, but should not write their own names on the cards. Redistribute cards in random order. Students determine the author.

Objective: Write a paragraph using *if/then* statements.

Warm-up: 15–20 minutes
Ask students to imagine what they would buy if they were given $1,000 to buy clothing. Individually, they should make a two-columned, itemized list of what they would buy and the estimated costs. Students can read their lists to the class. Discuss the differences and see who spent the most money. Read the word list on **pages 104 and 105**. Define each word and assign students to write sentences, using the words in context. Ask students to choose at least five words and create five complete sentences using these words. After a set time, have students close their dictionaries and review the sentences.

Introduction: State the objective.

Presentation 1: 15–20 minutes
Change direction by focusing student attention on the origin of clothing. Find out if anyone knows where jeans came from and when they were first created. Brainstorm hypotheses. Ask students to write *tie, jeans, suit,* and *poncho* on a piece of paper. Read **Words in Context** aloud and challenge students to listen for the places each item originated and take notes. Quiz them briefly with dictionaries closed. Introduce *if/then* statements. Show students how they can use *if* and *then* to describe what they would wear under different circumstances. For example: *If it rains, then I will wear a poncho or raincoat.* Review the future verb tense if necessary.

Practice 1: 10–12 minutes
Provide students with the following conditions for wearing different kinds of clothing:

If . . .	If . . .
it rains	I go to work
it is cold	I want to run
it is windy	I get married
it is 100 degrees	I go to a party

Ask students to complete the sentences with the *then* clause. Have students develop three additional conditions and sentences.

Evaluation 1: Students share their sentences.

Application: 20–22 minutes
Students should write a paragraph about what they would do and what they would wear if they went on a trip to Alaska or another cold destination.

Project

Students create an inventory for a clothing store of a particular style. The inventory should include prices and quantity on hand in the store. Use the three-column table template available on the **Activity Bank CD-ROM** to facilitate this activity.

Level ★

Objective: Identify types of sleepwear, underwear, and swimwear.

Warm-up: 7–10 minutes
Have students close their eyes and picture a sunny beach. Pose a question about what people are wearing on the beach. Choose another location students are familiar with, such as a bedroom, and ask about the clothing people wear to sleep. Write the responses on the board.

Introduction: State the objective.

Presentation 1: 15–20 minutes
Ask students to open their dictionaries to **pages 106 and 107.** Discuss each item with students and develop sentences using the words. Make a cluster diagram on the board and ask students to help complete it. The center circle should contain *intimate clothing.* Clearly define *intimate—the first layer of clothing on the body*—and give examples. The secondary circles are *sleepwear, swimwear,* and *underwear.* The tertiary circles are for items in the page spread. Hand out the cluster template on the Activity Bank CD-ROM.

Practice 1: 10–15 minutes
Divide students into groups of three and ask them to complete the cluster. All words from the dictionary's spread should be included in one of the circles.

Evaluation 1: Complete the cluster on the board with student input.

Presentation 2: 10–15 minutes
Have students cover the word list on **pages 106 and 107.** Alert students that this is a timed activity. Inform them that you will say an item's name and they should identify the item by its number, as listed in the dictionary. The challenge is to do this as quickly as possible. You might stage a friendly competition in which the student who calls out the proper number first wins.

Practice 2: 10–12 minutes
Pair students for quizzing each other. With word lists covered, partners should continue the activity from the Presentation.

Evaluation 2: Observe the activity.

Application: 8–10 minutes
Refer back to the Warm-up when students imagined different locations. Ask students to now think about their homes. Students should create a two-part inventory. The first part should include items from the word list that are found in their homes. The second part should include items found in their homes that are not in the dictionary. Provide time for sharing and define any new vocabulary that is discussed.

Sleepwear, Underwear, and Swimwear

Words in Context

Socks have a long history. Thousands of years ago, people wore animal skins on their feet. Knit socks appeared in the 3rd century in Egypt. They quickly became popular around the world. **Underwear** has a long history, too. Hundreds of years ago only very rich people wore underwear. However, in the 1700s, cotton became cheap and soon most people began to wear **boxer shorts, briefs,** or **underpants.**

106

Level ★ ★

Objective: Ask for prices.

Warm-up: 12–15 minutes
Warn students that they have five minutes to study **pages 106 and 107** before a pop quiz. When that time has elapsed, ask them to close their dictionaries and see how many items they can list, as suggested in *Words in Action #1.* After another few minutes, have students form groups.

Introduction: State the objective.

Presentation 1: 12–15 minutes
Go over each of the words on **pages 106 and 107** with students. Provide detailed explanations of each word and include these in *Word Partnerships.* As a class, make a list of the items on the board and come up with reasonable prices for each item. Base this on student experience. Then prepare students to perform this store conversation.

   Student A: *Excuse me. How much is the red nightgown?*

1 a clothesline
2 a clothespin
3 socks
4 tights
5 pantyhose / nylons
6 stockings
7 a swimsuit / a bathing suit
8 a bikini
9 (swimming) trunks
10 flip flops / thongs
11 slippers
12 a nightshirt

13 a (bath)robe
14 a nightgown
15 long underwear
16 a (blanket) sleeper
17 pajamas
18 a leotard
19 a bra
20 panties / underpants
21 a girdle
22 a camisole
23 a slip
24 an undershirt
25 a tank top

26 boxer shorts / boxers
27 briefs
28 an athletic supporter / a jockstrap

Word Partnerships

a terrycloth	(bath)robe
a silk	
a flannel	
knee	socks
sweat	
ankle	
dress	
a pair of	briefs
	boxer shorts
	socks
	slippers

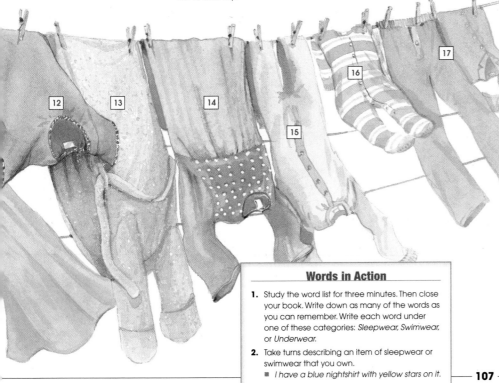

Words in Action

1. Study the word list for three minutes. Then close your book. Write down as many of the words as you can remember. Write each word under one of these categories: *Sleepwear, Swimwear,* or *Underwear.*

2. Take turns describing an item of sleepwear or swimwear that you own.
   - *I have a blue nightshirt with yellow stars on it.*

— **107**

Student B: *It is _____.*

Student A: *Thank you, I'll take it.*

Practice 1: 18–20 minutes
Hand out small cards on which students should write the names of three items. Collect the cards and shuffle them before redistributing in random order. Give instructions for a corners activity in which students will go into one of three corners—determined by the first word on their card. The corners are *sleepwear, swimwear,* and *underwear.* Once in the corner, students perform the conversation from the Presentation, using the first word on the card. Then, ask students to go to the corner associated with the next word and repeat the activity. Repeat the activity a third time.

Evaluation 1: Observe the activity.

Application: 20–22 minutes
With their final group, students discuss where they can buy these articles of clothing. After an allotted time, bring the groups together to discuss local stores in the community, comparing prices and selection.

Objective: Work as a team to solve marketing problems.

Warm-up: 8–12 minutes
Initiate a conversation by asking if anyone knows when socks were first used. Extend the conversation to include the original century people started wearing underwear. Request that students open their dictionaries to **pages 106 and 107** and give them two minutes to read *Words in Context* silently before closing their dictionaries. Give an oral quiz with comprehension questions about the paragraph.

Introduction: State the objective.

Presentation 1: 15–20 minutes
Study the word list on **pages 106 and 107** as a class and answer student questions. Create a table on the board with three headings: *sleepwear, swimwear,* and *underwear.* With dictionaries closed, students should attempt to classify as many items as they remember. Guide the activity so the class works together. After sufficient time, open the dictionary and add any missed items to the table. Ask if students are familiar with related clothing items that are not included in the picture. Discuss specifics and categorize those words properly. Discuss why some answers do not fit into one of the classifications.

Practice 1: 15–20 minutes
Assign students to groups of four. Members should imagine that they want to buy a specialized clothing store that only sells the items on the word list. Charge them with making a list of items that will sell the most quickly. All group members must agree on what the most popular items will be. Extend this activity by asking which clothing items are the most expensive.

Evaluation 1: Ask groups to report to the class.

Application: 30–40 minutes
Tell students that their clothing store has about 75 customers a day and that, of these customers, only about 45 buy merchandise. Students must organize the store so the most important items are near the front of the store. They order merchandise every two weeks. Based on this information, ask students to create a floor plan and an inventory list of the items on the word list.

Project

Mention a few famous designers that students might be familiar with. Encourage creative thinking as students design their own sleepwear, underwear, or swimwear item. Supply paper and colored pencils. Students present their new item to their classmates and explain how the item is different and better than the fashions already available.

Level ★

Objective: Ask for prices using *is* and *are*.

Warm-up: 7–10 minutes
Ask that all students stand. Make a series of statements using clothing words. Instruct students to sit when a statement applies to their clothing. Begin with students wearing sandals. Continue by having students wearing hats or scarves sit. As you call out each article of clothing, write it on the board and briefly review it. Include items from **pages 106 and 107** in order to refresh students' memories. Continue making statements until all students are seated.

Introduction: State the objective.

Presentation 1: 20–30 minutes
Ask students to open their dictionaries to **pages 108 and 109.** Go over the word list with students; review words used from the Warm-up and spend adequate time on those not yet discussed. Review singular and plural nouns. Write several examples of each on the board. Have students cover the word list as they are quizzed on item locations. Write *Where are* or *Where is* on the board and finish the question by reading aloud an item from the word list. Guide students to respond by pointing to the correct picture and saying *Here.* Alternatively, they can use prepositions of location to answer more explicitly.

Practice 1: 10–15 minutes
Continue the challenge by having students find an example of each item from the list on a classmate.

Evaluation 1: Create a class list on the board.

Presentation 2: 10–15 minutes
As a class, assign each item in the picture a price. You may choose to make all prices in dollars without cents, depending on student level and prior knowledge. Avoid teaching two objectives. Show students that *a* is required before each singular noun and it means *one.* Offer these examples: *How much are sandals? They are $25* and *How much is a handbag? It is $32.* Draw a table with two columns on the board. Ask students to classify the words from the spread under one of the two columns. Label the column headers *How much is . . . ?* and *How much are . . . ?*

Practice 2: 10–12 minutes
In groups, students should classify the remaining words and quiz each other on the prices. After some practice, ask that the word lists be covered.

Evaluation 2: Observe the activity.

Application: 7–10 minutes
Ask students to list the items they are wearing and the items they have at home. The second list should be ordered so that the items they have the most of should be first. Allow time for comparison.

Shoes and Accessories

Words in Context

Different **shoes** and **accessories** are popular in different cultures. For example, in Guatemala, many women wear **sandals**, long **earrings**, and bright **scarves, necklaces,** and **bracelets.** In India, women often wear a beautiful scarf, called a *dupatta*, and gold **rings.** What kinds of shoes and accessories are popular in your culture?

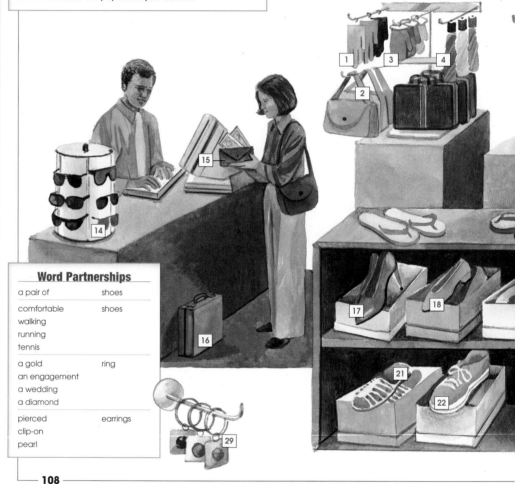

Word Partnerships

a pair of	shoes
comfortable	shoes
walking	
running	
tennis	
a gold	ring
an engagement	
a wedding	
a diamond	
pierced	earrings
clip-on	
pearl	

— 108 —

Level ★ ★

Objective: Make purchasing decisions.

Warm-up: 15–20 minutes
After presenting *Words in Action #1,* have students complete it with answers for three locations. Encourage the use of the dictionaries for reference. Expand this activity by including other clothing items as well. Place students in small groups to share their answers.

Introduction: State the objective.

Presentation 1: 15–20 minutes
Thoroughly go over each of the words from the word list on **pages 108 and 109** as a class. Make sure students understand what each item means and include the varieties in *Word Partnerships.* Develop a table with three columns labeled *grandfather, young adult man,* and *teenage girl.* As a class, identify a few items from the word list that person might wear.

1 gloves

2 a purse / a handbag

3 mittens

4 an umbrella

5 suspenders

6 a belt

7 a ring

8 a necklace

9 earrings

10 a bracelet

11 a (wrist)watch

12 a pin

13 jewelry

14 sunglasses

15 a wallet

16 a briefcase

17 a (high) heel

18 a pump

19 a loafer

20 a clog

21 a sandal

22 a sneaker

23 an athletic shoe

24 a hiking boot

25 a boot

26 a (knit) hat

27 a baseball cap / a baseball hat

28 earmuffs

29 a key chain

Words in Action

1. Name a place where you like to go. What shoes and accessories are good to wear to this place?

2. You need to buy three gifts: one for your 80-year-old grandfather, one for your 25-year-old brother, and one for your teenage sister. What shoes or accessories will you buy for each person?

109

Level ★ ★ ★

Objective: Make comparisons.

Warm-up: 12–15 minutes
Inform students that the lesson is about shoes and accessories. Define *accessories*. Guide students to read **Words in Context** on **page 108** and provide time for it to be read silently. Assign groups to discuss what accessories are popular in different countries and regions.

Introduction: State the objective.

Presentation 1: 15–20 minutes
Present the word list on **pages 108 and 109**. Make sure students understand each word and point out examples from students' clothing. With student help, expand the list, if possible. Describe particular accessories and see if students can identify the objects. For example, *This is something people wear on their fingers.* Ask questions, such as *What is the difference between pumps and high heels?* and *What is the difference between a necklace and a bracelet?*

Practice 1: 15–20 minutes
In groups, students should find and make as many comparisons between pairs of objects as possible. As an example, on the board write *The difference between gloves and mittens is that gloves have fingers and mittens don't.* They should practice saying sentences about the differences. Stage a competition in which the group with the most comparisons wins.

Evaluation 1: Listen to groups report by giving comparison sentences for pairs of objects.

Application: 30–40 minutes
Focus attention on the shoes and accessories being worn in class. Students should make comparisons and write complete sentences. Ask students to work in small groups to peer check. Have students read one sentence each to the class.

Practice 1: 15–20 minutes
As a group, have students decide how to answer **Words in Action #2.** Divide students into three evenly sized groups to complete the table. Each group should agree on all items. Then, have a representative for each group fill in one column on the board.

Evaluation 1: Ask groups to report to the class using the following wording:
We would buy _____ for our grandfather.

Application: 15–20 minutes
Individually, students make a list of special occasions for which they would buy gifts for family members. Have them make a second list to include the family members to receive the gifts. Students should then decide what each family member would receive as a gift for each special occasion. Encourage students to include items from both this lesson and the clothing lessons previously studied.

Project

In groups, students should design a shoe store. Where will the items in the store be? What might students sell besides shoes? How much of the store needs to be used as storage for inventory? After the design is complete, students should be directed to create a role-play situation at the store. Approve role-play suggestions to ensure they include situations applicable to the vocabulary. Students should write and improvise for the class.

Describing Clothes

Level ★

Objective: Describe clothing.

Warm-up: 10–15 minutes
Write *formal clothing* and *informal clothing* on the board. Describe the difference between the two by writing a few appropriate articles of clothing under each and using pantomime to illustrate what they are. For example, demonstrate what a tie is by pretending to straighten a tie, or straighten your own if you are wearing one. Ask students when they wear formal clothes and when they wear informal ones. Help them answer by giving suggestions and asking under which category you should write the occasions or places.

Introduction: State the objective.

Presentation 1: 20–30 minutes
Ask students to open their dictionaries to **pages 110 and 111.** Go over each item with students and practice the vocabulary by continuing to use hand signals to identify different items in the page spread. For example, point to your shirt or blouse and with a cutting motion, suggest that you have no sleeves. Then ask students to identify which item you are describing from the word list.

Practice 1: 10–15 minutes
Pair students to perform the activity just demonstrated in the Presentation. Students should work together to develop an action to describe each word.

Evaluation 1: Have volunteers stand and perform actions while their classmates guess the proper clothing vocabulary that the action describes.

Presentation 2: 10–15 minutes
As a class, name each person in the picture and maintain a list on the board. Write the following phrase: *John is wearing a violet button-down shirt.* There is no need to explicitly teach the present continuous for this activity, unless students are ready. They can learn the phrase above with little instruction. Prepare students to do the Practice.

Practice 2: 10–12 minutes
With a new partner, students practice aloud, describing what people in the picture are wearing. Sentences should all follow the same format: *Eliza is wearing _____.*

Evaluation 2: Have students present their descriptions to the class.

Application: 7–15 minutes
Read *Words in Action #1* and have students complete it.

Words in Context

Fashions come and go. For example, sometimes ties are **wide** and sometimes they're **narrow.** The length of **skirts** is always changing too. One year they're **long** and **straight,** and the next year they're **short** and **pleated.** It's hard to keep up with fashion!

Word Partnerships

fashionable	clothes
trendy	
designer	
work	
maternity	

7:00 — Casual Clothes 24

8:00 — Formal Clothes 25

110

Level ★ ★

Objective: Make comparisons.

Warm-up: 15–20 minutes
Place students in groups of three to develop descriptions of three classmates from other groups. Descriptions must solely focus on what they are wearing. Stage the exercise as a quiz so each group can read their sentences, such as *We are thinking of someone who is wearing . . .*

Introduction: State the objective.

Presentation 1: 15–20 minutes
Go over each of the words from the word list on **pages 110 and 111** as a class. Make sure students understand what each item is and then include *Word Partnerships.* As a class, name each person in the picture. Find two people in the picture who are wearing items similar in some way (e.g., color, length of sleeves). Draw a Venn diagram of the two people. There is a template on the Activity Bank CD-ROM to facilitate this activity.

1 a light jacket

2 a heavy jacket

3 a sleeveless shirt

4 a short-sleeved shirt

5 a long-sleeved shirt

6 a button-down shirt

7 a polo shirt

8 a wide tie

9 a narrow tie

10 flared jeans

11 straight leg jeans

12 baggy pants / loose pants

13 a V-neck sweater

14 a crew neck sweater

15 a cardigan sweater

16 a turtleneck sweater

17 a tight skirt

18 a straight skirt

19 a pleated skirt

20 a short skirt

21 a long skirt

22 high heels

23 low heels

24 informal clothes / casual clothes

25 formal clothes / dress clothes

Words in Action

1. Describe the clothes you and other people in class are wearing.

2. Which items of clothing in the picture are in fashion? Are any of the clothes not in fashion?

— 111 —

Level ★ ★ ★

Objective: Discuss fashions.

Warm-up: 8–10 minutes
In groups, students should discuss what other people in the class are wearing. Encourage them to be as descriptive and specific as possible.

Introduction: State the objective.

Presentation 1: 15–20 minutes
Direct students to the word list on **pages 110 and 111**. After ensuring clear comprehension of the differences, attempt to expand the list. Call for student input on listing similarities. The goal is to find the same item on more than one model. For example, three men and all five women are wearing long sleeves. Write *fashionable* on the board and ask students which model in the picture might be most fashionable and why. Lead the class in a discussion about the definition of *fashionable*, *stylish*, or *trendy*. Read **Words in Context** aloud. Write *dresses, skirts, men's and women's shirts*, and *shoes* on the board. Ask the class to give a name to each model.

Practice 1: 15–20 minutes
Divide students into small groups and ask them to discuss which people are wearing trendy or fashionable clothing. All students in the group must agree before attempting to rank the models from most to least fashionable.

Evaluation 1: Groups list their ranking on the board. Compare answers as a class and discuss reasons.

Application: 30–40 minutes
Generate a class conversation about well-known personalities, such as movie stars, news figures, and political leaders. On the board, list the first 20 names that are suggested. Back in their small groups, students should rank the people from most to least fashionable. Ask groups to add other well-known fashionable personalities.

Emphasize that Venn diagrams show similarities and differences. Examples can include: *Both John and Sam are wearing violet shirts, but John's is a button-down shirt and Sam's is a polo shirt.*

Practice 1: 15–20 minutes
Assign partners to create another Venn diagram for two other students. Supply copies of the template from the **Activity Bank CD-ROM**.

Evaluation 1: Ask students to describe their diagrams to the group.

Application: 15–20 minutes
Ask students to think about what styles of clothing they prefer: casual or formal, V-neck or crew neck, skirts or pants, etc. In pairs, have them describe a favorite outfit and when they wear it. Students should also mention what kinds of stores they like to shop at for their clothes. The listener in each pair should take notes. After 10 minutes of discussion in pairs, each student should describe his or her partner's preferences to the class.

Project

In groups, students should prepare a fashion show. They should describe what the models would wear. Consider having groups divided by theme, with each group focusing on a separate category, such as school clothing, party clothing, or formal clothing. Ask students to come to class ready to model their selections and stage a fashion show. Have students choose the roles of organizers, models, and narrators who will describe the clothing. Groups should have a script written for the narrator, which can be read to the class independently if students are reluctant to be models.

Fabrics and Patterns

Warm-up: 10–12 minutes
Explain the following identification game. State some of the basic vocabulary from the list and items of clothing from previous lessons. When students recognize an article of clothing, fabric, or pattern they are wearing, they should stand and remain standing. Continue the game until everyone is standing. Practice more by keeping the same rules but having students sit when they hear a clothing item this time. Proceed until everyone is seated.

Introduction: State the objective.

Presentation 1: 17–20 minutes
Read the vocabulary on **pages 112 and 113.** Instruct students to follow along as each item is studied. Let students know that you will be saying an article of clothing. They should respond with the material the item is made from. For example, if you say *blue jeans*, they should respond with *denim*. If you say *sweater*, they should answer *wool*. Help with pronunciation. Write all these combinations on the board. Practice writing a few sentences, using the words in context.

Practice 1: 12–15 minutes
Pair students to continue this quizzing activity.

Evaluation 1: Observe the activity and offer minimal guidance so students work independently.

Presentation 2: 12–15 minutes
Go over the patterns and give examples from the class. Prepare students to perform the following model conversation.

  Student A: *What will you wear later today?*

  Student B: *I will wear a denim dress and a cotton blouse.*

Have students create six other clothing options as a class and write them on the board. Show students how to substitute the information. Pass out small cards and ask students to write what they really will wear on the card, but tell them not to write their names. Collect the cards.

Practice 2: 10–12 minutes
Provide ample practice time and ask students to substitute the information on the board. Shuffle the cards and redistribute them randomly. Tell students that they should complete the exchange with as many students as necessary to find the student who wrote the information. They should not reveal what the card says or show their card until after performing the conversation.

Evaluation 2: Solicit volunteers to demonstrate.

Application: 7–10 minutes
Have partners complete *Words in Action #1.*

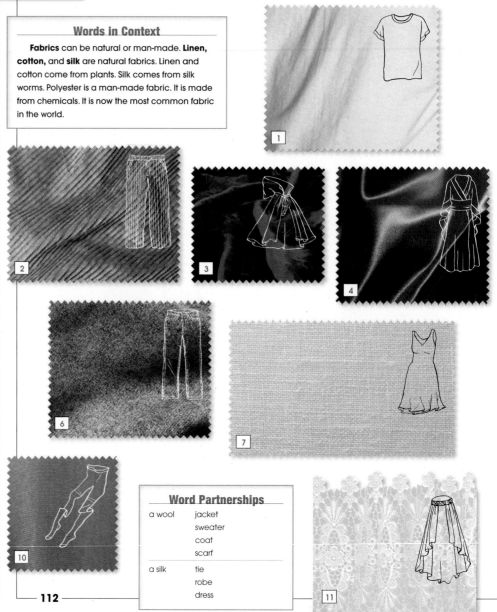

Words in Context

Fabrics can be natural or man-made. **Linen, cotton,** and **silk** are natural fabrics. Linen and cotton come from plants. Silk comes from silk worms. Polyester is a man-made fabric. It is made from chemicals. It is now the most common fabric in the world.

Word Partnerships

a wool	jacket
	sweater
	coat
	scarf
a silk	tie
	robe
	dress

112

Warm-up: 15–20 minutes
As students enter the classroom, hand each of them a small card on which to describe their clothing. Names are to be left off. Collect the cards and pass them out again in random order. Students should walk around the room and find the author of the card.

Introduction: State the objective.

Presentation 1: 15–18 minutes
Present each of the words from the word list on **pages 112 and 113.** Make sure students understand each item before lecturing on the terminology in *Word Partnerships*. Briefly teach the present continuous tense and create a chart on the board. Ask students to identify what different people in the class are wearing and determine similarities and differences. Start a list on the board. Be sure to include new vocabulary.

Fabrics	Patterns	
1 cotton	13 solid	17 paisley
2 corduroy	14 print	18 checked
3 velvet	15 polka dot	19 plaid
4 silk	16 floral	20 striped
5 leather		21 embroidered
6 denim		
7 linen		
8 suede		
9 cashmere		
10 nylon		
11 lace		
12 wool		

Words in Action

1. Work with a partner. Describe your partner's clothes.
   ■ *You're wearing brown corduroy pants and a blue and white striped cotton shirt.*
2. Design an outfit. Decide on the fabrics and patterns. Draw the outfit and describe it to your class.

113

Buying, Wearing, and Caring for Clothes

Level ★

Objective: Identify verbs for buying, wearing, and caring for clothes.

Warm-up: 7–10 minutes
While preparing for class, read *Words in Action #1* and develop five actions to perform for students. Begin class with a game of charades and split the class into two teams. As you pantomime a word from the list, teams should call out the answer when they recognize it. Whichever team correctly identifies the action first wins a point. Repeat four times and list correct answers on the board.

Introduction: State the objective.

Presentation 1: 15–20 minutes
Ask students to follow along as they open their dictionaries and read through the steps on **pages 114 and 115**. Present each item and ensure clear understanding. Repeat the pantomimes from the Warm-up and ask students to act out other words for classmates to guess.

Practice 1: 10–12 minutes
Divide students into small groups (3–4 students). Randomly assign each group four words to pantomime. Alert students that they will have the chance to teach the actions to the other students.

Evaluation 1: Students will perform one action each for the class. Classmates will guess the answers aloud.

Presentation 2: 10–12 minutes
Teach the simple present tense to students, paying special attention to the third person singular form. Create a chart for students to facilitate this presentation. Write several sentences to illustrate this grammar focus, using the verbs **on pages 114 and 115**.

Practice 2: 15–18 minutes
Ask students to write a sentence for each action on the word list, using the simple present tense.

Evaluation 2: Walk around the classroom and identify grammatically correct sentences. Choose one sentence per student to be written on the board.

Application: 7–10 minutes
Have students develop a three-column table and label the headers *I do this to my clothes, I have someone else do this to my clothes,* and *I never do this to my clothes*. List all 24 actions in the table. Use *Words in Action #2* as a guide.

Words in Context

Different clothes have different care instructions. Jeans are easy. You can **wash** them in the washing machine and then **dry** them in the dryer. However, a wool shirt needs special care. You shouldn't wash a wool shirt. Instead, you should **dry clean** it. To prevent wrinkles, always **hang up** clothes.

1	go shopping	5	buy	10	button	15	unzip
2	look for a jacket	6	take home	11	buckle	16	unbuckle
3	go into a dressing room	7	cut off	12	roll up	17	take off
		8	put on	13	wear	18	wash
4	try on	9	zip	14	unbutton	19	dry

— 114 —

Level ★ ★

Objective: Read labels and washing instructions.

Warm-up: 15–20 minutes
Simulate an action from **pages 114 and 115** that is suggested in *Words in Action #1*. See if students can define your action. Try a few more actions, and then have students continue the exercise in pairs.

Introduction: State the objective.

Presentation 1: 15–20 minutes
Study the word list on **pages 114 and 115** as a class. Make sure students understand the concepts before introducing *Word Partnerships*. Write the following instructions on the board: *Machine wash in cold water or dry clean. Do not tumble dry.* Ask if any students know what material or garment these directions might be attached to. Accept all reasonable answers. Write down all the possible washing and drying combinations students know.

Word Partnerships

20 dry clean

21 mend / repair

22 sew on

23 iron / press

24 hang (up)

hang it	on a hook
	on a hanger
	in the closet
wash it	in cold water
	in hot water
	by hand
zip	up
button	

Words in Action

1. Pretend to do one of the actions on the word list. Your partner will guess what you are doing. Take turns.

2. Explain how you care for your favorite piece of clothing.
   - *I never wash my leather jacket in the washing machine. I dry clean it.*

— 115 —

Include *tumble dry, machine wash and dry, dry clean, line dry, iron low heat,* and *don't use bleach.*

Practice 1: 15–20 minutes
Refer students to **pages 112 and 113.** Review fabrics, and then ask students to write what cleaning instructions should be used for each type of fabric or article of clothing. Have students discuss possibilities with a partner or a group.

Evaluation 1: Ask groups to report answers to the class.

Application: 15–20 minutes
Students should identify clothing that classmates are wearing. What items do they think might need special cleaning instructions? If the labels are easily accessible, ask students to read the labels. Converse about the benefits (pros) and drawbacks (cons) of washing and drying laundry compared to dry cleaning. Go around the room so students can each answer the question posed in *Words in Action #2.*

Warm-up: 15–20 minutes
Instruct students to open their dictionaries to **pages 114 and 115.** They should cover the word list and see how many verbs they can identify by making lists of their own. Stage a friendly competition to see which student can name the most verbs. If students do not know a word, they can make one up. Then compare answers.

Introduction: State the objective.

Presentation 1: 15–20 minutes
Go over the word list on **pages 114 and 115** as a class. Ensure that students understand each word and can use it in context. Students should choose three actions and write clear, concise sentences using their selected words in context. Review paragraph form with the class and remind them about the importance of indenting and writing within margins. Prepare students for a dictation.

Practice 1: 8–10 minutes
Use *Words in Context* as a dictation piece. Repeat if necessary. Before reopening dictionaries, answer any questions about the vocabulary or content of the reading.

Evaluation 1: Allow time for students to check their own accuracy against the paragraph on **page 114.**

Application: 40–60 minutes
Teach students about writing in chronological order. Explain how to include words such as *first, second, next, then, after that,* and *finally.* Then discuss a multi-paragraph essay, with the topic paragraph first and subsequent paragraphs giving details. Tell students that their goal is to write three paragraphs about a day in the life of Jane—the character in the dictionary. Ask students to use proper paragraph form. Although they do not need to include every action Jane performs, they should imagine what she is thinking while she is dong some of the pictured tasks. Advise students to limit her actions to a particular setting. Tell students to write a rough draft and then ask a partner to peer edit. Allow time for rewrites and final edits before turning in the stories.

Project

Assign students to small groups. They should imagine that they are shopping for two perfect outfits: one to wear to a job interview and the other to wear to a wedding. Students should write skits about where they search, find, try on, and buy clothing. Lower-level students might want to draw, present, and explain the outfits their groups created.

Sewing and Laundry

Level ★

Objective: Identify items associated with making and washing clothing.

Warm-up: 15–20 minutes
To begin, have students in groups make a list of all the kinds of clothing they see represented in the classroom. Groups should send representatives to put their lists on the board.

Introduction: State the objective.

Presentation 1: 15–20 minutes
Encourage students to open their dictionaries to **pages 116 and 117** and follow along as you describe each word. Practice vocabulary by pointing out examples and pantomiming. Next, have students cover the word lists. Read items 1 through 10 from the word list in random order. See if students can correctly identify the named item by pointing to its picture.

Practice 1: 7–10 minutes
Pair students to take turns quizzing each other. Allow sufficient time for all the words to be covered and students to reverse roles several times.

Evaluation 1: Observe the activity, making sure all students perform both roles.

Presentation 2: 10–15 minutes
Focus only on the items on **page 117** and practice that vocabulary with students. Read aloud items 11 through 30 from the word list in random order. Again, ask students to cover the word list and see if they can identify the item by pointing to it. Write the following sentence on the board: *The sewing machine is larger than the scissors.* Help students to say this sentence and understand its meaning.

Practice 2: 10–12 minutes
Individually, students should make a list of items 11–30 by size order. Ask students to put the largest item first and continue the list until the smallest item is last. Students can exchange papers and compare answers with a partner.

Evaluation 2: Students should create sentences similar to the example in Presentation 2, using their own lists. Students should also see if other pairs agree or disagree with their choices.

Application: 7–10 minutes
Read *Words in Action #2.* After discussing it briefly as a class, have students make a list. Compare answers.

Words in Context

Fashion designer Josie Natori comes from the Philippines. She sells her clothes all over the world. Her company started very small. At first, Natori worked alone in her living room with a **sewing machine, pins, needles, buttons, thread,** and **scissors.** Now her company has offices in Manila, Paris, and New York.

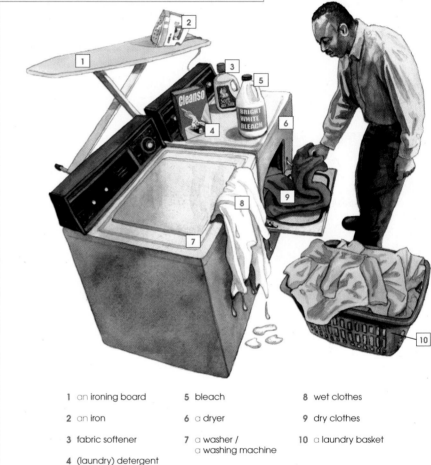

1 an ironing board	5 bleach	8 wet clothes
2 an iron	6 a dryer	9 dry clothes
3 fabric softener	7 a washer / a washing machine	10 a laundry basket
4 (laundry) detergent		

116

Level ★★

Objective: Describe a process.

Warm-up: 10–15 minutes
In small conversation circles, guide students to discuss the following questions: *How many people live in your home?, Who does the laundry?, How often does he, she, or they do the laundry?, Do people in your home iron?,* and *How often do they iron?*

Introduction: State the objective.

Presentation 1: 20–30 minutes
Go over each of the words from the word list on **pages 116 and 117** with students. Make sure they understand each item and include *Word Partnerships* in your presentation. Perform *Words in Action #1* as a class. Then write instructions for repairing or mending clothing as a class. Show students how they will use the imperative to give directions. There is an Activity Bank CD-ROM worksheet to facilitate this activity.

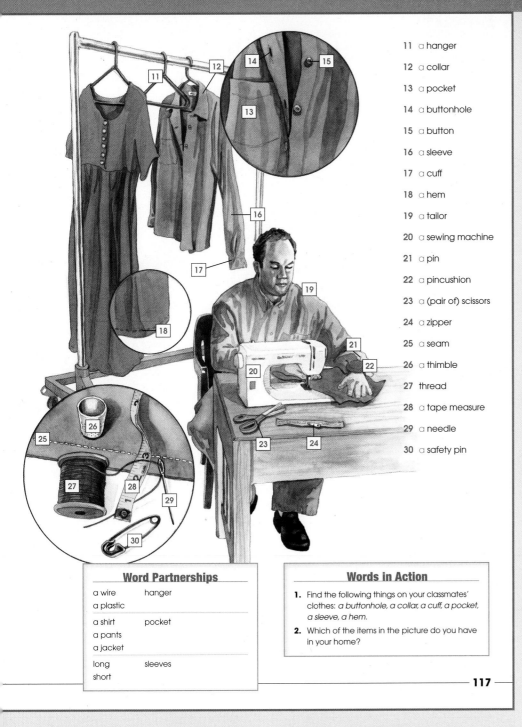

11 a hanger
12 a collar
13 a pocket
14 a buttonhole
15 a button
16 a sleeve
17 a cuff
18 a hem
19 a tailor
20 a sewing machine
21 a pin
22 a pincushion
23 a (pair of) scissors
24 a zipper
25 a seam
26 a thimble
27 thread
28 a tape measure
29 a needle
30 a safety pin

Word Partnerships

a wire	hanger
a plastic	
a shirt	pocket
a pants	
a jacket	
long	sleeves
short	

Words in Action

1. Find the following things on your classmates' clothes: *a buttonhole, a collar, a cuff, a pocket, a sleeve, a hem.*
2. Which of the items in the picture do you have in your home?

Objective: Describe a process in detail.

Warm-up: 8–10 minutes
Read and discuss *Words in Context.* Answer any vocabulary or comprehension questions before moving forward. Tell students that this is a "success story" and ask if they know other success stories about people in business.

Introduction: State the objective.

Presentation 1: 15–20 minutes
Present the word list on **pages 116 and 117.** Make sure students understand each word. Challenge students to help you add ten words to the list. Call for student descriptions of how to wash clothes. Add related verbs to the word lists, focusing on the details. Write on the board thorough instructions for doing laundry based on student response, and have the class copy the instructions for future study.

Practice 1: 15–20 minutes
When finished, shift focus from washing to mending. Have students write detailed instructions for mending clothes. Focus on a specific repair, such as sewing on a button, putting in a new zipper, or hemming pants or a skirt. Students may work with a partner for this activity. Use the Activity Bank CD-ROM worksheet to facilitate this exercise.

Evaluation 1: Ask pairs to share their processes.

Application: 20–25 minutes
Review types of clothing from other dictionary lessons. Narrow the focus down to one article of clothing. In pairs, students should write the process for making a piece of clothing. Instruct students to use the worksheet you supply from the Activity Bank CD-ROM.

Have several copies available so students can also use the worksheet for the upcoming practice about laundry. Read worksheet instructions as a class.

Practice 1: 20–30 minutes
In small groups, have students write instructions on how to do laundry. If they need prompting, put some of these phrases on the board: *sort the clothes, add bleach and detergent, choose the water temperature,* and *select a cycle.* Ask students to use at least five of the words from the page spread.

Evaluation 1: Ask groups to present. Compare directions.

Application: 10–12 minutes
Without referring back to their notes, have students describe the washing process in groups. With help from the group, they can further develop their directions and incorporate additional words from the list.

Project

Divide students into groups; ideally two men to represent a father and son and two women to signify a mother and daughter. Since they are to imagine they are a family, ask them to decide how often they need to do laundry, who will do it, and who will mend clothing. The family must also establish if anyone in the family will make clothes. Create a duty roster or chore schedule that includes frequency of each chore. There is a worksheet on the Activity Bank CD-ROM that will help create the duty roster.

Vehicles and Traffic Signs

Level ★

Objective: Identify vehicles and traffic signs.

Warm-up: 10–15 minutes
Ask all students what modes of transportation they use to get to school. Pose questions such as *Do you take the bus?*, *Do you walk?*, and *Do you drive a car?* Aid visual learners by writing or drawing on the board. Record any valid transportation answers. Take a class poll to determine what transportation method is most popular. Make a bar graph showing the results. Save a copy of this bar graph for use with the lesson on public transportation to come on **pages 128 and 129**.

Introduction: State the objective.

Presentation 1: 15–20 minutes
Ask students to open their dictionaries to **pages 118 and 119**. Present the traffic signs on **page 118** to the class and practice pronunciation of the vocabulary. If signs are unclear, demonstrate or have students pretend to be cars and demonstrate. After adequate time, ask students to cover the word list and point to the pictures as you say the words.

Practice 1: 8–10 minutes
Pair students to continue the quizzing exercise with one another. As in the Presentation, students should attempt this with the word list covered.

Evaluation 1: Observe the activity.

Presentation 2: 10–15 minutes
Introduce vehicles illustrated on **page 119** and discuss them as a class. Practice vocabulary with an oral listening activity. Say items 12 through 30 from the word list in random order. Students should cover the word list and try to identify the item by pointing to the correct picture. Generate opinions on what students consider to be the smallest and largest vehicles. As a class, identify the five largest vehicles, as suggested in *Words in Action #1.*

Practice 2: 10–12 minutes
In small groups, encourage students to continue the list started in the Presentation and ordering all vehicles from largest to smallest.

Evaluation 2: Groups place their lists on the board and compare answers. Discuss.

Application: 8–10 minutes
Divide students into small groups to discuss what vehicle each student owns or what each wants to own in the future. Guide the discussion to have students say what is good and what is bad about their current vehicles (*size, reliability, speed, style*). If time permits, bring magazines and have students find pictures of new cars they like. They should attempt to explain why they want to change vehicles.

Words in Context

Do you need a new car or truck? There is a lot to think about. Do you have children? A **compact car** may be too small. People with children often drive large **vehicles** like **station wagons, sedans,** and **SUVs.** Do you like to camp? An **RV** may be good for you. Do you like adventure? You might like a **motorcycle.** Do you often need to move large things? You may want a **pickup truck.** There are so many vehicles to choose from!

Signs

1. one way
2. stop
3. hospital
4. do not pass
5. do not enter
6. no left turn
7. railroad crossing
8. school zone
9. pedestrian crossing
10. yield
11. no U-turn

Vehicles

12. a school bus
13. a tow truck
14. a garbage truck
15. a pickup (truck)
16. an RV
17. a minivan
18. a limousine / a limo
19. a sedan
20. a van
21. a dump truck
22. an SUV

23. a trailer
24. a sports car
25. a semi / a tractor trailer
26. a police car
27. an ambulance
28. a fire engine
29. a station wagon
30. a compact (car)
31. a convertible
32. a motorcycle

118

Level ★★

Objective: Interact with a police officer at a traffic stop.

Warm-up: 10–15 minutes
Read and ask small groups to discuss *Words in Action #2.* Allow time for groups to report. Bring in magazine pictures or newspaper advertisements to discuss ideal vehicles.

Introduction: State the objective.

Presentation 1: 20–30 minutes
Study each of the words from the word list on **pages 118 and 119** as a class. Make sure students understand what each item means before tackling the phrases in *Word Partnerships.* Try to find other word partnerships with students. Ask students what they should say to a police officer if they are stopped for *running a stop sign.* Write the offense on the board. Also write *rolling through a stop sign* on the board. Prepare students to perform this conversation:

Word Partnerships

drive	a convertible
	a truck
	an SUV
ride	a motorcycle
ride in	a limousine
ride on	a bus

Words in Action

1. Work with a partner. Make a list of the five largest vehicles in the word list. Make another list of the five smallest vehicles.

2. Imagine you have enough money to buy a new vehicle. What vehicle will you buy? Explain your choice to the class.

119

Warm-up: 8–10 minutes
In small groups, assign students to read and discuss *Words in Context*. Answer any vocabulary or context questions. Have students try to answer the questions asked in the paragraph.

Introduction: State the objective.

Presentation 1: 15–20 minutes
Read aloud the word list on **pages 118 and 119.** Have students repeat each word after you pronounce it. Discuss each word in depth and have students quiz each other in pairs. Add to a list on the board any items related to vehicles or traffic signs that students can call out. Generate a discussion about who owns a car and ask experienced students to explain how to buy a new or used car. Explain that car buyers need to be prepared before they attempt to buy from a car dealership. Discuss how they can go online and get factory invoice prices. Bring the discussion to a close by discussing what options are available on vehicles. Write them on the board.

Practice 1: 20–25 minutes
With a partner, students should identify five cars they would like to buy. For each choice, they should list the type of car, make, model, year, color, and all the extras: moon roof, CD player, leather seats, etc. Partners should also explain why they chose a specific car. Continue by having students practice the information in a simulated role-play with one partner acting as a sales person at a new or used car lot. There is a vehicle worksheet on the Activity Bank CD-ROM that can facilitate this activity.

Evaluation 1: Encourage volunteers to perform their role-plays for the class.

Application: 18–20 minutes
In groups, students should discuss vehicles they own, how much the cars are worth, and what they like and dislike about the cars. Each group should choose one car to sell to another group. Have students from other groups try to buy the car. Discuss conversations and record the results on the board in chart form. What kinds of cars with which options sold at what prices?

Project

Bring in samples of an automobile blue book and the classified ads from a newspaper. Students should find their current automobile and discuss how much it is worth (or choose one to pretend is theirs). Compare answers. Challenge students to find one or two cars worth double the value of their current car and discuss the differences.

Officer: *May I please see your license and registration?*

Driver: *Yes, Officer. What seems to be the trouble?*

Officer: *You ran the stop sign back there.*

Driver: *I'm sorry. I did not see the sign.*

Officer: *OK, but I still need to give you a ticket. Sign here.*

Put the following sentences on the board: *You made an illegal left turn, You were driving the wrong way,* and *You were driving too fast in a school zone.*

Practice 1: 12–15 minutes
In pairs, have students practice the dialog, substituting offenses using those on the board. Ask the "police officer" to point to a sign that describes how the law was broken, prompting the "driver" to respond.

Evaluation 1: Ask for demonstrations.

Application: 18–20 minutes
Students should begin a new conversation to discuss driving experiences and other encounters with the police.

Level ★

Objective: Identify parts of a car.

Warm-up: 10–15 minutes
Write the word *safety* on the board. Help students to understand the definition. Present one or two examples of ways to stay safe. Have students help you make a list on the board of things that make people safe. Help them brainstorm by making suggestions, such as *locks on doors, fire extinguishers, traffic laws,* and automobile safety items such as *headlights* and *tires.*

Introduction: State the objective.

Presentation 1: 15–20 minutes
Have students open their dictionaries to **pages 120 and 121** and review the words together. Make a table on the board with three columns. Label the columns *inside the car, outside the car,* and *under the hood.* Define each of these categories and classify one item from the word list for each.

Practice 1: 7–10 minutes
Divide students into three groups to complete the table. Assign one category to each group and send group representatives to the board to fill in those columns.

Evaluation 1: Answer questions as students progress.

Presentation 2: 10–15 minutes
Prepare students to perform this model conversation.

> **Repairperson:** *May I help you?*
>
> **Customer:** *Yes, my battery is dead.*
>
> **Repairperson:** *OK, please sit down and I will be with you in a moment.*

Write other phrases on the board, such as *My car doesn't start, I have a flat tire, My car is overheating,* and *I need new windshield wipers.*

Practice 2: 10–12 minutes
Pair students to practice the exchange. Have students switch roles twice and substitute alternate phrases for the underlined phrase. Encourage students to develop other phrases from the word list or from personal experience. Hold a class discussion and ask students if any of them know how to fix any car problems on their own. Also discuss where they take cars for repairs.

Evaluation 2: Ask for volunteers to demonstrate in front of the class.

Application: 10–15 minutes
Read and allow time for students to do **Words in Action #2.** Bring in pictures of cars for students to copy or work from.

Parts of a Car

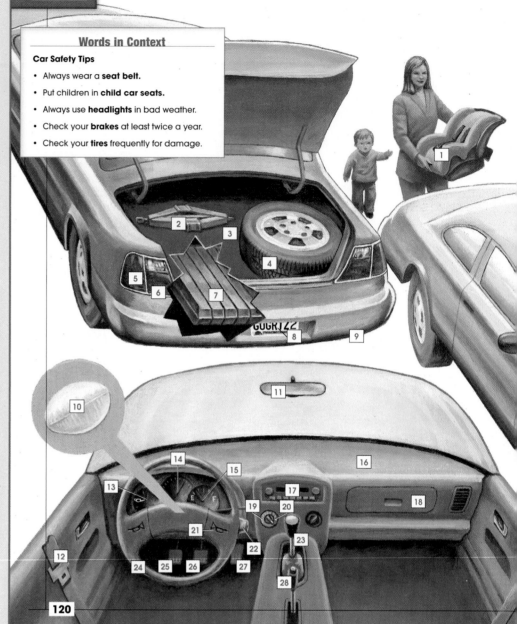

Words in Context

Car Safety Tips
- Always wear a **seat belt.**
- Put children in **child car seats.**
- Always use **headlights** in bad weather.
- Check your **brakes** at least twice a year.
- Check your **tires** frequently for damage.

120

Level ★ ★

Objective: Discuss proper car maintenance.

Warm-up: 10–15 minutes
In groups, students should read and discuss **Words in Action #1** on **page 121.** Set aside time to discuss their ideas.

Introduction: State the objective.

Presentation 1: 20–30 minutes
Direct attention to the word list on **pages 120 and 121.** After presenting, make sure students understand each item and then focus on **Word Partnerships.** Ask what other things students should *check* on the car. Help students understand the modal *should* and how to use it in giving advice. Consider drawing a chart to illustrate this modal's structure and use. Ask *How often should I check the battery?* Review other important areas to check on the car. Have another student respond: *Check it daily (weekly, monthly, twice a year, once a year).*

1 a child car seat
2 a jack
3 a trunk
4 a tire
5 a taillight
6 a brake light
7 a gas tank
8 a license plate

9 a bumper
10 an air bag
11 a rearview mirror
12 a seat belt
13 an oil gauge
14 a speedometer
15 a gas gauge
16 a dashboard
17 a radio

18 a glove compartment
19 air conditioning
20 heater
21 a horn
22 an ignition
23 a gearshift
24 a steering wheel
25 a clutch
26 a brake pedal
27 an accelerator / a gas pedal

28 an emergency brake
29 a windshield wiper
30 a hood
31 a fender
32 an engine / a motor
33 a battery
34 jumper cables
35 a radiator
36 a turn signal
37 a headlight

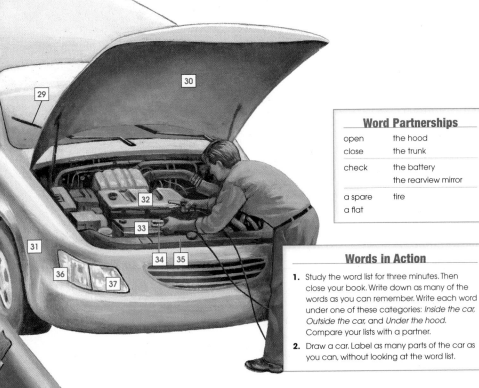

Word Partnerships

open	the hood
close	the trunk
check	the battery
	the rearview mirror
a spare	tire
a flat	

Words in Action

1. Study the word list for three minutes. Then close your book. Write down as many of the words as you can remember. Write each word under one of these categories: *Inside the car, Outside the car,* and *Under the hood.* Compare your lists with a partner.

2. Draw a car. Label as many parts of the car as you can, without looking at the word list.

— 121 —

Objective: Develop a safety brochure.

Warm-up: 8–10 minutes
Assign small groups to read and discuss *Words in Context.* Allocate time for questions about vocabulary or content.

Introduction: State the objective.

Presentation 1: 15–20 minutes
Present the word list on **pages 120 and 121.** Make sure students understand each word and have them practice writing a few sentences about car parts. If possible, expand the list with student assistance. Review *Words in Context.* As a class, divide the information into two categories, *maintenance* and *safety.* Ask students to help classify each item from the word list into the proper category. Include additional items students may think of, such as *follow traffic laws* and *get an oil change.*

Practice 1: 20–30 minutes
Find out if there are any car experts in the room. Assign one to each group, and have that person explain what could happen to the car if the owner doesn't follow maintenance tips. Others should ask questions based on the word list and *Word Partnerships.* One group member should take notes, and another (not the expert) should report the information to the class. If there are no experts, ask students to use their best judgment in guessing what could happen if maintenance tips are not followed.
Evaluation 1: Listen to reports and create a two-column *if/then* chart on the board as students speak. When completed, review the conditional tense using the examples raised by students.

Application: 20–30 minutes
Ask students to imagine that their assigned group works for the Department of Motor Vehicles or a driving school. Their supervisor has issued an order that they should design a safety brochure for new drivers based on the information from the Presentation and *Words in Context.* Ask that groups discuss and compile a list of car safety tips and car maintenance techniques they can distribute to the community. Consider distributing the published brochures to the school or other English classes.

Project

In groups, students should choose the 15 words from **pages 120 and 121** that they consider the most important. All members of the group must agree on which 15 words to select. Challenge students to make a new picture dictionary page for lower-level students. The cars should illustrate the 15 vocabulary words and safety tips. Encourage students to use and label car pictures/diagrams from magazines, newspapers, and the Internet.

Have students add other car maintenance questions for the class to answer.

Practice 1: 15–20 minutes
Have pairs work on new student questions about car maintenance. Ask students to convert their conversations into advice statements using *You should.* Students should individually write schedules for their cars.

Evaluation 1: Ask volunteers to share problem and advice conversations with the class.

Application: 15–20 minutes
Read *Words in Context.* Have students rate themselves on how well they follow the advice given in *Words in Context.* They receive two points for each thing they do as directed, they receive one point for each thing they do on occasion, and they receive zero points for each thing they never do. Students tally their totals and write their sums on pieces of paper (without their names). Create a bar graph of the class results. Utilize the template available on the Activity Bank CD-ROM to facilitate this activity.

Level ★

Objective: Identify road trip vocabulary.

Warm-up: 10–15 minutes
Initiate a conversation about car ownership and drivers' licenses. Ask which students drive, and expand the discussion by asking how many miles per week they drive. Survey the class. Make a bar graph of the information from the poll. Use the Activity Bank CD-ROM bar graph template to facilitate this activity.

Introduction: State the objective.

Presentation 1: 15–20 minutes
Direct students to dictionary **pages 122 and 123.** Review the word list at least once. Make a table on the board with three columns labeled *the car, the driver,* and *both the car and driver.* As a class, begin categorizing action words from the dictionary into the appropriate columns.

Practice 1: 7–10 minutes
Pair students to complete the table. Combine everyone into two large groups and assign a leader to coordinate the answers. One group leader should fill in column 1 on the board; the other can be responsible for column 2.

Evaluation 1: As a class, discuss the answers.

Presentation 2: 8–10 minutes
Prepare students to do *Words in Action #1* by pantomiming a few actions. Call for a student volunteer to pantomime an action for the class. Evaluate how students understand by seeing if they correctly identify the vocabulary.

Practice 2: 8–10 minutes
Pair students for this practice activity. They continue by performing actions for the rest of the word list. All students should master one action with the approval of their partners. Have students perform these select actions for the other groups to identify the words. Compare students' actions.

Evaluation 2: Observe the activity.

Application: 12–15 minutes
Begin a discussion about road trips. Encourage students to talk about their own personal road trips. Individually, students should list each item from this lesson's vocabulary that they have experienced on a trip. Review dictionary **pages 118 through 121** and ask how these lessons on safety and cars are related. For example, have students discuss road signs that appear during the road trip in the dictionary.

Road Trip

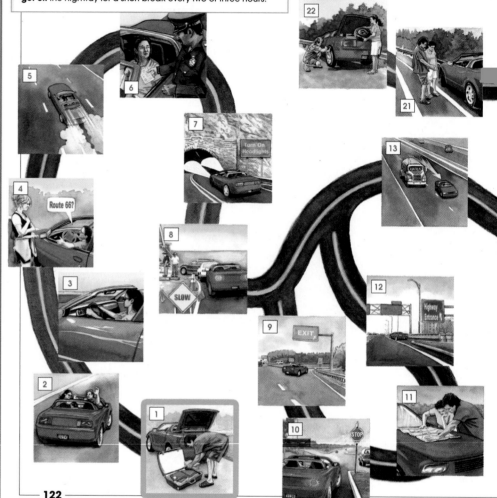

Words in Context

Here are some tips for a good **road trip.** Before you **leave,** make sure your car is running well. **Get** gas, **check** the oil, and **put** air in your tires. Take plenty of coins to **pay** tolls. Once you are on the road, **turn on** your headlights. Finally, make sure you **get off** the highway for a short break every two or three hours.

122

Level ★★

Objective: Use the past continuous tense to describe events.

Warm-up: 10–15 minutes
Ask students to open their dictionaries to **pages 122 and 123** and undertake *Words in Action #1.*

Introduction: State the objective.

Presentation 1: 20–30 minutes
Go over each of the words from the word list on **pages 122 and 123** with students. Present *Word Partnerships.* Ensure understanding before teaching the past continuous verb tense. Show students that to use this form, there must be two different events going on at the same time, or one event of shorter duration occurring (use simple past) during a longer event (use past continuous). Ask the class to name the two people pictured in the dictionary's road trip. Provide an example to show how *when* and *while* are used in different past tenses. Examples can

1 pack
2 leave
3 drive
4 ask for directions
5 speed up
6 get a speeding ticket
7 turn on the headlights
8 slow down

9 get off the highway
10 stop
11 look at a map
12 get on the highway
13 pass a truck
14 honk (the horn)
15 get gas
16 check the oil
17 wash the windshield
18 put air in the tires
19 have an accident
20 pull over
21 have a flat (tire)
22 change the tire
23 pay a toll
24 arrive at the destination
25 park (the car)

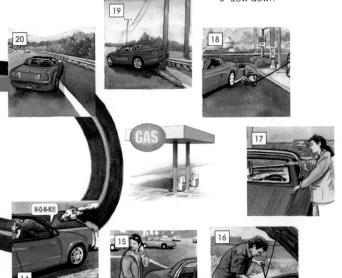

GAS

H-O-N-K!!!

Word Partnerships

pack	a suitcase
	a bag
stop	at a red light
	for gas
turn on	the windshield wipers
	the radio
	the air conditioning

Words in Action

1. Work with a partner. Act out a verb on the list. Your partner will guess the verb. Take turns.
2. Plan your "dream" road trip. Where will you go? What will you do on the trip?

— 123 —

include: *Jane was getting gas* <u>*when*</u> *John checked the oil* or *The phone rang* <u>*while*</u> *John and Jane* <u>*were leaving*</u>. Encourage students to use their imaginations.

Practice 1: 20–30 minutes
Make groups of two or three, depending on class size. Ask them to write 10 sentences about the picture using the past continuous and simple past. Encourage students to write five sentences with actions that happened simultaneously and five where one event concluded while another continued on.

Evaluation 1: Have students write some of their sentences on the board.

Application: 15–20 minutes
Ask students to write five sentences, each about something that happened to them while traveling or using public transportation. Tell them to use the simple past and the past continuous, including several sentences with actions happening at the same time and others describing two events with different durations. Schedule time for peer reading and editing.

Objective: Write a creative story.

Warm-up: 8–10 minutes
Direct attention to **pages 122 and 123.** Assign students to small groups to look over the pages and then read and discuss *Words in Context.*

Introduction: State the objective.

Presentation 1: 15–20 minutes
Go over the word list on **pages 122 and 123.** Make sure students understand the meaning of each item and can give a detailed description. Have students cover the word list in the dictionary. Explain that you will say a number and they should identify what is happening in the picture. Have students study the order of the road trip actions. Then, distribute scissors and copies of the worksheet available on the Activity Bank CD-ROM. Tell students that the worksheet should be cut into cards. With dictionaries closed, students should attempt to put the cards in the order that appears in the dictionary. Reopen the dictionaries and have students check their work.

Practice 1: 20–30 minutes
Place students in small groups to create a story using the past tense(s). Stories should be about the dictionary characters on **pages 122 and 123.** Pose a few questions to start. *Where did they go? Why did they go? How long were they gone?* Explain that students should answer the questions: *Who?, What?, When?, Where?, Why?* and *How?* In doing so, they will have the details needed to build a solid paragraph. To limit the length of the story, have students choose only five cards from Presentation 1 on which to base their stories.
Evaluation 1: Ask a volunteer from the group to tell the story that the group has created.

Application: 20–30 minutes
Students should recall a personal experience about public transportation or a road trip and tell this story to their assigned group. Do not let students use notes about the trip, but members of the group can assist. Allow time for students to think about the memories and then discuss. After group members ask questions, students should write their experiences in a paragraph, adding information that other students inquired about.

Project

Supply maps and atlases for classroom use. Students should work in groups to plan a road trip. They should plot their starting points and destinations, as well as five stops along the way. Additionally, ask them to identify where they will fill the car with gas, how long it will take them to drive to their destinations, and why they chose this route.

Level ★

Objective: Identify airport vocabulary.

Warm-up: 10–15 minutes
Divide students into small groups. Tell students to think of and list as many kinds of transportation as they can. Set a time limit dependent on students' prior knowledge and vocabulary skills. This is an ideal time to review previous lessons. Have students go through the dictionary. The group with the longest list records answers on the board while others offer more suggestions.

Introduction: State the objective.

Presentation 1: 15–20 minutes
Refer students to dictionary **pages 124 and 125.** Prepare students to do the activity suggested in **Words in Action #1** by formally reading the word list. Students will be able to hear the correct pronunciation as well as familiarize themselves with the vocabulary. Call out words randomly and ask students to point to the corresponding picture. Repeat this several times before having students cover the list.

Practice 1: 7–10 minutes
Pair students to continue the activity suggested in **Words in Action #1.** One student should cover the word list. The other reads the words and checks the answers. Encourage questions and discussion as you move about the room.

Evaluation 1: Observe the activity.

Presentation 2: 8–10 minutes
Prepare students to do **Words in Action #2** by starting a three-column table on the board, using the Activity Bank CD-ROM template. Teach the grammar rule that *nouns are people, places, and things.* Then, add the three categories of nouns as column headers. Place one example from the word list into each classification.

Practice 2: 10–15 minutes
In pairs, students should complete the table as suggested in **Words in Action #2.** Combine the class into three larger groups and assign each group one of the three categories to check through. Ask groups to fill in the column they are responsible for on the board.

Evaluation 2: With student help, check the final version of the table for accuracy.

Application: 10–15 minutes
Students should make a list of all the new vocabulary they learned from this lesson. Ask them to place a star next to five words they consider the most important to know from the lesson. Then have students make meaningful sentences with these words. Provide time for sharing and comparison.

Airport

Words in Context

Air travel is changing. **Airports** now have **automated check-in machines.** A **passenger** can quickly check in, choose a **seat,** and get a **boarding pass.** In the future, some **airplanes** will be bigger and some will fly much faster.

Airport

1 a terminal
2 a ticket
3 a photo ID
4 a ticket counter / a check-in counter
5 baggage / luggage
6 a passenger
7 an automated check-in machine
8 a boarding pass

124

Level ★ ★

Objective: Write sentences using airport vocabulary.

Warm-up: 10–15 minutes
Inform students that the lesson is about airports. In three columns, write the phrases: *people in an airport, places in an airport,* and *things in an airport.* Divide the class into three groups and assign each group to come up with as many nouns as they can under one

column's topic. Groups should put their lists on the board.

Introduction: State the objective.

Presentation 1: 20–30 minutes
Go over each of the words from the word list on **pages 124 and 125** as a class. Make sure students understand what each item is before presenting **Word Partnerships.** As a class, take the first few words on the word list and decide on a verb that can be associated with it. Ask students to write sentences for each noun/verb combination.

9 a metal detector

10 a security checkpoint

11 arrival and departure monitors

12 a helicopter

13 a runway

14 a gate

15 a pilot

16 a carry-on bag

17 customs

18 a customs (declaration) form

19 the baggage claim (area)

20 immigration

21 a line

Airplane / Plane

22 first class

23 economy (class) / coach (class)

24 an overhead compartment

25 an emergency exit

26 a flight attendant

27 a seat

28 a seat belt

29 an aisle

Word Partnerships

an aisle	seat
a middle / a center	
a window	
an electronic / an e-	ticket
a paper	
an arrival	terminal
a departure	
an international	

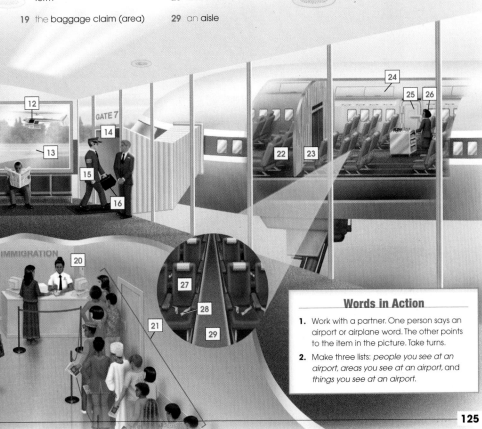

Words in Action

1. Work with a partner. One person says an airport or airplane word. The other points to the item in the picture. Take turns.

2. Make three lists: *people you see at an airport, areas you see at an airport,* and *things you see at an airport.*

125

Practice 1: 20–30 minutes
Divide the remaining words and assign pairs to write sentences for the other words on the word list. Students should first create a noun/verb list before attempting to write their sentences. Move about the room and help with grammar as needed.

Evaluation 1: Choose at least one sentence from each pair to be written on the board.

Application: 15–20 minutes
Review the simple past tense and past continuous of verbs and have students write five sentences in the past tense about things they have done or seen at an airport. Sentences should be grammatically correct. Combine students into small groups for sharing. Choose several exemplary sentences to be read to the class. Lead a discussion about these experiences and use airport vocabulary as often as possible.

Objective: Develop definitions.

Warm-up: 8–10 minutes
In groups, students should read and discuss *Words in Context*. Allow time for a class discussion and questions about the vocabulary and content.

Introduction: State the objective.

Presentation 1: 15–20 minutes
Study the word list on **pages 124 and 125** as a class. Discuss each item and make sure a general idea is understood for each. Challenge students to think about beginning English students and write a brief dictionary for their use. Pick two words from the word list and together write formal definitions for each. Evaluate how well students do. Write the following phrases on the board: *This is something that . . . , This is someone who . . . ,* and *This is a place where . . . .* Create a few complete definitions as a class.

Practice 1: 20–30 minutes
Place students in small groups to create definitions. Distribute small cards made before class with one of the vocabulary words written on each card. Prepare two cards for every word so students will be able to compare two definitions and learn how more than one can be correct. Students write the definitions on the opposite sides of the cards. After students have written their definitions, collect the cards and read the definitions to the other groups. See how well students define the word.

Evaluation 1: Use the flashcards to evaluate progress.

Application: 20–30 minutes
Ask students to create a personal set of flashcards. They should write their own definitions based on previously suggested definitions plus their own input. Additionally, challenge them to help define their words by classifying each as a person, place, or thing—as in *Words in Action #2.* Ask groups to share their definitions with classmates.

Project

Have students imagine they are taking a trip. Place students in groups and have members choose any destination they wish to travel to. The only requirement is that they travel by plane. Students should submit a scenario of events beginning with leaving home for the airport and ending with leaving their destination airport. All vocabulary from the word list should be used in chronological order and may be written as a dialog. To cap this activity, students perform a skit, using as many of the words from the list as possible. Stage a competition where the group that uses the most words wins.

Taking a Flight

Level ★

Objective: Identify flight vocabulary.

Warm-up: 10–15 minutes
Preview the lesson and develop actions to accompany key words on the list. When students arrive, tell them to think of verbs to describe your actions or define your location. Pantomime departure preparation, getting on an airplane, and in-flight activities. Encourage students to guess what verbs denote the actions you are performing. Include a few challenges, such as getting stopped when you go through the metal detector.

Introduction: State the objective.

Presentation 1: 15–20 minutes
Ask students to open their dictionaries to **pages 126 and 127**. Concentrate on words that are new to students. Read the list aloud or play audio to help students with pronunciation. Create pantomimes for items one through five on the word list. Quiz the class on those five out of order.

Practice 1: 7–10 minutes
Divide the class into groups and assign each group a portion of the word list. Group members should create pantomimes of the different actions assigned to their group.

Evaluation 1: Members stand in front of the classroom and perform their pantomimes while the class guesses.

Presentation 2: 8–10 minutes
Answer any questions about the word list and help students learn words that can be associated with the verbs. Say one of the nouns from the word list, such as *gate*, and see if students can associate the word with a verb. For example, say *gate* and help students respond with *wait at the gate* or *go to the gate*. Repeat this several times with several words. Alert students that there can be multiple answers. Accept any reasonable answers and respond to questions as they arise.

Practice 2: 10–15 minutes
Pair students for a quizzing exercise. By now, they should feel comfortable giving each other words and associating them with verbs—without referring to the word list.

Evaluation 2: Observe the activity. Assist with pronunciation.

Application: 10–15 minutes
Describe *time or chronological order* in terms students will understand. Let them imagine they are going on a trip. Each student should write what actions he or she would take and list them in chronological order. Ask *When you go on a trip, what do you do first?* to get them started.

Words in Context

Air Travel Tips

- **Check in** early.
- When you **board** the plane, **stow** your carry-on bag.
- Drink plenty of water.
- **Stretch** often.
- **Ask for** a pillow. Put your seat back, and try to sleep as much as possible.

126

1 check in
2 show your ID
3 check your baggage
4 get your boarding pass
5 go through security
6 check the monitors
7 wait at the gate
8 board the plane
9 find your seat
10 stow your carry-on bag
11 turn off your cell phone
12 fasten your seat belt
13 take off
14 ask for a pillow
15 turn on the overhead light
16 put on your headphones
17 listen to music
18 put your tray table down
19 stretch
20 choose a meal
21 land
22 unfasten your seat belt
23 get off the plane
24 claim your bags

Level ★ ★

Objective: Form questions.

Warm-up: 10–15 minutes
Students should pretend that they are taking a three-hour flight (pick a destination three hours from your location) and that they will be gone for three days. Ask them to make a list of all the items they will take on the trip. Ask volunteers to report to the class. Encourage use of the dictionary pages.

Introduction: State the objective.

Presentation 1: 20–30 minutes
Present all vocabulary from the word list on **pages 126 and 127** and ask students to provide meanings through definition, pantomime, or sentence formation. Ensure understanding of what each item means before including **Word Partnerships**. Ask if students can add to the **Word Partnerships**. Brainstorm with students about what the people in the dictionary picture are saying to each other, maintaining focus on questions people

Pillow, please.

Word Partnerships	
wait	for a boarding call
	in line
go through	a metal detector
	customs
	immigration

Words in Action

1. Work with a partner. Pretend to do one of the actions on the word list. Your partner will guess what action you are doing. Take turns.

2. Make a list of things you can do on a plane to be safe. Make another list of things you can do to be comfortable.

127

Objective: Create a test.

Warm-up: 8–10 minutes
Provide a few minutes for students to peruse **pages 126 and 127**. Read *Words in Action #2* and ask students to complete the task. Use the two-column table template from the Activity Bank CD-ROM to title and create the lists. Discuss as desired. Finally, ask one volunteer to read *Words in Context* aloud to the class. Allot time for students to add new items to their lists.

Introduction: State the objective.

Presentation 1: 15–20 minutes
Discuss the word list on **pages 126 and 127**. Before proceeding, students should understand each item and be able to describe it in detail. Formally present types of test questions and include matching, multiple-choice, short-answer, and fill-in-the-blank. Write an example of each type of question. Be selective in your examples. You may wish to make a few examples from the page, but feel free to use words from previous lessons. This will offer a review of other lessons and save words for students to use.

Practice 1: 20–40 minutes
Assign groups and ask students to imagine they are new teachers. In order to place students in the correct English class and check vocabulary, they will ask new students to take a test. Encourage creativity as they create a 30-question entrance examination and include all the question types from the Presentation. Each group should supply an answer key for their test.

Evaluation 1: Observe the activity and assist.

Application: 20–30 minutes
Copy the tests and hand them to other groups to take. Have the original groups score the tests, using the answer keys they developed. Ask students to critique the tests by offering opinions about which questions were too easy or too hard. Save one group's test to use as a review quiz later in the unit.

might ask when traveling. Review question formation with students.

Practice 1: 20–30 minutes
Form groups and have students create a question that corresponds to what the person might be asking for or responding to in each of the 24 pictures. Encourage students to rely on personal experiences. Depending on allotted time and class size, divide the pictures among groups.

Evaluation 1: Students can write some of their questions on the board. Have groups share questions with the class.

Application: 10–15 minutes
Generate a class conversation about personal experiences on board airplanes. Call for stories about plane trips students have taken and discuss the different airlines. Pose a question about what experiences are similar among airlines. Then, ask questions about differences among airlines. Students should write five questions that they might ask if flying on an airplane in the future.

Place students in groups and have them write an instruction manual for first-time airplane travelers. The manual should be written in chronological order and contain a list of frequently asked questions and responses that travelers and airport employees might discuss. Have someone in the group describe "a typical airplane trip."

Level ★

Objective: Identify modes of transportation.

Warm-up: 10–15 minutes
Review the lesson from **pages 118 and 119.** Go around the room so students can tell what modes of transportation they used to get to school. Pose questions such as *Did you come by bus?, Did you walk?,* and *Did you drive a car?* Take a class poll to determine what the members of the class use most and make a pie graph showing the results. Utilize the template found on the Activity Bank CD-ROM.

Introduction: State the objective.

Presentation 1: 15–20 minutes
Refer students to **pages 128 and 129** and follow along as new vocabulary is presented. Help students with pronunciation. As a class, divide the word list into different sections, including *bus, taxi, train,* and *subway.* Students may offer other modes of transportation, such as *bicycle, motorcycle, car, boat,* and *plane.* Start a cluster activity with the center circle labeled *transportation.* The secondary circles will be the modes of transportation, and the tertiary circles, which will be completed in the Practice, should be from the dictionary word list.

Practice 1: 10–15 minutes
In pairs, students should complete the cluster diagram. They may reference previous lessons. Each secondary circle should have a minimum of three tertiary circles. Distribute the cluster template from the Activity Bank CD-ROM.

Evaluation 1: Complete the cluster on the board.

Presentation 2: 10–15 minutes
Teach **Word Partnerships.** Prepare students to perform this model conversation.

  Student A: *How do you like to travel in the city?*

  Student B: *I like to take the bus.*

Review other possible answers.

Practice 2: 10–15 minutes
To get information for the exchange, students should speak with five classmates using variations of the conversation above. Students will complete a table with student names listed along the left and transportation methods along the top. Distribute the table outline from the Activity Bank CD-ROM.

Evaluation 2: Discuss the results.

Application: 10–15 minutes
Students rank transportation methods by preference. Share lists with the class.

Public Transportation

Words in Context

There are three ways to get from JFK Airport in New York to Manhattan. The first way is by **cab.** You can get a cab at the **taxi stand.** The **fare** is about $35.00. The second way is by **bus.** You can catch a bus from the **bus stop** outside the airport. The **ticket** is about $13.00. The bus will take you to a Manhattan **train station** or hotel. The third way is by **subway.** Go to the JFK Airport **subway station.** The subway will take you into Manhattan. This is the cheapest way. It costs only $2.00.

1 a taxi stand	13 a conductor
2 a meter	14 a track
3 the fare	15 a strap
4 a taxi / a cab	16 a (subway) line
5 a taxi driver / a cab driver	17 a ferry
6 a passenger	18 a subway (train)
7 a bus stop	19 a platform
8 a bus driver	20 a token
9 a bus	21 a fare card
10 a ticket window	22 a schedule
11 a ticket	23 a turnstile
12 a train	

128

Level ★ ★

Objective: Form sentences.

Warm-up: 15–20 minutes
Have students peruse the words and pictures on **pages 128 and 129** before dividing into small groups. One group member should read *Words in Action #1* aloud. Schedule a limited time for groups to ask and answer the questions posed.

Introduction: State the objective.

Presentation 1: 20–30 minutes
Teach the word list on **pages 128 and 129** in lecture format. Make sure students understand what each item means before proceeding to *Word Partnerships.* Prepare students to do the activity suggested in *Words in Action #2.* Challenge students to attempt this activity without writing any information. They should try to be as spontaneous as they can with their reactions and sentences. Students should strive to be understood, but not lose time making each sentence perfect.

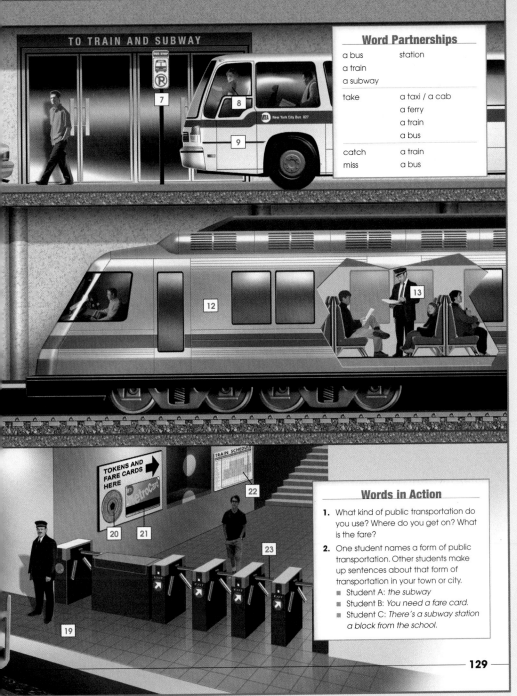

Word Partnerships

a bus	station
a train	
a subway	
take	a taxi / a cab
	a ferry
	a train
	a bus
catch	a train
miss	a bus

Words in Action

1. What kind of public transportation do you use? Where do you get on? What is the fare?

2. One student names a form of public transportation. Other students make up sentences about that form of transportation in your town or city.
   - Student A: *the subway*
   - Student B: *You need a fare card.*
   - Student C: *There's a subway station a block from the school.*

— **129** —

Objective: Write a paragraph.

Warm-up: 20–30 minutes
Begin with students creating a list of every word they know that is associated with public transportation. After they complete their lists, they should draw a line below the last word. Ask them to find two new items from five other students for a total of ten additional items to write below the line. Set aside student discussion time. In small groups, students should organize their lists into meaningful categories.

Introduction: State the objective.

Presentation 1: 15–20 minutes
Discuss the word list on **pages 128 and 129** as a class. Make sure students understand the meaning of each item and can use the words in sentences. Read *Words in Context* with students and discuss how people can travel from the school to important areas in their community. Discuss the function of transitional expressions and provide examples. Focus on how and why transitions are used in the paragraph on **page 128**. Review paragraph structure. Write the following information on the board:

From Disneyland to LAX—34 miles

Forms of transportation: airport shuttle, bus, and taxi.

As a class, decide the best transportation for this trip. Discuss potential costs. If possible, investigate the costs and make a bar graph depicting the differences.

Practice 1: 20–30 minutes
Ask students to write a paragraph, paying close attention to form. Their topic sentence should be about traveling from a city airport to a famous place. They may use *Words in Context* as a model.

Evaluation 1: Review the paragraphs as a class. Have other students ask questions if information is confusing or unclear.

Application: 20–30 minutes
Ask students to write a paragraph about traveling to a landmark or the local airport. Their paragraphs should explain the pros and cons of using different methods of public transportation to get there.

Project

In groups, students can decide on the most popular landmarks in the community. Have them make a map showing the different places and then write directions from the school to one place on the map not in walking distance. The directions should instruct people to use the best mode of public transportation for that location.

Practice 1: 10–15 minutes
In groups, students should write sentences about each mode of public transportation on **pages 128 and 129,** beginning with *taxi*. Each member should give a unique sentence to the group before moving on to the next form of transportation. Encourage students to help and teach one another.

Evaluation 1: Observe the activity.

Application: 15–20 minutes
Pick a local landmark that can be arrived at by bus, taxi, and two other forms of transportation. Assign one area of the room to each of these forms of transportation. Ask students how they prefer to travel and send them to that area. Once in the corner, students discuss why they chose this mode of transportation. Remind them to use their sentences from the practice to get their conversations started. Call out a new landmark and have students switch corners for another conversation.

Up, Over, Around

Level ★

Objective: Give street directions.

Warm-up: 10–15 minutes
Ask questions about where students live. Discuss how many miles or kilometers they live from the school. Make a line graph showing the various distances students live from school. Show students how to calculate the average distance.

Introduction: State the objective.

Presentation 1: 15–20 minutes
Ask students to open their dictionaries to **pages 130 and 131.** Have students follow the roller coaster track with a finger to review each direction with a partner. Discuss the word list, paying special attention to any words new to students. Concentrate on teaching correct pronunciation. Next, draw a new map on the board or overhead projector as you describe directions from the school to a place in the community. Go over the map a second time and write sentences to describe the directions. Ask students to help provide the return directions. Use *turn right, turn left, go straight,* and *turn around* to put the direction words in useful context. In this first presentation, avoid using prepositions of location like *under* and *over.*

Practice 1: 10–15 minutes
Choose three places in the community. In pairs, students should write round-trip directions to these places, using the sentences on the board as a model.

Evaluation 1: Check for accuracy when student volunteers write the directions on the board.

Presentation 2: 10–15 minutes
Review prepositions of location and other descriptive words that can be added to the directions students gave in the previous practice. Make a list of buildings and landmarks that students would pass to get to the first designated location from the Presentation. Focus student attention on how the directions can be improved by identifying landmarks.

Practice 2: 10–15 minutes
Schedule time for students to add to the directions they have written. They should include landmarks one would pass by.

Evaluation 2: Move about the room and help as needed. Ask for volunteers to read their directions with landmarks.

Application: 10–15 minutes
Students should write descriptive directions from their homes to the school. Additionally, have them reverse the directions as if they have invited a classmate over after class and he needs directions. For fun, complete the activity in *Words in Action #2.*

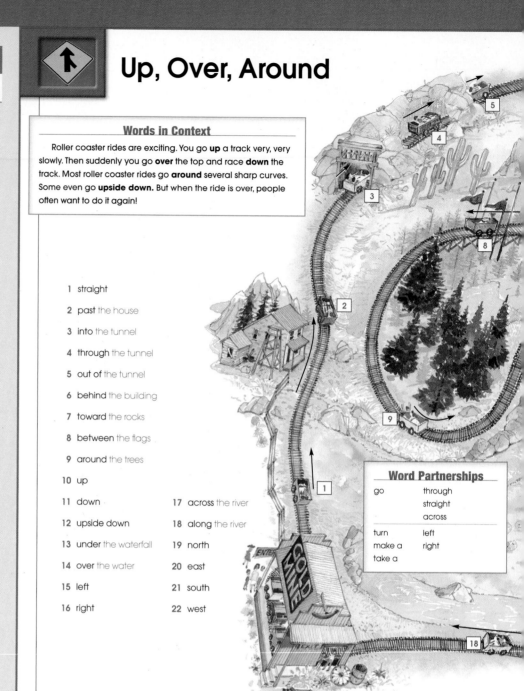

Words in Context

Roller coaster rides are exciting. You go **up** a track very, very slowly. Then suddenly you go **over** the top and race **down** the track. Most roller coaster rides go **around** several sharp curves. Some even go **upside down.** But when the ride is over, people often want to do it again!

1 straight
2 past the house
3 into the tunnel
4 through the tunnel
5 out of the tunnel
6 behind the building
7 toward the rocks
8 between the flags
9 around the trees
10 up
11 down
12 upside down
13 under the waterfall
14 over the water
15 left
16 right
17 across the river
18 along the river
19 north
20 east
21 south
22 west

Word Partnerships

go	through
	straight
	across
turn	left
make a	right
take a	

130

Level ★★

Objective: Ask for and give directions.

Warm-up: 10–15 minutes
In groups, students should discuss the question asked in **Words in Action #1.** Note if students use prepositions and direction words.

Introduction: State the objective.

Presentation 1: 20–30 minutes
Go over each of the words from the word list on **pages 130 and 131.** Review each item and include the phrases in **Word Partnerships.** After that, write this model conversation on the board.

Student A: *Excuse me. Can you give me directions?*

Student B: *Sure. Where do you want to go?*

Student A: *I need to go to the post office.*

Student B: *OK, I think I can help you.*

Identify four places: *the post office, a bank, a restaurant,* and *the city hall.*

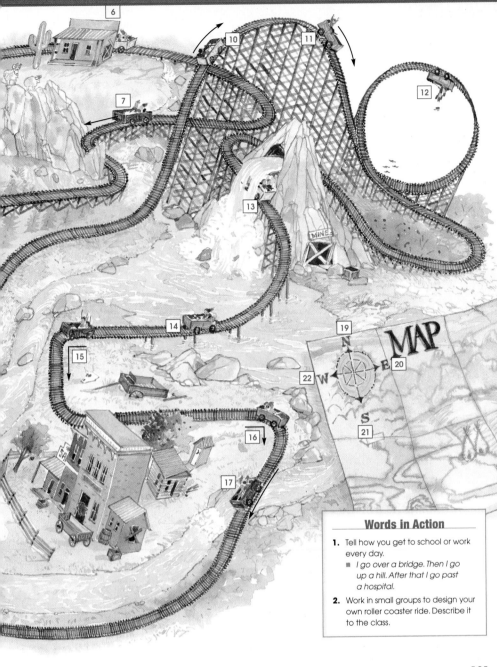

Words in Action

1. Tell how you get to school or work every day.
   - *I go over a bridge. Then I go up a hill. After that I go past a hospital.*
2. Work in small groups to design your own roller coaster ride. Describe it to the class.

— **131**

Objective: Describe a trip.

Warm-up: 15–20 minutes
Ask students if they have ever been to an amusement park. Stimulate discussion about what they liked and didn't like. Form groups and ask students to read *Words in Context*. Encourage questions and discussion about vocabulary and content.

Introduction: State the objective.

Presentation 1: 15–20 minutes
Present the word list on **pages 130 and 131**. Make sure students understand the meaning of each item. Describe a trip you have taken by car, bus, or train. Have students refer to **pages 122 and 123** as you describe the trip. Review any necessary definitions. Be sure to use the vocabulary from the word list as well as the *Word Partnerships*. Tell the story a second time and focus students' attention to the terms from **pages 130 and 131**. As you are telling your story again, students should point to corresponding words.

Practice 1: 20–30 minutes
Give students the following as dictation and repeat if necessary.
   My___(wife, husband, friend) and I took a road trip to Palm Springs, California. We live in Las Vegas, Nevada. We drove for five hours. We had to drive over a mountain pass. It was beautiful. We drove along a riverbed for several miles. When we reached the top, we found ourselves between two mountain peaks. What a wonderful view!

Evaluation 1: Write the paragraph on the board and ask students to evaluate their own dictations. Note problems or questions they have. Ask students to come to the board and underline new vocabulary. Discuss.

Application: 20–30 minutes
Using the Practice paragraph above as a model for student writing, assign students to write a paragraph about a road trip they have taken. Before beginning, lead students through a brainstorming session, discussing destinations and events that took place on their trips. Suggest that students jot down ideas and then create a time line for their paragraphs. Remind them to use proper paragraph format and complete sentences.

Practice 1: 15–20 minutes
Students should find a partner and arrange to give appropriate directions to the four places suggested in the Presentation. Consider switching partners for each location. Have students select other popular locations and devise directions.

Evaluation 1: Students demonstrate in front of the class. Assist as needed.

Application: 15–20 minutes
Supply a list of other less-known places in the community, such as small restaurants, stores, or government offices that are necessary but not often visited. Students can ask for and give directions to these places. They should each pick two places they are curious about and move around the room until they find someone who actually knows the directions. Bring in maps of the local community, if available. Many communities have maps on the Internet.

Project

Have students make a map of their community in groups. Ask them to write a brochure with directions to important nearby landmarks. Share the different brochures and take the best ideas from each to create one brochure for the class. Distribute copies to students to share with new students.

The Human Body

Level ★

Objective: Identify parts of the body.

Warm-up: 8–10 minutes
Instruct students to stand. Tell them to listen carefully and follow directions. Name different parts of the body and have students point to or touch that part. Students may follow other students' lead.

Introduction: State the objective.

Presentation 1: 15–20 minutes
Ask students to open their dictionaries to **pages 132 and 133.** Go over the new vocabulary. Read the list aloud to help students learn how to pronounce all words correctly. Say a part of the body and see if students can point to it in their dictionaries. Repeat this several times.

Practice 1: 8–10 minutes
In pairs, have students do *Words in Action #1.* Allow adequate time for discussion and presentation.

Evaluation 1: Observe the activity.

Presentation 2: 10–15 minutes
Prepare students to perform this model conversation.

Student A: *Where is the <u>wrist</u> in the picture?*

Student B: <u>*The wrist is here, number 7*</u> (points to where the part of the body is labeled).

Student A: *Is there another <u>wrist</u> in the picture?*

Student B: *Yes, there is one here* (points to another picture) or *No, there are no other <u>wrists</u> in the picture.*

Student A: *Where is your <u>wrist</u>?*

Student B: *My <u>wrist</u> is right here (points).*

Review plural nouns if necessary. Allow time for questions.

Practice 2: 10–15 minutes
With a partner, students should practice the exchange and substitute other words for the underlined one.

Evaluation 2: Volunteers demonstrate in front of the class.

Application: 10–15 minutes
Set aside time for quizzing. Students stand and face a partner. They take turns pointing to a part of their own body and their partner identifies it without the dictionary. Set a timer to ring every two minutes. After each signal, students switch partners and repeat the activity.

Words in Context

Always prepare for exercise. A ten-minute warm-up will stretch your **muscles** and get your **body** ready. Roll your **head** around in a circle. Move your **shoulders** up and down. Stretch your **arms** out and swing them in a circle. Bend your **knees,** and then stretch out your **legs.** Now you are ready to exercise.

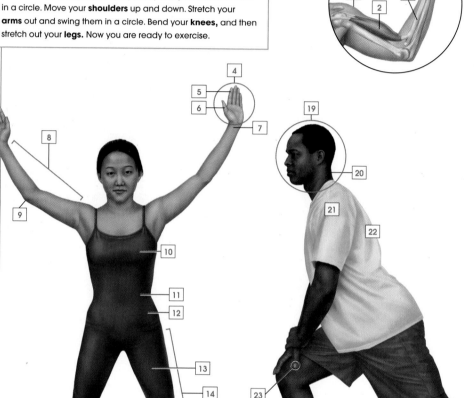

132

Level ★★

Objective: Express ailments.

Warm-up: 10–15 minutes
Tell students that the lesson focuses on parts of the body. Assign groups to create a list of parts of the body that they know. Stage a friendly competition to see which group can make the longest list of words. Have each group read their list and delete any items that other groups already have.

Introduction: State the objective.

Presentation 1: 20–30 minutes
Present the words on **pages 132 and 133.** Include **Word Partnerships.** Tell students that different parts of your body can hurt. Write *What is the matter?* on the board. Prepare students to perform this model conversation.

Student A: (pantomimes having a <u>headache</u>)

Student B: *What is the matter?*

Student A: *My <u>head</u> hurts.*

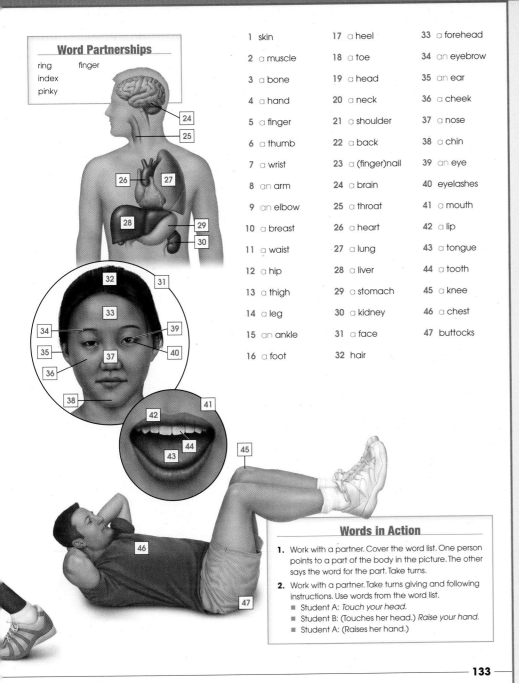

Word Partnerships

ring	finger
index	
pinky	

1	skin	17	a heel	33	a forehead
2	a muscle	18	a toe	34	an eyebrow
3	a bone	19	a head	35	an ear
4	a hand	20	a neck	36	a cheek
5	a finger	21	a shoulder	37	a nose
6	a thumb	22	a back	38	a chin
7	a wrist	23	a (finger)nail	39	an eye
8	an arm	24	a brain	40	eyelashes
9	an elbow	25	a throat	41	a mouth
10	a breast	26	a heart	42	a lip
11	a waist	27	a lung	43	a tongue
12	a hip	28	a liver	44	a tooth
13	a thigh	29	a stomach	45	a knee
14	a leg	30	a kidney	46	a chest
15	an ankle	31	a face	47	buttocks
16	a foot	32	hair		

Words in Action

1. Work with a partner. Cover the word list. One person points to a part of the body in the picture. The other says the word for the part. Take turns.

2. Work with a partner. Take turns giving and following instructions. Use words from the word list.
   - Student A: *Touch your head.*
   - Student B: (Touches her head.) *Raise your hand.*
   - Student A: (Raises her hand.)

— **133** —

Objective: Offer advice about exercise.

Warm-up: 15–20 minutes
Teach students to research exercise habits by asking other students if they exercise regularly and what they do specifically. Consider having students first gather information about classmates in a group setting. Continue by sending group representatives to meet with other groups in an effort to gain more information. Create a list of statistics about exercise habits and make a pie chart of exercise frequency per week.

Introduction: State the objective.

Presentation 1: 15–20 minutes
Discuss the word list on **pages 132 and 133**. Clearly define each word and ensure understanding. Initiate a conversation about what the people on the pages are doing. As a class, make a list of different exercises. Be prepared to demonstrate exercises, such as jumping jacks, sit-ups, and push-ups. Read *Words in Context* aloud as a class. Expand the discussion by focusing on warm-up activities. Review with students how to use *should* as a modal. Call for students to respond with other activities people can do to prepare for exercise. Have volunteers demonstrate.

Practice 1: 20–30 minutes
In groups, students should create a pamphlet on a proper warm-up. The pamphlet should explain a few exercises and why they are good for you. Encourage students to use the modal *should* as much as possible in this context.

Evaluation 1: Collect the finished products and share them with the other groups.

Application: 20–30 minutes
In small groups of three or four, students complete a list of pains and bodily injury. After brainstorming a list of possible remedies for the ailments, group members must agree on the best solution for each problem. Have students write their solutions in complete sentences using the word *should*.

Student B: *I'm sorry. Do you want an aspirin?*

Practice 1: 10–15 minutes
Students should choose a partner. Have them practice the exchange and substitute different problems and solutions. Generate a classroom discussion in which students name the ailments they discussed and the medical advice they offered.

Evaluation 1: Each pair should demonstrate one of their exchanges for the class. Discuss names for treatments as they come up.

Application: 20–22 minutes
Individually, students should make a list of the types of body pains they have most often. Encourage the group members to suggest solutions as students share their problems with a group. Bring the class together for a general session on pain or injury and medical solutions suggested. Tally the types of problems to see what are the most common health problems.

Project

As a class, discuss gyms and personal trainers. After guiding students toward health and exercise, divide them into groups of three or four. Group members should imagine that they are personal trainers. They should complete an exercise regimen for their client that includes exercises for 10 parts of the body.

Illnesses, Injuries, Symptoms, and Disabilities

Level ★

Objective: Identify illnesses and injuries.

Warm-up: 8–10 minutes
Ask students how they are today. The answer will probably be *fine* or *good*. Ask students what they say when they are sick. Ask them how often they get sick—for example, *once a week, once a month, three times a year.* Take a class poll.

Introduction: State the objective.

Presentation 1: 15–20 minutes
Have students open their dictionaries to **pages 134 and 135.** Go over the new vocabulary. Help students learn how to pronounce all words correctly. Write *illness, injury, symptom,* and *disability* on the board. Explain how these words are different. Give students one example of each. Make a table with four columns: *illness, injury, symptom,* and *disability.* Show students how to complete the table.

Practice 1: 10–15 minutes
Form groups and ask students to put all the words from the word list into the table. Discuss disabilities other than those pictured.

Evaluation 1: Complete the table as a class.

Presentation 2: 10–15 minutes
Prepare students to play Bingo. Ask students to choose and write eight words on a piece of paper or use the Bingo cards from the **Activity Bank CD-ROM.**

Practice 2: 10–15 minutes
Read the word list aloud. Tell students that the first one to hear and cross off all eight words should yell "Bingo!" To make this activity more of a challenge, pantomime the problem or use it in a sentence or paragraph.

Evaluation 2: Observe students.

Application: 7–10 minutes
Ask students to list five injuries or illnesses that they have had in the past five years. Ask them to share their list with a group. Help students use the verbs *had* and *was* appropriately. When they finish, have students write what they said in sentences. Students may want to keep their lists private. Explain that privacy is important in certain areas, such as medical conditions and financial information.

Words in Context

There are many reasons people visit the doctor's office. In winter, many people get a **sore throat**, a **cough**, or the **flu**. In summer, bad **sunburns** are common. **Earaches, stomachaches,** and **backaches** are common problems all year round.

Word Partnerships

a head	cold
a bad	
catch	a cold
have	a cold
	the flu
	a sore throat
feel	dizzy
	nauseous

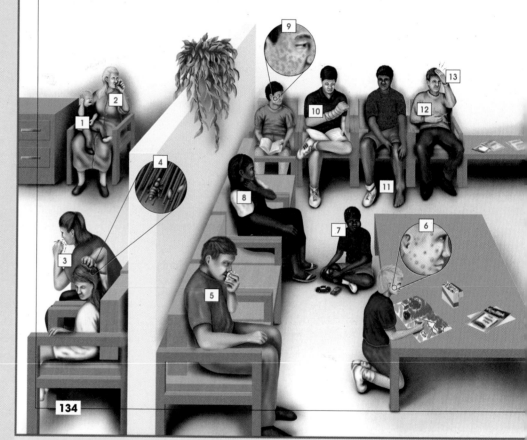

Level ★ ★

Objective: Make a doctor's appointment.

Warm-up: 10–15 minutes
Ask students to do the activity suggested in *Words in Action #2.* To make the task more challenging, have students add *symptoms* and *disabilities* to their lists. Then ask students to share their lists with partners.

Introduction: State the objective.

Presentation 1: 20–30 minutes
Go over each of the words from the word list on **pages 134 and 135** with students. Make sure they understand what each item means and include the *Word Partnerships.* Ask students to make a quick list of their illnesses and injuries in the last few years. Share a few of your own. Take a class poll of how many people have broken an arm or leg in their lives. Ask them how often they visit a doctor's office. Make a bar graph of the frequency of students' visits to doctors for

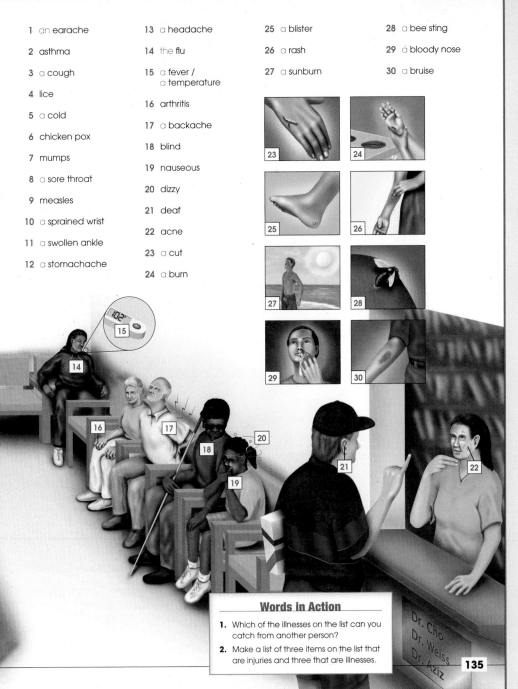

1 an earache
2 asthma
3 a cough
4 lice
5 a cold
6 chicken pox
7 mumps
8 a sore throat
9 measles
10 a sprained wrist
11 a swollen ankle
12 a stomachache

13 a headache
14 the flu
15 a fever / a temperature
16 arthritis
17 a backache
18 blind
19 nauseous
20 dizzy
21 deaf
22 acne
23 a cut
24 a burn

25 a blister
26 a rash
27 sunburn

28 a bee sting
29 a bloody nose
30 a bruise

Words in Action

1. Which of the illnesses on the list can you catch from another person?
2. Make a list of three items on the list that are injuries and three that are illnesses.

135

Level ★ ★ ★

Objective: Give advice on preventative measures.

Warm-up: 15–20 minutes
Draw a table on the board with four columns. The columns are headed by the four seasons. Ask students in groups to complete the chart by listing the most common illnesses and injuries that may occur in each season. Ask groups to share their results with the class. Then read *Words in Context* as a class and discuss it. Discuss reasons why certain injuries and illnesses seem to occur during different times of year.

Introduction: State the objective.

Presentation 1: 15–20 minutes
Go over the word list on **pages 134 and 135.** Make sure students understand the meaning of each item. Discuss what causes each illness. For example, sunburn may occur if one stays out in the sun too long. As a class, discuss possible causes for the illnesses, injuries, symptoms, and disabilities. Causes might include eating habits, exposure to contagious illnesses, improper clothing, accidents, etc.

Practice 1: 20–30 minutes
Ask students to discuss in groups how to prevent the items listed on the board. Ask each group to write down ideas.

Evaluation 1: Discuss the ideas as a class.

Application: 20–30 minutes
Review the use of should and shouldn't in giving advice or warning. Also remind students that they can use alternative phrases like: *It's a good idea to . . . , You might try to . . . , It is important to . . . ,* etc. Write these words on the board. Ask students to prepare a pamphlet describing ways to prevent many common symptoms, illnesses, and injuries. There is a worksheet on the Activity Bank CD-ROM to facilitate this activity.

checkups or health problems. Prepare students to do the following conversation.

Patient: *Hello, this is Julio Valentina. I need to make an appointment.*

Receptionist: *What is the problem?*

Patient: *I have a sore throat.*

Receptionist: *A sore throat —OK, we can schedule you for 2:00 today.*

Teach students when to use *a* and *the*, as in *the* mumps or *a* cold. Also teach students when to use *to have* or *to be*

with certain words on the list, such as *I am dizzy* and *I have a sore throat.*

Practice 1: 8–10 minutes
Ask students to perform the conversation, substituting different problems.

Evaluation 1: Ask for volunteers to demonstrate in front of the class.

Application: 20–30 minutes
Form groups and ask students to prepare and perform a skit for the class about scheduling and going to a doctor's appointment.

Project

Ask groups to imagine that they are working in an emergency room. Tell them that all the patients need help. Give a name to every individual on the page spread. Ask groups to prioritize the problems (to rank problems from the most important to the least important) and take patients in order of need. Also determine how much time the doctor(s) will probably take with each patient. If there are healthcare workers in the classroom, defer to their expertise as often as possible.

Level ★

Objective: Identify hurting and healing vocabulary and describe feelings.

Warm-up: 8–10 minutes
After informing students that a common question in English is *How are you?*, go around the room and ask each student to answer. Provide examples of responses, including *Terrible, Not bad, A little sick, Fine, thanks,* and *Great.* Allow time for students to ask and answer this question amongst themselves. Tell them that they can respond in any way they want except *Fine.* Show students other ways to phrase the question like a doctor or nurse might. Include *How are you feeling today?*

Introduction: State the objective.

Presentation 1: 10–15 minutes
Instruct students to open their dictionaries to **pages 136 and 137.** Go over the new vocabulary and the pronunciations. Warn students that this lesson contains words with many meanings. Point out how to use the items from the word list and *Word Partnerships* that start with *be.* Prepare students to do *Words in Action #2.* Students should respond with the problem or merely point to the picture from the dictionary.

Practice 1: 10–15 minutes
Schedule time for pairs to do *Words in Action #2.* As in the Presentation, students respond with the problem or merely point to the picture from the page spread.

Evaluation 1: Observe.

Presentation 2: 15–20 minutes
Demonstrate how students can describe how they feel by identifying a list of statements. Add to and adjust the list as necessary. Include: *I am in pain, I am sick, I have a cold, I have the flu, I am coughing a lot today, I am sneezing a little today, I am vomiting a lot today, I am having an allergic reaction to something,* and *I have a fever.* Prepare students to perform this model conversation.

Doctor: *How are you feeling today?*

Patient: *I am in pain.*

Doctor: *I will see what I can do for you.*

Practice 2: 8–10 minutes

In pairs, students practice the exchange, substituting information from the list you created.

Evaluation 2: Ask volunteers to demonstrate.

Application: 10–15 minutes
In small groups, students should talk about the last time they went to the doctor, but ask them to use the simple present tense as if it were happening at this moment.

Hurting and Healing

Words in Context

Are you **coughing** and **sneezing**? You probably have a cold. **Drink** plenty of fluids and **rest** as much as possible. Do you feel hot? **Take** your temperature. You might have the flu. **Make** an appointment with your doctor. He will **examine** you. You may need to **take** pills or get a shot. Follow your doctor's instructions. You will soon **feel** better.

1 be in pain
2 be unconscious
3 bleed
4 be in shock
5 break a leg
6 burn yourself
7 choke
8 cut yourself
9 drown
10 swallow poison
11 overdose (on drugs)
12 have an allergic reaction
13 have a heart attack
14 get a(n electric) shock
15 fall

Word Partnerships		
be	injured	
	hurt	
feel	much	better
	a little	

136

Level ★★

Objective: Describe emergencies.

Warm-up: 10–15 minutes
Initiate a conversation about car accidents. Volunteers can describe what happened in their accidents. Choose to share any personal anecdotes at this time. Proceed by determining who has called 911 for help and allow time to discuss these experiences.

Introduction: State the objective.

Presentation 1: 20–30 minutes
Go over each of the words from the word list on **pages 136 and 137** with students. Make sure they understand what each item means and include *Word Partnerships.* Talk to students about appropriate 911 calls and vote on which situations depicted on the page spread might lead to a 911 call. Talk about the situations where it would be wrong to call 911. Show students how to use the vocabulary in such a call. Offer explanations as necessary. Prepare students to perform this model conversation.

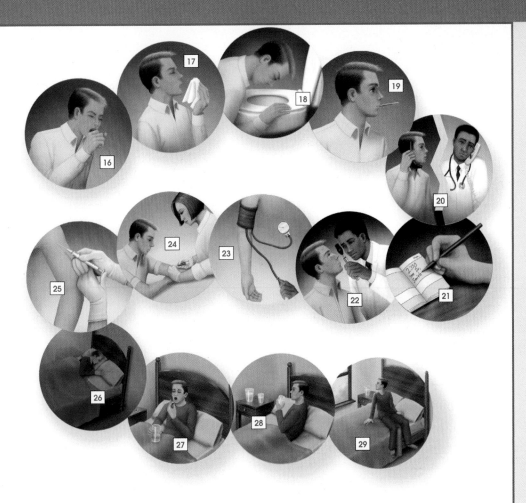

16 cough

17 sneeze

18 vomit / throw up

19 take your temperature

20 call the doctor

21 make an appointment

22 examine the patient

23 check his blood pressure

24 draw his blood

25 give him a shot

26 rest

27 take a pill

28 drink fluids

29 feel better

Words in Action

1. Look at page 136. Which things on the list are more likely to happen to adults? Which are more likely to happen to children?

2. Work with a partner. One person pretends to have one of the medical problems on the list. The other guesses the problem. Take turns.

— 137 —

Level ★★★

Objective: Give advice.

Warm-up: 15–20 minutes
Read *Words in Context* as a class and then assign students to small groups. Group members should discuss the differences between a cold and the flu. Compare group answers and create a master grid on the board.

Introduction: State the objective.

Presentation 1: 15–20 minutes
Present the word list on **pages 136 and 137** and include *Word Partnerships*. Make sure students understand the meaning of each item. Define *first aid* and encourage questions. Make a list on the board of certain *first aid techniques* that would be appropriate for the emergency situations described on the dictionary pages. Students should imagine that they are nurses in a clinic. Pose these questions: *What would a nurse say to patients with the ailments described? What would the advice be?* Help students to begin thinking of answers to these questions by running a brainstorming session.

Practice 1: 20–30 minutes
In groups, challenge students to write as many ailments as they can think of on a separate piece of paper. Have them name new situations or ailments not already included in the dictionary. For each problem, students should compile a list of what a doctor might say. Utilize the worksheet designed with a special table on the **Activity Bank CD-ROM** to facilitate this activity.

Evaluation 1: Have groups share their information with other groups and/or with the class.

Application: 20–30 minutes
Ask the same groups to create skits. The skits should include a person with an ailment, a telephone call to make a doctor's appointment, and a visit to the doctor. The conclusion of the skit must contain a nurse's or doctor's diagnosis and treatment.

---

911 Operator: *911. Can I help you?*

Caller: Yes. *There has been a car accident.*

911 Operator: *Is anyone hurt?*

Caller: Yes. *I think a woman is in shock!*

911 Operator: *I will send the paramedics immediately.*

Depending on comprehension, add name, address, and other pertinent information to the conversation. Remind students to never hang up until the operator tells them it's all right.

Practice 1: 8–10 minutes
Request that partners perform the conversation substituting different problems. Add questions about names and addresses if students are confident.

Evaluation 1: Evaluate class performances.

Application: 22–25 minutes
In groups, students should discuss what first aid might be required for each problem while awaiting 911. Ask for help from students trained in first aid.

Project

Supply each student with a small card listing an ailment. Begin by having students decide if their ailment is more likely to happen to an adult or a child, as suggested in *Words in Action #1*. After comparing answers, divide students into two groups: child ailments and adult ailments. Groups should create a safety pamphlet including *Dos* and *Don'ts (healthcare tips)* that might prevent these ailments.

Hospital

Level ★

Objective: Identify hospital vocabulary.

Warm-up: 8–10 minutes
Teach or review how to give location directions with students. Review lessons in which directions and prepositions of location were taught. In a classroom discussion, ask where the nearest hospital is and how to get there. Draw a map on the board and practice giving directions to the hospital. Students can practice doing this with a partner.

Introduction: State the objective.

Presentation 1: 10–15 minutes
Direct students to open their dictionaries to **pages 138 and 139** and follow along as you present each new vocabulary word from the list. Help students learn how to pronounce all words correctly. Prepare students to do the activity suggested in *Words in Action #1*. Draw a table on the board with three columns labeled *people, places,* and *things*. As a class, put one item from the word list in each column. Discuss why each was categorized the way it was.

Practice 1: 10–15 minutes
Assign three groups to do *Words in Action #1* by completing the three-column table started on the board. Supply copies of the template from the Activity Bank CD-ROM to help students with this activity.

Evaluation 1: Listen to group reports.

Presentation 2: 7–10 minutes
Ask students to cover the word list in preparation for an oral quiz. Say an item from the word list. Students should be able to point to the item and tell you if it is a *person, a place,* or *a thing*.

Practice 2: 10–12 minutes
Pairs should continue the quizzing exercise from the Presentation. Set aside time for students to switch partners a few times.

Evaluation 2: Observe the activity.

Application: 15–20 minutes
In groups, students should complete *Words in Action #2*. Half the students should write complete sentences about a patient's room, using words from the list. The other half should write sentences describing an operating room. Group students by which room they were describing and have them share, compare, and discuss their sentences.

Words in Context

Here are some things to look for in a **hospital:**
• Are the **doctors** and **nurses** friendly and helpful?
• Are there plenty of nurses at each **nurses' station**?
• Are the **patients** happy with the hospital?

1 a nurses' station
2 a nurse
3 an intensive care unit
4 an IV / an intravenous drip
5 an operating room
6 an X-ray
7 an anesthesiologist
8 an operating table
9 blood

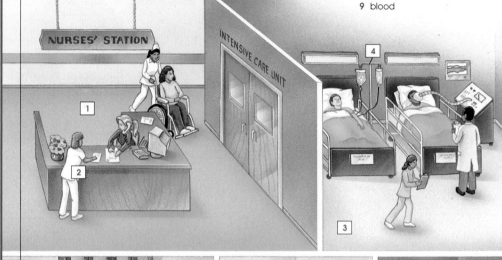

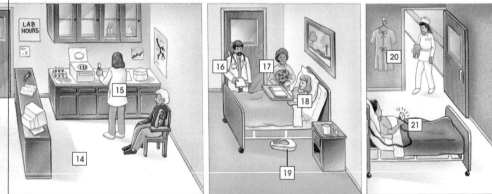

138

Level ★ ★

Objective: Describe actions in a hospital.

Warm-up: 15–20 minutes
Ask students to keep their dictionaries closed. Tell them that the lesson is about a hospital and hospital vocabulary. Make a four-column table on the board with the following headers: *emergency room, nurses' station, laboratory, patient's room,* and *operating room*. In groups, students should categorize as many people and things as possible for each room. After a time limit of 5–10 minutes, ask students to open their dictionaries to **pages 138 and 139.** Refer students to previous lessons in this unit for more help.

Introduction: State the objective.

Presentation 1: 15–20 minutes
Go over each of the words from the word list on **pages 138 and 139** as a class. Make sure students understand what each item means and then include

10 a surgeon

11 an operation

12 latex gloves

13 a (surgical) mask

14 a lab / a laboratory

15 a lab technician

16 a doctor

17 a visitor

18 a patient

19 a bedpan

20 a hospital gown

21 a call button

22 an orderly

23 a wheelchair

24 CPR / cardiopulmonary resuscitation

25 an emergency room

26 a paramedic / an EMT

27 a stretcher

28 stitches

29 an ambulance

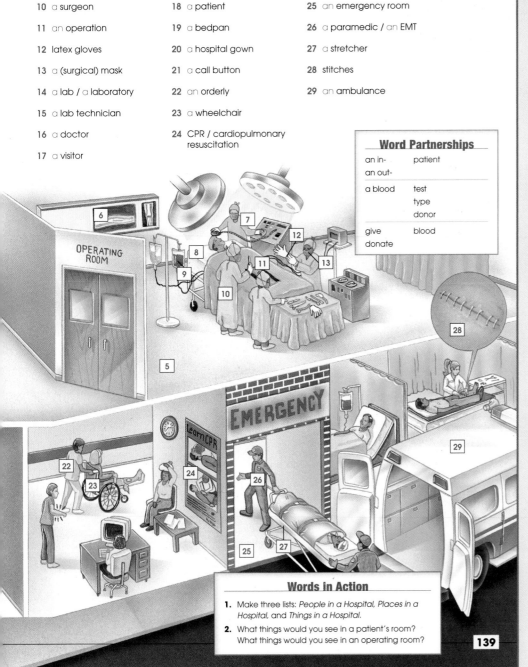

Word Partnerships

an in- an out-	patient
a blood	test type donor
give donate	blood

Words in Action

1. Make three lists: *People in a Hospital*, *Places in a Hospital*, and *Things in a Hospital*.

2. What things would you see in a patient's room? What things would you see in an operating room?

139

Word Partnerships. As a whole group, identify what people are doing on these two pages. Write a couple of example sentences on the board.

Practice 1: 15–20 minutes
Ask each student to write five sentences about what might be happening in this hospital. Have students choose actions to pantomime what they've written. Set up a charades game in which students act out their sentences for a group and see if the group members can reproduce the sentence.

Evaluation 1: Ask volunteers to demonstrate for the class.

Application: 15–20 minutes
Ask students to write a short paragraph about the hospital and what people are doing in it. Teach students the proper technique for sentence combining, so they may merely combine the sentences they already wrote in the Practice. Students should then add three new sentences to their paragraphs. Sentences should be complete and contain several words from the word list on **pages 138 and 139.**

Level ★

Objective: Identify medical center vocabulary.

Warm-up: 8–10 minutes
Begin by discussing where students go when they are sick. Some students might say they go to the hospital or doctor's office. Focus the discussion on specific types of medical care and ask students where they go if they have a toothache. Write *dentist* on the board. Then ask if students know where to go for glasses. Write *optometrist* on the board. Continue by suggesting other medical issues and adding the type of doctor to the list started.

Introduction: State the objective.

Presentation 1: 12–15 minutes
Ask students to open their dictionaries to **pages 140 and 141** and follow along as new vocabulary is presented. Spend time focused on clear pronunciation. Help students learn how to pronounce all multi-syllabic words correctly. Prepare students to do the activity suggested in *Words in Action #1.* Choose a student to help demonstrate if needed.

Practice 1: 8–10 minutes
In pairs, have students perform the activity detailed in *Words in Action #1.*

Evaluation 1: Observe the activity.

Presentation 2: 12–15 minutes
As a class, compile a two-column table, using the Activity Bank CD-ROM template, of all the medical people from the word list. Write the medical specialist in the first column. Write the body parts and/or type of people they treat in the second column. Write *dentist* in the first column. Have students write *teeth* in the second. Present the word *pediatrician.* Show students that they should write *children* in the second column. Write sentences on the board, using the information from student tables. Examples include: *A dentist works on teeth. A pediatrician works with children.*

Practice 2: 8–10 minutes
With a partner, students should make sentences about all the medical professionals. If students show that they know the word list well, ask that they keep the list covered and just rely on their two-column tables.

Evaluation 2: Students read and write sentences on the board.

Application: 12–15 minutes
Assign small groups to identify how often students go to different doctors. Make a list on the board of the doctors from the medical center and ask students to write the frequency of their visits. Suggest *once a month, once a year,* and *once every two years* to get students started. Groups can share answers with the class.

Medical Center

Words in Context

During a **physical,** a doctor does several tests. She listens to the patient's heart and lungs with a **stethoscope.** She checks the patient's blood pressure with a **blood pressure monitor.** For patients over 40, the doctor may also give the patient an **EKG.**

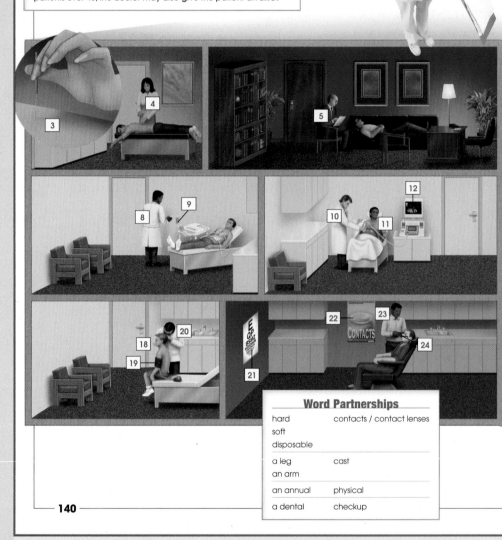

Word Partnerships

hard	contacts / contact lenses
soft	
disposable	
a leg	cast
an arm	
an annual	physical
a dental	checkup

140

Level ★ ★

Objective: Discuss medical jobs.

Warm-up: 15–18 minutes
Write *cast* on the board. Explain what it is. Follow with *crutches* and *sling.* Add dental words, such as *braces* and *fillings.* Explain what all these items are. Ask students to discuss in groups who has had any of these things, as suggested in *Words in Action #2.*

Introduction: State the objective.

Presentation 1: 15–20 minutes
Study each of the words from the word list on **pages 140 and 141** with students. Make sure students understand what each item means. Where appropriate, present the phrases in *Word Partnerships.* Ask students which doctors they are most nervous to visit. Discuss frequency of visits to different types of doctors. Students should offer their opinions about which medical person has the most difficult job and which has the easiest job. Encourage explanations for their thoughts.

1 a stethoscope

2 a medical chart

3 acupuncture

4 an acupuncturist

5 a psychologist

6 a waiting room

7 a pediatrician

8 a cardiologist

9 an EKG /
   an electrocardiogram

10 an obstetrician

11 a pregnant woman

12 a sonogram /
    an ultrasound

13 a sling

14 a crutch

15 a cast

16 a receptionist

17 an orthopedist

18 a physical (exam) /
    a checkup

19 a blood pressure
    monitor

20 a GP /
    a general practitioner

21 an eye chart

22 a contact (lens)

23 an optometrist

24 (eye)glasses

25 a (dental) hygienist

26 a dentist

27 a filling

28 a tooth

29 braces

30 gums

31 a drill

32 a cavity

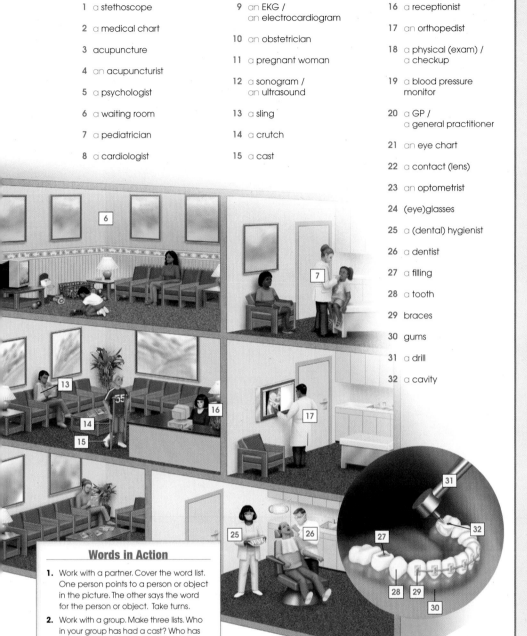

141

Words in Action

1. Work with a partner. Cover the word list. One person points to a person or object in the picture. The other says the word for the person or object. Take turns.

2. Work with a group. Make three lists. Who in your group has had a cast? Who has had a sling? Who has had crutches?

Objective: Compare and contrast healthcare systems.

Warm-up: 8–10 minutes
Generate opinions about what qualities make a good hospital. Accept all reasonable answers. As a class, read *Words in Context*. Encourage questions and discussion about the vocabulary.

Introduction: State the objective.

Presentation 1: 20–30 minutes
Formally present the word list on **pages 140 and 141**. It is necessary that students have a clear understanding of each item and practice defining the words before moving forward. Have students consider how many hours a year they spend in doctors' offices. Students should compute the hours but maintain a different time total for each type of doctor. Create a class bar or pie graph and discuss the implications of the busiest doctor or professional. There is a template for bar graphs on the Activity Bank CD-ROM.

Practice 1: 20–30 minutes
In groups, students should discuss the healthcare industry. Present information if students do not know much about it. Lead them to list the pros and cons of the current healthcare system. Have the groups expand their discussions and choose one other country to compare the current healthcare system to. How are they different? How are they similar? Have students complete a Venn diagram to describe their responses. Utilize the template for Venn diagrams located on the Activity Bank CD-ROM.

Evaluation 1: Compare Venn diagrams and discuss the differences.

Application: 20–30 minutes
Students write a paragraph about the similarities and differences in two healthcare systems. Encourage them to use the information already compiled from one of the Venn diagrams. They can take that information and write a well-organized paragraph with a strong topic sentence and a concluding statement.

Practice 1: 15–20 minutes
Place students in small groups to discuss and then rank the top three most difficult medical center jobs and the three that interest them most. All group members should try to agree before proceeding. For each medical professional named, groups should explain their choices. Students may want to include other jobs not mentioned in the dictionary, such as physician's assistant, nurse practitioner, and registered nurse.

Evaluation 1: Listen to group reports.

Application: 15–20 minutes
Assign each student one type of doctor or medical professional taught in the lesson. Students should imagine they are that type of doctor and write a few sentences about why they may or may not enjoy that job. When sentences are completed, students should join classmates who were assigned the same doctor and discuss their sentences.

Project

Review the floor plans for the medical center on **pages 140 and 141**. Assign students to create a floor plan for a new medical center. Where would certain offices be located? For each section of the floor plan, students should have reasons for their design. What other types of medical offices should be included that aren't in this building? Post the students' plans around the classroom.

Level ★

Objective: Identify pharmacy vocabulary.

Warm-up: 13–15 minutes
Ask students *Do you use home remedies?* Explain that home remedies are things they might use to help them when they are sick that do not come from a pharmacy or doctor. Give examples such as tea, honey, soft drinks, and chicken soup. Call for suggestions as to where people can go if they need to buy medicine. Make a list of suggested places where medicine can be purchased. As a class, make a list of medications students take for their ailments. Be prepared to discuss *prescriptions* versus *over-the-counter medicine*.

Introduction: State the objective.

Presentation 1: 15–30 minutes
Refer students to dictionary **pages 142 and 143.** Present the new vocabulary in detail. Take time to help students learn how to pronounce all words correctly. Make a list on the board of the following ailments: *cough, stomachache, itching eyes, headache, burns,* and *cuts*. Develop pantomimes for each of the ailments. Practice performing the pantomimes while students identify the problem. Prepare students to perform this model conversation.

> **Student A:** (Coughs) *I feel terrible.*
>
> **Student B:** *You should take cough syrup.*

Provide students with substitution phrases for the underlined portion, such as *take an antacid, use eye drops, take aspirin, use ointment,* and *get a bandage.*

Practice 1: 7–10 minutes
Pair students to first determine what medical problem requires each of the solutions given. Students should then practice the exchange with their partner, substituting actions and phrases for different ailments. Have students switch roles twice.

Evaluation 1: Volunteers can demonstrate in front of the class.

Presentation 2: 8–10 minutes
Ask students to cover the word list. Say particular items from the pharmacy and have students identify the item by pointing to it in the picture and saying its number.

Practice 2: 8–10 minutes
In pairs, students can quiz each other by continuing the activity from the Presentation.

Evaluation 2: Observe the activity.

Application: 12–15 minutes
Read **Words in Action #1.** Allow time for students to discuss, make a personal list of items, and present their findings. If they have most things, tell them to say what they <u>don't</u> have at home.

Pharmacy

Words in Context

Follow these steps to treat a cut.

- Press **gauze** on the cut. This will help stop the bleeding.
- Lift the cut above the heart.
- Clean the cut with soap and water. Then put **antibacterial ointment** on it.
- Cover the cut with a **sterile pad** and **sterile tape.**

Remember—accidents happen. Always keep a **first-aid kit** in your home.

1 a tablet
2 a capsule
3 a pill
4 prescription medicine
5 a pharmacist
6 over-the-counter medication
7 cough syrup
8 an antacid
9 (throat) lozenges
10 cough drops
11 an inhaler
12 a nasal (decongestant) spray
13 eyedrops
14 antihistamine
15 a prescription
16 a warning label
17 a cane
18 a knee brace
19 an elastic bandage
20 vitamins
21 a heating pad
22 hydrogen peroxide

142

Level ★ ★

Objective: Make purchases at a pharmacy.

Warm-up: 18–20 minutes
Write and discuss the following medications on the board: *cough drops, throat lozenges, aspirin, vitamins, antacid, nasal spray, cough syrup,* and *antibiotic ointment.* In groups, students should identify as many ailments as they can think of that these medications can help. Alert students that these products can often help more than one ailment. Schedule time for group reports.

Introduction: State the objective.

Presentation 1: 15–20 minutes
Read the words from the word list on **pages 142 and 143** and discuss definitions. Make sure they understand what each item means and then present the verbs in **Word Partnerships.** As a class, put a price estimate on each item in the word list. Prepare students to perform this model conversation.

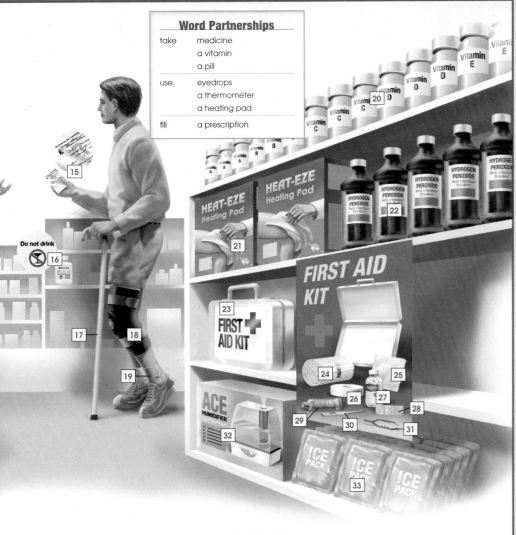

Word Partnerships

take	medicine
	a vitamin
	a pill
use	eyedrops
	a thermometer
	a heating pad
fill	a prescription

23 a first-aid kit

24 gauze

25 a sterile pad

26 sterile tape

27 aspirin

28 an adhesive bandage

29 antibacterial ointment / antibacterial cream

30 a thermometer

31 tweezers

32 a humidifier

33 an ice pack

Words in Action

1. Which pharmacy items on the word list do you have in your home?

2. Which pharmacy items are good for a cold? Which are good for a cut? Which are good for a sprain? Discuss with a partner.

Level ★ ★ ★

Objective: Discuss healthy lifestyles.

Warm-up: 8–10 minutes
Generate a discussion about *first aid* and determine who has experience giving first aid. Pose the question about what students would do if they had a very bad cut. Read **Words in Context** as a class and then allow time for students to discuss it in groups.

Introduction: State the objective.

Presentation 1: 15–25 minutes
Go over the word list on **pages 142 and 143** as a class. Make sure students understand the definitions of each word and can use the verbs in **Word Partnerships**. Assign all students a word from the word list and have them write a sentence using that word in context. Next, find out what students do to stay healthy and expect answers such as *exercise* and *sleep well*. Guide the discussion to include preventative medicine like *vitamins*. Determine what types of medicine students already have at home.

Practice 1: 20–30 minutes
Divide students into small groups to discuss ways to stay healthy. Challenge them to create a daily and weekly plan to do so. Suggest they begin with a plan for staying healthy but create another plan for when they do get sick. In the plan, students should list the items every home should have in case of medical emergency and/or illness.

Evaluation 1: Listen to group presentations.

Application: 20–30 minutes
Individually, students should evaluate their current health and set goals for themselves to avoid getting sick. When thinking about their medical conditions, each student should submit a list of items they don't currently have, but should keep, in the medicine cabinet.

Pharmacist: *Can I help you?*

Customer: *Yes. I need* <u>ointment</u> *and* <u>cough syrup</u>.

Pharmacist: *That is* <u>ointment</u> *and* <u>cough syrup</u>, *right?*

Customer: *That's right.*

Pharmacist: *Your total is $_____.*

Practice 1: 12–15 minutes
Partners should practice the exchange until they have replaced the underlined items with every word from the word list at least once.

Evaluation 1: Each set of partners should demonstrate.

Application: 15–20 minutes
Individually, students should list the five items they purchase most often and the five they buy least often. For each, they should be able to tell their classmates why they buy so much or so little of each item. If time permits, students can discuss where they purchase these items and how much they cost.

Project

In groups of five, students should be encouraged to imagine that they are in a new home with no medical supplies. Ask them to make a shopping list of items to buy at the pharmacy for a family of five with children, teenagers, and adults. Have each group write its list on the board and compare with other lists. Students can state their rationales for their inclusions and deletions.

Level ★

Objective: Identify soap, comb, and floss vocabulary.

Warm-up: 8–10 minutes
Plan to bring examples of several word list items to class. Write *comb* and *brush* on the board. Act out using each and use examples brought to class. Pantomime using a *hair dryer, lipstick,* and *nail clippers*. Write these words on the board. Determine which students have each product at home and see how many words the class can list on the board.

Introduction: State the objective.

Presentation 1: 10–15 minutes
Direct students to open their dictionaries to **pages 144 and 145.** Go over the new vocabulary and encourage discussion and questions. Set aside time to help students learn how to pronounce all words correctly. Review the pantomimes developed in the Warm-up.

Practice 1: 8–10 minutes
Divide students into two large groups to come up with additional pantomimes for every item on the word list. Students should then find a partner from the other group. Partners should perform the pantomimes, as suggested in *Words in Action #2.*

Evaluation 1: Each pair should perform one or two of their pantomimes for the class.

Presentation 2: 10–12 minutes
Create a table on the board with two columns. Label one column *men* and the other *women*. Students should determine the products used mostly by women and the products used mostly by men. Categorize one item from the word list into each column as an example.

Practice 2: 12–15 minutes
Pairs should complete the table. If necessary, explain how to make a Venn diagram or review Venn diagrams created in earlier lessons. Ask partners to place their results into a Venn diagram. Provide copies of the template available on the Activity Bank CD-ROM.

Evaluation 2: Observe the activity.

Application: 12–15 minutes
Students should make a list of the items currently in their homes. They should write how many they have next to each item and mark a check next to the items they use every day. Allow time for discussion and focus attention on the differences between products for men and women.

Soap, Comb, and Floss

Words in Context

Did you know?

- The first **combs** were fish bones.
- Before **toothbrushes** and **toothpaste,** people cleaned their teeth with charcoal, lemon juice, or tobacco.
- In ancient Egypt, both men and women wore **makeup.**
- The Egyptians used red berries to make **rouge.**
- The Egyptians used bright red insects to make **lipstick.**

1 hairspray
2 shampoo
3 conditioner
4 hair gel
5 a curling iron
6 a blow dryer / a hair dryer
7 a barrette
8 a comb
9 rollers / curlers
10 a (hair)brush
11 nail polish
12 a nail clipper
13 dental floss
14 toothpaste
15 a toothbrush
16 shaving cream
17 aftershave
18 a razor
19 an electric shaver / an electric razor
20 deodorant
21 perfume
22 sunscreen
23 lotion
24 soap
25 tissues

Makeup
26 face powder
27 lipstick
28 blush / rouge
29 eye shadow
30 mascara
31 eyeliner

144

Level ★ ★

Objective: Determine uses and users of products.

Warm-up: 15–18 minutes
Write *cosmetics* or *toiletries* on the board. Split students into groups of all men and all women. They should create a list of all the *cosmetics* they can think of. Discuss the types of cosmetics men use, such as shaving cream and skin lotion, and compare with the types of cosmetics the women listed. Bring the groups together by listing products both men and women use.

Introduction: State the objective.

Presentation 1: 15–20 minutes
Go over each of the words from the word list on **pages 144 and 145** and pay special attention to items that were not mentioned in the Warm-up. Make sure students understand what each item means before including the words in *Word Partnerships.* Call for student opinions about what they consider to be

Verbs

32 wash

33 rinse

34 comb

35 (blow) dry

36 brush

37 cut

Word Partnerships

a disposable a dull	razor
nail polish	remover
hand face antibacterial	soap
hand body	lotion
put on wear	aftershave mascara lipstick

Words in Action

1. What things from the list do you use every day?
2. Work with a partner. One person pretends to use one of the items from the list. The other guesses what it is. Take turns.

145

Objective: Discuss makeup use.

Warm-up: 8–10 minutes
Initiate a group conversation about hair care and encourage students to offer their own personal daily hair care techniques. Have students recommend specific products and make a list. Read *Words in Context* and allow students time to discuss the reading with a small group.

Introduction: State the objective.

Presentation 1: 15–25 minutes
Formally present the word list on **pages 144 and 145.** Ensure clear comprehension of each item's function. Start a class discussion about what makeup students consider to be designed only for women. Expand the discussion to include opinions about which items women like to use. Ask men if they think makeup is important. Allow time for argument on this topic. Continue the discussion by posing similar questions about amounts of makeup and styles of makeup.

Practice 1: 20–30 minutes
Divide students into groups of all males and all females. Encourage them to expand their thoughts on the ideas from the Presentation. The groups should report on what they can agree upon. Note general ideas on the board as the groups present. As a class, determine common themes of the women's groups and those of the men's groups.

Evaluation 1: As a class, compare comments the female groups had in common with the male groups. Note any differences that men and women have about makeup. Encourage discussion and questions.

Application: 20–30 minutes
Ask students to create a list of 10 products from **pages 144 and 145** that they think are most important to have at home. For each, they should have a reason why that product is important. Let students know that their reasons can be based on who lives in the home. Students can share ideas with a group and take note of generalizations.

the most important things on the list for men and for women. Add any missing vocabulary students mention.

Practice 1: 10–15 minutes
Back in groups, students should rank the items from most needed to least needed for both men and women. All groups should create lists for both genders.

Evaluation 1: Listen to groups report to the class and compare their answers.

Application: 20–30 minutes
Divide students into gender-mixed groups and encourage them to imagine that they have a store that sells only the items pictured in the dictionary. Tell students that approximately 100 people buy things in their store every day and that they receive new merchandise once a month. Challenge students to make an inventory of the stock they should keep. Include number of items, prices, and sales of the item per week. Supply copies of the worksheet available on the **Activity Bank CD-ROM** for students to use as they develop their stock.

Project

In groups, students should create companies that sell their products from a catalog. Group members should decide which items from the word list they will feature and what colors and quantities each product is available in. Different sizes, colors, and combinations should then be priced. Supply magazines, markers, and colored pencils for students to create pages for their catalogs. Allow time for presentations.

Level ★

Objective: Identify job titles.

Warm-up: 10–12 minutes
Start a list on the board titled *jobs*. Write *teacher, student,* and *homemaker* so students understand what the goal is. Ask students to think of more jobs and have them name 10 to 15 jobs, depending on class level. Accept any reasonable job title. Go around the room and ask students what jobs they currently have. Have students describe their jobs.

Introduction: State the objective.

Presentation 1: 10–15 minutes
Direct students to open their dictionaries to **pages 146 and 147.** Move through the word list and pay special attention to words not previously covered in the Warm-up. Help students learn how to pronounce all words correctly. Form pairs, and allow time for them to practice. Call out jobs from the list in random order. Have students identify the job they hear by pointing to the correct picture and saying the corresponding number.

Practice 1: 7–10 minutes
In pairs, students should continue the quizzing activity with one partner saying job titles and the other responding by pointing to the pictures and saying the correct numbers. Ask them to switch roles an equal number of times.

Evaluation 1: Observe the activity.

Presentation 2: 10–12 minutes
Create a three-column table on the board labeled with *in offices, in stores,* and *outside.* Place one example in each category before asking students to help complete the chart. Use the template on the **Activity Bank CD-ROM** to facilitate this activity. Prepare students to perform this model conversation.

> **Student A:** *Where does a gardener work?*
>
> **Student B:** *A gardener works outside.*

Practice 2: 8–10 minutes
Ask partners to practice the exchange and substitute at least 10 jobs and locations each. Then have students reverse roles.

Evaluation 2: Listen to student exchanges. List jobs on the board and have volunteers write where each person in this job works.

Application: 15–20 minutes
Students should make a list of the five jobs from the word list they would most like to have. Divide students into conversation groups where they can compare lists and expand on why they chose those five jobs.

Jobs 1

Words in Context

What kind of work is right for you? Do you like to work with your hands? You could be a **carpenter**, an **assembler**, or a **construction worker**. Do you want to help people? You could be a **babysitter**, a **home health aide**, or a **doctor**. Are you creative? You could be a **hairstylist**, a **florist**, or an **architect**. Are you good with numbers? You could be an **accountant** or an **engineer**.

1 an accountant	9 a delivery person	17 a barber
2 a dentist	10 a computer technician	18 an assembler
3 an artist	11 a janitor / a custodian	19 an architect
4 a cook	12 a doctor	20 a butcher
5 a hairstylist / a hairdresser	13 a homemaker	21 a (home) health aide / a (home) attendant
6 a construction worker	14 a florist	22 an engineer
7 a graphic artist	15 a housekeeper	23 a businessman / a businesswoman
8 a gardener	16 an editor	

146

Level ★ ★

Objective: Write a job posting.

Warm-up: 10–15 minutes
Begin a discussion about students' hopes and dreams. Students should state why they are learning English and how English might help them in their future plans. Before students look at the dictionaries, ask them to make lists of different jobs or professions that might interest them in the future.

Introduction: State the objective.

Presentation 1: 20–30 minutes
Present the word list on **pages 146 and 147.** Make sure that students understand what each item means and can classify the items as *part-time, well-paid, blue-collar,* or *white-collar* jobs, as in **Word Partnerships.** Focus attention on where they might go to look for a job. Talk about job postings and create a posting on the board or show examples from local *help wanted ads.* Include *part-time, full-time, benefits, contact, experience,*

Word Partnerships

a	part-time	job
	well-paid	
	blue-collar	
	white-collar	
look for	a job	
apply for		
get		
lose		

24 a cashier

25 an actor

26 a carpenter

27 an electrician

28 a firefighter

29 a garment worker

30 a babysitter

Words in Action

1. Look at the list. What are the best five jobs to have? Why?
2. Which jobs are done in offices? Which are done in shops? Which are done outdoors? Make three lists.

147

Objective: Discuss talents and future plans.

Warm-up: 10–15 minutes
Explain to the class that the activity will be a timed competition. Set a time limit and have students write as many job titles as they can think of. Then, set a time limit for students to work in pairs to share and add to their lists. The pairs should repeat the timed exercise with another pair. The group with the most legitimate job titles is the winner.

Introduction: State the objective.

Presentation 1: 25–35 minutes
Read the word list on **pages 146 and 147** and make sure students understand the meaning of each item. Generate a conversation about what jobs students believe they have the most talent for and what those specific talents are. Suggest that their talents might include *working with hands or being creative*. Ask students which jobs need which talents. Start a table with two columns for *job* and *talents or skills*. Students can fill in the job titles for those jobs that require specific talents. Read *Words in Context* with students and discuss the jobs in more detail.

Practice 1: 20–30 minutes
Focus students' attention on their own individual talents and have students clearly express what they can do well. Students should create a second list of talents they want to develop. Once students have completed their lists, they should share their ideas with a small group. Have groups discuss and respond to the question in *Words in Action #1*.

Evaluation 1: Check for comprehension.

Application: 20–30 minutes
Ask students to write responses in complete sentences to the following questions.

What are your talents?
What do you like to do?
What do you do now?
What do you want to do in the future?

Review with students how to complete a Venn diagram. Show that the purpose is to find similarities and differences. Using the answers to each question, students should create four seperate Venn diagrams with a partner. Hand out copies of the Activity Bank CD-ROM template.

etc. Show possible abbreviations. Explain that there are no rules for abbreviations in ads. Ask students how they think postings would look for a few of the jobs in the dictionary.

Practice 1: 15–20 minutes
Divide students into small groups and assign each an equal number of jobs from the dictionary. Within groups, students should write advertisements for these jobs. The advertisements should include experience needed, contact person/number, and salary.

Have students mimic the help wanted ads online or in newspapers.

Evaluation 1: Evaluate group presentations.

Application: 15–20 minutes
Within the same groups, students should choose a job for each person. For each of these jobs, the group submits to the class a job posting. Have students read their postings aloud to the class. Provide time for students to compare and contrast job postings written for the same position.

Project

In groups, students should make a chart of the different jobs on the word list and include an estimated starting salary for each position. Groups should discuss reasons why people in some positions earn more than people in others. Write sample job postings for several of the positions. Follow up with Internet research.

Level ★

Objective: Identify job titles.

Warm-up: 5–8 minutes
Pantomime the actions of the following jobs: *mechanic, salesperson, taxi driver,* and *painter.* Write the words on the board as students guess correctly. Generate opinions from students about which person they think makes more money or has a higher salary. Define *salary* or any of the occupations as necessary.

Introduction: State the objective.

Presentation 1: 10–15 minutes
Instruct students to open their dictionaries to **pages 148 and 149.** Go over the new vocabulary in detail and teach proper pronunciation for all of the words. Review the pantomimes that were developed in the Warm-up. Create several more pantomimes as a class by calling for student suggestions.

Practice 1: 15–25 minutes
In groups, ask students to create additional pantomimes for every job on the word list. Explain that they will be performing their pantomimes for the class.

Evaluation 1: Ask for volunteers from groups to quiz the class.

Presentation 2: 8–10 minutes
Create a table on the board with two columns. Label one column *college education /vocational training necessary* and the other *only on-the-job training/no academic training.* See if students can find a job from the word list to go into each column. List a few examples as a class. Discuss the differences between a college education and vocational training. For the examples listed in column 1, discuss how much education is needed.

Practice 2: 12–15 minutes
Group students into teams. Each team should attempt to complete the table with the rest of the words in the list. For column 1, they should discuss which jobs require a college education and which require vocational training.

Evaluation 2: Hold a class discussion about students' ideas. There may be different opinions about the level of education each job requires.

Application: 10–15 minutes
Students should list the five jobs from the word list they would most like to have. For each, they should write a complete sentence about why that job appeals to them.

Jobs 2

Words in Context

There are many **jobs** in my family. I'm a **reporter** for a newspaper. My sister is a **musician.** My brother likes to work with animals, so he is a **veterinarian.** My other brother travels a lot. He's a **truck driver.** Our parents are **teachers.** They taught us to love work.

1 a reporter	10 a mechanic	20 a realtor
2 a manicurist	11 a police officer	21 a salesperson
3 a lawyer	12 a photographer	22 a tour guide
4 a soldier	13 a stockbroker	23 a pilot
5 a receptionist	14 a (house)painter	24 a musician
6 a physical therapist	15 a plumber	25 a writer
7 a locksmith	16 a scientist	26 a truck driver
8 a security guard	17 a taxi driver	27 a travel agent
9 a teacher / an instructor	18 a server	28 a veterinarian / vet
	19 a nurse	

148

Level ★ ★

Objective: Discuss tools for jobs.

Warm-up: 10–15 minutes
Focus attention on **pages 148 and 149** and divide students into groups to answer the question posed in *Words in Action #1.* The group members should negotiate and agree on the selected jobs. Discuss as a class.

Introduction: State the objective.

Presentation 1: 20–30 minutes
Present each of the words from the word list on **pages 148 and 149** to students. Make sure they understand each item and can understand adjectives, as demonstrated in *Word Partnerships.* Write *tools* and *equipment* on the board. Explain to students what these words mean. Call on students to indicate tools or equipment used in each of the jobs listed. Inform students that vehicles can also be considered equipment.

Word Partnerships

a fashion	photographer
a wedding	
a registered	nurse
a school	
a commercial	pilot
a private	
a fighter	

Words in Action

1. Look at the list. Which are the five most difficult jobs? Why? Which are the five easiest? Why?

2. Look at the list. Which people use vehicles in their jobs? What vehicles do they use? Which people use equipment in their jobs? What equipment do they use?

149

Working

Objective: Identify job actions and use the modal *can*.

Warm-up: 5–8 minutes
Write *office* on the board. Generate students' opinions about what people do in office settings. Pantomime some of the actions. Examples include *write, read, type, make copies, use a computer,* and *talk on the phone.* Be prepared to clarify or define these words for students. Help by writing them on the board.

Introduction: State the objective.

Presentation 1: 30–40 minutes
Direct attention to dictionary **pages 150 and 151.** Thoroughly discuss the new vocabulary. Help students learn how to pronounce all words correctly. Introduce *can* to students. Show them how *can* is followed by the base of the verb. Present a grammar chart on the board to aid comprehension. Review subject pronouns, specifically *he* and *she.* Prepare students to perform this model conversation.

Student A: (points to a picture) *What can she do?*

Student B: *She can take care of babies.*

Explain to students that most of the words on the list need additional vocabulary to complete the descriptions. Teach students these words and ask them to write them in their dictionaries. Because of the number of words being introduced, you may choose to have students practice with only a few.

Practice 1: 8–10 minutes
Allow time for students to practice the exchange with a partner. After they use the examples done as a class, ask them to write some sentences for other pictures.
Evaluation 1: Observe the activity.

Presentation 2: 8–10 minutes
Teach students how to do a Johari Squares activity by working with a student to complete one on the board. There is a template for Johari Squares on the Activity Bank CD-ROM. The squares include *I can do, my partner can do, my partner and I can do,* and *my partner and I can't do.*

Practice 2: 8–10 minutes
Ask partners to use the verbs from the word list to complete a four-part Johari Squares template on the Activity Bank CD-ROM. Change the squares categories to read *my partner and I can do; my partner can't do and I can do; my partner can do and I can't do; my partner and I can't do.*
Evaluation 2: Observe the activity.

Application: 8–10 minutes
Students should choose the five verbs from the word list they would most like to do on the job. They should mention if they already have experience doing each task.

Words in Context

Needed: Office Assistant

Can you answer phones, **take** messages, **schedule** appointments, and **file**? Can you **use** a computer and a fax machine? Can you **type** 50 words per minute? You may be the right person for this job. Call 555-9389 to schedule an appointment for an interview.

1 cook	9 take care of
2 examine	10 act / perform
3 speak	11 sing
4 arrest	12 take a message
5 open mail	13 hire
6 load	14 sell
7 deliver	15 repair / fix
8 type	16 plan

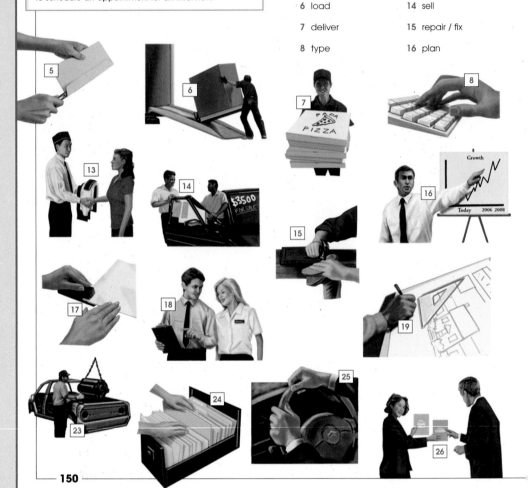

150

Objective: Use the present continuous verb tense.

Warm-up: 10–15 minutes
Read the word list on **pages 150 and 151** and allow time for students to consider the activity suggested in *Words in Action #1.* They should make a list and discuss their choices with a group. Have students write *I can take a message* and *use a computer*, varying the underlined portions.

Introduction: State the objective.

Presentation 1: 20–30 minutes
Teach each of the words from the word list on **pages 150 and 151.** Students should include the phrases in *Word Partnerships.* Introduce the present continuous in a grammar table on the board. Show students how they can describe all the verbs on the word list. Write *What is she doing?* on the board.

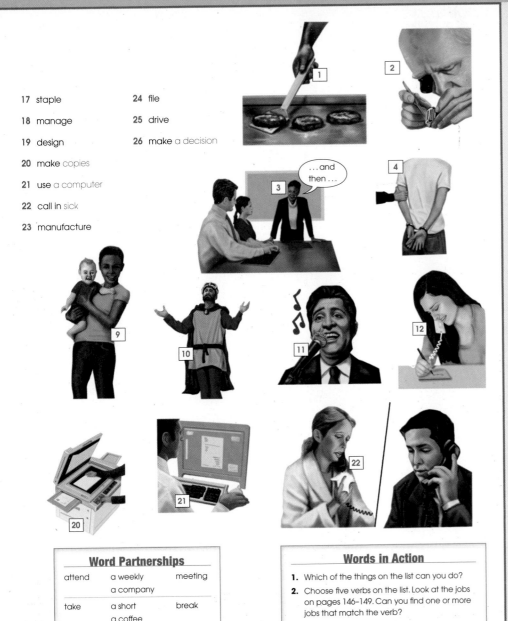

17 staple
18 manage
19 design
20 make copies
21 use a computer
22 call in sick
23 manufacture

24 file
25 drive
26 make a decision

…and then …

Word Partnerships

attend	a weekly a company	meeting
take	a short a coffee	break
make	a tough an easy a good a bad	decision

Words in Action

1. Which of the things on the list can you do?
2. Choose five verbs on the list. Look at the jobs on pages 146–149. Can you find one or more jobs that match the verb?

Have students answer and ask the question several times about different pictures. Review **pages 146 through 149** for names of jobs.

Practice 1: 15–20 minutes
Students should find a partner and complete the activity described in *Words in Action #2.* Then, combine jobs and verbs into sentences that are written in the present continuous. Challenge students to find as many verb matches as they can for each job.

Evaluation 1: Ask students to write sentences on the board and review them as a class.

Application: 15–20 minutes
Individually, have students write five sentences describing what five family members or friends from outside of the classroom do. For each, they should include the job title and a few tasks associated with it. Schedule time for students to discuss the different jobs they wrote about.

Objective: Interview for a job.

Warm-up: 15–20 minutes
Start a conversation about what jobs students have or have had and what tasks are most important in these positions. Discuss this as a class. Then read *Words in Context* aloud and incorporate that content into group conversation. Assign small groups to answer the following questions: 1) *Are all these tasks necessary to work in an office?*, 2) *Have you ever worked in an office? If so, what did you do?*, 3) *What was most difficult about working in an office?*

Introduction: State the objective.

Presentation 1: 15–25 minutes
Present the word list on **pages 150 and 151.** Make sure students understand the definition for each item. Discuss what jobs each verb might be associated with. As a class, make a list of questions that might be asked during a job interview. Start with generic questions that can apply to any job. Guide students to think of more specific questions and suggest a question for a pizza delivery person, such as *Can you drive a car?* Review how to form questions.

Practice 1: 20–30 minutes
In groups, students should list 10 general interview questions that are possible for any job. Individually, students should create 10 questions that are specific to one of the positions in the dictionary pictures. Pass out small cards and ask students to write their questions without the job title listed. Group members should exchange cards and try to identify the jobs. Expand the activity by exchanging cards with other groups.

Evaluation 1: Repeat the activity by selecting a few cards and reading them to the class.

Application: 20–30 minutes
Pair students to practice interviewing each other for a position from the list. Use the questions from the Practice. Discuss difficult questions that students are unsure how to answer.

Project

In groups, members should choose one job from those on **pages 146 through 151.** Ask the groups to submit a job interview questionnaire, an advertisement, and a job description for the position. Additionally, have the groups prepare a few questions that they would ask a potential candidate.

Level ★

Objective: Identify farm vocabulary.

Warm-up: 10–12 minutes
Remind students what a pantomime is. Challenge them to pantomime different jobs in front of the class and make them difficult enough to stump the teacher. Allow students to review **pages 146 through 151** before beginning the activity. Address any job vocabulary that students do not recall. Stage a game of charades and split students into two teams. Each team should think of 10 pantomimes to be performed for the other group. Whichever group correctly guesses the most jobs wins the friendly competition.

Introduction: State the objective.

Presentation 1: 10–15 minutes
Direct students to open their dictionaries to **pages 152 and 153.** Thoroughly discuss the new vocabulary. Help students learn how to pronounce all words correctly. Prepare students to complete the Practice by drawing items on the board and having students guess what the items are. Ask volunteers to draw a few items on the board.

Practice 1: 10–15 minutes
Carry out the activity suggested in *Words in Action #2.* Have this activity completed with dictionaries open. After a set time, ask students to close their dictionaries.

Evaluation 1: Observe the activity.

Presentation 2: 8–10 minutes
Start a cluster activity on the board. Hand out copies of the cluster template available on the Activity Bank CD-ROM. Label the center circle *farm.* Three secondary circles are *people and animals, things,* and *places.* Lead the class to find one example for a tertiary circle.

Practice 2: 12–15 minutes
Assign small groups to complete the cluster together. Move about the classroom to offer help as needed.

Evaluation 2: With student help, complete the cluster on the board.

Application: 10–15 minutes
Ask students to make lists of all the new words they learned in this lesson. For each word on the list, ask students to use it in a complete sentence. Students should read their sentences to the class. For an extended activity, have students draw a map of a farm they would like to have and include new vocabulary of different crops and/or animals.

Farm

Words in Context

Jimmy Carter was the 39th president of the U.S. He grew up on a **farm** full of animals. There were **dogs, turkeys, horses,** and **cows** on the farm. Carter did many jobs around the farm. He **milked** the cows each day after school. He also **picked** cotton and peanuts in the **fields.**

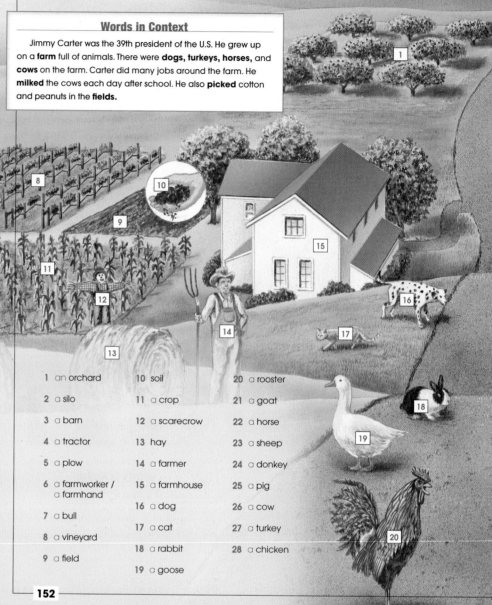

1 an orchard	10 soil	20 a rooster
2 a silo	11 a crop	21 a goat
3 a barn	12 a scarecrow	22 a horse
4 a tractor	13 hay	23 a sheep
5 a plow	14 a farmer	24 a donkey
6 a farmworker / a farmhand	15 a farmhouse	25 a pig
	16 a dog	26 a cow
7 a bull	17 a cat	27 a turkey
8 a vineyard	18 a rabbit	28 a chicken
9 a field	19 a goose	

152

Level ★★

Objective: Describe animals.

Warm-up: 10–15 minutes
Ask students to do the suggested activity in *Words in Action #1* on **page 153.** Students should each create a list with the three categories and share them with a small group.

Introduction: State the objective.

Presentation 1: 20–30 minutes
Go over each of the words from the word list on **pages 152 and 153** with students. Make sure they understand each item and include the names of common baby animals. Talk about colors and different parts of animals. Address the following vocabulary: *fur, feathers, paw, beak, udder, horn,* and *hoof.* Describe a few animals by making statements such as *I am thinking of an animal with black and white fur. This animal has four legs and four paws.* If no one responds, say *Its baby is called a puppy.*

Verbs

29 plant
30 water
31 pick
32 milk
33 feed

Animal	Baby Animal
dog	puppy
cat	kitten
chicken	chick
pig	piglet
sheep	lamb
cow	calf
goat	kid

Words in Action

1. Study the word list for three minutes. Then close your book. Write down as many of the words as you can remember. Write each word under one of these categories: *People and animals on a farm, Things on a farm, Places on a farm.*

2. Choose a word and draw a picture of it on the board. The first classmate to guess the word gets a point and draws the next picture on the board.

153

Objective: Prepare a schedule and a test.

Warm-up: 8–10 minutes
Tell students that they will learn about farms and farm work in this lesson. Have students individually list farm animals they know. Set aside time for students to compare lists. Collect the lists and create one master list of farm animals for the class to reference throughout the lesson.

Introduction: State the objective.

Presentation 1: 15–25 minutes
Present the word list on dictionary **pages 152 and 153.** Develop clear definitions for students as needed. At this point, students can add any additional names of farm animals to their lists from the Warm-up and to the master list on the board. Read and discuss *Words in Context.* Encourage discussion by asking students to imagine they are farmers. Ask them how they might schedule their activities on the farm, from the moment they wake up in the morning to the time they go to sleep at night.

Practice 1: 20–30 minutes
Have students work in pairs and use the daily planner template on the **Activity Bank CD-ROM** to outline their farm's daily activities.

Evaluation 1: Observe the activity.

Application: 20–30 minutes
In the same pairs, have students develop quizzes on farm vocabulary. Have pairs create 10 multiple-choice questions, 10 true/false questions, and 10 short-answer questions. They should use most of the new vocabulary in the quizzes and develop answer keys. Schedule time for pairs to exchange quizzes. After sufficient time has elapsed, have pairs correct each other's work.

Practice 1: 15–20 minutes
In pairs, students should attempt to describe animals, as modeled in the Presentation. Allow students to work together to develop descriptions. Combine pairs into groups of four and ask students to quiz each other with the descriptions they wrote.

Evaluation 1: Observe the activity.

Application: 15–18 minutes
Individually, students should make a list of animals they or their family members have owned. Descriptions should follow and include animal type, color, number of legs, size, and type of hair or fur. Help students as needed. Schedule time for sharing.

Project

In groups, have students design a farm different from the one in the dictionary. Challenge them to create their farm without referring to the dictionary's farm. Ask students to keep their dictionaries closed and give them the vocabulary words. See which group can design a farm using the most words from the lesson. Have students illustrate the farm if they are artistic; otherwise they need only create a diagram or floor plan of the farm.

Level ★

Objective: Identify office vocabulary.

Warm-up: 15–20 minutes
Select a student and borrow a pencil or pen. Pretend to write a letter. Solicit guesses as to what you are doing with the pen. Write *tools for the office* on the board. Write *pen* and *pencil* underneath. As a class, ask for students' help in compiling a complete list. Prompt them by describing many objects. Even if students don't understand a lot of the vocabulary in the descriptions, encourage them to listen for any familiar words and use these to help guess. For example, say *This machine is used to type letters* in an effort to gain the response *a typewriter* or *a computer.*

Introduction: State the objective.

Presentation 1: 20–30 minutes
Ask students to open their dictionaries to **pages 154 and 155.** Present the new vocabulary. Review the use of prepositions of location by referring to objects by their placement in the picture. For example, state *The appointment book is on the desk, in the right corner.* Review *in, on, next to, between, in front of, behind, by,* and *on top of.* Prepare students to perform this model conversation.

    Student A: *Where is the fax machine?*

    Student B: *The fax machine is between the binders and the copy machine.*

Practice 1: 8–10 minutes
Arrange for pairs to practice the exchange. Have them substitute new words each time and reverse roles an equal number of times.

Evaluation 1: Observe the activity.

Presentation 2: 8–10 minutes
Start a cluster activity on the board. Pass out copies of the cluster template available on the Activity Bank CD-ROM. Label the center circle *office* and the secondary circles *machines, tools, supplies,* and *other.*

Practice 2: 8–10 minutes
In small groups, give students time to complete the cluster with words from the list.

Evaluation 2: With students' help, complete the cluster on the board.

Application: 10–15 minutes
Question students about what items they have at home, as suggested in **Words in Action #1.** Provide time for students to share with small groups. Have students make lists of office supplies they don't have but that might be helpful at home.

Office

Words in Context

Offices are very different today than they were 100 years ago. Back then there were no **computers, fax machines,** or **photocopiers.** People used **typewriters** to write letters. However, some things are the same. Most offices still have **file cabinets** and use supplies like **staplers, paper clips,** and **rubber bands.**

154

Level ★ ★

Objective: Describe uses for office supplies.

Warm-up: 10–15 minutes
Encourage students to look around the classroom and list all the items that can be found in an office. Ask them to walk around the room and share ideas with three other students, if possible.

Introduction: State the objective.

Presentation 1: 20–30 minutes
Study each of the words from the word list on **pages 154 and 155.** Make sure students understand each item and include the terms in **Word Partnerships.** Discuss the meaning of an item from the list by describing its use. For example, consider this model: *This is a tool that holds sheets of paper together.* Teach the construction of this sentence. Solicit students' help and put a few additional sentences on the board.

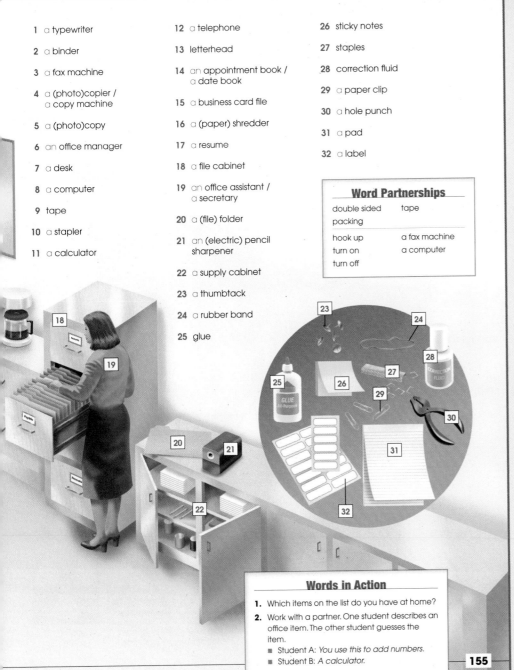

1 a typewriter

2 a binder

3 a fax machine

4 a (photo)copier / a copy machine

5 a (photo)copy

6 an office manager

7 a desk

8 a computer

9 tape

10 a stapler

11 a calculator

12 a telephone

13 letterhead

14 an appointment book / a date book

15 a business card file

16 a (paper) shredder

17 a resume

18 a file cabinet

19 an office assistant / a secretary

20 a (file) folder

21 an (electric) pencil sharpener

22 a supply cabinet

23 a thumbtack

24 a rubber band

25 glue

26 sticky notes

27 staples

28 correction fluid

29 a paper clip

30 a hole punch

31 a pad

32 a label

Word Partnerships

double sided packing	tape
hook up	a fax machine
turn on	a computer
turn off	

Words in Action

1. Which items on the list do you have at home?
2. Work with a partner. One student describes an office item. The other student guesses the item.
   - Student A: *You use this to add numbers.*
   - Student B: *A calculator.*

155

Practice 1: 15–20 minutes
Form small groups and have students write sentences describing the functions of six to eight other items from the dictionary's office. Play a game in which groups write their sentences on the board and ask the other groups to decide what item is being described. The winning group is the one that can write the most descriptions that can be correctly guessed.

Evaluation 1: Judge the accuracy of student sentences and comprehension.

Application: 15–18 minutes
Ask students to describe three things in the room, using the same sentence construction. Focus on correct grammar. Collect sentences from students and quiz the class.

Level ★ ★ ★

Objective: Interview for a clerical job.

Warm-up: 8–10 minutes
Call for opinions about what qualifications might be necessary for a clerical job. Think of a list of positions that are considered clerical, such as *an administrative assistant*, *an office assistant*, *a secretary*, and *a medical receptionist*.

Introduction: State the objective.

Presentation 1: 15–25 minutes
Explain the words covered on **pages 154 and 155**. Make sure students understand the meaning of each item. Ask students to add to their lists from the Warm-up. Read and discuss *Words in Context*. As a class, write an advertisement for a clerical job. Include required words per minute (WPM), filing experience, education, and computer experience. Supply copies of local classified advertisements and discuss similarities and differences between the class's work and the postings in the newspaper.

Practice 1: 20–30 minutes
Divide students into groups of four and have them imagine they are hiring someone. Ask them to write 10 questions that could be asked in a job interview for the clerical job advertisement written in the Presentation.

Evaluation 1: Listen as groups report their questions to the class.

Application: 20–30 minutes
Tell groups to imagine they are a hiring committee assigned to interview up to four people for a clerical job. Offer time for them to review the questions they will ask. Send one person from every group to another group for an interview. Schedule five to seven minutes for the interview and then send students back to their original groups. Repeat. After all students have been interviewed, ask interviewees whom they would like to work for. Then, ask the interviewers whom they would like to hire. Encourage discussion.

Project

Have students form small groups and imagine they are in charge of an office. Pose questions such as *What do they do?*, *How many employees are there?*, *What tools and equipment do they need?*, and *What other products should be kept in stock?* Arrange for students to report to the class.

Level ★

Objective: Identify factory vocabulary.

Warm-up: 15–20 minutes
Write *Be careful!* on the board and ask students for definitions. Follow with other words they may be familiar with, such as *caution.* Write *boots* on the board and next to that, write *feet.* Create a matching activity. Write *safety glasses, safety boots, hard hat,* and *safety vest* on one side. On the other side, randomly write the parts of the body the items protect. First, have students try the matching in groups, without pictures or explanations. Then, add pictures to confirm their guesses.

Introduction: State the objective.

Presentation 1: 20–30 minutes
Have students follow along as the words are presented from **pages 156 and 157**. Focus on reviewing the safety equipment. As a class, carry out the exercise described in **Words in Action #1**. Expand by creating a list of all the protective equipment and the body parts they protect. Have students find other safety items in the dictionary's factory. These include *fire extinguisher* and *signs.* The picture can be divided into different locations. Ask students to make five columns, each representing a designated locale. Include *the front office, the warehouse, the loading dock, the assembly line,* and *the parts department.* Ensure that students understand what each location is and discuss what they would see in each place.

Practice 1: 8–10 minutes
Form pairs and have students categorize items from the dictionary's factory into the appropriate columns. Expand by challenging students to include items not found on the word list.

Evaluation 1: Share group reports.

Presentation 2: 8–10 minutes
Review the *to be* verb and its use in question writing. Write *Where is the conveyor belt?* and *Where are the workers?* Show students how to answer the questions with *It is in the assembly line area* and *They are in the assembly line area, the front office, the parts department, and the loading dock.* Focus attention on the differences between singular and plural subjects.

Practice 2: 8–10 minutes
In pairs, students should ask and answer questions about locations of people and things.

Evaluation 2: Observe the activity.

Application: 10–15 minutes
Have students make a list of safety items they use in their homes. They can include items beyond those in the dictionary, such as a *telephone* and *two exits.* Allow time to share lists with the class.

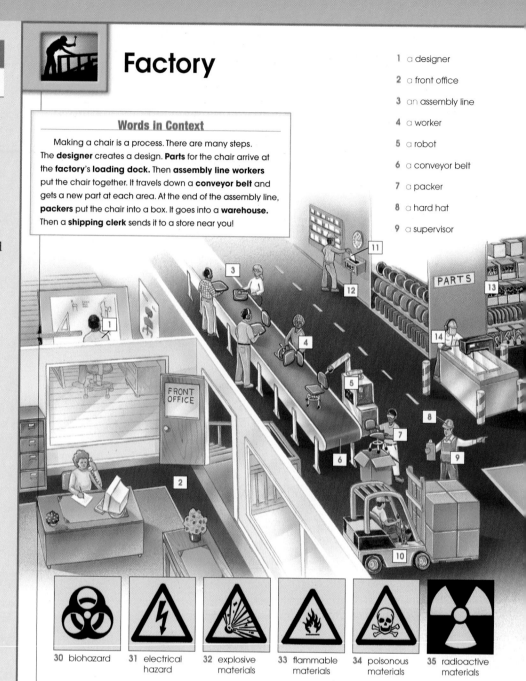

Factory

1 a designer
2 a front office
3 an assembly line
4 a worker
5 a robot
6 a conveyor belt
7 a packer
8 a hard hat
9 a supervisor

Words in Context

Making a chair is a process. There are many steps. The **designer** creates a design. **Parts** for the chair arrive at the **factory's loading dock.** Then **assembly line workers** put the chair together. It travels down a **conveyor belt** and gets a new part at each area. At the end of the assembly line, **packers** put the chair into a box. It goes into a **warehouse.** Then a **shipping clerk** sends it to a store near you!

30 biohazard
31 electrical hazard
32 explosive materials
33 flammable materials
34 poisonous materials
35 radioactive materials

156

Level ★ ★

Objective: Converse in a factory setting.

Warm-up: 10–15 minutes
Focus attention on **pages 156 and 157.** Students should identify the people in the picture and make a list of all the jobs represented. Form groups and have students read and discuss answers to **Words in Action #1.**

Introduction: State the objective.

Presentation 1: 20–30 minutes
Go over each of the words from the word list on **pages 156 and 157.** Ensure that students understand what each item means and include **Word Partnerships** where appropriate. Ask students to imagine what every person in the factory is saying. Write the ideas on the board. Suggest examples, such as the receptionist saying, *"Hello, this is Acme Chair Factory,"* and the supervisor saying, *"Please take these boxes to the loading dock."* Answer any questions

10 a forklift	20 a hairnet
11 a time card	21 a safety visor
12 a time clock	22 a respirator
13 parts	23 safety goggles
14 a machine operator	24 earplugs
15 a warehouse	25 safety glasses
16 a shipping clerk	26 a particle mask
17 a fire extinguisher	27 a safety vest
18 a loading dock	28 safety boots
19 a hand truck / a dolly	29 safety earmuffs

Word Partnerships

a factory	worker
an assembly line	
a forklift	operator
a shift	supervisor
	worker
punch	a time card

Words in Action

1. Make a list of the people in this factory. Which job is the most interesting to you? Which is the least interesting? Why?

2. What part of the body do each of these pieces of safety equipment protect: earplugs, a hard hat, safety boots, safety goggles, a safety visor, safety earmuffs, safety glasses, a particle mask, a hairnet.

— **157** —

Objective: Describe a process.

Warm-up: 8–10 minutes
Find an item in the classroom that has been manufactured. The item could be a chair, a table, a computer, clothing, processed food, a book, or anything else that was produced through a manufacturing process. Have students work in groups to imagine all the steps that were involved in getting the item to the classroom. Ask students to submit a list of people who might be involved in each step and how they contribute to the process. The people might include assembly line workers, designers, packaging people, warehouse workers, salespeople, and/or delivery people. Groups share their work with the class.

Introduction: State the objective.

Presentation 1: 20–30 minutes
Teach the word list on **pages 156 and 157.** Provide clear definitions for each word and clarify student understanding with context questions. Students may add any appropriate words to the list. Read and discuss *Words in Context*. Ask students to summarize the process by writing a numbered list. Transcribe their lists to the board.

Practice 1: 20–30 minutes
Have students close their dictionaries and find partners. Pairs should describe the process of manufacturing a chair by following the steps they listed. They are not to read the list but rather discuss the process, much like the text of *Words in Context*. Have Student A present the first step in the process in his or her own words. Then, have students carry on a conversation in which Student B interrupts with a question after every two steps. Student B might say *What happens next?* or *Where do they do the designing?*

Evaluation 1: Ask pairs to demonstrate.

Application: 20–30 minutes
Individually, students choose an item in the classroom and write a description of the process from its conception to its delivery. Students start by making a list and continue by writing a paragraph, following the model in *Words in Context*.

that come up regarding new vocabulary needed to complete this exercise.

Practice 1: 15–20 minutes
Assign students to small groups to write skits about performing jobs in a factory.

Evaluation 1: Watch skit performances.

Application: 15–20 minutes
On the board, write these situations for pairs to role-play.

1. *A shipping clerk speaks to a worker. The shipping clerk can't find a box of chairs. The chairs are in a box in the front office.*

2. *An assembly line worker needs help with the seats of the chairs. They are damaged. The assembly line is still moving. She/he doesn't know what to do.*

3. *A manager sees a worker with no hard hat or safety glasses.*

Project

Form groups and have students imagine they are running a factory. Students may choose any product for their factory to manufacture except chairs. Groups should design the factory, assign each member a job title, and discuss the process of manufacturing the selected product.

Level ★

Objective: Identify hotel vocabulary.

Warm-up: 15–20 minutes
Write *vacation* on the board. Explain what it means. Generate a conversation about where students take vacations. Make suggestions to help them understand. Provide an example by describing a personal vacation. Display a calendar or the names of the months on the board. Review **pages 6 and 7** in the dictionary. Show students the months that school is in session and describe what one might do during the weeks or months when he or she is off from school or work. Ask students to talk about whether they travel or stay at home.

Introduction: State the objective.

Presentation 1: 15–20 minutes
Ask students to open their dictionaries to **pages 158 and 159.** Go over the new vocabulary. Have students cover the word list and identify different items on the page spread. Prepare students to perform this model conversation.

> **Student A:** *Where is the lobby?*
>
> **Student B:** *The lobby is here* (points to the picture of the lobby).

Practice 1: 8–10 minutes
Have pairs of students practice the exchange, substituting different words from the word list.

Evaluation 1: Observe the activity and find out if any students have stayed in a hotel or have worked in a hotel. Use these students as sources for helping with definitions of the words.

Presentation 2: 8–10 minutes
Prepare students to do *Words in Action #1.* Start a three-column table on the board and distribute the template from the **Activity Bank CD-ROM.** Label the headers *people in a hotel, places in a hotel,* and *things in a hotel.* Find one example per column.

Practice 2: 8–10 minutes
In three groups, students should complete the table. Assign each group one of the three categories to focus on. A representative from each group should fill in the assigned column on the board.
Evaluation 2: Complete the table as a class.

Application: 10–15 minutes
Arrange a corners activity. Assign to each corner of the room a different hotel job from the word list. They might be *housekeeper, concierge, bellhop,* and *desk clerk.* As a class, identify what responsibilities each person has. Then, ask individuals to go to the corners of the jobs they would prefer. Within corners, students can discuss why they chose this job. If time permits, have students go to the job they would choose last or like least and discuss their reasoning.

Hotel

Words in Context

There's a **hotel** in Sweden made completely of ice! You **check in** at the ice **lobby.** All the **rooms** and **suites** are made of ice, too. **Room service** brings you a hot drink in the morning. You can go to the **sauna** to warm up. Room rates are high, but the Ice Hotel is very popular. Be sure to **make** a reservation before you go!

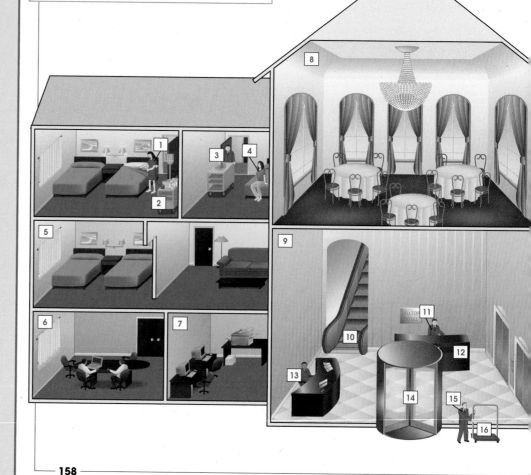

158

Level ★ ★

Objective: Make reservations for a hotel.

Warm-up: 10–15 minutes
Encourage students to imagine they are going to a hotel in a nearby city. In groups, they should list all the employees and features they would see at the hotel.

Introduction: State the objective.

Presentation 1: 20–30 minutes
Study each of the words from the word list on **pages 158 and 159** and incorporate *Word Partnerships.* Make sure students understand the definition of each word. Initiate discussion about what students think the cost for a night's stay in this hotel might be. Develop a range of prices. List the names of some popular hotels. Prepare students to perform this model conversation.

> **Desk Clerk:** *Hello. Harper Hotel. Can I help you?*
> **Guest:** *Yes, I want to reserve a room for Tuesday.*

Verbs

24 make a reservation

25 check in

26 order room service

27 check out

1 a housekeeper
2 a housekeeping cart
3 room service
4 a (hotel) guest
5 a suite
6 a meeting room
7 a business center
8 a ballroom
9 a lobby
10 an escalator
11 a desk clerk

12 a registration desk
13 a concierge
14 a revolving door
15 a bellhop
16 a luggage cart
17 a (double) room
18 a (single) room
19 a fitness center
20 a sauna
21 a (swimming) pool
22 a gift shop
23 valet parking

Word Partnerships

a luxury	hotel
a budget	
room	rates
an indoor	(swimming) pool
an outdoor	
a heated	

Words in Action

1. Make three lists: *People in a Hotel*, *Places in a Hotel*, and *Things in a Hotel*.

2. Role-play with a partner. One of you is the desk clerk at a hotel. The other is calling with questions about the hotel.
   - Student A: *How much is a double room?*
   - Student B: *It's $50 a night for a double.*
   - Student A: *Is there a swimming pool?*

Objective: Identify hotel amenities and special offers.

Warm-up: 8–10 minutes
Call for students' opinions on unusual hotels or hotels with interesting amenities. Encourage brainstorming as you ask what amenities students would like to see in a hotel. They might discuss special pools with waterfalls or restaurants or attractive interior designs. If possible, have some pictures from travel brochures to share. In groups, students should read *Words in Context* and discuss.

Introduction: State the objective.

Presentation 1: 20–30 minutes
Present the word list on **pages 158 and 159** and have students write definitions. Incorporate *Word Partnerships* and have students give examples from hotels they have visited. Encourage them to add other appropriate vocabulary to the list. Start a conversation with ideas from students about what they look for in a hotel when traveling. Talk about each room or area in the dictionary's hotel.

Practice 1: 20–30 minutes
Students should organize ideas about amenities and other features to look for when choosing a hotel. Hand out copies of the hotel amenities worksheet located on the Activity Bank CD-ROM for students to use during the Practice. Students should list details to look for in each type of room or facility.

Evaluation 1: Students present individual reports.

Application: 20–30 minutes
In small groups, students should take the information they compiled in the Practice and create a *Hotel Shopper's Guide*. Supply copies of the Activity Bank CD-ROM worksheet to facilitate this activity.

Desk Clerk: *Do you want a double or single room?*

Guest: *Single. How much is the room?*

Desk Clerk: *It's $75 a night. For that price, you can also use the pool.*

For the list of hotels on the board, students should imagine each hotel has different amenities (pool, spa, tennis courts, etc.). Write the amenities next to the hotel. Students can use previous experiences or their imaginations to add to the list.

Practice 1: 15–20 minutes
Pairs practice the conversation, substituting the information from the board. Encourage them to incorporate the adjectives from *Word Partnerships*.

Evaluation 1: Ask for volunteers to demonstrate in front of the class.

Application: 15–20 minutes
Have pairs create a new conversation and perform it in front of the class. They can either use the model on the board and *Words in Action* #2 or introduce new characters.

Project

Form groups and tell them that they are families about to embark on a 20-day vacation. They will stay in a hotel for 15 fun-filled days. The five remaining days will be used for car travel, during which they will stay with relatives. Groups should submit a budget for their family, including hotel, gasoline, entertainment, and food costs. If possible, students should choose an actual hotel to study. Supply travel brochures or printouts from the Internet for students to use. Also provide copies of the vacation budget worksheet available on the **Activity Bank CD-ROM**.

Level ★

Objective: Identify common tools and supplies.

Warm-up: 15–20 minutes
Write *carpenter* on the board. Ask students to identify what a carpenter does. This might best be described by pantomiming a carpenter's actions with tools or the items he or she makes. Develop a list with the class of things carpenters or people in construction make. Include items such as *furniture* and *buildings*. Write the following job titles on the board: *electrician, plumber,* and *gardener.* Describe these professions by pantomiming actions.

Introduction: State the objective.

Presentation 1: 20–30 minutes
Direct students to **pages 160 and 161.** Read *Words in Context* and go over the new vocabulary. Ask for student input on what each tool is used for. If possible, bring in the items and let students handle them before saying what they think the tools are used for. Consider pantomiming the uses of the items. Since many students may not be involved in construction, identifying the tool names may be enough; but try to personalize the words by associating certain tools with simple tasks around the house. Make sure students are comfortable with a minimum of the terms, such as *screwdriver, hammer, wrench, pliers, ruler, shovel, lightbulb, handsaw,* and *drill.* Ask students what might be most important to have in every household.

Practice 1: 8–10 minutes
Individually, students make a priority list of tools that are most important to keep in the house. Form groups to rank the items from most necessary to least necessary.

Evaluation 1: Have the groups report their findings.

Presentation 2: 8–10 minutes
Prepare students to play Bingo. Have them write eight *tools* and *supplies* from the list on a piece of paper. Help students understand the difference between tools and supplies. A blank Bingo card template is available on the Activity Bank CD-ROM. Also available as lesson worksheets are Bingo cards with tools and supplies already filled in.

Practice 2: 10–15 minutes
Pantomime the use of tools in random order. When students see one of the tools on their list pantomimed, they cross it out. When someone says *Bingo!*, review the crossed out actions to ensure the participant is correct.

Evaluation 2: Review the pantomimes.

Application: 8–10 minutes
Ask students to make two lists: tools they have in their homes and tools they need to buy.

Tools and Supplies 1

Words in Context

I go to hardware stores a lot because I work in construction. I keep my **wrench**, my **hammer**, and my **screwdriver** in my **tool belt**. Those are the **tools** I use the most.

Hand Tools

1 a utility knife	7 a file	13 a vise	19 electrical tape
2 a C-clamp	8 a caulking gun	14 a chisel	20 an extension cord
3 a sledgehammer	9 a hammer	15 pliers	21 wire
4 a shovel	10 a wrench	16 a level	22 a lightbulb
5 an ax	11 a hacksaw	17 a ruler	23 a wire stripper
6 a handsaw	12 a tool belt	18 a screwdriver	24 (pipe) fittings

160

Level ★ ★

Objective: Discuss household problems.

Warm-up: 10–15 minutes
Place students in groups and focus attention on *Words in Action #1* on page 161. Have students explain when and how to use the tools.

Introduction: State the objective.

Presentation 1: 20–30 minutes
Go over each of the words from the word list on **pages 160 and 161** with students. Make sure they understand what each item means, including those in *Word Partnerships*. Present or invent a story about a problem in your house. For example, talk about an occasion when a pipe burst and a room flooded. Explain that the plumber used a pipe wrench and pipe fittings. During the course of the flood, other things were damaged and required replacement, such as the kitchen cabinets. Ask if students have ever had similar problems. Make a list of household problems.

Electrical

Plumbing

Power Tools

25 a pipe wrench

26 a pipe

27 a router

28 a drill

29 a drill bit

30 a blade

31 a circular saw

32 a power sander

Word Partnerships	
a tool	bench
	box
a Phillips	screwdriver
a flathead	
an electric	drill
a cordless	

Words in Action

1. Which items on the list have you used? What job did you do with each item?

2. Which tools would you use to:
   - build a bookcase?
   - wire a house?
   - install a sink?

— **161** —

Warm-up: 10–15 minutes
Focus attention on *Words in Action #2* on **page 161.** Assign groups to complete the activity. Schedule time for representatives to talk with other groups and then share ideas with their original groups. Arrange for groups to report to the class.

Introduction: State the objective.

Presentation 1: 20–30 minutes
Present the word list on **pages 160 and 161.** Make sure students understand the meaning of each item. Encourage them to add anything they can to the list. Identify possible problems people could have around the house or in an apartment. Ask students whom they call about a problem in a rental unit. Ask students if they have ever written a complaint letter and if so, what was written. Try to elicit responses such as a clear and direct identification of the specific problem, the tenants' expectations of repair including date, and other standard letter-writing information. Explain the proper format for a complaint letter. Use the sample letter from the Activity Bank CD-ROM to model or create a letter as a class about an imaginary problem.

Practice 1: 20–30 minutes
Present students individually, in pairs, or in groups (depending on their abilities) with the following problem: *Every time you use the toaster oven and the microwave at the same time, your power goes out.* Ask students to write a letter of complaint, following the standards described in the Presentation.

Evaluation 1: Read the letters.

Application: 20–30 minutes
Have students write a letter to their own landlord if they are having problems. If they own a home, they can write a letter to a company that provided bad service for a recent household problem. Schedule time for students to exchange letters and explain that they will respond to the letter of complaint, pretending to be the company or landlord.

Practice 1: 15–20 minutes
Using the household problems listed during the Practice, ask students to make a cluster identifying the tools needed. Distribute copies of the cluster template available on the Activity Bank CD-ROM to facilitate this activity. The center circle should read *problems around the house.* The secondary circles should be labeled with the specific problems and the tertiary circles should be labeled with the tools used to correct the problems.

Evaluation 1: Ask groups to report to the class.

Application: 15–20 minutes
Pairs or small groups discuss specific problems they have personally experienced in their homes and how they resolved those issues. Encourage use of vocabulary from the word list. Have students compile a list of tools they (or a professional) used to fix the problem. Additionally, ask students if they've ever built anything and encourage them to share their stories in groups.

Project

In groups, have students make a *Tools and Their Uses* pamphlet for the different tools. Have students include drawings and mention ways the tools could be useful, such as appliance repair or furniture building.

Tools and Supplies 2

Level ★

Objective: Identify construction tools and supplies.

Warm-up: 10–15 minutes
Pantomime preparing and painting a wall and have students guess your actions. Allow time for several guesses. After students guess correctly, either have them state what is needed to prepare and paint a wall, or pantomime again and after every action, have them name the tools used. Make a list on the board. To prepare a wall for painting, consider pantomiming *scraping any extra material off the wall, using putty to cover holes, sanding down the putty, priming the wall with paint and a brush, painting all the edges first with a brush,* and *rolling the walls.*

Introduction: State the objective.

Presentation 1: 15–20 minutes
Ask students to open their dictionaries to **pages 162 and 163** and follow along as words are read and discussed. Prepare samples in advance if some items are unfamiliar to students. Encourage students to help as much as possible. If there are any students in construction, ask for their help with this part of the lesson. Have students cover their word lists and point to items when new vocabulary is mentioned. Prepare and read sentences that include the new vocabulary and see if students can recognize the words and point to the corresponding pictures. For example, say *In dark places, you need a flashlight to see.* Develop a scenario, such as remodeling a kitchen, and ask students to point to each item as it is mentioned.

Practice 1: 8–10 minutes
Arrange students in pairs to quiz each other by having one partner say random words from the word list. With the word list covered, the other partner will then point to the object on **pages 162 and 163.**

Evaluation 1: Observe the activity.

Presentation 2: 8–10 minutes
As a class, make a list of built-in items in a home. For example, guide students to include *doors, windows, cabinets,* and *toilets.* Consider asking students to help you by referring to other pages in the dictionary. Review **pages 72 through 75.**

Practice 2: 12–15 minutes
Assign small groups to list the tools that might be associated with the built-in items the class listed in the Presentation.

Evaluation 2: Have groups report.

Application: 8–10 minutes
Have students make individual lists of tools they have in their homes and tools they need to buy. Include vocabulary from **pages 160 through 163.**

Words in Context

How to Hang a Picture on a Wall

- With a **tape measure** or ruler, measure 66 to 68 **inches** above the floor.
- Put a small piece of **masking tape** on the wall.
- Put a **nail** through a picture **hook,** and pound it in through the masking tape.
- Hang your picture.

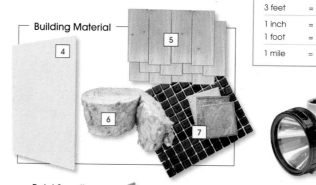

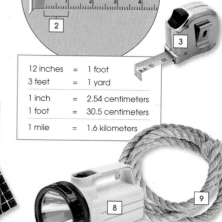

12 inches	=	1 foot
3 feet	=	1 yard
1 inch	=	2.54 centimeters
1 foot	=	30.5 centimeters
1 mile	=	1.6 kilometers

Building Material

Paint Supplies

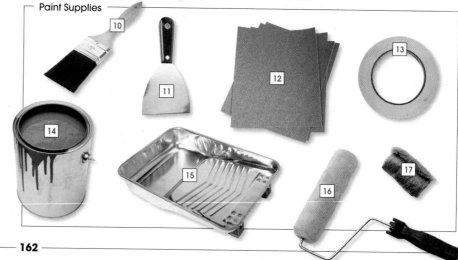

162

Level ★ ★

Objective: Write instructions.

Warm-up: 10–15 minutes
Ask students to open their dictionaries to **pages 162 and 163** and complete **Words in Action #1.**

Introduction: State the objective.

Presentation 1: 20–30 minutes
Go over each of the words from the word list on **pages 162 and 163.**

Review the phrases included in **Word Partnerships.** Read **Words in Context** aloud and discuss any vocabulary that students find difficult. Teach the use of the *imperative* to give directions. Create a grammar chart on the board to remind students of the use and form of the imperative. Students should understand that every new verb generally requires a new sentence. Review other possible uses of this verb form, such as writing recipes and giving directions, and giving "how-to" instructions. Identify people in the classroom who might have expertise in

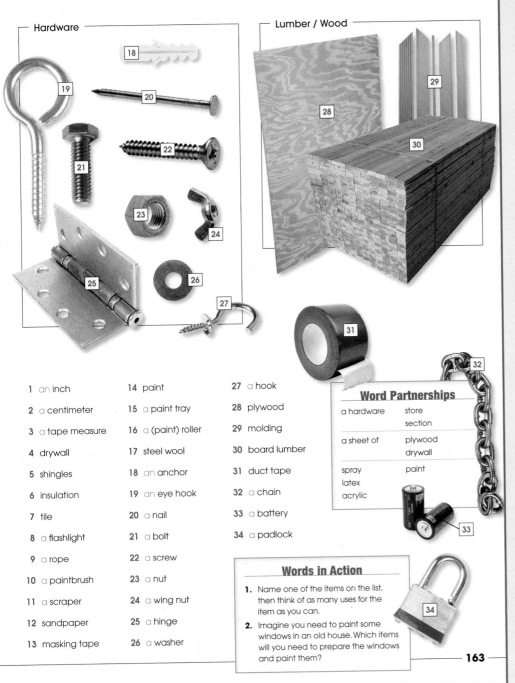

Hardware

Lumber / Wood

1 an inch	14 paint	27 a hook
2 a centimeter	15 a paint tray	28 plywood
3 a tape measure	16 a (paint) roller	29 molding
4 drywall	17 steel wool	30 board lumber
5 shingles	18 an anchor	31 duct tape
6 insulation	19 an eye hook	32 a chain
7 tile	20 a nail	33 a battery
8 a flashlight	21 a bolt	34 a padlock
9 a rope	22 a screw	
10 a paintbrush	23 a nut	
11 a scraper	24 a wing nut	
12 sandpaper	25 a hinge	
13 masking tape	26 a washer	

Word Partnerships

a hardware	store
	section
a sheet of	plywood
	drywall
spray	paint
latex	
acrylic	

Words in Action

1. Name one of the items on the list, then think of as many uses for the item as you can.
2. Imagine you need to paint some windows in an old house. Which items will you need to prepare the windows and paint them?

163

Level ★

Objective: Use the present continuous verb tense.

Warm-up: 10–15 minutes.
Generate a conversation about where students live and guide them to answers such as *a house, an apartment, a mobile home,* or other housing. Encourage students to refer to or review **pages 62 and 63** in the dictionary. Make a bar graph on the board of types of housing represented in the class. Utilize the template on the Activity Bank CD-ROM to facilitate this activity.

Introduction: State the objective.

Presentation 1: 15–20 minutes
Have students open their dictionaries to **pages 164 and 165** and follow along as the new vocabulary is read and discussed. Generate student suggestions for the purpose of each action. Make this conversation as interactive as possible. Call for students who are in construction or good with home repair to help those students with no building experience. Write *verbs* and *direct objects* on the board. Teach both parts of each phrase on the word list. Students should offer examples as complete sentences. Prepare students to do *Words in Action #2* by pantomiming a few actions and seeing if students can identify them.

Practice 1: 8–10 minutes
Schedule time for students to practice *Words in Action #2* with a partner.

Evaluation 1: Stage a class game of charades.

Presentation 2: 8–10 minutes
As a class, decide on a name for each individual in the construction site on **pages 164 and 165.** Students can write the names on the word list, on the picture, or on a separate piece of paper. Review the present continuous with students. Create a grammar chart on the board and discuss the use of this tense. Show students how to use the present continuous tense to write sentences about activities in the dictionary. Ask: *What is happening at the construction site today?*

Practice 2: 10–15 minutes
Divide the word list among students. Ask them to write five to ten sentences in the present continuous about different pieces of the picture.

Evaluation 2: Select students to write some of their sentences on the board.

Application: 10–15 minutes
Combine the two Practices. One student performs an action and the other writes a sentence describing the action in the present continuous. Students should only choose actions that they are familiar with.

Drill, Sand, Paint

Words in Context

In 1980, Edouard Arsenault, a Canadian fisherman, began to make buildings with old glass bottles. He used thousands of bottles. He **mixed** cement. Then, instead of **laying** bricks, he laid rows of bottles in the wet cement. After he **put up** the glass walls, he **installed** skylights. Many people visit these buildings each year.

Word Partnerships

paint	a wall
	a room
	a house
install	a phone line
	a water heater
shovel	gravel
	snow

164

Level ★ ★

Objective: Write sentences.

Warm-up: 10–15 minutes
Focus attention on **pages 164 and 165** and read *Words in Action #1.* Allow time for students to work in groups to complete the task to the best of their ability before the words are discussed in detail.

Introduction: State the objective.

Presentation 1: 20–30 minutes
Present each of the words from the word list on **pages 164 and 165** to the class. Make certain all students understand what each item means before including *Word Partnerships.* Help students see how some of the verbs on the list can be used in other contexts. For example, people can *read a book* or *climb a mountain.* Discuss other direct object possibilities with students as a class.

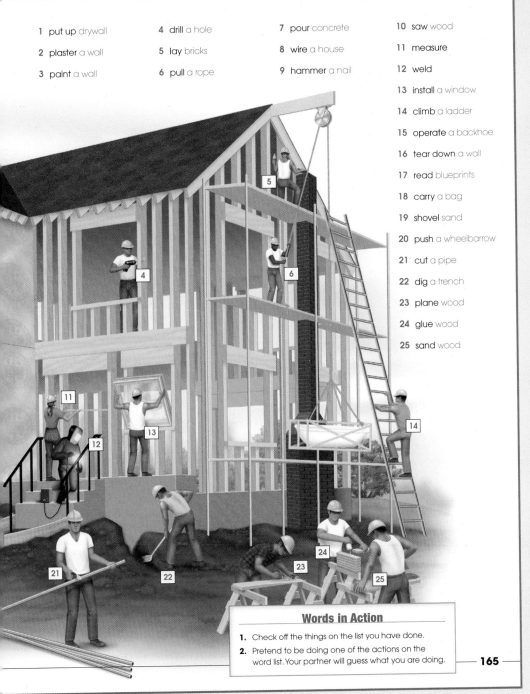

1 put up drywall
2 plaster a wall
3 paint a wall
4 drill a hole
5 lay bricks
6 pull a rope
7 pour concrete
8 wire a house
9 hammer a nail
10 saw wood
11 measure
12 weld
13 install a window
14 climb a ladder
15 operate a backhoe
16 tear down a wall
17 read blueprints
18 carry a bag
19 shovel sand
20 push a wheelbarrow
21 cut a pipe
22 dig a trench
23 plane wood
24 glue wood
25 sand wood

Words in Action

1. Check off the things on the list you have done.
2. Pretend to be doing one of the actions on the word list. Your partner will guess what you are doing.

— 165 —

Weather

Level ★

Objective: Identify weather vocabulary.

Warm-up: 15–20 minutes
Write *summer, fall, winter,* and *spring* on the board. Make sure students understand what these seasons are and when they take place. Direct attention to **pages 104 and 105** in the dictionary and ask students what clothing they should wear in your region in each of the seasons. Draw a table with four columns for the four seasons. Ask groups to complete the table with clothing from the dictionary picture.

Introduction: State the objective.

Presentation 1: 15–20 minutes
Focus attention on **pages 166 and 167** as the new vocabulary is presented. Generate a conversation about today's weather. Focus on items 25–30. Together, explain that the weather vocabulary can be associated with a particular season. Use basic vocabulary to convey this question. Write *How is the weather today?* on the board. Allow time for students to practice asking this question. Prepare students to perform this model conversation.

> **Student A:** *How is the weather today (in winter, in spring, in August, etc.)?*
> **Student B:** *It is (It's) windy today (in winter).*

Create a pantomime to describe the weather types with students. Then ask the question from the exchange and ask students to answer based on the pantomime. Repeat for each weather pattern.

Practice 1: 8–10 minutes
Pair students to practice the conversation with the actions, as demonstrated in the Presentation.

Evaluation 1: Observe the activity.

Presentation 2: 8–10 minutes
Teach the vocabulary of a thermometer and the difference between Celsius and Fahrenheit. Review the other weather patterns and vocabulary. Prepare students to do the following exchange while pointing to different weather items.

> **Student A:** *How is the weather outside?*
> **Student B:** *It's hot. There's a lot of sun.*

Show students the difference between plural and singular nouns. Decide which words from the list can be used in this exchange. Write them on the board and put *is* or *are* next to each word.

Practice 2: 10–15 minutes
Pairs practice. Student A points to a picture and asks how the weather is. Student B responds.

Evaluation 2: Observe the activity.

Application: 10–15 minutes
Have students list aspects of their favorite weather forecast.

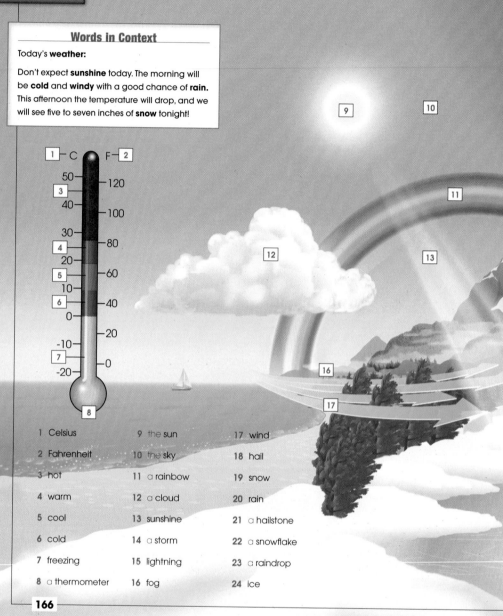

Words in Context

Today's **weather:**

Don't expect **sunshine** today. The morning will be **cold** and **windy** with a good chance of **rain.** This afternoon the temperature will drop, and we will see five to seven inches of **snow** tonight!

1 Celsius	9 the sun	17 wind
2 Fahrenheit	10 the sky	18 hail
3 hot	11 a rainbow	19 snow
4 warm	12 a cloud	20 rain
5 cool	13 sunshine	21 a hailstone
6 cold	14 a storm	22 a snowflake
7 freezing	15 lightning	23 a raindrop
8 a thermometer	16 fog	24 ice

166

Level ★★

Objective: Express likes and dislikes.

Warm-up: 10–15 minutes
Before opening dictionaries, students write what clothing they wear in the winter. Place students in small groups and have them discuss what kinds of weather they experience in winter in your region. Group members should list all the winter weather vocabulary they can think of and share.

Introduction: State the objective.

Presentation 1: 20–30 minutes
Discuss each of the words from the word list on **pages 166 and 167** with students. Make sure they understand what each item means before reviewing adjectives and including *Word Partnerships*. Individually, students should start a list of weather features they like and dislike. Share preferences. Explain why you like or dislike some weather patterns and phenomena. Ask volunteers to share their opinions.

25 It's sunny.
26 It's cloudy.
27 It's windy.
28 It's snowing.
29 It's foggy.
30 It's raining.

Word Partnerships

25	degrees	Celsius
77		Fahrenheit
a cold	wind	
a bitter		
a heavy	rain	
a light		
a blue	sky	
a gray		
a cloudless		

Words in Action

1. Describe the weather today. Then describe yesterday's weather.
   ■ *It's rainy and cool today. Yesterday was sunny and warm.*
2. What is your favorite kind of weather? Why?
   ■ *I like sunny weather because I can go to the beach.*

167

Level ★ ★ ★

Objective: Write a descriptive paragraph.

Warm-up: 10–15 minutes
Initiate a class discussion about students' favorite weather. Ask students if they listen to the daily weather report on TV or on the radio. Prepare students for dictation and use the content in **Words in Context.** Direct students to open their dictionaries to **pages 166 and 167** and ask them to check their dictations for accuracy.

Introduction: State the objective.

Presentation 1: 20–30 minutes
Present the word list on **pages 166 and 167.** Clearly define each word and encourage questions as the class moves through the list. Review the form and function of a descriptive paragraph, reminding students that an important component is adjectives. Study **Word Partnerships** as a class and add any other adjectives generated in a brainstorming session. Consider words such as *ugly, frightening, torrential, gentle, beautiful, breathtaking,* and *romantic.*

Practice 1: 20–30 minutes
Have students write descriptive sentences about the weather when it is the best or when it is the worst in their opinions. Remind students to include times of day from **pages 4 and 5.** Encourage students to use adjectives to make their sentences stronger. Students need to write at least four sentences.

Evaluation 1: Select students to write their sentences on the board.

Application: 20–30 minutes
After reviewing topic sentences and paragraph format, have students put their sentences together in a descriptive paragraph. Guide them by writing a paragraph as a class and use the sample paragraph worksheet from the Activity Bank CD-ROM. Alert students that their paragraphs will be checked for use of descriptive adjectives in well-constructed sentences.

Practice 1: 10–15 minutes
Explain how to complete a Johari Squares exercise and have students choose partners. There is a Johari Squares template available on the Activity Bank CD-ROM. Label the four squares *weather only I like, weather only my partner likes, weather we both like,* and *weather we both don't like.* Ask students to express why they like their favorites using *because.*

Evaluation 1: Ask students to report their partners' likes and dislikes.

Application: 20–30 minutes
In groups, students should discuss their favorite weather, as suggested in **Words in Action #2.** Dedicate enough time for all students to have two minutes of sharing time in the group setting. Students should describe what they do in their favorite weather conditions. For example, *I go sailing when it's windy* or *I go to the beach when it's sunny.* Review student opinions in a class discussion.

Project

Schedule time for students to research weather around the world. Consider assigning students or groups to a specific continent or country. Students should create a script for a country's weather report and present it to the class. Scripts should be modeled after reports heard on local newscasts or the **Words in Context** paragraph.

Level ★

Objective: Identify earth surface vocabulary.

Warm-up: 15–20 minutes
Write *vacation* on the board and explain the meaning by giving examples of popular places for vacations. Offer personal preferences. Ask students to name their favorite places or regions and why they want to go there for vacation.

Introduction: State the objective.

Presentation 1: 15–20 minutes
Ask students to open their dictionaries to **pages 168 and 169.** Study the new vocabulary in depth by teaching both the definitions and pronunciation. Try to identify similar places in or around the school. For example, define *mountains* and see if students can state where mountains are located. Say different items on the word list and ask students to point to those items, indicating a place in the world where those items are located.

Practice 1: 8–10 minutes
Pair students to continue the exercise demonstrated in the Presentation. Student A points to a topographical item and Student B says the name and an example of it. Remind them that they should switch roles several times and include as many vocabulary words as possible.

Evaluation 1: Observe the activity.

Presentation 2: 8–10 minutes
Prepare students to play Bingo by reminding them that they should choose eight words and put them on a list. Call out words in random order. When students hear a word on their list, they cross it out. The first student to get all eight words wins. Repeat several times. Stage a formal game of Bingo using the Bingo cards available on the **Activity Bank CD-ROM.**

Practice 2: 10–15 minutes
Schedule time for a Bingo game. Consider bringing in prizes. In order to win a prize, students who get Bingo should define the words that they crossed out.

Evaluation 2: Observe the activity.

Application: 10–15 minutes
Having covered all vocabulary from this spread, revisit the travel destination conversation. Do students still want to visit the same place? Do some students now want to visit a mountainous region? Encourage discussion and make a list of places to find specific topographical formations.

The Earth's Surface

Words in Context

The land changes across the United States. There are **mountains** in the West, **hills** in the East, and wide **plains** in between. There are **deserts, canyons,** miles of coastline, and thousands of **lakes.**

168

Level ★★

Objective: Describe a vacation.

Warm-up: 10–15 minutes
Ask students what they enjoy doing in their free time and share their ideas with a small group. Groups should choose a spokesperson to report on each member to the class.

Introduction: State the objective.

Presentation 1: 20–30 minutes
Formally present each of the words from the word list on **pages 168 and 169.** Make sure students understand what each item means and then include **Word Partnerships.** As a class, extend the list by adding new vocabulary. Pose the question *What verbs can go along with some of the items on the list?* The list might include *hike, fish, camp, ski, explore, sail, climb, swim,* and *fly.* Have students write some topographical categories and list these verbs under each

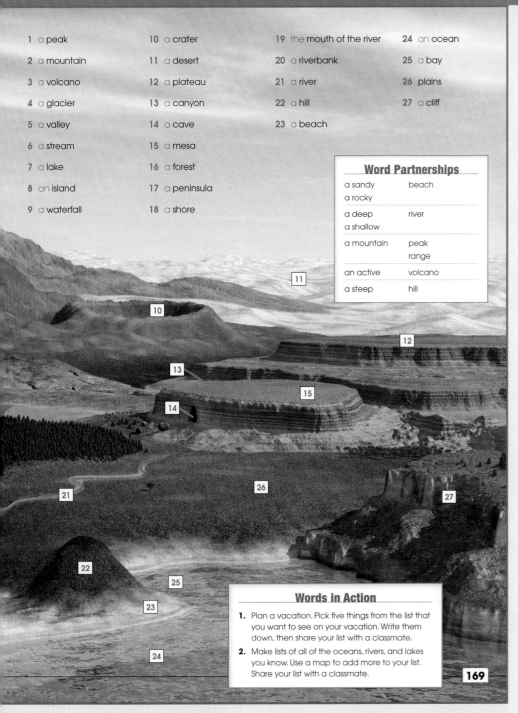

1 a peak	10 a crater	19 the mouth of the river	24 an ocean
2 a mountain	11 a desert	20 a riverbank	25 a bay
3 a volcano	12 a plateau	21 a river	26 plains
4 a glacier	13 a canyon	22 a hill	27 a cliff
5 a valley	14 a cave	23 a beach	
6 a stream	15 a mesa		
7 a lake	16 a forest		
8 an island	17 a peninsula		
9 a waterfall	18 a shore		

Word Partnerships

a sandy a rocky	beach
a deep a shallow	river
a mountain	peak range
an active	volcano
a steep	hill

Words in Action

1. Plan a vacation. Pick five things from the list that you want to see on your vacation. Write them down, then share your list with a classmate.

2. Make lists of all of the oceans, rivers, and lakes you know. Use a map to add more to your list. Share your list with a classmate.

169

Objective: Discuss and plan a family vacation.

Warm-up: 10–15 minutes
Write *mountains, beach, lakes,* and *caves* on the board. Hand out "ballots" and ask students to mark the spot where they would like to be taking a vacation right now. Collect responses. Read *Words in Context* as a class and discuss it. Make sure students maintain a clear understanding of the content. Provide a map if possible.

Introduction: State the objective.

Presentation 1: 20–30 minutes
Tell students to follow along as the word list on **pages 168 and 169** is presented. Define each term in detail. Read *Words in Action #2* together as a class. Discuss how people might visit one of these places and what they might like to do. Discuss what equipment might be taken and how much time would be spent there. Encourage interaction and lead the discussion so all students have the opportunity to participate.

Practice 1: 20–30 minutes
Place students in groups of four. Inform the groups that they are now a family unit about to embark on a family trip. Ask them to plan the necessary details and answer the following questions: *How much time will you be gone? Where will you go? What modes of transportation will you use? What will you do when you get there? What food do you need? How much money do you need?* and *What equipment do you need to bring?* Have students develop a budget. Supply maps or travel brochures for reference.

Evaluation 1: Ask students to report to the class.

Application: 20–30 minutes
Schedule time for students to work one-on-one with a partner to discuss their favorite vacation spots. Partners will then prepare a short oral report to be presented to the class.

---

category. Show students how they might write sentences using this vocabulary.

Practice 1: 10–15 minutes
Ask that students write sentences about what activities they like to do outside, and in what areas they perform those activities. Students should each write a minimum of three sentences.

Evaluation 1: Students write their sentences on the board.

Application: 20–30 minutes
Assign students to groups to discuss their favorite vacations, as suggested in *Words in Action #1.* Encourage students to express why certain destinations are their favorites. Tell students that they will choose from four different vacations: *skiing in the mountains, fishing on a lake, camping in a forest,* or *exploring caves.* Lead a corners activity. Assign a different corner to each vacation trip. Instruct students to pick the corner that corresponds to their choice. Within the corner, students can discuss any similar trips they have taken or wish to take.

Project

Students should draw a map of their own countries or home regions, complete with topographical features. Ask them to display where mountains, rivers, beaches, and any of the items from the word list would be located on the map. Ask them to use as much new vocabulary as possible.

Energy, Pollution, and Natural Disasters

Level ★

Objective: Identify pollution and natural disaster vocabulary.

Warm-up: 15–20 minutes
Write *natural disasters* on the board, and below that add these vocabulary words: *fire, earthquake,* and *flood.* Help students understand each of these disasters and discuss examples. Take a poll to see how many students have experienced any of the three disasters and allow them to talk about their knowledge. Create a bar graph in which each of the three disasters has a bar and *none* is the fourth bar. There is a template for bar graphs on the Activity Bank CD-ROM to facilitate this activity.

Introduction: State the objective.

Presentation 1: 15–20 minutes
Ask students to open their dictionaries to **pages 170 and 171.** Discuss the words on the list and encourage questions. Make sure students understand the definitions, and review pronunciation. Present and explain each of the three dictionary categories to the class. Concentrate on natural disasters for this presentation. Tell students that there are earthquakes in California and hurricanes in Florida. Generate a discussion about where students would rather live: in California or in Florida.

Practice 1: 8–10 minutes
Assign students to small groups to rank disasters from the worst to the most tolerable. Approach each by encouraging students to discuss where they would rather live; for example, a place with fires or a place with floods.

Evaluation 1: Ask groups to write their rankings of items 1 through 12 on the board and discuss them as a class.

Presentation 2: 8–10 minutes
Briefly talk about pollution and energy. Discuss the students' opinions about what the worst kind of pollution is.

Practice 2: 12–15 minutes
Ask groups to rank types pollution from the worst to the least harmful. Next, compare the students' rankings for the best and worst forms of energy.

Evaluation 2: Compare rankings after they're written on the board and discuss how students came to these conclusions.

Application: 8–10 minutes
Students should identify forms of pollution and the natural disasters they have experienced. Each student should present a personal report to the class.

Words in Context

Automobile exhaust creates **air pollution.** Air pollution can turn into **acid rain.** Acid rain kills plants and animals. Some new cars run on **solar energy.** These cars don't create air pollution.

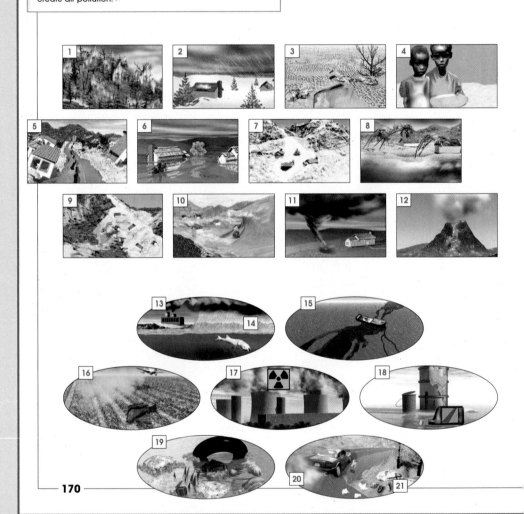

170

Level ★ ★

Objective: Describe a natural disaster.

Warm-up: 10–15 minutes
Ask students to open their dictionaries to **pages 170 and 171.** Read *Words in Action #1.* Allow time for students to complete the task together.

Introduction: State the objective.

Presentation 1: 20–30 minutes
Focus attention on each of the words from the word list on **pages 170 and 171.** Make sure students understand the definitions prior to incorporating *Word Partnerships.* As a class, add adjectives to the list and lead a brainstorming session to think of as many words as possible to describe the other disasters. Ask students if they have experienced any of the disasters. Review the simple past tense with students, as well as phrases such as *there was, we had,* and *we lived near.*

Natural Disasters

1   a forest fire
2   a blizzard
3   a drought
4   a famine
5   an earthquake
6   a flood
7   an avalanche
8   a hurricane
9   a mudslide
10 a tsunami / a tidal wave
11 a tornado
12 a volcanic eruption

Pollution

13 air pollution / smog
14 acid rain
15 an oil spill
16 pesticide poisoning
17 radiation
18 hazardous waste
19 water pollution
20 automobile exhaust
21 litter

Energy

22 natural gas
23 oil / petroleum
24 wind
25 geothermal energy
26 coal
27 solar energy
28 nuclear energy
29 hydroelectric power

Word Partnerships

a long	drought
a severe	
a flash	flood
a minor	earthquake
a major	
environmental	disasters
	pollution

Words in Action

1. Work with a group. Choose two or three natural disasters. In what parts of the world has each disaster happened? Make a list for each disaster.

2. Which kind of energy source do you use to heat your home? Which do you use to cook? Which do you use to dry your clothes? Discuss with a group.

171

Objective: Write a cause-and-effect paragraph.

Warm-up: 10–15 minutes
As students begin class, present the questions posed in *Words in Action #2.* Students should perform this activity individually for a set time limit. After students finish working, put them into groups to discuss answers. Finally, discuss as a class.

Introduction: State the objective.

Presentation 1: 20–30 minutes
Explain the words in the list on **pages 170 and 171.** Make sure students understand the meaning of each item. Relate the words to the conversation held during the Warm-up. Read *Words in Context* as a class. Ask students to think about how pollution affects the way people live. Start the conversation by giving the example that air pollution can cause acid rain and automobile exhaust can cause air pollution. Encourage students to incorporate examples from their home cities, states, or countries. Discuss local news events about these issues.

Practice 1: 10–15 minutes
Define cause and effect. Provide students with several examples. Divide students into groups of four or five and challenge them to find as many cause-and-effect relationships in the dictionary picture as they can.

Evaluation 1: Groups orally report to the class.

Application: 20–30 minutes
Students should think of a well-known natural disaster and write a cause-and-effect paragraph detailing the events leading up to the disaster and the results of the disaster. Reinforce the components of a cause-and-effect paragraph and review topic sentences and any relevant grammar. Remind students to pay attention to their grammar.

Practice 1: 10–15 minutes
Allow time for groups of students to discuss their personal experiences with natural disasters. Should few students have detailed stories, have others relate programs they've seen on TV about disasters, or schedule time for the class to research historical disasters and share their findings.

Evaluation 1: Observe the activity.

Application: 20–30 minutes
Ask students to make a list of all the natural disasters they have experienced or have lived near. Ask that they incorporate the adjectives from *Word Partnerships* whenever possible. Disasters from their lists, along with the appropriate adjectives, should be converted into complete sentences using the past tense. Schedule time for student reports.

Project

In groups, students should try to determine the causes of pollution. Encourage them to discuss each type in the *Pollution* word list. For each cause, students should submit ideas for solutions. If appropriate, allow time for research in the school computer lab or library. To extend the activity, have groups create flyers about how individuals can help fight pollution by changing their own habits and how the community can achieve environmental goals together. Combine their ideas to share with other English classes.

Level ★

Objective: Read a map.

Warm-up: 10–15 minutes
Focus attention on the United States and see how many states students can name, as you list them on the board. Then mention Canada and see how many provinces students can name. Extend the conversation by determining how many students have visited places in these countries. Begin compiling a list of states or provinces that have been visited by students in the class. Allow time for students to write individual lists and compare them in a class discussion.

Introduction: State the objective.

Presentation 1: 15–20 minutes
Ask students to open their dictionaries to **pages 172 and 173** and follow along as new vocabulary is presented. Ask students to close their books and use the state names in a spelling test. Students can check for accuracy and then discuss the pronunciation. Draw attention to states that sound different from the way they are spelled. For example, mention *Arkansas, Illinois, Michigan,* and *Connecticut.* Review the different regions of the country and prepare students for a corners activity. Label the four corners *west, east, north,* and *south.* Challenge students to point to the different locations as you mention them. Also call out specific states for students to classify. Prepare students to perform this model conversation.

Student A: *Where is California?*
Student B: *California is in the west of the United States.*

Practice 1: 8–10 minutes
Pair students and have them ask each other where states are in the United States, using the exchange modeled in the Presentation.

Evaluation 1: Observe the activity.

Presentation 2: 10–12 minutes
Show students that states and provinces are designated by color on the map. Teach students how to recognize the capital cities. Prepare students to perform this model conversation.

Student A: *Where is Arizona?*
Student B: *Arizona is in the Southwest.*
Student A: *What is the capital of Arizona?*
Student B: *The capital is Phoenix.*

Practice 2: 15–20 minutes
Students practice the conversation several times.

Evaluation 2: Ask for volunteers to present.

Application: 10–15 minutes
Ask students to draw maps of their countries and list landmarks and cities in the north, south, east, and west.

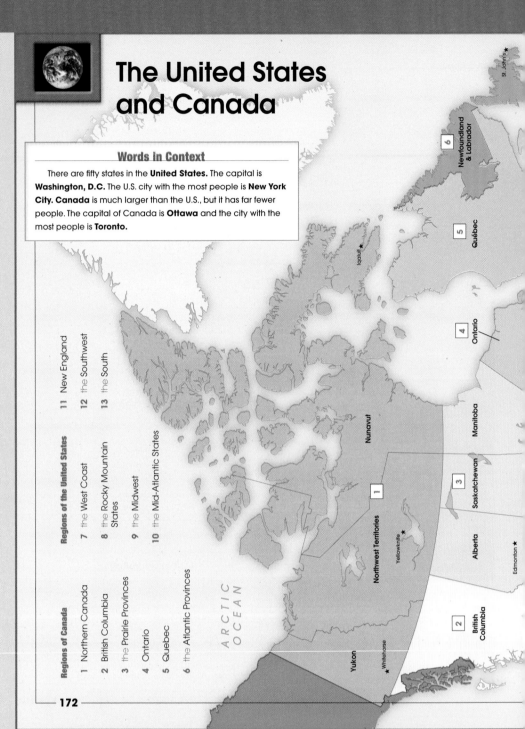

The United States and Canada

Words in Context

There are fifty states in the **United States.** The capital is **Washington, D.C.** The U.S. city with the most people is **New York City.** **Canada** is much larger than the U.S., but it has far fewer people. The capital of Canada is **Ottawa** and the city with the most people is **Toronto.**

Regions of the United States
11 New England
7 the West Coast
12 the Southwest
8 the Rocky Mountain States
13 the South
9 the Midwest
10 the Mid-Atlantic States

Regions of Canada
1 Northern Canada
2 British Columbia
3 the Prairie Provinces
4 Ontario
5 Quebec
6 the Atlantic Provinces

172

Level ★ ★

Objective: Read a map and describe locations.

Warm-up: 10–15 minutes
Pair students and ask them to read **Words in Action #1** together. Schedule time for them to name at least one state in each region.

Introduction: State the objective.

Presentation 1: 20–30 minutes
Go over each of the words from the word list on **pages 172 and 173** with students. After covering the different regions, teach the nouns included in **Word Partnerships.** Show students how to identify a location by saying it is *east of, west of, north of,* and *south of.* Also introduce *northeast, southeast, northwest,* and *southwest.* Review *large, small, larger, smaller, southern, northern, eastern, midwestern,* and *western.* Teach students how they might describe a state

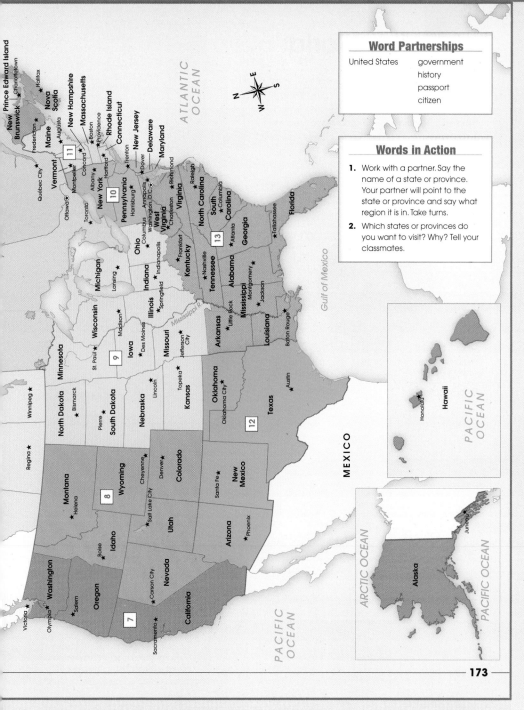

Word Partnerships

United States   government
                    history
                    passport
                    citizen

Words in Action

1. Work with a partner. Say the name of a state or province. Your partner will point to the state or province and say what region it is in. Take turns.

2. Which states or provinces do you want to visit? Why? Tell your classmates.

173

Objective: Discuss weather and topography diversity.

Warm-up: 10–15 minutes
Place students in small groups and pose the question suggested in *Words in Action #2.* Each student should have a chance to participate in the discussion. After students finish working, discuss answers as a class.

Introduction: State the objective.

Presentation 1: 20–30 minutes
Present the word list on **pages 172 and 173.** Determine comprehension by having students write sentences using several of the states and regions in context. Read *Words in Context* as a class. Discuss what people in the class know about the different regions. Ask students what they would expect the weather to be in each region. They may refer to **pages 166 and 167** for vocabulary if needed. Consider an additional assignment or class project to research the weather in each region. Encourage stories from personal experience.

Practice 1: 15–18 minutes
Assign students to one of seven groups. Members should discuss what they would expect the weather to be like in different seasons in the different regions of the United States. Review the seasons from **pages 6 and 7.** Ask students to include a discussion of the topography for each region. After ample time, focus each group on a particular region. Each group will then present its findings on an assigned region. As a large group, students should discuss how the United States regions are similar and different. Give students the option of discussing the regions of another country if interested.

Evaluation 1: Listen to group reports.

Application: 15–18 minutes
Revisit the conversation from the Warm-up in which students discussed their preferences of places to visit. Extend this activity by asking students to include information about topography and weather.

by giving the example *Montana is a northern Rocky Mountain state near the Canadian border. It is just north of Idaho and Wyoming.*

Practice 1: 15–20 minutes
Pass out small cards to students. Students should write descriptions of states on the cards without writing their names. After a few minutes, divide students into small groups. Students should read their descriptions and see if they are accurate and clear enough for other group members to identify the states. Each group can write five to ten descriptions.

Evaluation 1: Stage a card exchange in which groups share their cards with other groups. See if the other groups can guess which state is being described.

Application: 15–17 minutes
Students should describe their favorite state and ask classmates to guess which one it is. While sharing, classmates can offer suggestions to add to or improve the description.

Ask students to make a map of another country. Or, write names of different countries on cards, have students choose a card, and ask them to draw maps of those countries. Encourage students to get help from someone from that country or use the computer. Ask them to label the map with as many cities as possible, as well as topographical features and weather patterns.

Level ★

Objective: Read a world map.

Warm-up: 10–15 minutes
Focus attention on world travel and see how many countries students can name. List them on the board. Extend the conversation by determining how many countries and continents students have visited. Begin compiling a second list of countries that students have visited. Allow time for students to write their individual lists and compare them in a large-group discussion. Expand the activity by discussing the different languages spoken in each country students listed and/or visited.

Introduction: State the objective.

Presentation 1: 15–20 minutes
Ask students to open their dictionaries to **pages 174 and 175.** Plan a spelling test using the 14 words in the word list. Suggest that students spell what they hear. Check for accuracy and then discuss how the spelling patterns match or differ from the way the words are pronounced. Practice pronunciation. Prepare students to do *Words in Action #1.*

Practice 1: 10–12 minutes
Pair students to perform *Words in Action #1.* After practice, arrange all students in a circle around the room and repeat the activity. When students can't think of a country for their letter, they leave the circle. The last student in the circle wins.

Evaluation 1: Observe the activity.

Presentation 2: 10–12 minutes
Call out a few country names in random order and see if students can point to them in the dictionary. Choose a few students to select countries to find. Prepare students to perform *Words in Action #2.*

Practice 2: 10–12 minutes
Ask students to continue practicing with *Words in Action #2.* Set time limits and after each elapsed time period, students should switch partners and repeat the activity. Challenge students to use as many countries as possible during the exercise.

Evaluation 2: Ask for volunteers to present in front of the class.

Application: 10–15 minutes
Students should identify places on the map where they would like to visit and share the information with a partner. For each place selected, students should state why they want to visit.

The World

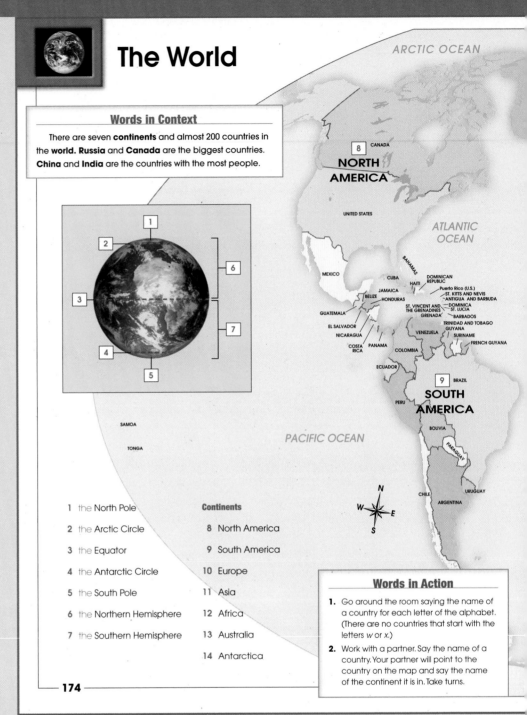

Words in Context
There are seven **continents** and almost 200 countries in the **world. Russia** and **Canada** are the biggest countries. **China** and **India** are the countries with the most people.

1	the North Pole		Continents
2	the Arctic Circle	8	North America
3	the Equator	9	South America
4	the Antarctic Circle	10	Europe
5	the South Pole	11	Asia
6	the Northern Hemisphere	12	Africa
7	the Southern Hemisphere	13	Australia
		14	Antarctica

Words in Action
1. Go around the room saying the name of a country for each letter of the alphabet. (There are no countries that start with the letters w or x.)
2. Work with a partner. Say the name of a country. Your partner will point to the country on the map and say the name of the continent it is in. Take turns.

174

Level ★ ★

Objective: Read a map and describe locations.

Warm-up: 10–15 minutes
Ask students to keep their dictionaries closed. Review the use of *where is?* and *where are?* Pose questions about some of the vocabulary from the word list. Check for understanding and see how much students already know.

Introduction: State the objective.

Presentation 1: 20–30 minutes
Go over each of the words from the word list on **pages 174 and 175** with students. Make sure they understand where each place is located on the dictionary world map. Incorporate phrases from *Word Partnerships.* Quiz students by asking them in which continents certain countries are located. Expand questioning to include the hemispheres where countries are located. Go around the room and ask each student to state which country they think has the greatest population.

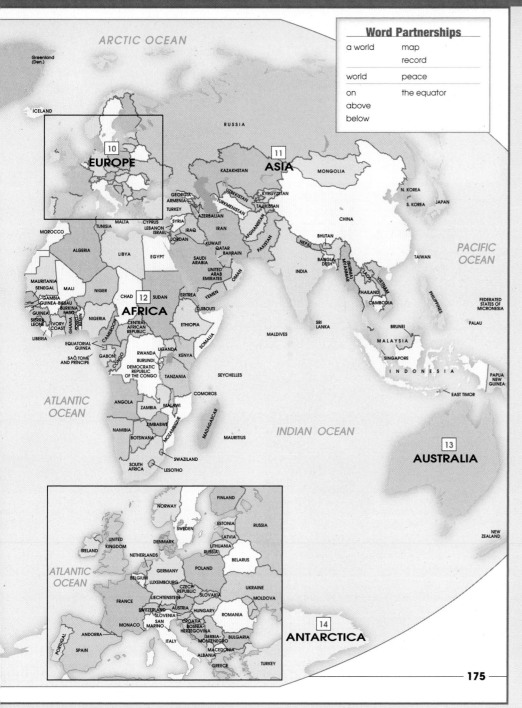

Word Partnerships

a world	map
	record
world	peace
on	the equator
above	
below	

Level ★ ★ ★

Objective: Prepare a test.

Warm-up: 10–15 minutes
Give students names of countries and ask them to describe where the places are with dictionaries closed. Help them to identify places by continent. Pose questions such as *Is Brazil in South America or North America?* Form pairs and have students quiz each other. One student has the dictionary open while the other guesses the continent. Allow time for students to switch roles.

Introduction: State the objective.

Presentation 1: 20–30 minutes
Study the word list on **pages 174 and 175.** List the seven continents on the board and ask students to choose the most populous or well-known countries to write under each continent. Discuss who has been to different places. Read ***Words in Context*** as a class. Learn what people in the class know about the different regions. Show students how to write multiple-choice questions and display a few examples of questions and answers on the board.

Practice 1: 15–18 minutes
Place students in groups and ask them to imagine they are a team of teachers. They all teach a required course on world geography and must plan a test for their students. Each test consists of 20 multiple-choice questions related to the world map. They should create these tests and also provide answer keys.

Evaluation 1: Observe the activity.

Application: 15–18 minutes
Collect the tests and supply photocopies if possible. Students give their tests to classmates from other groups. Students also take responsibility for retrieving the tests and scoring them. Pull some of the more challenging questions and read those as part of an oral quiz for the whole class. Extend the activity by converting multiple-choice questions into fill-in-the-blank, matching, and true/false questions. Discuss which type of question is easiest to write and which is easiest to answer.

Practice 1: 15–20 minutes
In groups, students should discuss what countries have the largest populations. Groups should make a list of the 10 countries they think have the largest populations.

Evaluation 1: Ask groups to write their lists on the board. Consider investigating the real data as a class. The pertinent data from 2004 is below.

1. China: 1,300,000,000
2. India: 1,087,000,000
3. United States: 294,000,000
4. Indonesia: 238,000,000
5. Brazil: 179,000,000
6. Pakistan: 159,000,000
7. Russia: 144,000,000
8. Bangladesh: 141,000,000
9. Nigeria: 137,000,000
10. Japan: 128,000,000

Application: 15–20 minutes
Group members should state whether they would prefer living in heavily populated or less populated areas of the world. Discuss the pros and cons.

Project

Divide students into seven groups and assign each group one of the continents. Allow time for students to do intensive research. As an alternative, supply travel books or provide access to a set of encyclopedias. Have students write an essay about their assigned continent and include details about the land, weather, population, food, cultures, economics, and politics. Review lessons on land and weather on **pages 166 through 169** in the dictionary.

Level ★

Objective: Identify space vocabulary.

Warm-up: 12–15 minutes
Start class by asking if anyone saw the moon the night before. Draw a picture of the moon in different phases and explain what each one is called. Find out if any students can classify what the moon phase is at the present time. *Is it a full moon?* Mention that the newspaper often has pictures of current moon phases, and show examples if possible. Extend the discussion by calling for student input about other objects in the sky.

Introduction: State the objective.

Presentation 1: 17–20 minutes
Direct students to open their dictionaries to **pages 176 and 177.** Discuss the vocabulary in depth and note that most of these words have more than one syllable. Take this opportunity to explain syllables. Begin a pronunciation lesson and focus on splitting the words into syllables. Define each word and make sure that students understand the given explanations. Say different items from the word list and have students identify each item by pointing to it.

Practice 1: 8–10 minutes
Form pairs and have students continue the quizzing activity. Student A says an item from the word list and Student B points to the item. After each pair has practiced with the list exposed, set a new challenge and time limit for pairs to practice with the list covered.

Evaluation 1: Observe the activity.

Presentation 2: 8–10 minutes
Start a two-column table on the board. Label the column headers *man-made* and *natural.* Guide the group to categorize a few items from the list into the proper columns.

Practice 2: 8–10 minutes
Assign small groups to categorize the remaining items from the word list.

Evaluation 2: Complete the table on the board.

Application: 10–15 minutes
Arrange discussion groups in which students should answer the following questions: *Do you want to be an astronaut? Do you want to visit space one day? Do you like telescopes? Do you want to know more about space? Do you like science fiction?* If time permits, encourage groups to compare answers.

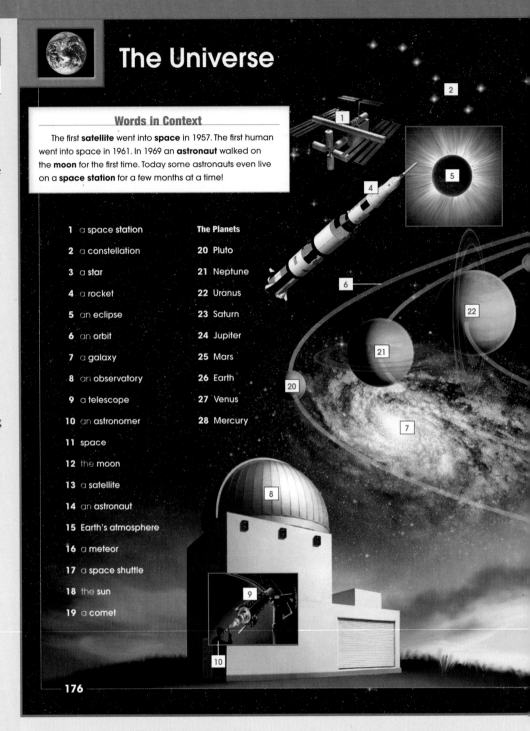

The Universe

Words in Context
The first **satellite** went into **space** in 1957. The first human went into space in 1961. In 1969 an **astronaut** walked on the **moon** for the first time. Today some astronauts even live on a **space station** for a few months at a time!

1 a space station
2 a constellation
3 a star
4 a rocket
5 an eclipse
6 an orbit
7 a galaxy
8 an observatory
9 a telescope
10 an astronomer
11 space
12 the moon
13 a satellite
14 an astronaut
15 Earth's atmosphere
16 a meteor
17 a space shuttle
18 the sun
19 a comet

The Planets
20 Pluto
21 Neptune
22 Uranus
23 Saturn
24 Jupiter
25 Mars
26 Earth
27 Venus
28 Mercury

176

Level ★★

Objective: Use comparatives and yes/no questions.

Warm-up: 10–15 minutes
Read *Words in Action #1* and have students reference **pages 176 and 177.** Go around the room and have students answer the question and state their reason.

Introduction: State the objective.

Presentation 1: 20–30 minutes
Present each of the words from the word list on **pages 176 and 177.** Use each word in a sentence so that context can aid understanding of the vocabulary. Where appropriate, include **Word Partnerships.** Teach *larger than* and *smaller than.* Describe planets by their size. For example, state *Jupiter is larger than Mercury.* Review other identifying factors for objects in the solar system. Talk about which things are *man-made* and which are *natural.* Review yes/no question formation.

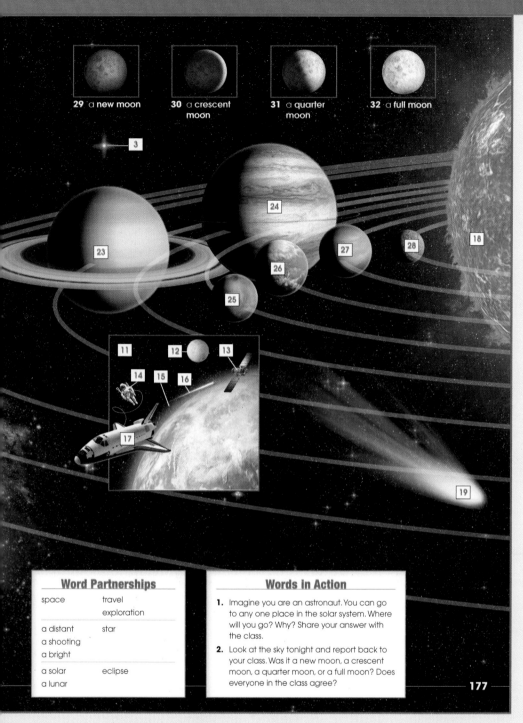

29 a new moon   **30** a crescent moon   **31** a quarter moon   **32** a full moon

Word Partnerships

space	travel
	exploration
a distant	star
a shooting	
a bright	
a solar	eclipse
a lunar	

Words in Action

1. Imagine you are an astronaut. You can go to any one place in the solar system. Where will you go? Why? Share your answer with the class.

2. Look at the sky tonight and report back to your class. Was it a new moon, a crescent moon, a quarter moon, or a full moon? Does everyone in the class agree?

177

Objective: Discuss the future.

Warm-up: 10–15 minutes
Read *Words in Context* aloud and discuss it as a class. Extend the discussion by finding out what students know about other advancements in space technology. Accept any reasonable answers. Make a master list on the board.

Introduction: State the objective.

Presentation 1: 20–30 minutes
Refer to the word list on **pages 176 and 177** and encourage students to follow along as each of the words is defined and used in a sentence. Have students help to create sentences. Using the words in context will help them understand the definitions. Review the use of the future verb tense. Discuss the different ways to express the future. For example, if students use *will*, they are expressing more certainty than if they use *planning to* or *going to*. Teach students to use the modals *might* and *could* to express possibility. For example, write *In the future, the space shuttle might travel to Mars.* Allow sufficient time to explain grammar, as this is often a difficult concept. Develop a grammar chart on the board to display the forms and functions of the future tense and modal formations.

Practice 1: 15–18 minutes
In groups, have students discuss future possibilities based on the rate of technological advances. Focus the discussion on the universe and ask students to incorporate words from the word list. Ask groups to craft 10 sentences describing the subject.

Evaluation 1: Ask students to write their sentences on the board and review them as a class.

Application: 15–18 minutes
Teach proper paragraph formation and review topic sentences. Students should use their sentences from the Practice to create paragraphs about their predictions for the future of technology. They should alter the sentences appropriately to reflect their personal opinions but retain the use of the vocabulary, future tense, and modals.

Practice 1: 15–20 minutes
Give instructions for playing Twenty Questions and divide students into small groups. One student per group thinks of an item from the dictionary pages. The other members of the group ask him or her yes/no questions. The questions can be about size, shape, man-made versus natural, or any other defining characteristics. Group members take turns until they guess the item. Have each student lead a round of yes/no questioning.

Evaluation 1: Observe the activity.

Application: 15–17 minutes
Ask students to write questions they have about the universe and pose them to the class. Discuss possible answers and make a list of resources one could use to learn the correct responses. See if there are any students who would like to complete this research before the next class. If there are volunteers, reserve five minutes of the following class period for them to report their findings.

Project

Divide students into groups and have them create a model of the solar system and present it to the class. Have props available or have students designate a popular type of ball for each planet. Suggest that a basketball could symbolize Jupiter, since it is the largest planet.

Level ★

Objective: Identify garden vocabulary.

Warm-up: 12–15 minutes
Remind students what a *yard* is and take a poll to see how many classmates have one. Encourage students to talk about the things they have in their yards at home. Accept any reasonable answers. If students don't know how to say certain words, invite them to draw pictures on the board. Involve all students as much as possible, even though some of them will not have their own yards to discuss.

Introduction: State the objective.

Presentation 1: 17–20 minutes
Ask students to open their dictionaries to **pages 178 and 179**. Explain each of the new words. Make sure students understand what each item means and review pronunciation with them. Create a table consisting of four columns labeled *types of flowers, parts of flowers, types of trees,* and *parts of trees.* Generate class input and find one example for each category.

Practice 1: 8–10 minutes
Divide students into four equally sized groups and have them classify the remaining words on the word list into the four categories. As students near completion of the table, focus each group's attention on one of the four categories and ask that the members concentrate on making sure they have all relevant words listed. Send one representative from each group to the board to complete their assigned column.

Evaluation 1: Discuss differences in answers until a final, correct version is reached.

Presentation 2: 8–10 minutes
Ask the class which plants from the word list grow in other countries. Find out if their favorite plants grow in your area. Ask students descriptive questions about the color, shape, size, smell, and feel of these plants. Model the questions and answers for them. Then, write the questions you asked on the board, with student responses. Make sure students understand both the questions and answers.

Practice 2: 10–12 minutes
Have students ask each other what their favorite plants are and proceed to ask them the questions you wrote on the board.

Evaluation 2: Have each student tell the class about his or her partner's favorite plant, including its shape, size, smell, and feel.

Application: 15–18 minutes
Individually, have students do *Words in Action #1.* Schedule time for students to share ideas with partners and then with the class.

Garden

Words in Context

There are 350,000 kinds of plants. Most plants grow from a **seed**. First **roots** grow from seeds, then **stems**, and then **leaves**. In **pine trees**, seeds come from the **pinecones**. In **lilacs, poppies, sunflowers,** and many other plants, seeds come from inside the **flowers**.

Parts of a Tree

Parts of a Flower

178

Level ★★

Objective: Describe things in a garden.

Warm-up: 10–12 minutes
Write *garden* on the board. Poll students to see who has gardens in or around their homes. Describe garden types.

Introduction: State the objective.

Presentation 1: 20–30 minutes
Present each of the words from the word list on **pages 178 and 179** to the class.

When discussing *trees, flowers,* and *roses,* incorporate the adjectives from **Word Partnerships**. Brainstorm adjectives that could be associated with other words from the list. Write several examples on the board. Describe a tulip. For example, state: *The tulip has red petals. It is a larger flower with round petals.* Be sensitive to the fact that students may not be familiar with these particular trees and flowers, and encourage them to describe plants from their native countries as well.

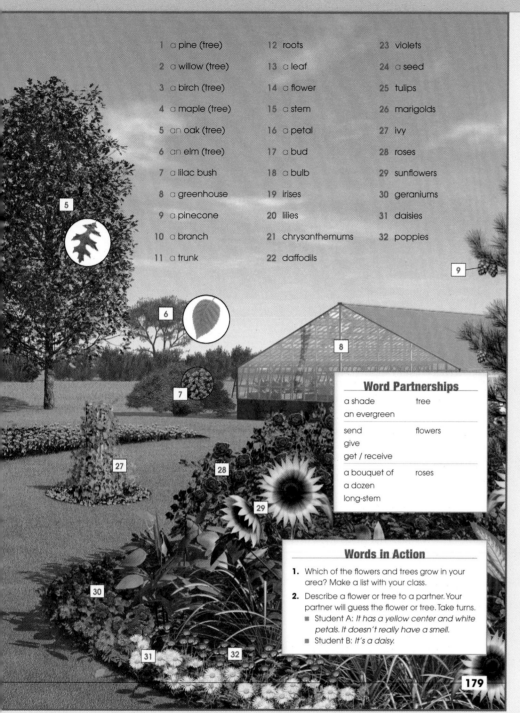

1 a pine (tree)	12 roots	23 violets
2 a willow (tree)	13 a leaf	24 a seed
3 a birch (tree)	14 a flower	25 tulips
4 a maple (tree)	15 a stem	26 marigolds
5 an oak (tree)	16 a petal	27 ivy
6 an elm (tree)	17 a bud	28 roses
7 a lilac bush	18 a bulb	29 sunflowers
8 a greenhouse	19 irises	30 geraniums
9 a pinecone	20 lilies	31 daisies
10 a branch	21 chrysanthemums	32 poppies
11 a trunk	22 daffodils	

Word Partnerships

a shade	tree
an evergreen	
send	flowers
give	
get / receive	
a bouquet of	roses
a dozen	
long-stem	

Words in Action

1. Which of the flowers and trees grow in your area? Make a list with your class.
2. Describe a flower or tree to a partner. Your partner will guess the flower or tree. Take turns.
   - Student A: *It has a yellow center and white petals. It doesn't really have a smell.*
   - Student B: *It's a daisy.*

179

Level ★ ★ ★

Objective: Write a descriptive paragraph.

Warm-up: 10–15 minutes
Read **Words in Context** and discuss it as a class. Call on students for ideas about where to find gardens near their homes or in their local communities. Mention a city botanical garden.

Introduction: State the objective.

Presentation 1: 20–30 minutes
Discuss descriptive language with students. Review the form and function of adjectives. Point attention to **Word Partnerships** and discuss how these adjectives can help create a picture of the word in the readers' minds. Read the word list on **pages 178 and 179**. For each of the words, brainstorm at least two adjectives that would describe it. List the adjectives on the board.

Practice 1: 15–20 minutes
Review the format of a paragraph and ask students to write a short paragraph describing the scene depicted in the page spread.

Evaluation 1: Students write a few of the sentences from their paragraphs on the board and review them as a class.

Application: 15–20 minutes
Arrange for students to participate in a roundtable activity in small groups. Each member of the group has an opportunity to write sentences as part of a larger story. The groups should consist of four or five students. All students start a story with a topic sentence that is set in a garden. Encourage students to use the descriptive language they produced in the Practice. After all students write a topic sentence, they pass each paper to another group member, who adds a new sentence. Continue until the stories have progressed through every member. Groups will have four or five stories, depending on how many students are in their group. Share the stories with the rest of the class.

Practice 1: 15–18 minutes
Prepare students for a quizzing exercise. After pairing students, one student describes a flower and the other guesses what it might be. Reverse roles several times. Extend the activity by challenging students to develop a quiz for the other students.

Evaluation 1: Observe the activity.

Application: 15–18 minutes
Students should choose their favorite flower and describe it in writing. Allow time for organizing. Students should name their favorite flower and list as many appropriate adjectives as possible. Encourage them to share with other classmates to expand their lists. Review sentence structure and have students write several descriptive sentences about the flower. The descriptions should be detailed. Ask students to think about whether or not the flower reminds them of a person or event in their lives. If so, they should incorporate this story into their paragraphs. If necessary, review the simple present and simple past tenses.

Project

Bring in leaves and flowers from a variety of trees and plants that grow in the local area. In groups, students should guess what type of tree the leaf came from or what kind of flower it is. Allow time for students to talk. Bring simple nature guide books if possible so students can research the names themselves. Reveal the answers after sufficient time.

Level ★

Objective: Identify desert vocabulary.

Warm-up: 10–15 minutes
See which students prefer cold weather and which would choose warm weather. Extend the conversation by asking about preferences for rain or snow. Write some contrasting words on the board and ask for student preferences: *sand/dirt, hot/cold, insects (bugs)/animals, windy/calm, dry/humid.* Discuss preferences with the class. Write *desert* on the board. Use a map or describe what this word means. Choose words from the previously discussed contrasting pairs that might best describe a *desert.* **Note:** All of the words, except *humid* and *snow,* could be associated with a desert. Accept any reasonable answers. For example, the desert can be very cold at night. Encourage discussion.

Introduction: State the objective.

Presentation 1: 15–20 minutes
Request that students open their dictionaries to **pages 180 and 181** and follow along as new vocabulary is presented. Make sure students understand what each item means and review pronunciation with them. Create a table with two columns. The columns should be labeled *living* and *nonliving.* Help students start the table by putting one item from the word list in each column.

Practice 1: 8–10 minutes
In groups, students attempt to complete the table with all words from the list. Allow groups to compare answers before calling the class together and creating one master list on the board.

Evaluation 1: Ask groups to report to the class.

Presentation 2: 8–10 minutes
Prepare students for Bingo. Students should choose eight items from the word list and write them on a piece of paper. Remind them how to play. Consider using the Bingo cards from the Activity Bank CD-ROM.

Practice 2: 8–10 minutes
Play Bingo. Use the target vocabulary in random order. For more of a challenge, say sentences containing the words or don't say the words at all and merely describe the items. Be sure descriptions include details, such as whether the items are *living* or *nonliving* and *bugs* or *animals.*

Evaluation 2: Observe student responses.

Application: 12–15 minutes
Do *Words in Action #2.* Discuss the question as a class.

Desert

Words in Context

Fourteen percent of the earth's surface is **desert.** Deserts contain mostly sand and **rocks.** They get very little rain. Many animals and **insects,** like camels, lizards, snakes, ants, and spiders, live in the desert. The largest desert in the world is the Sahara Desert in North Africa. It has an area of about 900 million square kilometers.

Word Partnerships

a red	ant
a black	
a fire	
a carpenter	
a swarm of	ants
	flies
a poisonous	snake
	spider

Level ★ ★

Objective: Describe animals, insects, and things associated with a desert.

Warm-up: 12–15 minutes
Have students describe things in the room. Play the "I'm thinking of" game. Students describe things in the room and classmates guess what the things are. Give the example *I am thinking of something blue and large. It is in the corner of the room.* Students then guess *the door.*

Introduction: State the objective.

Presentation 1: 20–30 minutes
Present the word list on **pages 180 and 181.** Make sure students understand each item. Review adjectives and concentrate on *Word Partnerships.* Ask students what adjectives could be associated with the other nouns. Write examples on the board. For example, *A snake can be poisonous. It is a long animal with no legs and big teeth.* Refer to the Activity Bank CD-ROM lesson worksheet on describing desert animals for alternate practice activities.

1 a hawk	7 a palm tree	13 a rat	**Insects / Bugs**
2 an owl	8 a camel	14 a snake	18 a spider
3 a boulder	9 a vulture	15 an oasis	19 a grasshopper
4 a coyote	10 a lizard	16 a cactus	20 a fly
5 a mountain lion	11 a rock	17 a pebble	21 a moth
6 a sand dune	12 a tortoise		22 a cricket
			23 a scorpion
			24 an ant

Words in Action

1. One student chooses a word from the word list. The other students ask "Yes / No" questions to gather information and try to guess the word.
   - Student A: *Is it an animal?*
     Student B: *No.*
   - Student C: *Is it an insect?*
     Student B: *Yes.*
   - Student D: *Does it have wings?*
     Student B: *Yes.*
   - Student D: *Is it a fly?*
     Student B: *Yes!*
2. Imagine you are taking a trip to the desert. What things do you want to see? Discuss this with your class.

181

Level ★ ★ ★

Objective: Discuss living in a desert.

Warm-up: 10–15 minutes
Determine which students have lived in or near a desert and have these students describe what it was like. Read **Words in Context** and discuss it as a class.

Introduction: State the objective.

Presentation 1: 20–30 minutes
Define all the words in the list on **pages 180 and 181**. Challenge students to use the words correctly in context during the ensuing conversation. Explain descriptive language and concentrate on **Word Partnerships** to show how adjectives are used. Write new words on the board that describe items in the word list. Ask students what they might need to survive for any length of time in the desert. Make a list on the board.

Practice 1: 15–20 minutes
Arrange an outside/inside circle activity. Place the same number of students in an outside circle and in an inside circle. Ask students to face one another and discuss questions about living in a desert. Impose a five-minute time limit. When the time limit has elapsed, the students on the inside circle should rotate so each student is facing a new student. Repeat the process as time allows. If the room isn't large enough for two circles, form two parallel lines. Offer these questions for discussion: *What would your home be like? Where would you get your water? Would you have a car? How far would you live from a city? Would you own a gun? How could you protect yourself from animals, insects, and the weather?*

Evaluation 1: Observe the activity.

Application: 15–18 minutes
Ask students to do a Venn diagram where they talk about preferences. With a partner, students discuss what they like and don't like about the desert. Supply copies of the Venn diagram template available on the **Activity Bank CD-ROM**.

Practice 1: 10–15 minutes
Read **Words in Action #1** and have students play 20 Questions. Student pairs should reverse roles so both have the chance to ask questions and guess the answers. For a more challenging activity, have student pairs think of verbs that describe the action a particular animal makes. Pairs should read the actions to the class and have the class guess the animal.

Evaluation 1: Observe the activity. Assist students in question formation during 20 Questions.

Application: 18–20 minutes
Ask students to identify the animals in the picture they would most like to see in and around their homes and explain why. Ask them to describe the animals to their groups. For each animal, students should say if they have ever seen that animal. If so, they should describe where it was and what it did. Review the simple past if necessary. Additionally, students should discuss which of the animals are considered sacred or evil in particular cultures.

Project

Have students form groups of three. On a piece of paper, each student should make a numbered list of four words from the word list. Then, each group compares the first word each member wrote and tries to find a common bond between the words. Once the group finds a link, it tries to connect the second word each member wrote by a common feature. On a separate piece of paper, groups should write their four sets of three words each and the link for each set. For example: *tortoise, boulder, palm tree: heavy.* Have students consider size, color, texture, body parts, species, and abilities.

Level ★

Objective: Identify rain forest vocabulary.

Warm-up: 10–15 minutes
Write *animals* on the board. Draw two columns on the board and label them *wild* and *domestic*. Explain the difference and as a class, make a list of animals that could be classified under each. Students may not have the vocabulary but can describe the animals by sound or action. You may list animals that are not included in the word list.

Introduction: State the objective.

Presentation 1: 15–20 minutes
Direct students to dictionary **pages 182 and 183.** Discuss the new vocabulary and have students use two or three words in sentences to make sure they understand them. Review pronunciation as students read their sentences aloud. Create a three-column table with the headers *plants*, *animals*, and *insects*. As a class, categorize one item from the page spread into each column.

Practice 1: 8–10 minutes
Divide students into small groups to complete the table, as suggested in *Words in Action #1.* Compare answers and discuss any discrepancies.

Evaluation 1: Complete the table as a class.

Presentation 2: 8–10 minutes
Write *dangerous* on the board. Ask students to identify which animal is the most dangerous. Make a class decision about which animal is least dangerous. Show the least and the most dangerous animals at opposite ends of a line, with plenty of space in between. Ask students to rank the animals and insects from the most dangerous to the least dangerous.

Practice 2: 8–10 minutes
Reconvene into small groups and have students complete ranking the animals from least to most dangerous. Compare answers and discuss different rationales.

Evaluation 2: Complete a ranking that the entire class agrees on.

Application: 12–15 minutes
Individually, students should make a list on small cards of animals they have seen in person. They should not write their names on the cards. Collect the cards and redistribute them randomly. Ask students to find the authors of the cards they are holding. Write this model question on the board. *Have you ever seen a gorilla?* Have students use this model question as they aim to find the authors.

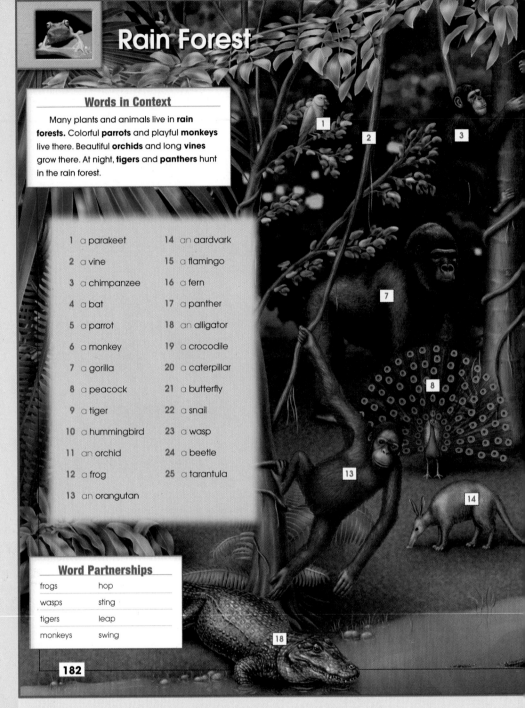

Rain Forest

Words in Context

Many plants and animals live in **rain forests**. Colorful **parrots** and playful **monkeys** live there. Beautiful **orchids** and long **vines** grow there. At night, **tigers** and **panthers** hunt in the rain forest.

1	a parakeet	14	an aardvark
2	a vine	15	a flamingo
3	a chimpanzee	16	a fern
4	a bat	17	a panther
5	a parrot	18	an alligator
6	a monkey	19	a crocodile
7	a gorilla	20	a caterpillar
8	a peacock	21	a butterfly
9	a tiger	22	a snail
10	a hummingbird	23	a wasp
11	an orchid	24	a beetle
12	a frog	25	a tarantula
13	an orangutan		

Word Partnerships

frogs	hop
wasps	sting
tigers	leap
monkeys	swing

182

Level ★★

Objective: Use prepositions to describe location.

Warm-up: 10–15 minutes
Write *zoo* on the board. Ask the class to brainstorm a cluster activity revolving around *zoo*. Use the templates located on the Activity Bank CD-ROM. Help students choose secondary and tertiary circles and categories.

Introduction: State the objective.

Presentation 1: 20–30 minutes
Study each of the words from the word list on **pages 182 and 183** with students. Make sure they understand what each item means and include *Word Partnerships.* Review prepositions of location and list common prepositions on the board for reference. Ask students where certain items are in the picture. Add to the vocabulary list when necessary.

Verbs

26 swing

27 hop

28 hang

Words in Action

1. Work with a partner. Put the words into groups of plants, animals, and insects.

2. Choose one of the animals on the list that makes a noise. Make that animal's noise. Your partner will guess the animal. Take turns.

183

Objective: Write a descriptive paragraph.

Warm-up: 10–15 minutes
Read *Words in Action #2* in pairs or in groups. Extend the activity by having students decide what sound each animal on the list makes. Ask for volunteers to imitate the animal sounds for the class and let others guess which animal it is.

Introduction: State the objective.

Presentation 1: 20–30 minutes
Present the word list on **pages 182 and 183.** Make sure students have a clear understanding of the words and have them use one or two words in sentences. Discuss descriptive language with students and focus on adjectives. Write any new words that are generated from the conversation on the board. Read *Words in Context* together as a class and the adjectives, such as *colorful* and *playful.*

Practice 1: 15–20 minutes
Place students in small groups and challenge them to think of two more adjectives for each animal on the word list. Adjectives should focus on the appearance of the animal. Challenge students to think about size and color, as well as words such as *beautiful* or *ugly.*

Evaluation 1: Ask for group reports and write ideas on the board.

Application: 15–20 minutes
Ask students to write paragraphs, similar to the one in *Words in Context,* describing the rain forest. Remind students to adhere to proper paragraph format and use complete sentences. Take time to review these concepts if necessary. Teach about paragraph indentation and the use of margins if they are not familiar with these rules. Paragraphs should be approximately six to eight sentences.

Practice 1: 15–18 minutes
Pair students for listening quizzes that identify items by their locations. Student A says that he or she is thinking about something that is in the water. The student may add more information, such as *It is a dangerous animal.* Student B guesses. Ask them to reverse roles.

Evaluation 1: Observe the activity.

Application: 15–18 minutes
Extend the quizzing by following the same rules but describing things around the classroom, the school, or the community. Partners should develop 10 descriptions that include locations. Team partners with another set of partners so they can give their quizzes to each other. If time allows, switch groups again or allow students to quiz the class as a whole.

Project

Review *Word Partnerships* on **page 182.** For each animal on the word list, students should determine the best verb to describe its movements. Allow students to work with a partner or small group. Create a list of all the new verbs after everyone has had the opportunity to report.

Grasslands

Words in Context

Animals in the **grasslands** have different sources of food. **Giraffes** and **elephants** graze on the tallest trees. **Buffalo** and **gazelles** graze on grasses. The large cats, like **lions, leopards,** and **cheetahs,** feed on other animals.

Level ★

Objective: Identify grassland vocabulary.

Warm-up: 15–17 minutes
Find a world map or use the one on **pages 174 and 175.** Students should identify countries where they might find lions and elephants. As a class, describe parts of Africa they are familiar with. If the class includes students from Africa, ask them to lead the discussion. In these discussions, very few complete and correct sentences are produced at this level; however, it is often productive to write vocabulary as students identify things by pointing, speaking, acting, or drawing. Try to avoid the temptation of discussing the subject in anything other than English.

Introduction: State the objective.

Presentation 1: 17–20 minutes
Direct students to open their dictionaries to **pages 184 and 185** and follow along as new vocabulary is presented. Clearly define each word from the list and use it in context. Take the time to review pronunciation. Call out items and ask students to point to them on the page spread.

Practice 1: 8–10 minutes
Have students form pairs. They should quiz each other, as demonstrated in the Presentation. After a few minutes, ask students to cover the word list and continue the quizzing.

Evaluation 1: Observe the activity.

Presentation 2: 10–12 minutes
Review simple prepositions of location, such as *by* and *next to.* Provide several examples describing items in the classroom. Prepare students to perform this model conversation.

> **Student A:** *Where is the lion?*
>
> **Student B:** *The lion is next to the ostrich* (points to the picture).

Practice 2: 8–10 minutes
Ask students to practice the exchange using various animals. If time permits, take an opportunity to have students review the animals from **pages 180 through 183** as well.

Evaluation 2: Ask for volunteers to demonstrate in front of the class.

Application: 10–15 minutes
Students should identify which animals they would like to keep in a zoo or nature preserve for wild animals. Form groups to discuss the best environment for these animals as well as the individual animals' needs. For example, students may want to install fences or ponds, or plant grass or trees. Students may refer to lessons in Unit 6 for vocabulary ideas.

Level ★ ★

Objective: Describe animals by specific body parts and features.

Warm-up: 15–17 minutes
Write *featherless biped* on the board. Explain to students that many animals are described by what they do or what features they have. See if students can determine what this expression means. Discuss what *featherless* means. Discuss what *biped* means. Ask students if people could be *featherless bipeds.* Extend the Warm-up by having students brainstorm other animals that also meet this description. Have students open to **pages 182 and 183** and identify any animals that might be featherless bipeds.

Introduction: State the objective.

Presentation 1: 15–20 minutes
Go over each of the words from the word list on **pages 184 and 185** with students. Make sure they understand what each item means and incorporate

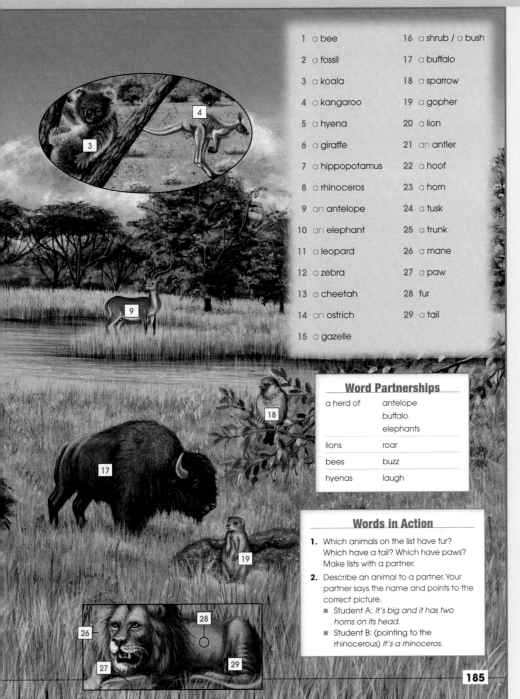

1 a bee	16 a shrub / a bush
2 a fossil	17 a buffalo
3 a koala	18 a sparrow
4 a kangaroo	19 a gopher
5 a hyena	20 a lion
6 a giraffe	21 an antler
7 a hippopotamus	22 a hoof
8 a rhinoceros	23 a horn
9 an antelope	24 a tusk
10 an elephant	25 a trunk
11 a leopard	26 a mane
12 a zebra	27 a paw
13 a cheetah	28 fur
14 an ostrich	29 a tail
15 a gazelle	

Word Partnerships

a herd of	antelope
	buffalo
	elephants
lions	roar
bees	buzz
hyenas	laugh

Words in Action

1. Which animals on the list have fur? Which have a tail? Which have paws? Make lists with a partner.

2. Describe an animal to a partner. Your partner says the name and points to the correct picture.
   - Student A: *It's big and it has two horns on its head.*
   - Student B: (pointing to the rhinocerous) *It's a rhinoceros.*

185

Objective: Discuss grassland animal habitats.

Warm-up: 10–15 minutes
Ask students to think of as many zoo animals as possible and write them on the board. Next to each animal, identify as a class one country where you might find one in the wild.

Introduction: State the objective.

Presentation 1: 20–30 minutes
Formally present the word list on **pages 184 and 185**. Make sure that students understand the meaning of each word and can use it in a sentence. Discuss descriptive language and the importance of adjectives in helping to create a mental picture. Students should think of two adjectives to describe each animal listed. Write new words on the board. Read *Words in Context* together as a class and discuss it. Introduce the use of *would* to students. Practice its use by generating a conversation about what would happen if the animals in the grasslands were really in such close proximity to one another. Prepare students to continue the conversation during the Practice.

Practice 1: 15–20 minutes
Form groups and ask students to discuss the question posed in the Presentation. Group members should elect a group leader. The leader should make sure all students participate.

Evaluation 1: Observe the activity.

Application: 10–15 minutes
Within the same groups, encourage students to imagine that they are responsible for maintaining this grasslands area and protecting the animals. They should identify where they might put fences, which animals they would separate, and which they would leave together.

Word Partnerships when appropriate. Pay special attention to items 21–29 and show students how they can use these words to describe animals.

Practice 1: 15–20 minutes
Form pairs and ask students to do *Words in Action #1* and then *Words in Action #2.* For each animal in the word list, students should think of at least two adjectives.

Evaluation 1: Observe the activity.

Application: 15–17 minutes
Ask students to make a list of the five animals that most interest them and then to describe them to a partner. Consider including the animals from previous lessons from the desert and rain forest as well. Review **pages 180 through 183**. Discuss lists once they have completed the task and have students make observations, such as why they prefer rain forest animals to grassland animals.

Project

Form small groups and have students design a zoo. They should put similar animals together. For example, the gorillas, orangutans, and monkeys should all be in the same vicinity. Students should classify animal groups and decide which ones to place next to each other in their zoos. Use vocabulary from **pages 180 through 185**.

Level ★

Objective: Identify vocabulary for polar lands.

Warm-up: 10–15 minutes
Start a conversation about clothing one wears in the snow. Accept any reasonable answers and begin a vocabulary list on the board. Include *jacket* or *coat*. Ask students to reference the lesson on **pages 104 and 105** and find words that might be appropriate. Bring the discussion back to winter and see if students know where snow falls all year round. Use a map and identify polar regions. Reference the maps on **pages 172 through 175.**

Introduction: State the objective.

Presentation 1: 15–20 minutes
Have students open their dictionaries to **pages 186 and 187.** Formally present the word list and use each word in a sentence. Make sure students understand what each item means and review pronunciation with them. Start a table with three columns on the board, as described in *Words in Action #2.* Review *flippers, wings,* and *claws.* As a class, identify one animal from the word list for each of these three body parts.

Practice 1: 8–10 minutes
Assign students to three groups to complete the table. After a set time, assign one category to each of the three groups and have them send representatives to the board to fill in that column.

Evaluation 1: Review the table as a class.

Presentation 2: 8–10 minutes
Prepare students to play Bingo. Remind them of the rules as they write eight words from the word list on a piece of paper. Consider using the Bingo cards available on the *Activity Bank CD-ROM.*

Practice 2: 8–10 minutes
Describe items from the page spread without saying the word. Use *claws, flippers,* or *wings* as a part of animal descriptions. Keep a list of all possible answers so as to check accuracy later. If students have the word on their list, they should cross it out. The first student to cross out all eight words wins. Play several rounds.

Evaluation 2: Observe the activity.

Application: 12–15 minutes
Hand out photocopies of the pages or have students make sketches of the animals. Instruct students how to make flashcards with the picture of the animal on one side and the name and important information on the reverse side. For example: penguin—where: South Pole, food: fish, interesting fact: doesn't fly.

Polar Lands

Words in Context

Many animals live on the ice or in the waters near the North Pole. They stay warm in different ways. The **whale** and the **walrus** have thick layers of body fat. The arctic **fox** and the **polar bear** stay warm in their thick, white fur. Even **moss** finds a way to stay warm. It grows over rocks facing the sun.

Word Partnerships

a humpback	whale
a blue	
a Canada	goose
a wild	
a pack of	wolves
a flock of	birds

186

Level ★ ★

Objective: Use the present continuous tense.

Warm-up: 15–17 minutes
Ask students to open their dictionaries and work with a group to answer the questions posed in *Words in Action #1.* Schedule time for groups to report.

Introduction: State the objective.

Presentation 1: 15–20 minutes
Go over each of the words from the word list on **pages 186 and 187** with students. Define each and include the phrases from *Word Partnerships.* Review the forms and functions of the present continuous verb tense. Draw a chart on the board to remind students of its construction. Ask students to make a list on paper of all the animals from polar lands. Write the following verbs on the board: *stand, lie, fly, look, watch, run, kiss, listen, snuggle,* and *walk.*

1 a goose
2 a moose
3 a reindeer
4 a wolf
5 a (grizzly) bear

6 moss
7 an otter
8 a (polar) bear
9 a (bear) cub
10 an iceberg

11 a fox
12 a seal
13 a penguin
14 a whale
15 a walrus

16 whiskers
17 a tusk
18 a flipper
19 a falcon
20 a beak

21 a wing
22 a claw
23 a feather

Parts of a Bird

Words in Action

1. Which polar animals eat meat? Which eat plants? Discuss these questions with your classmates.

2. In a group, make one list of the polar animals with wings, a second list of the animals with flippers, and a third list of the animals with claws. Compare lists among groups.

187

Objective: Compare and contrast animals.

Warm-up: 10–15 minutes
Read and discuss *Words in Context* as a class. Divide students into small discussion groups before holding a class discussion. Address any vocabulary questions.

Introduction: State the objective.

Presentation 1: 20–30 minutes
Present the word list on **pages 186 and 187.** Make sure students understand the meaning of each item by asking them to write sentences containing several of the words in context. Student sentences should show how these animals are different from the ones in previous lessons of the dictionary. Take the opportunity to review **pages 180 through 185.** Carefully discuss the features that keep polar animals warm. Remind students how to use comparative language like *larger than* and *smaller than.* Provide one sentence as an example.

Practice 1: 15–20 minutes
In groups, students should make a list of the things that are the same and the things that are different about animals. Compare the animals from this page spread with ones from previous lessons on the desert, rain forest, and grasslands. Remind students how to complete a Venn diagram. Group members should create several Venn diagrams comparing the animals. Utilize the Venn diagram template available on the **Activity Bank CD-ROM.**

Evaluation 1: Groups should share their Venn diagrams.

Application: 15–17 minutes
With a conversation group, students should discuss which domesticated animals they might have as pets and how these animals compare and contrast to the animals from polar lands. Groups should then complete Venn diagrams for these as well.

Practice 1: 18–20 minutes
Ask students to use each of these verbs in a sentence describing the scene. Sentences must contain the present continuous verb tense and be complete.

Evaluation 1: Students write their sentences on the board and discuss them as a class.

Application: 12–15 minutes
Ask students to use the same verbs to describe what familiar people and animals are currently doing. Students should write in complete sentences and use the present continuous verb tense. Share sentences.

Project

Students should focus on one animal whose home is in a polar region. They should try to imagine how this creature stays warm, what it eats, and how it survives. Ask students to write a short paragraph entitled "A Day in the Life of a _____." Their paragraphs should be written from the viewpoint of the animal.

Level ★

Objective: Identify and describe sea creatures.

Warm-up: 10–15 minutes
Start a cluster activity on the board. Label the center circle *animals*. The secondary circles should be labeled with different categories of animals that students volunteer during the discussion. Take the opportunity to review previous lessons from this unit for reference. The tertiary circles will consist of specific animals. Supply copies of the Activity Bank CD-ROM template to facilitate this activity.

Introduction: State the objective.

Presentation 1: 15–20 minutes
Ask students to open their dictionaries to **pages 188 and 189** and follow along as the new vocabulary is explained. Make sure students understand what each item means and review pronunciation with them. Identify the fish and other creatures by color. Notice that there are very few creatures in the pages that are the same color. Prepare students to perform this model conversation.

> **Student A:** *This creature is* <u>*orange*</u>.
>
> **Student B:** *It is an* <u>*octopus*</u>.

Practice 1: 8–10 minutes
Form pairs to practice the exchange by substituting different colors and sea creatures.

Evaluation 1: Ask for volunteers to demonstrate in front of the class.

Presentation 2: 8–10 minutes
Write *smallest* and *largest* on the board and ask students to help identify which two creatures are the smallest and the largest. Illustrate on the board how to make a continuum from smallest to largest.

Practice 2: 8–10 minutes
Divide students into groups of three or four. Assign them to put the creatures in order from smallest to largest.

Evaluation 2: Compare the answers.

Application: 12–15 minutes
Individually, students should list the sea creatures they consider to be the most interesting. They should include at least five. For each creature, they should state why they chose it as one of the most interesting. Place students in groups to share their lists and rationales.

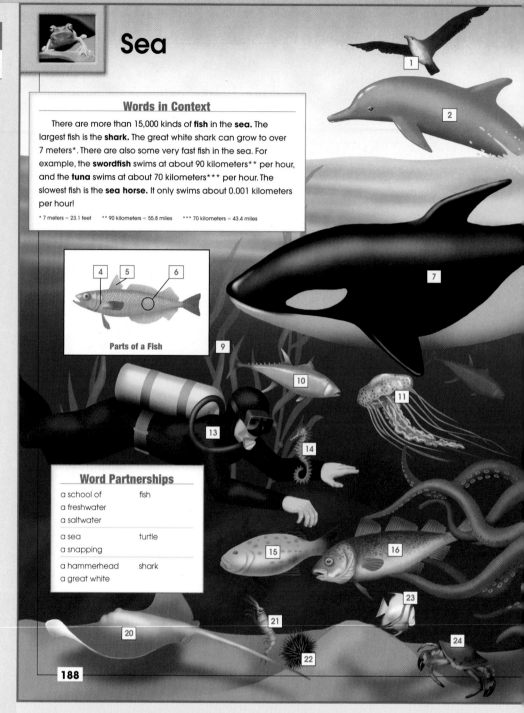

Sea

Words in Context

There are more than 15,000 kinds of **fish** in the **sea**. The largest fish is the **shark**. The great white shark can grow to over 7 meters*. There are also some very fast fish in the sea. For example, the **swordfish** swims at about 90 kilometers** per hour, and the **tuna** swims at about 70 kilometers*** per hour. The slowest fish is the **sea horse**. It only swims about 0.001 kilometers per hour!

* 7 meters = 23.1 feet   ** 90 kilometers = 55.8 miles   *** 70 kilometers = 43.4 miles

Parts of a Fish

Word Partnerships

a school of	fish
a freshwater	
a saltwater	
a sea	turtle
a snapping	
a hammerhead	shark
a great white	

188

Level ★ ★

Objective: Describe sea creatures.

Warm-up: 10–15 minutes
Read *Words in Action #1* aloud to students and have them make individual lists of sea animals they have seen. Then place them in small groups to compile the individual lists into one group list. Listen to the groups report. Have students open their dictionaries to **pages**

188 and 189 and add items that they may have forgotten.

Introduction: State the objective.

Presentation 1: 15–20 minutes
Go over each of the words from the word list on **pages 188 and 189** with students. Make sure they understand what each item means and incorporate *Word Partnerships* where appropriate. Discuss all the adjectives that can be associated with the sea creatures. Include color, size, shape, movement, and

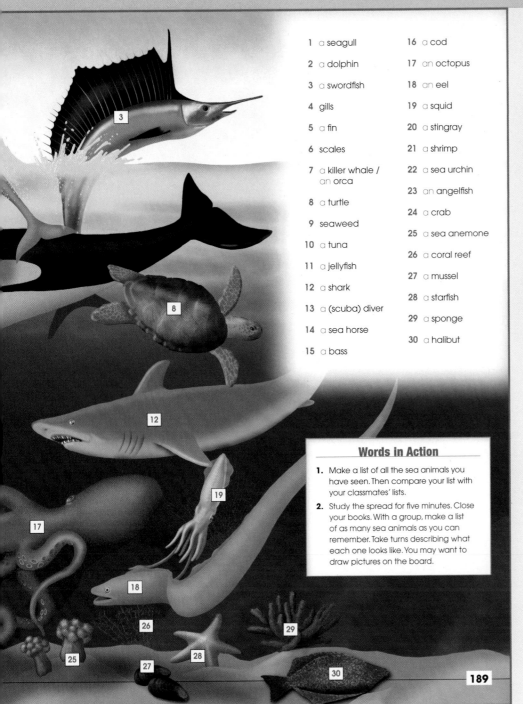

1 a seagull
2 a dolphin
3 a swordfish
4 gills
5 a fin
6 scales
7 a killer whale / an orca
8 a turtle
9 seaweed
10 a tuna
11 a jellyfish
12 a shark
13 a (scuba) diver
14 a sea horse
15 a bass

16 a cod
17 an octopus
18 an eel
19 a squid
20 a stingray
21 a shrimp
22 a sea urchin
23 an angelfish
24 a crab
25 a sea anemone
26 a coral reef
27 a mussel
28 a starfish
29 a sponge
30 a halibut

Words in Action

1. Make a list of all the sea animals you have seen. Then compare your list with your classmates' lists.

2. Study the spread for five minutes. Close your books. With a group, make a list of as many sea animals as you can remember. Take turns describing what each one looks like. You may want to draw pictures on the board.

189

Objective: Write a story.

Warm-up: 15–20 minutes
Divide students into teams and prepare them for a friendly competition. Describe the activity suggested in *Words in Action #2*. Before they open their dictionaries, they should strategize with their teams on ways to remember all the words. Suggest that one strategy might be to have different members of the team study different words. Set a timer for five minutes and begin. The team with the most correct words wins.

Introduction: State the objective.

Presentation 1: 20–30 minutes
Present the word list on **pages 188 and 189.** Clearly define the words and use them in context. Read *Words in Context* as a class. Discuss the variety of sea creatures. Students should imagine they are scuba divers. Pose the questions *What would you be looking for in the sea?*, *Why would you go diving?*, *Where would you dive?*, and *What kind of equipment would you need?* Students can suggest other questions. Prepare students to write answers in complete sentences. Review the parts of a sentence, including nouns, verbs, adjectives, and adverbs. Take this opportunity to discuss rules of punctuation and capitalization for sentences.

Practice 1: 15–20 minutes
Ask students to write answers to each of the questions using correct grammar, punctuation, and capitalization.

Evaluation 1: Write each student's best answer on the board for analysis.

Application: 10–15 minutes
Expand the sentences into paragraphs. First, review proper paragraph formatting. Students should write a story about what might happen if they went diving.

features. Help students begin to describe different creatures.

Practice 1: 18–20 minutes
Students should choose partners for this activity. One student gives a description and the other student draws a picture of a creature and writes its name. The student drawing the picture doesn't show it to his or her partner until it is complete. Both students compare the drawing to the picture in the dictionary.

Evaluation 1: Check drawings for accuracy.

Application: 12–10 minutes
Review adjectives and their importance in descriptions. Encourage students to imagine that they have a fish tank at home. Have them describe the creatures they would include in it. If students already own a fish tank, they can describe their fish or any that they would like to add.

Project

Students should review the maps from the lessons on **pages 172 through 175.** With the help of classmates, they should determine the best countries and cities to find the sea creatures near. Discuss the best travel destinations for diving.

Level ★

Objective: Identify woodland creatures.

Warm-up: 10–15 minutes
Ask students to name all the different kinds of animals they might have as pets. Go around the room and solicit information from all students about their pets and the names they've given their pets. Tell personal stories and anecdotes to encourage students to share. Finally, ask students what animals live outside near their homes. Discuss answers, but don't write them.

Introduction: State the objective.

Presentation 1: 15–20 minutes
Prepare students for a spelling test and use the words from the word list. After the test, ask them to check their answers as you progress through a formal presentation of the words. Ask students to open their dictionaries to **pages 190 and 191**. Go over the new vocabulary. Make sure students understand what each item means and review pronunciation with them. Say items from the picture and ask students to point to them.

Practice 1: 8–10 minutes
Have students cover the word list. Give a description of different items from the dictionary woodlands. When students recognize the picture you are describing, they should write the word and its number on a separate piece of paper.

Evaluation 1: Check student work for accuracy.

Presentation 2: 8–10 minutes
Teach certain prepositional phrases of location to the class. Include *on the tree stump, on a tree branch, underground, on a tree, in the grass*, and *in the air*. Use each expression in a sentence to describe creatures in the woods.

Practice 2: 8–10 minutes
Pair students and ask them to describe the locations of all the items from the word list. Suggest that one partner says an animal name from the word list and the other partner gives its location.

Evaluation 2: Ask for volunteers to demonstrate in front of the class.

Application: 12–15 minutes
Students should make a list of animals from the dictionary that they have seen in the wild. Then, they should make a second list of animals they have seen in a zoo. Allow time for students to share their lists and stories with groups.

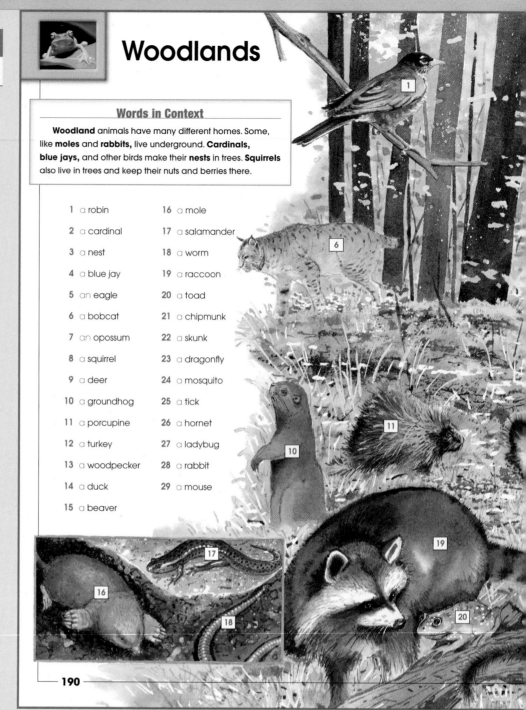

Woodlands

Words in Context

Woodland animals have many different homes. Some, like **moles** and **rabbits**, live underground. **Cardinals**, **blue jays**, and other birds make their **nests** in trees. **Squirrels** also live in trees and keep their nuts and berries there.

1	a robin	16	a mole
2	a cardinal	17	a salamander
3	a nest	18	a worm
4	a blue jay	19	a raccoon
5	an eagle	20	a toad
6	a bobcat	21	a chipmunk
7	an opossum	22	a skunk
8	a squirrel	23	a dragonfly
9	a deer	24	a mosquito
10	a groundhog	25	a tick
11	a porcupine	26	a hornet
12	a turkey	27	a ladybug
13	a woodpecker	28	a rabbit
14	a duck	29	a mouse
15	a beaver		

190

Level ★ ★

Objective: Describe woodland creatures.

Warm-up: 15–20 minutes
Read *Words in Action #1* aloud to students and place them in small groups. After making their two lists, groups should report to the class. Encourage discussion.

Introduction: State the objective.

Presentation 1: 15–20 minutes
Present each of the words from the word list on **pages 190 and 191**. Make sure students understand the definitions. Explain what an idiom is and present those listed in **Word Partnerships**. Lead a cluster activity. The center circle should be labeled *describing animals*. The secondary circles should be *physical characteristics*, *homes*, and *actions*. Fill in several tertiary circles as a class.

Word Partnerships

as quiet as a mouse

as busy as a beaver

as prickly as a porcupine

as scared as a rabbit

Words in Action

1. What animals live on or near water? What animals live on land? Make lists with a partner.

2. Choose three animals on the list. Write a list of at least three things you know about each of the animals.

   Ducks
   1. They have wings.
   2. They live on water.
   3. Baby ducks follow their mother.

191

Objective: Develop supporting arguments.

Warm-up: 15–20 minutes
Direct attention to *Words in Context* on **page 190** and read it aloud. Divide students into small groups to discuss different places animals live. Brainstorm reasons why some animals live underground and others live in trees.

Introduction: State the objective.

Presentation 1: 20–30 minutes
Study the word list on **pages 190 and 191.** Make sure students can use each of the words in a complete sentence. Explain that in an ecosystem, each animal is important. Ask students which animal they think might be the most important and why. List the students' suggestions on the board and encourage questions and discussion.

Practice 1: 15–20 minutes
Reconvene in groups to discuss the animals in the woodlands. Students should decide which five animals are most important to human beings and why. Assign one person in each group to be a secretary. As a group, students take notes and make a report for the class. Show students how they might do this.

Evaluation 1: Groups share their answers. Encourage other students to ask questions about why certain animals were chosen.

Application: 10–15 minutes
Individually, students should create a report on one specific animal. Students should write about the animal they believe is the most important to human beings. Students may use supporting details from the Practice and add more of their own. Students should submit a persuasive paragraph, listing supporting arguments for why their animal is the most important.

Practice 1: 15–20 minutes
Form groups and have students complete *Words in Action #2.* Challenge students to think of more than three facts for each animal.

Evaluation 1: Compare group answers and add to the cluster on the board with combined input from all groups.

Application: 15–20 minutes
Students should describe a pet that someone might have, using the three areas discussed in the Presentation. Review the function of an adjective and have students use as many adjectives as possible in their final versions.

Project

Review all the animal lessons from Unit 13. Answer any questions students might have. Challenge them to create a dictionary for new students of English. First, they should alphabetize all the animals. For each entry, they should write at least one adjective and draw a picture. Supply colored pencils or markers to make the pictures more realistic.

Level ★

Objective: Identify mathematical shapes and symbols.

Warm-up: 15–20 minutes
Draw a circle, square, triangle, oval, and rectangle on the board. Ask students to find examples of these shapes in the classroom. Combine students into groups of four and compile one list of all items identified. Schedule time for each group to report back to the class. Create one master list of all items identified on the board.

Introduction: State the objective.

Presentation 1: 15–20 minutes
Ask students to open their dictionaries to **pages 192 and 193.** Go over the new vocabulary. Make sure students understand what each item means and review pronunciation with them. Say different items from the word list and ask students to point to the items in the dictionary. Or, have them point to something in the classroom that is related to each word.

Practice 1: 8–10 minutes
Ask students to cover their word lists before proceeding. Prepare students to quiz each other. One partner says an item and the other points to it. Students should reverse roles and use all the words from the word list.

Evaluation 1: Observe the activity.

Presentation 2: 8–10 minutes
Prepare students for a drawing game. As you draw an item on the board, they should call out the word when they recognize it. Then have students draw examples of items as you say them. They can copy the examples from the dictionary. Eventually, have them close their dictionaries and draw from memory.

Practice 2: 8–10 minutes
With dictionaries closed, prepare students for dictation from the word list. Answers should include both words and drawings.

Evaluation 2: Schedule time for peers to correct each other's work.

Application: 10–15 minutes
Students should identify shapes they see in the community. Suggest they begin by focusing on the road system near the school. They could identify, for example, parallel or perpendicular streets. Consider drawing a rough map on the board for students to reference.

Math

Words in Context

You use **math** every day. You use **subtraction** to balance your checkbook. You use **fractions** to cook. You use **addition** to add up the total on a restaurant bill. You may even use **geometry** to decorate your home. Geometry can help you figure out how much wallpaper you need for your walls and how much carpet you need for your floors.

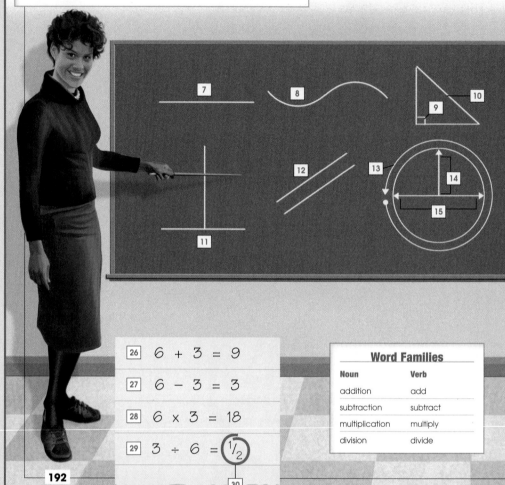

Word Families	
Noun	**Verb**
addition	add
subtraction	subtract
multiplication	multiply
division	divide

26 6 + 3 = 9
27 6 − 3 = 3
28 6 × 3 = 18
29 3 ÷ 6 = ½

Level ★★

Objective: Read mathematical symbols and equations.

Warm-up: 15–17 minutes
Read *Words in Action #1* aloud. Place students in small groups and ask them to find examples of each shape, either in the room or think of examples in the world.

Introduction: State the objective.

Presentation 1: 15–20 minutes
Present each of the words from the word list on **pages 192 and 193.** Use the words in sentences to help students understand them. Teach *Word Families*. Practice reading items 1–6 and equations 26–29 with students. Write the following on the board:

7×5=	22×43=	33×3=	10×20=
12+144=	17+456=	7+45=	6+6=
450−439=	15−4=	236−12=	6−6=
10÷5=	12÷4=	144÷12=	200÷10=

1 plus

2 minus

3 equals

4 percent

5 multiplied by / times

6 divided by

7 a straight line

8 a curved line

9 an angle

10 a side

11 perpendicular lines

12 parallel lines

13 the circumference

14 the radius

15 the diameter

16 a circle

17 an oval

18 a rectangle

19 a triangle

20 a square

21 a pyramid

22 a cube

23 a sphere

24 a cone

25 a cylinder

26 addition

27 subtraction

28 multiplication

29 division

30 a fraction

31 geometry

32 algebra

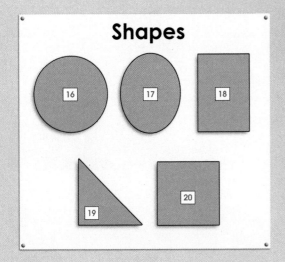

Shapes

Solids

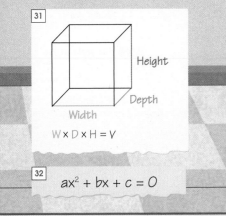

Height

Depth

Width

$W \times D \times H = V$

31

32

$ax^2 + bx + c = 0$

Words in Action

1. Look around your classroom. Find an example of each of the shapes on the list. Share your ideas with the class.
   - *My desk is a rectangle and the clock is a circle.*

2. Work with a partner. One student writes down a math problem. The other student figures out the answer, then reads the problem and the answer out loud.
   - Student A: (writes: *3 + 3*)
   - Student B: *Three plus three equals six.*

— **193**

Objective: Discuss the use of math in everyday life.

Warm-up: 15–20 minutes
Direct students to open their dictionaries to **pages 192 and 193**. Prepare them for a memory quiz. Tell them that they will have five minutes to study the pictures and word list. After studying, they must write down or draw as many symbols or shapes from the word list as they can remember. The student with the most correct answers is the winner.

Introduction: State the objective.

Presentation 1: 20–30 minutes
Read the word list on **pages 192 and 193** to students and have them repeat the words to practice pronunciation. Make sure students understand the meaning of each item by having them write sentences using the words in context. Read *Words in Context* together and discuss it. Lead a discussion to find other examples of when students use math as described in the paragraph.

Practice 1: 15–20 minutes
Divide students into groups of three or four. Have the groups discuss the use of math in everyday life. Members should list times when they could use each of the operations described in the dictionary. Let them start with the ideas listed in *Words in Context* and then expand.

Evaluation 1: Arrange for students to share their ideas with the class. Hold a class discussion to answer any questions.

Application: 15–18 minutes
In the same groups, students should create an example using one or more of their ideas from the Practice. For example, suggest that they write a paragraph about a shopping spree, develop a recipe, create a sales slip, or design a room with measurements. Schedule time for sharing the different ideas.

As a class, perform these operations and find solutions.

Practice 1: 15–20 minutes
Pair students and tell them that they will be practicing math. Read *Words in Action #2* and have students repeat it several times. Remind them to switch roles.

Evaluation 1: Ask volunteers to write their equations on the board and have the class compute the results.

Application: 15–20 minutes
Focus attention on why these vocabulary words are so important. Have students think of some real-world examples of when math is required. Suggest situations such as shopping, using recipes, and reading maps. With a partner, students should write some equations that exemplify these circumstances.

Project

Individually, students should think about purchasing their dream house. They should design their home and include all measurements in a floor plan. They should also incorporate three or four shapes from the word list into their descriptions. Ask students to describe their work.

Level ★

Objective: Identify science vocabulary.

Warm-up: 7–10 minutes
Write *science* on the board and ask students to define it. Think of some examples that might help students and list any suggestions on the board. For example, consider beginning by writing *biology, chemistry,* and *physics* on the board. Pantomime a chemist mixing chemicals or a biologist looking through a microscope. Encourage students to pantomime as well.

Introduction: State the objective.

Presentation 1: 15–20 minutes
Ask students to open their dictionaries to **pages 194 and 195.** Study the word list as a class and discuss each word to make sure students understand what each item means. Review pronunciation by discussing the spelling patterns of the words. Say different items from the word list and ask students to point to the corresponding pictures in the dictionary's science lesson.

Practice 1: 8–10 minutes
Ask students to cover the word lists and form pairs for a quizzing activity. Ask partners to quiz each other by having one student choose an item and the other student point to it. If this is challenging, students may begin by using the word list.

Evaluation 1: Observe the activity.

Presentation 2: 8–10 minutes
Prepare students to play Bingo. Students should write eight of the words from the list on a piece of paper. Consider using the Bingo card templates available on the Activity Bank CD-ROM. As an alternate activity, students can use the Science Bingo worksheets, which are also on the Activity Bank CD-ROM.

Practice 2: 13–15 minutes
Give students words from the word list in random order. Students cross out the words on their lists as they hear them. The first student to cross out all eight words is the winner. Before being declared a winner, the student could define all the words on his or her list.

Evaluation 2: Check for accuracy as students recite definitions.

Application: 10–15 minutes
Individually, students should list any items from the word list that they have had personal experience with and write sentences about when and how they used the words.

Science

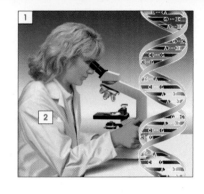

Words in Context

The famous **physicist** Albert Einstein won the Nobel Prize in **Physics** for his ideas about space and time. He is also famous for his **formula** $E = mc^2$. There is even an **element** in the **periodic table** named after Einstein. It's called *einsteinium.*

1	biology	21	a dropper
2	a biologist	22	a stopper
3	chemistry	23	a beaker
4	a chemist	24	a flask
5	physics	25	a microscope
6	a physicist	26	a magnifying glass
7	a prism	27	a funnel
8	forceps	28	a slide
9	a balance	29	a petri dish
10	a solid	30	a magnet
11	a liquid		
12	a gas		
13	a test tube		
14	a Bunsen burner		
15	the periodic table		
16	an element		
17	an atom		
18	a molecule		
19	a formula		
20	a graduated cylinder		

Word Partnerships

a biology	class
a chemistry	lab / laboratory

Word Families

Noun	Adjective
atom	atomic
magnet	magnetic
microscope	microscopic
liquid	liquid
solid	solid

— **194** —

Level ★ ★

Objective: Describe items by their functions.

Warm-up: 15–18 minutes
Have students follow along as you prepare them to complete *Words in Action #2.*

Introduction: State the objective.

Presentation 1: 15–20 minutes
Present each of the words from the word list on **pages 194 and 195** to the class. Make sure students understand what each item means and include examples from *Word Partnerships.* Write the following sentences on the board:

1. *This is something scientists use to study very small things.*
2. *This is something used to pour liquid into a beaker.*
3. *This is something used to hold drops of liquid.*
4. *This is the opposite of liquid.*
5. *This is something that can float in the air.*

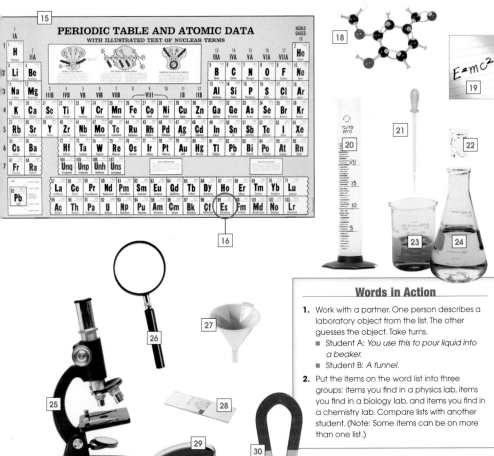

Words in Action

1. Work with a partner. One person describes a laboratory object from the list. The other guesses the object. Take turns.
   - Student A: *You use this to pour liquid into a beaker.*
   - Student B: *A funnel.*
2. Put the items on the word list into three groups: items you find in a physics lab, items you find in a biology lab, and items you find in a chemistry lab. Compare lists with another student. (Note: Some items can be on more than one list.)

195

Objective: Discuss scientific advancements.

Warm-up: 15–20 minutes
In groups, students should develop a definition for *science*. Set a reasonable time limit. After groups have had a few minutes to write definitions on paper, ask them to write their definitions on the board. Encourage questions and discuss the similarities and differences between the definitions.

Introduction: State the objective.

Presentation 1: 20–30 minutes
Have students follow along as you read aloud the word list on **pages 194 and 195.** Make sure students understand the meaning of each item and can think of an example of how each item is used. Read and discuss *Words in Context* together as a class. Lead a class discussion about the way of life 100 years ago. Ask students to identify any inventions that have changed or improved our lives over the last 100 years. Begin a cluster activity, using the cluster template from the Activity Bank CD-ROM.

Practice 1: 15–20 minutes
Have students work in groups to complete the cluster activity. Supply copies of the cluster template from the Activity Bank CD-ROM so each student can maintain his or her own copy.

Evaluation 1: Ask representatives of each group to visit other groups and compare their clusters. Create one master version of the cluster on the board that incorporates all the students' answers.

Application: 10–15 minutes
Place students into groups of four. With their groups, students choose which five advancements are most important. Answers must be restricted to inventions and developments that have taken place in the past 100 years. Have groups rank their choices from most important to fifth most important. Allow time for all groups to present their lists and state their rationale for the rankings.

6. *This is something that compares two weights.*
7. *This is something so small you can't see it without a microscope.*
8. *This is something that measures liquid.*
9. *This is something that attracts metal.*
10. *This is something used for picking up small items.*

Practice 1: 20–22 minutes
Divide students into small groups to name the items. Group members should all agree on the same answers, and a few questions can have more than one answer. Compare answers and discuss questions the groups answered differently. In pairs, students should perform *Words in Action #1.*

Evaluation 1: Have volunteers demonstrate in front of the class.

Application: 10–12 minutes
Ask students to describe items in the classroom by their functions.

Project

In groups, students should develop a new invention that will help advance today's world. Groups should describe their invention in a paragraph and a diagram, incorporating as many words from the word list as possible. Schedule an "invention convention" for students to showcase their developments.

Writing

Level ★

Objective: Identify punctuation.

Warm-up: 7–10 minutes
Have students write their names on a piece of paper. Each student should write a sentence with his or her name in it. Give a sample sentence using your name, such as *Sally is from New York*. Label each of these parts: *word, letter,* and *sentence.* Circle the period and the capital letter in the example sentence on the board. Have students identify what the parts are. Use a few student examples and label these as well.

Introduction: State the objective.

Presentation 1: 15–20 minutes
Ask students to open their dictionaries to **pages 196 and 197.** Present the new words and write sentences using words and/or punctuation marks. Make sure students understand the meaning and pronunciation of each item. As a class, read *Words in Context* and identify the punctuation.

Practice 1: 10–15 minutes
Students should make a list of punctuation marks (items 10–19). Divide the class into small groups and have them review the *Words in Context* sections from previous dictionary lessons. Ask them to find several examples of each punctuation mark. Note that most of the punctuation is represented, with the exception of quotes, semicolons, and parentheses. Groups should maintain a list of page numbers for their examples.

Evaluation 1: Listen to group reports.

Presentation 2: 7–10 minutes
Discuss the use of each punctuation mark. Create a list of specific uses for students to reference.

Practice 2: 8–10 minutes
Ask students to copy the sentences in the dictionary where they found each punctuation mark. They can use the *Words in Context* sections again, or as a challenge, write their own sentences using the targeted punctuation mark.

Evaluation 2: Observe the activity.

Application: 15–20 minutes
Supply copies of newspapers or magazines for students to complete *Words in Action #1.* Students may also find other punctuation marks such as bullets or dashes. They should copy the sentences. Then discuss the meanings together.

Words in Context

Writing an **essay** is a process. First you **brainstorm** ideas. Next you **write** an outline, and then you write a draft. Before you **edit**, you **get** feedback. Are you ready to write the final draft? Before you do, make sure the **punctuation** is correct. Have you used **capital letters** for the first letter of each **word** in the **title**? Have you indented each **paragraph**? If so, now you are ready to write the final draft.

1 a letter
2 a word
3 a sentence
4 a paragraph
5 a paper / an essay
6 an indentation
7 a margin

8 a title
9 punctuation
10 a period
11 a comma
12 a question mark
13 an exclamation point / an exclamation mark

14 an apostrophe
15 parentheses
16 quotation marks
17 a colon
18 a semicolon
19 a hyphen

Verbs

20 brainstorm ideas

21 write an outline

22 write a draft

23 get feedback

24 edit your essay

25 type your final draft

196

Level ★★

Objective: Outline an idea.

Warm-up: 15–18 minutes
Write the word *brainstorm* on the board and ask students to guess its meaning. Divide the word into two parts, *brain* and *storm*, and discuss the definitions of these words. Show students a sample of a cluster. Explain how to brainstorm. Explore a common subject, such as

healthy food, in a cluster so students learn the concept through practice.

Introduction: State the objective.

Presentation 1: 15–20 minutes
Go over each of the words from the word list on **pages 196 and 197** with students. Where appropriate, incorporate the adjectives from *Word Partnerships*. Teach students basic outlining techniques and show them how to turn the sample cluster into an outline. The center circle of the cluster can become the first, or

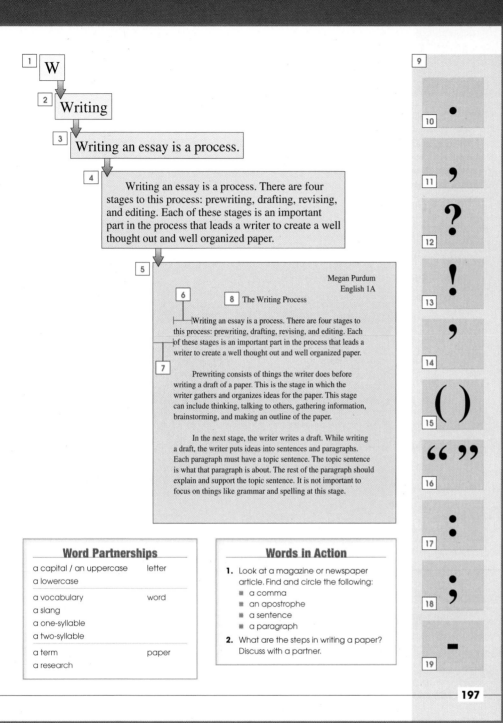

Word Partnerships

a capital / an uppercase	letter
a lowercase	
a vocabulary	word
a slang	
a one-syllable	
a two-syllable	
a term	paper
a research	

Words in Action

1. Look at a magazine or newspaper article. Find and circle the following:
   - a comma
   - an apostrophe
   - a sentence
   - a paragraph
2. What are the steps in writing a paper? Discuss with a partner.

9
10 .
11 ,
12 ?
13 !
14 ,
15 ( )
16 " "
17 :
18 ;
19 -

197

Level ★ ★ ★

Objective: Discuss and practice the writing process.

Warm-up: 15–20 minutes
Place students into groups of four to read **Words in Context** and discuss it. Groups should make a numbered list of the steps in the writing process. Supply copies of the local newspaper for students to peruse articles and discuss whether or not the paragraphs conform to the mechanics outlined in **Words in Context.**

Introduction: State the objective.

Presentation 1: 20–30 minutes
Focus student attention on the word list on **pages 196 and 197.** Students should display their understanding of each word by using it in a sentence or pointing out an example from a newspaper article or a lesson in the dictionary. Give students a sample outline (See level 2 Presentation for an example.) and discuss ways the outline can be transformed into an essay. This essay should be simple and use basic vocabulary and sentence structure.

Practice 1: 15–20 minutes
Discuss general topics that students can write about. Students should choose one topic and write a simple essay following the punctuation and outline methods previously discussed.

Evaluation 1: Check students' work as they write and peer edit.

Application: 10–15 minutes
Ask students to edit their own essays and then attempt to write a final draft. Students at this level may or may not be ready to write a simple essay without close direction and guidance. If students are ready for the challenge, ask them to carefully advance through the steps of the writing process to create essays on their chosen topics. Explain that essays will be collected and graded.

introductory, heading. Consider labeling this Roman numeral I. The secondary circles might be the next Roman numerals, and finally the tertiary circles can be capital letters. For example:

I. Introduction—healthy food
II. Fruits and Vegetables
  A. Bananas
  B. Carrots

Start the outline with students.

Practice 1: 15–20 minutes
Ask students to work with a partner to complete the outline.

Evaluation 1: Put a final outline on the board.

Application: 15–20 minutes
As a class, write a simple essay or paragraph using the outline. Students at this level may not be completely ready to write essays. This is merely an exercise to prepare them for the future. Make the activity as interactive as possible as the essay develops.

Project

In groups, students should create a visual list or poster of the writing process. Discuss each step in depth so that students can create visual pictures in their minds. After the list is complete and the entire group agrees on the steps, students should draw pictures to remind them of each step. Remind them to be as thorough as possible so that students at lower levels can use their pictures to follow the process.

Level ★

Objective: Identify verbs and develop a personal time line.

Warm-up: 15–20 minutes
Create a time line on the board about someone's life. If you choose someone well known or historical, prepare information in advance. On the time line, note the person's birth date, school dates, and work background. Consider using the time line worksheet on the **Activity Bank CD-ROM**. Hand out copies of the worksheet time line to students and indicate that exercise A is an example. Read it together. Students should use the blank time line on the worksheet to detail their own life. Request that students make their personal time lines in pencil so that they can update them later.

Introduction: State the objective.

Presentation 1: 15–20 minutes
Ask students to open their dictionaries to **pages 198 and 199.** Study the new vocabulary in depth and make sure students understand what each item means. Take the time to focus on the final *s* sound of many of the verbs and review pronunciation. Ask students to point to different items from the word list as you read them out loud. As a class, create pantomimes for the first five words on the list. Sometimes the pantomimes may be difficult, but students should help each other understand.

Practice 1: 10–15 minutes
Divide the remaining words from the list among different groups. Each group should create pantomimes for their words.

Evaluation 1: Stage a charades game.

Presentation 2: 15–20 minutes
Write *verbs* on the board and ask students if they can identify verbs from the list. As a class, help students see how to use the first 10 words in sentences about their own lives. Review the simple present and make a chart on the board. Emphasize when to use the third-person singular *s*.

Practice 2: 20–30 minutes
In groups, have students work together to write new sentences with the second half of the word list. Students may need help with vocabulary. If this task becomes too difficult, ask each group to work on a different part of the list.

Evaluation 2: Group representatives can write sentences on the board.

Application: 10–15 minutes
Ask students to look at the time lines they made in the Warm-up and revise them to include vocabulary they learned in this lesson.

Explore, Rule, Invent

Words in Context

Humans have achieved amazing things. We have **composed** operas and poetry. We have **discovered** cures for diseases. We have **sailed** the world's oceans and **explored** the continents. We have **launched** rockets into space and **reached** the moon.

1 Humans **migrate** from Asia to the Americas.
2 Mesopotamians **produce** the first wheel.
3 The Egyptians **build / construct** pyramids.
4 The Vikings **sail** to present-day Canada.
5 The Chinese **grow** tea.
6 Joan of Arc **defends** France.
7 Montezuma I **rules** the Aztecs.
8 Amerigo Vespucci **explores** the Amazon.
9 Sir Isaac Newton **discovers** gravity.
10 Ludwig van Beethoven **composes** his first symphony.
11 The Suez Canal **opens.**
12 Thomas Edison **invents** the lightbulb.
13 The Wright brothers **fly** the first plane.
14 World War II **ends.**
15 The Soviet Union **launches** the first satellite.
16 Martin Luther King Jr. **wins** the Nobel Peace Prize.
17 Japan **introduces** the high-speed "bullet" train.
18 Apollo 11 astronauts **reach** the moon.
19 The Berlin Wall **falls.**
20 South Africa **elects** Nelson Mandela president.

Word Partnerships	
win	a war
	a contest
compose	a song
	a letter
elect	a prime minister
	a president
	a mayor
build	a road
	a bridge

— 198 —

Level ★ ★

Objective: Describe past events.

Warm-up: 10–15 minutes
Students should do *Words in Action #1.* They should attempt this activity without looking at the list. As they work, evaluate what students already know.

Introduction: State the objective.

Presentation 1: 20–30 minutes
Present each of the words from the word list on **pages 198 and 199.** Make sure students understand what each item means and discuss the examples in *Word Partnerships.* Review regular past-tense verbs and their pronunciation. Pronunciation of the past tense is often difficult at this level, and the pronunciation of the *ed* ending will improve with use, so be cautious not to deliberate too long. Identify the 16 regular verbs from the word list and

Words in Action

1. Work with a partner. Cover the sentences. One student points to a picture. The other says the event. Take turns.

2. Work with a partner. One student says one of the verbs from the verb list. The other student uses that verb in a sentence.
   - Student A: *Invent*
   - Student B: *Alexander Graham Bell invented the telephone.*

Objective: Discuss past events.

Warm-up: 15–20 minutes
Go around the room and have all students state the most important event in their lives. Suggest some major life events, such as the birth of a baby or a marriage. Ask them what they think is the most important event in history. Consider splitting students into groups for this activity and then have groups report on five major historical events. Encourage questions and discussion.

Introduction: State the objective.

Presentation 1: 20–30 minutes
Read the word list on **pages 198 and 199**. Make sure students understand the meaning of each item. See if the class can create new sentences using each of the verbs. Read **Words in Context** together and discuss it. Review the use of the simple past tense. Describe the events on the list using the past tense. Also review the use of the past perfect tense to describe when one event occurred relative to another. For example, say *Thomas Edison had invented the light bulb before the Wright Brothers flew the first plane.*

Practice 1: 13–15 minutes
Ask students to write sentences comparing two events. Then challenge them to write sentences containing three events.

Evaluation 1: Students should write at least one sentence on the board.

Application: 13–15 minutes
In groups, students should discuss other events that might have been included in the dictionary time line. Give the example of Columbus's voyage to America in 1492. Ask students what other events could be added, especially from their native countries. Suggest ideas such as a revolutionary war, a special election, or major inventions. Have students describe where these events might fit into the time line. Encourage use of the past perfect if students are familiar with this tense.

discuss the five irregular verbs. Review the past tense of a few irregular verbs students should know, such as *be* and *have*.

Practice 1: 10–12 minutes
In pairs, students should read and practice the dialog as suggested in **Words in Action #2**. Have students change roles and incorporate as many examples from the word list as possible within the allotted time.

Evaluation 1: Observe the activity.

Application: 20–30 minutes
Ask students to make a personal time line of their lives. Consider developing a time line about yourself, a well-known person, or a fictitious character you create so students will have an example from which to work. Supply copies of the worksheet available on the Activity Bank CD-ROM. Students should use past-tense verbs in their time lines.

Project

Ask students to make a new time line of events in the history of the world or their own countries. If the class is from a single country, form groups of students to choose various countries or various eras in their country's history. Schedule time for students to share their time lines in formal presentations to the class.

U.S. Government and Citizenship

Level ★

Objective: Identify government vocabulary.

Warm-up: 7–10 minutes
As a class, discuss world leaders and their titles. Match leaders to their countries and write the country names on the board along with each country's type of government. Start with the President of the United States. Include leaders representing all the students' native countries as well as any others students suggest.

Introduction: State the objective.

Presentation 1: 15–20 minutes
Focus attention on **pages 200 and 201.** Explain the words in the list and have students use them in sentences or create sentences with the students. Formally review pronunciation by having students repeat the words after you. Say different items from the word list and ask students to point to the corresponding pictures.

Practice 1: 10–15 minutes
Students should form pairs to continue the quizzing activity. One partner points to an item on the word list and the other responds by identifying the proper picture. The student responding can use the word list at first but should cover it after a prearranged time limit for study.

Evaluation 1: Observe the activity.

Presentation 2: 8–10 minutes
Explain the distinction between verbs and nouns. Create a table on the board with the categories *people, places, other nouns,* and *verbs.* Start filling in the table as a class with the new vocabulary. Include one example for each category.

Practice 2: 10–15 minutes
Ask students in groups to complete the table. Ask them to include any other words they might know and arrange time to discuss.

Evaluation 2: Complete the table on the board with feedback from the groups.

Application: 10–15 minutes
Ask students to make a list of the five words from the word list they consider the most important. Then ask volunteers to share their lists with the class. For each word selected, students should have a reason for choosing it. Encourage questions and discussion.

Words in Context

The U.S. **government** has three parts. These parts are called *branches.* The executive branch includes the **president** and the **vice president.** The legislative branch includes the **House of Representatives** and the **Senate.** There are 100 **senators** in the Senate and 435 **congressmen** and **congresswomen** in the House of Representatives. The judicial branch includes nine **Supreme Court justices.**

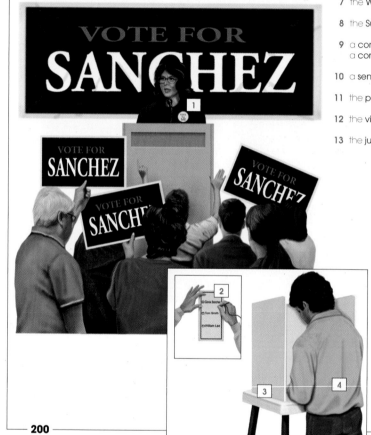

1 a (political) candidate

2 a ballot

3 a voting booth

4 a citizen

5 the U.S. Constitution

6 the Capitol (Building)

7 the White House

8 the Supreme Court

9 a congresswoman / a congressman

10 a senator

11 the president

12 the vice president

13 the justices

200

Level ★ ★

Objective: Discuss and compare governments.

Warm-up: 10–15 minutes
Ask students to study the activities on the word list (numbers 14 through 19) and form groups to rank them from most important to least important. Students should discuss their rankings and agree on a new master list.

Remind students that all the activities may be very important.

Introduction: State the objective.

Presentation 1: 20–30 minutes
Present each of the words from the word list on **pages 200 and 201.** Make sure students understand what each item means and include *Word Partnerships.* Start a conversation about items 14 through 19.

We the People

Legislative Branch

Congress

House of Representatives → ← Senate

Executive Branch

Judicial Branch

Verbs

14 vote

15 obey the law

16 pay taxes

17 serve on a jury

18 protest / demonstrate

19 serve in the military

Word Partnerships

a United States	citizen
	senator
	congressman

Words in Action

1. Compare the U.S. government with the government of another country. How are they similar? How are they different?

2. Discuss which branch of the U.S. government you think is most important. Explain your reasons.

201

Level ★ ★ ★

Objective: Write a paragraph.

Warm-up: 15–20 minutes
Generate a conversation about the governments in the U.S. and other countries. See what students already know about government in the United States. Read **Words in Context.** Give students five full minutes to study and tell them that there will be a quiz afterward. After the time has elapsed, ask students to close their dictionaries and answer the following questions:

1. *How many branches or parts of government are there?*
2. *Who are the leaders in the executive branch?*
3. *How many senators are there?*
4. *In the Supreme Court there are nine _____.*

Review the answers together as a class.

Introduction: State the objective.

Presentation 1: 15–18 minutes
Go over the word list on **pages 200 and 201.** Ask students to relate each word to the government system in the United States. Students should be able to use the words in context. Review what each branch of government does and what it means to have *checks and balances.*

Practice 1: 15–18 minutes
Ask students to write sentences describing the branches of the U.S. government. Provide them with the sentence starter *The executive branch is important because . . .* They should complete the same sentence for each of the different branches.

Evaluation 1: Ask students to write their sentences on the board.

Application: 15–18 minutes
Students should use the sentences on the board, along with new ones they create, to form a paragraph that addresses the question posed in *Words in Action #2.* If necessary, review proper paragraph form and transition words.

Write the following questions on the board:
1. *Do you vote in the U.S./your native country? How often?*
2. *Do you obey speed limits on the highway? What are they?*
3. *Does the U.S./your native country have a jury system?*
4. *Is it legal to protest in the U.S./in your native country?*
5. *Does the U.S./your native country have a large military?*
6. *Do you pay taxes?*

Discuss the meaning of each question.

Practice 1: 15–20 minutes
Ask students to form pairs to ask one another the questions. Set aside time for students to discuss their answers. Encourage them to take notes.

Evaluation 1: Observe the activity.

Application: 15–18 minutes
Ask students to do **Words in Action #1** or discuss the question as a class using the ideas generated in the Practice.

Project

In groups, have students imagine they are going to teach a U.S. citizenship course. The group should develop a simple chart describing the form of government in the U.S. and another describing the government system of another country. Ask groups to present their charts to the class.

Level ★

Objective: Identify fine arts vocabulary.

Warm-up: 10–15 minutes
Write the following words across the board with space between them: *table, chair, apple, cat,* and *spider.* Ask volunteers to draw a picture under each word. Consider drawing one of them yourself and mention that beautiful art is not expected or required. Write *ART* on the board in large letters and point to each of the drawings. Pantomime other forms of art, such as sculpting or taking a photograph. Ask students to identify what you are doing. Write the forms of art on the board and ask students to pantomime any others they can think of. If possible, bring art samples to class.

Introduction: State the objective.

Presentation 1: 15–20 minutes
Ask students to open the dictionaries to **pages 202 and 203** and follow along as the new vocabulary is presented. Make sure students understand what each item means and review pronunciation. Start a cluster on the board. Label the primary circle *art materials.* Draw four secondary circles and label the first one *painting.* Add one tertiary circle to that labeled *paintbrush.* Have students add as many tertiary circles as possible. There is an Activity Bank CD-ROM template available to facilitate this activity.

Practice 1: 10–15 minutes
Ask students to complete the cluster. For this cluster activity, students should label the three other secondary circles and create new tertiary circles.
Evaluation 1: As a class, complete the cluster started in the Presentation.

Presentation 2: 8–10 minutes
Prepare students to perform this model conversation.
   Student A: *Do you <u>draw</u> (paint, take photographs, sculpt, make pots)?*
   Student B: *Yes OR No.*
   Student A: *Do you prefer to look at art or create art?*
   Student B: *I like to <u>create</u> art.*

Next, prepare students to do a corners activity. Each corner of the room represents one of the secondary circles from Practice 1. Assign each corner an art form.

Practice 2: 8–10 minutes
Tell students to go to the corner representing the art form they prefer. Encourage them to talk with students in their corner, using the model conversation.
Evaluation 2: Observe conversations.

Application: 10–15 minutes
Have students imagine they will take a course about one of the art forms described in the dictionary. They should make a list of supplies they will need.

Fine Arts

202

Level ★ ★

Objective: Describe a scene.

Warm-up: 10–12 minutes
Have students form pairs and discuss the questions posed in **Words in Action #2.**

Introduction: State the objective.

Presentation 1: 20–30 minutes
Explain each of the words from the word list on **pages 202 and 203.** As a class, create definitions the students agree on and pay special attention to **Word Partnerships.** Students should describe what they see in the picture. Write a few sentences on the board. Make a list of a few adjectives and adverbs they can use and incorporate the **Word Partnerships.** Review the forms and functions of adjectives and adverbs as well as correct word order for the English language. Explain that the adjective usually comes before the noun unless it follows the *be* verb. Explain that adverbs are usually placed near the verb.

1 a frame

2 a still life

3 a portrait

4 a landscape

5 a model

6 a palette

7 a painting

8 a paintbrush

9 a painter

10 paint

11 an easel

12 a canvas

13 a sketchpad

14 a sketch

15 a mural

16 a sculpture

17 a sculptor

18 pottery

19 a potter

20 a potter's wheel

21 clay

22 a photograph

23 a photographer

Verbs

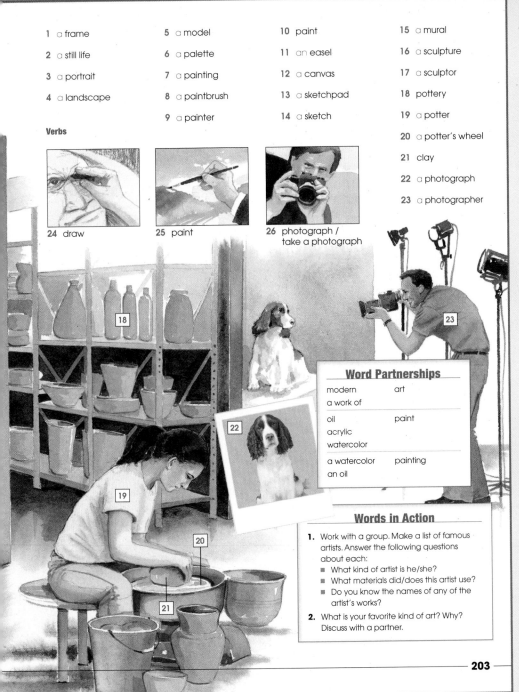

24 draw

25 paint

26 photograph /
take a photograph

Word Partnerships

modern	art
a work of	
oil	paint
acrylic	
watercolor	
a watercolor	painting
an oil	

Words in Action

1. Work with a group. Make a list of famous artists. Answer the following questions about each:
   - What kind of artist is he/she?
   - What materials did/does this artist use?
   - Do you know the names of any of the artist's works?

2. What is your favorite kind of art? Why? Discuss with a partner.

203

Level ★ ★ ★

Objective: Plan an art supply store.

Warm-up: 15–20 minutes
Form groups and ask students to read *Words in Context* before discussing their opinions about art. Then lead a class discussion. Consider extending the conversation by asking for student opinions about modern art and preferences among still life, portraits, and sketches. Encourage students to name famous artists or specific pieces of artwork.

Introduction: State the objective.

Presentation 1: 15–20 minutes
Formally present the word list on **pages 202 and 203**. Make sure students understand the meaning of each item and can write a sentence using the term in context. As a class, complete a table with four columns labeled *painting, sculpture, pottery,* and *photography*. Consider incorporating the group activity outlined in *Words in Action #1*. Use the table template on the Activity Bank CD-ROM. Ask students to share their personal experiences with art and knowledge about famous painters.

Practice 1: 15–20 minutes
Divide students into small groups and ask them to add to the word list. Encourage them to discuss the supplies they would need if they were opening an art supply store. Then send representatives from each group to the other groups to gather more ideas.

Evaluation 1: Observe the activity.

Application: 15–20 minutes
Within their groups, students should take the inventory lists they created in Practice 1 and make the following decisions about their art supply stores:
1. *Choose a name.*
2. *Decide how they will advertise.*
3. *Identify prices for items for sale.*

Schedule time for group reports and discussion.

Practice 1: 15–17 minutes
Individually, students should write a description of the scene in the dictionary on **pages 202 and 203** and use as many adjectives and adverbs as they can. Challenge students to use at least one adjective and adverb per sentence, but remind them to consider correct English word order.

Evaluation 1: Students write their sentences on the board and discuss each one. Assist with grammar and pronunciation.

Application: 15–20 minutes
Students select and describe a favorite picture from a previous dictionary lesson. Ask students to write several sentences describing their selection and encourage them to use adjectives and adverbs.

Project

Bring in informational pamphlets or postcards from a local art museum's collection. Printouts from a Web site work as well. Have students identify what types of art are in the museum. What time periods or cultures are represented? How is the museum organized? Have small groups specialize in particular sections of the museum and describe what visitors would see there. Each group should describe a few pieces of art in detail, discussing the medium, size, shape, history, artist, and title of the piece. A highlight of this project would be to bring students to the museum and then have them discuss their assigned sections afterward.

Level ★

Objective: Identify performing arts vocabulary.

Warm-up: 10–15 minutes
Write *dance, act,* and *sing* on the board. Ask students to help you define these words through actions or examples. Ask for examples of famous dancers, actors, and singers. Make a list on the board. Continue the conversation by discussing examples of names of dances and songs. Ask if any students are involved in performing arts, or have been in the past.

Introduction: State the objective.

Presentation 1: 15–20 minutes
Ask students to open their dictionaries to **pages 204 and 205.** Go over the new vocabulary. Make sure students understand what each item means and review pronunciation. Prepare students to play Bingo. Print out the Performing Arts Bingo cards (with pre-selected words) from the Activity Bank CD-ROM worksheet folder, or have students choose eight words from the list and write them on the blank Bingo cards from the Activity Bank CD-ROM template folder.

Practice 1: 10–15 minutes
Read words from the list in random order. Ask students to cross out the words as they hear them. The first student to cross off all eight words is the winner. Challenge the winning students to also give definitions after they yell, "Bingo!"

Evaluation 1: Observe the activity.

Presentation 2: 8–10 minutes
Prepare students for a focused listening activity. Remind them that they may look at the dictionary pages while they listen.

Practice 2: 8–10 minutes
Tell students that they should listen and point to the performing arts items as they hear them in the following paragraph. If time permits, read the paragraph again slowly and ask students to write each vocabulary word they hear.

I went to a <u>ballet</u> yesterday. I went to the <u>ballet</u> early because I didn't have <u>tickets</u>. The <u>box office</u> was really busy. I saw a beautiful <u>dancer</u>. She was wearing a long, dark <u>costume</u>. I liked this much better than the <u>play</u> I went to where the <u>actor</u> didn't have a <u>microphone</u>. I couldn't hear him! This time, the <u>orchestra</u> was excellent. I am so lucky I could go. Next time, I want to go see an <u>opera</u>.

Evaluation 2: Observe the activity.

Application: 10–15 minutes
Ask for opinions from all students about which activity they like the most: a ballet, an opera, a rock concert, a play, or something else.

Performing Arts

Words in Context

Different **performing arts** began in different countries around the world. For example, theater began in ancient Greece. The **actors** wore **masks** and performed **plays** in large outdoor theaters. **Opera** began in Italy at the end of the 16th century, and soon became popular in France and Germany. **Ballet** also began in Italy at the end of the 16th century, and it became very popular in France while Louis XIV was king.

1	a ballet	6	a stage
2	a balcony	7	a conductor
3	a dancer	8	an orchestra
4	a mask	9	an audience
5	a costume		

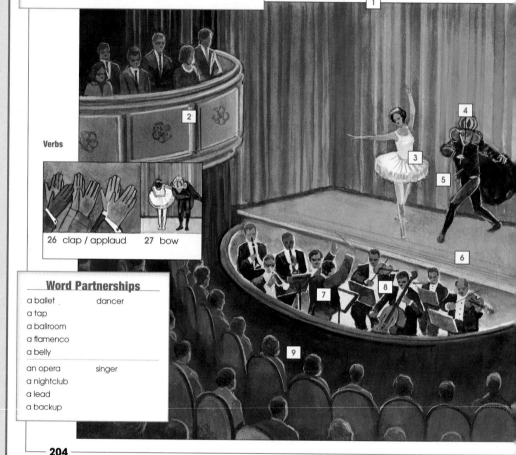

Verbs

26 clap / applaud   27 bow

Word Partnerships

a ballet	dancer
a tap	
a ballroom	
a flamenco	
a belly	
an opera	singer
a nightclub	
a lead	
a backup	

204

Level ★ ★

Objective: Use the present continuous tense.

Warm-up: 15–17 minutes
Divide students into small groups and ask them to complete the activity suggested in *Words in Action #1.* Have groups choose their favorite form of performing arts.

Introduction: State the objective.

Presentation 1: 15–18 minutes
Go over each of the words from the word list on **pages 204 and 205** with students. Make sure they understand what each item means. When discussing *dancer* and *singer,* include the adjectives in *Word Partnerships.* Review the present continuous tense and make a chart on the board. As a class, choose a verb to go with each of the items from the word list. The nouns can be associated with the verbs as either a subject or a direct object. Explain the

10 a (rock) concert
11 a spotlight
12 a drummer
13 a microphone
14 a singer
15 a guitarist
16 backup singers
17 a play

18 an actor
19 a set
20 a seat
21 an usher
22 a ticket
23 a program
24 a box office
25 an opera

Words in Action

1. Have you ever seen a ballet? An opera? A play? Choose your favorite and tell a partner about it.

2. Imagine you are the directors of a new arts center. What kinds of concerts, plays, and other performances will you present this year? Discuss with your group.

205

difference between the two. Give students a few examples: *A dancer bows* and *An usher gives a program.*

Practice 1: 20–30 minutes
Students should work with a partner to form a sentence for each of the pairs of verbs and nouns from the chart on the board. Verbs should be used in the present continuous. For example: *A dancer is bowing* and *An usher is giving a program.* An Activity Bank CD-ROM lesson worksheet on the present continuous is available to assist with this practice.

Evaluation 1: Ask students to write their sentences on the board and discuss them.

Application: 10–15 minutes
Have students continue writing sentences using the present continuous. Encourage students to think about activities that are happening both in the performing arts spread and in pictures from previous lessons. Review the fine arts picture on **pages 202 and 203** and help with vocabulary.

Objective: Manage a performing arts center.

Warm-up: 15–20 minutes
Begin a conversation in which students discuss how much money they spend on entertainment on weekends. Students can explain what they enjoy doing for entertainment. They should write their favorite types of entertainment and be prepared to share with the entire class. Take a poll and see what students like to do in their free time. Group entertainment activities together in categories and make a bar graph. There is a bar graph template available on the Activity Bank CD-ROM to facilitate this activity.

Introduction: State the objective.

Presentation 1: 10–15 minutes
Present the word list in its entirety on **pages 204 and 205.** Make sure students understand the meaning of each item and can use the words in sentences. Read *Words in Context* with students and discuss it, focusing on the use of vocabulary. Write *rehearsals* on the board. Ask students for opinions on how much rehearsal is necessary for a theater or musical production. Expand the conversation by asking students to share personal performing arts experiences. Review the grammatical concept of reported speech versus quoted speech. Also discuss the proper use of verbs for each.

Practice 1: 15–17 minutes
Place students in small groups to complete the discussion described in *Words in Action #1.* Students should describe why they prefer one form of performing arts to another. Tell students that they will present information about one other group member to the rest of the class. Remind them to focus on proper grammar for reported speech.

Evaluation 1: Observe the activity and then discuss the question as a class. Ask students to report on someone else so that they have the opportunity to use reported speech.

Application: 20–30 minutes
Assign students to work on *Words in Action #2.* Students should develop a calendar for six months of performances and rehearsal time. They should also include more than one or two forms of performing arts. Think of specific plays, ballets, and musical groups to invite.

Project

Assign students to attend a local theater performance and write a short essay reviewing their experience and using new vocabulary words. Have students call ahead to ask about group rates and student discounts available at many theaters.

Instruments

Level ★

Objective: Identify musical instruments.

Warm-up: 10–15 minutes
Write *music* on the board and initiate a conversation about what kinds of music students enjoy listening to. Make a list on the board of different kinds of music. Expand the conversation to include types of musical instruments students play or enjoy listening to. Be prepared to use a lot of hand gestures and pantomimes to help students understand.

Introduction: State the objective.

Presentation 1: 15–20 minutes
Ask students to open their dictionaries to **pages 206 and 207.** Formally present the new vocabulary and make sure students understand what each item means. Review pronunciation as a class by having students repeat the words. Say an item and ask students to point to the corresponding pictures. Initiate a game where identifying the instruments is the goal. There are five categories of instruments on the two pages. Ask students to do something different each time you say an instrument in a different category. For example, have them stand up and sit down any time you mention a percussion instrument. Have them raise their right hands for brass and their left hands for woodwinds. Other actions might include clapping or putting their hands to their ears. Practice a few times.

Practice 1: 8–10 minutes
Say the names of instruments in random order and ask students to perform the actions developed in the Presentation.

Evaluation 1: Observe the activity.

Presentation 2: 8–10 minutes
Start a two-column table on the board and label the headers *familiar* and *unfamiliar.* Describe what the headers mean. Provide one example for each column so students understand.

Practice 2: 8–10 minutes
Ask students to complete the table individually for both the familiar instruments they have listened to before and the unfamiliar ones they think they have never heard.

Evaluation 2: Provide time for students to share their lists in groups.

Application: 12–15 minutes
Have students rank the instruments that they are familiar with from the most beautiful sound to the least. Students can compare answers for the most beautiful instruments using Venn diagrams from the template available on the **Activity Bank CD-ROM.**

Words in Context

Percussion instruments are thousands of years old. **Drums** are one of the oldest percussion instruments. They were part of African culture as early as 6000 B.C. The **tambourine** is also thousands of years old. Many countries, from Japan to Morocco to England, use tambourines in their music. Other percussion instruments include **maracas,** from Latin America, and **cymbals,** from China.

Word Partnerships

play	an instrument
tune	
practice	the piano
	the violin
	the cello
an acoustic	guitar
an electric	
a bass	

206

Level ★ ★

Objective: Describe instruments.

Warm-up: 15–20 minutes
In groups, ask students to list as many musical instruments as possible. Dictionaries should remain closed. If students don't know a word in English, let them draw a picture of it. After 10 minutes, the group with the most words wins. Make a master list of the words on the board.

Introduction: State the objective.

Presentation 1: 15–18 minutes
Go over each of the words from the word list on **pages 206 and 207** with students. Make sure they understand what each item means and include *Word Partnerships.* Review shapes by referring to **page 193.** Also review colors and materials such as brass, nickel, silver, plastic, and wood. Flutes are made of silver and/or nickel; brass instruments and saxophones are made of brass; clarinets, oboes, and bassoons are made of wood

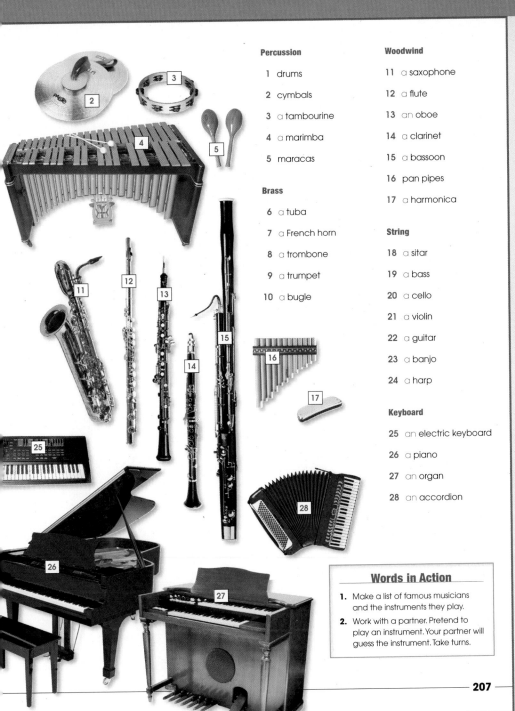

Percussion

1 drums
2 cymbals
3 a tambourine
4 a marimba
5 maracas

Brass

6 a tuba
7 a French horn
8 a trombone
9 a trumpet
10 a bugle

Woodwind

11 a saxophone
12 a flute
13 an oboe
14 a clarinet
15 a bassoon
16 pan pipes
17 a harmonica

String

18 a sitar
19 a bass
20 a cello
21 a violin
22 a guitar
23 a banjo
24 a harp

Keyboard

25 an electric keyboard
26 a piano
27 an organ
28 an accordion

Words in Action

1. Make a list of famous musicians and the instruments they play.

2. Work with a partner. Pretend to play an instrument. Your partner will guess the instrument. Take turns.

207

Level ★ ★ ★

Objective: Write a paragraph from an outline.

Warm-up: 8–10 minutes
Ask students to complete the task suggested in *Words in Action #1*.

Introduction: State the objective.

Presentation 1: 10–15 minutes
Read the word list on **pages 206 and 207**. Encourage discussion and questions and encourage students to offer personal stories. Read *Words in Context* with students and discuss it. Initiate a conversation in which students state their favorite category of instruments: *percussion, brass, woodwind, string,* or *keyboard.* Write the following information on the board.

I.   The first horn
A. animal horn
B. different sizes—different sounds or tones

II. The first trumpet
A. metal and bronze
B. 1500 BC
C. from Egypt

III. French horn
A. first horn in the orchestra
B. from England

IV. Trombone
A. first horn to play all notes
B. nine feet long when stretched out

Practice 1: 30–40 minutes
Students should use the information presented on the board to write a paragraph about the history of brass instruments. Work together to create an interesting topic sentence. Students can use *Words in Context* as a model.

Evaluation 1: Ask volunteers to read their paragraphs to the class.

Application: 50–60 minutes
Ask students to write another outline and paragraph about their favorite instrument(s) and why they like it/them. Prepare some background information to have available in class.

Project

Project A) Supply pictures or brochures of local bands or orchestras. Ask students to determine what instruments are represented in each musical group.

Project B) If students are willing, have them bring in instruments they play and answer questions from their classmates. Have students summarize the experience of talking to the musicians in class.

---

and/or plastic. String instruments are usually made of wood. Prepare students to model this conversation.

Student A: *It is an instrument made of wood. It is black, long, and straight.*

Student B: *Is it a clarinet?*

Student A: *Yes (OR No).*

Practice 1: 20–30 minutes
In pairs, students quiz one another by describing an instrument and seeing if their partner can identify it from the description.
Evaluation 1: Observe the activity.

Application: 10–12 minutes
Students should write a description of their favorite instrument on a small card without including their own name or the instrument's name. Collect the cards and redistribute them randomly. Make sure no student gets his or her own card. Ask students to go around the room and try to find the author of the card they received. They may not read the descriptions out loud but should only ask questions such as *Is your favorite instrument the <u>saxophone</u>?*

Level ★

Objective: Describe TV and movie viewing habits.

Warm-up: 10–15 minutes
Write *listen to music, watch TV,* and *go to a movie* on the board and go around the room asking students to state their preferences. Take a poll and tell students they can only vote once. Make a bar graph of the results. There is a bar graph template on the Activity Bank CD-ROM.

Introduction: State the objective.

Presentation 1: 15–20 minutes
Have students open their dictionaries to **pages 208 and 209.** Go over the new vocabulary. Make sure students understand what each item means and review pronunciation. Focus on movies and films. Call for students to identify any recent movies or films they have seen. Write their responses on the board. To assist in this discussion, review **pages 38 and 39** in the dictionary. Ask students what *feelings* horror films evoke.

Practice 1: 8–10 minutes
In groups, students should decide what feelings or emotions might accompany watching each of the other types of films listed in the dictionary.

Evaluation 1: Listen to group reports.

Presentation 2: 15–20 minutes
Determine how many hours a day students watch TV. Extend the conversation to include how many hours they listen to music. Create two more bar graphs to reflect these class polls. Utilize the Activity Bank CD-ROM bar graph template to facilitate this activity. Make a sample pie chart that shows percentages. Divide it in various ways so students understand how to estimate a percentage. Give students the following information about Margie.

watches the news 50% of the time

watches game shows 15% of the time

watches sitcoms 30% of the time

watches sports 5% of the time

Practice 2: 8–10 minutes
Ask students to make a pie chart of the information about Margie and give it a title. Supply copies of the pie chart template available on the Activity Bank CD-ROM.

Evaluation 2: Students copy their charts to the board and discuss them as a class.

Application: 10–15 minutes
Ask students to make a pie chart based on their own television-watching habits.

Film, TV, and Music

Words in Context

My husband and I never agree on **films.** For example, my husband always wants to see **action** films or **horror movies.** I usually prefer **dramas** or **comedies.** But we have children, so we usually end up at **animated** films!

Films / Movies

1 action / adventure
2 comedy
3 mystery / suspense
4 drama
5 romance
6 science fiction
7 western
8 fantasy
9 horror
10 documentary
11 animated

Word Partnerships

an independent a foreign	film
a funny a scary	movie
satellite cable	TV
a TV	station commercial
loud soft	music

208

Level ★ ★

Objective: Describe feelings.

Warm-up: 15–17 minutes
As a class, complete *Words in Action #1.*

Introduction: State the objective.

Presentation 1: 15–20 minutes
Study each of the words from the word list on **pages 208 and 209** with students. Make sure they understand what each item means before including *Word*

Partnerships. Ask students how they feel when they listen to classical music. Some students might say that they are bored and others might express excitement or other feelings. Prepare students for an interview by reviewing the following questions.

Where do you listen to music?

What type of music do you listen to?

When do you listen to music?

How often do you listen to music?

TV programs

12 news
13 sitcom
14 cartoon
15 game show
16 soap opera
17 talk show
18 nature program
19 children's program
20 sports
21 reality show

Music

22 pop
23 jazz
24 rock
25 blues
26 R&B / soul
27 hip hop
28 classical
29 country and western

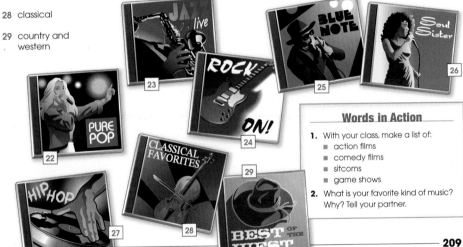

Words in Action

1. With your class, make a list of:
   - action films
   - comedy films
   - sitcoms
   - game shows
2. What is your favorite kind of music? Why? Tell your partner.

Why do you listen to music?
How does music make you feel?

Practice 1: 20–30 minutes
Ask students to interview four students in the class with these questions and take notes.

Evaluation 1: Students report information about the classmates they interviewed. Have students use the student information grid templates available on the **Activity Bank CD-ROM** to collect the information.

Application: 20–30 minutes
Have students interview classmates about their interests in TV shows and movies. Students should be thorough in their answers.

Objective: Express agreement and disagreement.

Warm-up: 15–17 minutes
Students should find a partner and discuss the question posed in *Words in Action #2.*

Introduction: State the objective.

Presentation 1: 20–30 minutes
Present the word list on **pages 208 and 209** and ask students to suggest an example for each word. Read *Words in Context* with students and discuss it. Discuss the movie-rating system. Ask students why there is a rating system. Explain that the ratings are guidelines for parents of children and teenagers. Some parents don't allow their children to see movies containing violence or other adult content. Most of these guidelines have to do with sex, impolite language, or violence. Teach students conversational expressions to show agreement and disagreement. For example, teach them *I agree, That makes sense, I don't agree, That is your opinion, not mine,* and *I (don't) think it is a good idea.* Also, teach expressions for asking for more information, such as *Why do you say that?, Can you explain what you mean?,* and *I don't know what you mean.*

Practice 1: 15–18 minutes
In groups, students should expand on the discussion about the movie-rating system and incorporate their personal opinions. Each group should elect a secretary to take notes. Notes should include whether each member agrees or disagrees with the movie-rating system. Encourage students to check their statements to make sure they use the examples given in the Presentation. Suggest that they elaborate on their opinions and point out pros and cons of the system.

Evaluation 1: Listen to group reports.

Application: 10–15 minutes
In small groups, have students discuss how much TV a child should be allowed to watch a day. Have students make a chart of which TV shows are good for children and which aren't. Ask students why they think some shows are inappropriate for children.

Project

Ask groups to develop a survey about film, TV, and music. The survey should have 10 questions, including the following:
1. *How much TV should children watch?*
2. *How does rock music make you feel?*
3. *Do movies today have too much violence?*

Schedule time for students to survey other classes and tabulate the results.

Level ★

Objective: Describe beach vocabulary.

Warm-up: 8–10 minutes
Write *sand*, *water*, *towel*, and *swim* on the board. Explain what each of these words means. Tell students that the lesson relates to these words and see if students can determine what these things have in common. After the lesson topic is revealed, ask if students have ever been to a beach and take a poll to find out if they liked it.

Introduction: State the objective.

Presentation 1: 15–20 minutes
Ask students to open their dictionaries to **pages 210 and 211.** Go over the new vocabulary. Make sure students understand what each item means and review pronunciation. Prepare students for a quizzing exercise by naming different items in the dictionary and asking students to point to the corresponding pictures.

Practice 1: 8–10 minutes
Pair students by level and have them continue the quiz. Student A points to an item and Student B says the corresponding word from the list. After a few minutes, students cover the word list and continue.

Evaluation 1: Listen to group reports.

Presentation 2: 10–15 minutes
Present the four verbs listed. Brainstorm verbs to accompany other words from the list. Write these items and verbs on the board: *sailboat—sail, water-skier—ski, snorkel—go snorkeling, sunbather—sunbathe,* and *shovel—dig.* Review the meaning of each word. Assign a name to each person in the dictionary. Prepare students to perform this model conversation.

> **Student A:** *What does Mary like to do at the beach?*
>
> **Student B:** *She likes to sunbathe.*

Practice 2: 8–10 minutes
Have students practice the exchange substituting underlined words.

Evaluation 2: Ask for volunteers to demonstrate in front of the class.

Application: 12–15 minutes
Continue the exchange from Practice 2 but substitute personal information for the underlined words. Write the following on the board.

> **Student A:** *What do you like to do at the beach?*
>
> **Student B:** *I like to _____.*

Students should talk with four classmates and record their responses. Use the student information grid template from the *Activity Bank CD-ROM.*

Beach

Words in Context

There is a **beach** in Japan with perfect weather every day of the year. How is it possible? The beach at Ocean Dome is indoors! **Sunbathers** put their beach towels on the **sand** and relax. There is no sun, but it feels warm and sunny inside. **Swimmers swim** in a man-made **ocean**, and **surfers surf** on man-made **waves**!

Verbs

30 surf   31 dive

32 swim   33 float

210

Level ★★

Objective: Use the past continuous tense.

Warm-up: 15–17 minutes
Assign small groups to complete the task presented in *Words in Action #2.*

Introduction: State the objective.

Presentation 1: 15–20 minutes
Go over each of the words from the word list on **pages 210 and 211** with students. Define each item and include the adjectives from **Word Partnerships.** Incorporating the adjectives from **Word Partnerships,** describe the scene as a class. Write sentences to describe what is happening and describe the beach itself. Write on the board *I am looking at the area by the sunbather. What is happening?* Review the present continuous. As a class, come up with something that might happen. For example: *She was sunbathing when a fly landed on her nose.* Make a chart and teach students the past continuous.

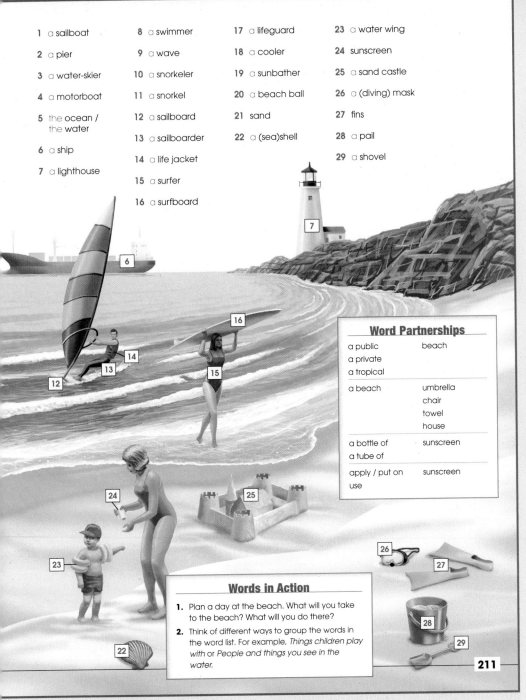

1 a sailboat

2 a pier

3 a water-skier

4 a motorboat

5 the ocean / the water

6 a ship

7 a lighthouse

8 a swimmer

9 a wave

10 a snorkeler

11 a snorkel

12 a sailboard

13 a sailboarder

14 a life jacket

15 a surfer

16 a surfboard

17 a lifeguard

18 a cooler

19 a sunbather

20 a beach ball

21 sand

22 a (sea)shell

23 a water wing

24 sunscreen

25 a sand castle

26 a (diving) mask

27 fins

28 a pail

29 a shovel

Word Partnerships

a public	beach
a private	
a tropical	
a beach	umbrella
	chair
	towel
	house
a bottle of	sunscreen
a tube of	
apply / put on use	sunscreen

Words in Action

1. Plan a day at the beach. What will you take to the beach? What will you do there?

2. Think of different ways to group the words in the word list. For example, *Things children play with* or *People and things you see in the water.*

211

Objective: Discuss safety tips.

Warm-up: 10–15 minutes
Begin a conversation about the beach and poll the class to see if students prefer the beach in warm or cold weather. Determine if any students like to go to the beach in cold weather. Discuss why or why not. Make lists of activities students like to do on the beach in the summer and what they like to do on the beach in the fall. Read *Words in Context* as a class before dividing into small groups to discuss it.

Introduction: State the objective.

Presentation 1: 20–30 minutes
Present the word list on **pages 210 and 211** and ask students to create a sentence for each word. Make sure students understand the meaning of each item. Begin a conversation about safety and ask students to suggest accidents that can happen at the beach. Focus attention on the lifeguard and create a list of reasons why a lifeguard is important. Discuss the word *drowning*. Write the following words on the board: *avoid, fall, drown, accompany, never, alone, sunscreen, protection, caution, life jacket,* and the modal *should.* Include any other related words students suggest. Review the function of modals and give examples using *should.*

Practice 1: 10–15 minutes
In groups, students should use the words on the board to write sentences expressing advice about the beach. They must use each word at least once but may include more than one word in the same sentence. Additionally, they must include the modal *should.* Suggest thinking of signs they see at the beach as a starting point.

Evaluation 1: Groups should select their three best sentences to be shared with the class.

Application: 10–15 minutes
Ask students to make a DO and DON'T chart on the board. The chart should contain safety tips for the beach.

Make sure they understand that they may need to accompany the past continuous clause with a simple past clause, as in the example.

Practice 1: 20–30 minutes
Put students in small groups and ask them to write five more sentences using the past continuous and five sentences using the present continuous. Focus on the differences in form and make sure students are using them correctly. Teach students to focus on *when* events are

happening so they can best determine which tense to use.

Evaluation 1: Have group representatives write sentences on the board.

Application: 10–15 minutes
Ask students to write past-continuous sentences about things they did the previous day or the last day they went to the beach. Schedule time for students to read their sentences out loud. Encourage questions and discussion.

Project

Place students in groups and have them imagine they are friends who are taking a vacation at the beach. Ask them to complete the task described in *Words in Action #1.* Remind students to think of any food and safety objects they should bring as well as any items they should purchase.

Level ★

Objective: Describe camping vocabulary.

Warm-up: 8–10 minutes
In small groups, students should brainstorm activities that they can do outside. Tell them that they can look through the dictionary for ideas, but don't reveal what the lesson for the day is. Start a table on the board with two columns. Label the columns *outside* and *inside*. Individually, students should write three things they like to do inside and three things they like to do outside. To help them understand the activity, consider creating a sample table about yourself on the board.

Introduction: State the objective.

Presentation 1: 15–20 minutes
Ask students to open their dictionaries to **pages 212 and 213.** Go over the new vocabulary. Make sure students understand what each item means and review pronunciation. Create a new table on the board with four columns. Label the headers *people, sleeping and resting, tools or equipment,* and *other*. As a class, help students classify at least one item from the word list into each category. Discuss the reasons why the words belong in these columns.

Practice 1: 8–10 minutes
Divide students into four groups and ask them to complete the table. Each group should attempt to fill in all the columns. After a set time, assign each group one category to focus on.

Evaluation 1: Ask students to complete the table on the board and discuss.

Presentation 2: 10–15 minutes
Teach alphabetical order by writing the alphabet across the full length of the board. Students should list as many words as possible that start with the first three letters of the alphabet.

Practice 2: 8–10 minutes
Ask students to participate in a competition where they put all the items from the word list in alphabetical order. Consider making this a group activity. The first group of students to complete the list in correct alphabetical order and with no misspelled words or omissions wins.

Evaluation 2: Correct any errors.

Application: 20–30 minutes
Have students complete the activity suggested in *Words in Action #1.* They should imagine that they are a family and need supplies for everyone. Schedule time for group reports.

Camping

Words in Context

The Appalachian Trail is a 2,174-mile* **trail** in the U.S. It starts in Maine and goes all the way to Georgia. Some people **hike** a small part of the trail for a day. Others hike longer portions of the trail. These **hikers** usually bring a **backpack**, a **tent**, and a **sleeping bag**, along with other camping equipment like a **trail map**, a **compass**, a **water bottle**, and a **pocket knife.** Hiking the whole trail takes an entire season!

*3,478.4 kilometers

Word Partnerships

a camping	trip
	site
a fishing	boat
a ski	
a street	map
a city	
a road	

212

Level ★ ★

Objective: Discuss money and make purchases.

Warm-up: 15–17 minutes
Divide students into groups to complete *Words in Action #1.* They may not refer to the dictionary.

Introduction: State the objective.

Presentation 1: 15–20 minutes
Present each of the words from the word list on **pages 212 and 213.** Make sure students understand what each item means before including *Word Partnerships.* Ask students to describe the scene. As a class, decide which items in the picture can be purchased. Remind students how to discuss prices. Teach them to say *two dollars and ninety-five cents* as opposed to *two dollars ninety-five.* Assign prices to two of the items. Write on the board *I think it should cost _____., _____ is more expensive than _____.,* and *It should be _____.*

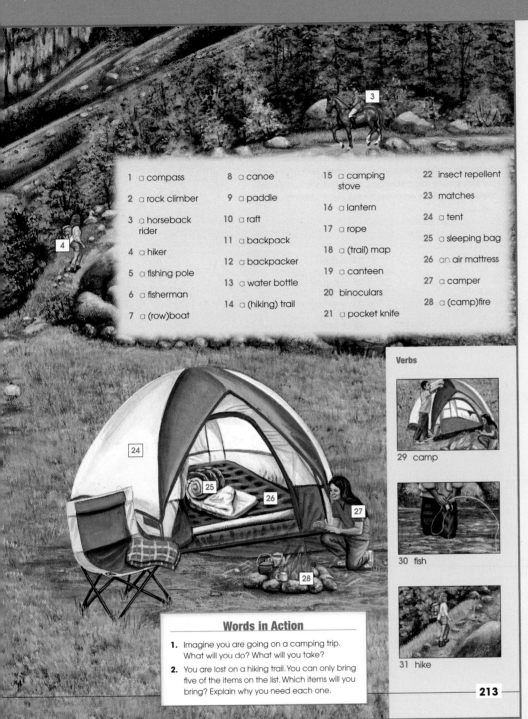

1 a compass	8 a canoe	15 a camping stove	22 insect repellent
2 a rock climber	9 a paddle		23 matches
3 a horseback rider	10 a raft	16 a lantern	24 a tent
	11 a backpack	17 a rope	25 a sleeping bag
4 a hiker	12 a backpacker	18 a (trail) map	26 an air mattress
5 a fishing pole	13 a water bottle	19 a canteen	27 a camper
6 a fisherman	14 a (hiking) trail	20 binoculars	28 a (camp)fire
7 a (row)boat		21 a pocket knife	

Verbs

29 camp

30 fish

31 hike

Words in Action

1. Imagine you are going on a camping trip. What will you do? What will you take?

2. You are lost on a hiking trail. You can only bring five of the items on the list. Which items will you bring? Explain why you need each one.

213

Objective: Use the conditional tense.

Warm-up: 10–15 minutes
Tell students that today's lesson covers camping vocabulary. Poll the class to find out who has gone on a camping trip. Brainstorm a list of words that students think are in the dictionary.

Introduction: State the objective.

Presentation 1: 20–30 minutes
Present the word list on **pages 212 and 213.** Make sure students understand the meaning of each item and can define it by its use. Allow time for students to add more words to the list created in the Warm-up. As a class, read *Words in Context.* Discuss the different items people would take on a hike. Ask students what could go wrong or could be dangerous on a long hike. Ask students to share stories from personal experiences. Call for students' opinions about what to do if lost while hiking or camping. Teach them the correct use of the conditional. Write the following on the board:

> *If I were lost, I would . . .*
> *If I lost my canteen, I would . . .*
> *If a bear ate my food, I would . . .*
> *If I lost my paddle, I would . . .*
> *If I had no matches, I would . . .*
> *If I lost my compass, I would . . .*

Practice 1: 15–20 minutes
In groups, students should discuss possible endings to these statements and then complete the sentences. Group members should decide which solution they think best fits each sentence.

Evaluation 1: Groups write their best sentences on the board. Allow time to discuss the various solutions offered.

Application: 15–20 minutes
Ask students to complete *Words in Action* #2 and have them use the conditional structure taught in this lesson.

Practice 1: 20–30 minutes
In small groups, students should develop a price list for all commercial items. Group members should agree on a final price list to present to the class. An Activity Bank CD-ROM lesson worksheet is available for more practice discussing prices while using camping vocabulary.

Evaluation 1: Group representatives share their answers. Review the prices as a class and discuss reasons why prices differed among groups.

Application: 10–15 minutes
Students should create dialogs between a store owner and a customer in a supply store. Conversations should range from six to ten sentences and the store owner and customer should discuss prices, supplies, and uses for camping supplies.

Project

Divide students into small groups and ask them to imagine that they are opening a camping supply store. They should put together an inventory list, design the layout of the store, and decide how they will advertise. Schedule time for formal presentations.

City Park

Level ★

Objective: Use vocabulary related to parks and recreation.

Warm-up: 8–10 minutes
Ask students to think of any parks located in their neighborhoods or near the school. List things found in parks. Since students may not know many vocabulary words, encourage them to draw the items on the board. Draw a seesaw as an example. Label the pictures. Write *amusement parks* and *carnivals* on the board. Help students understand what these places are by drawing more pictures and labeling them.

Introduction: State the objective.

Presentation 1: 15–20 minutes
Ask students to open their dictionaries to **pages 214 and 215**. Discuss the new vocabulary. Take time to pronounce and define each word for students. As a class, make a list of things people can bring to a park. Start a table with two columns and label the headers *younger children* and *older children*. Clearly explain the classifications and place one vocabulary word in each category.

Practice 1: 8–10 minutes
In groups, ask students to complete the table by listing things in the dictionary park that younger children would like and things that older ones would like. Explain what *older* and *younger* mean but don't provide specific ages. Tell students that some items can fit into both columns.

Evaluation 1: Complete the table on the board with help from the groups.

Presentation 2: 10–15 minutes
Come up with appropriate verbs for several of the scenes and use them in sentences on the board. Teach students the use of *can*. Sentences might include *People can watch puppet shows at the park*, *People can eat hot dogs from street vendors at the park*, *People can swing on swings at the park*, *People can have picnics at the park*, *People can skate on in-line skates at the park*, and *People can ride bicycles at the park*. Prepare students to perform this model conversation.

Student A: *What can people do at the park?*

Student B: *They can have picnics at the park.*

Practice 2: 8–10 minutes
Partners should practice the exchange.

Evaluation 2: Observe the activity.

Application: 20–30 minutes
Have students make a list of things they see at parks in their neighborhoods.

Words in Context

Central Park is a beautiful **park** in the middle of New York City. It is about two miles* long and has something for everyone. For adults, there are bicycle and jogging paths. For children, there is a **playground** with a **sandbox, monkey bars,** and **swings.** There is even an old **carousel,** an ice rink, and a zoo.

*3.218 kilometers

1. a kite
2. swings
3. monkey bars
4. a playground
5. a slide
6. a jungle gym
7. a seesaw
8. a sandbox
9. a trash can / a garbage can
10. a puppet show
11. a picnic
12. a picnic basket
13. a picnic table
14. a carousel / a merry-go-round
15. a Ferris wheel
16. a roller coaster
17. a bridge
18. a (park) bench
19. a pond
20. a jogger
21. a skateboard
22. a skateboarder
23. a skater
24. (in-line) skates
25. a cyclist
26. a bicycle / a bike
27. a path
28. a street vendor
29. a pigeon

Word Partnerships

a local	park
a national	
an amusement	
ride	a bike
	a carousel
have	a picnic
go on	
fly	a kite

214

Level ★ ★

Objective: Express preferences.

Warm-up: 10–15 minutes
In groups, students should read **Words in Action #2** and then complete the task with their dictionaries closed.

Introduction: State the objective.

Presentation 1: 20–22 minutes
Go over each of the words from the word list on **pages 214 and 215** with students.

Make sure they understand what each item means and include **Word Partnerships**. As a class, describe the scene. Students should point to the place in the dictionary's park where they would prefer to spend time. Teach students vocabulary to help them express preferences, such as *I like . . .*, *I prefer . . .*, and *Not me, I think* skating *is more fun.* Teach students questions to use, such as *What do you like to do?*, *Where do you like to spend time?*, and *What is your favorite thing to do (place to go)?*

Words in Action

1. Work with your class. Discuss your dream park. Draw a picture of the park on the board. Each student adds an item to the park and labels this item.

2. When did you last go to a park? What did you do? What did you see? Tell a partner.

215

Objective: Write a descriptive paragraph.

Warm-up: 10–15 minutes
Divide students into small groups and have them read *Words in Context* and discuss it. Focus their conversations on familiar parks and ask students to compare them to the park in the dictionary. Allow time for students to list items from the dictionary that they have seen in a local park. Have them make a separate list of things not available nearby. Compare and contrast group lists.

Introduction: State the objective.

Presentation 1: 20–30 minutes
Formally present the word list on **pages 214 and 215**. As the list is presented, discuss spelling patterns and how the patterns are reflected in the pronunciation of the words. Proceed by describing the scene in detail and having students concentrate on the pronunciation of the words. Review verb tenses, focusing on the present continuous and simple present. Remind students of when each should be used. Teach the formation of adjectives and discuss where they fit into English word order. Remind students that in order to write well and help the reader create vivid images, they must incorporate a variety of adjectives.

Practice 1: 20–30 minutes
Students should describe the scene with plenty of adjectives. Their sentences should contain the two verb forms presented. Encourage the use of adverbs as well. Let students reference previous lessons as they search for appropriate adjectives and adverbs.

Evaluation 1: Students write some of their sentences on the board and discuss them as a class.

Application: 20–30 minutes
Teach students how to tie their sentences together to form a well-written paragraph. Have students turn in a final version for scoring. Explain that the paragraphs will be checked for proper use of verb tenses and adjectives.

Practice 1: 20–30 minutes
Divide students into small groups to discuss each member's preferences. Encourage students to incorporate as many words as possible from the word list and write sentences about a local park. Schedule time for groups to share their favorites.

Evaluation 1: Observe the activity.

Application: 10–15 minutes
Teach students how to complete a Johari Squares chart. Students should work in pairs for this activity. Ask students to label the four squares *my preferences, my partner's preferences, not our preferences,* and *our preferences.* Set aside time for pairs to complete the activity.

Project

In groups, ask students to complete the task described in *Words in Action #1,* but have students make and decorate posters to put up in the class. Ask students to label all features clearly.

Level ★

Objective: Identify places of entertainment in the community.

Warm-up: 8–10 minutes
Write *vacation* on the board. Take a poll to find out what students like to do on vacation and find out how much vacation people take a year. Discuss vacation time offered by different businesses and compare allotted vacation times in different countries. Complete a bar graph of the information using the bar graph template from the Activity Bank CD-ROM.

Introduction: State the objective.

Presentation 1: 18–20 minutes
Ask students to open their dictionaries to **pages 216 and 217**. Present the new vocabulary. Make sure students understand what each item means and review pronunciation with them. Ask students to identify places children would like to visit. Make a list. Ask students where they would like to visit.

Practice 1: 8–10 minutes
Divide students into small groups of either all men or all women. Ask groups of women to list what they like to do and ask groups of men to compile another list of what they like to do for fun.

Evaluation 1: Compare and contrast the lists.

Presentation 2: 10–15 minutes
Prepare students to practice this model conversation.

> **Student A:** *What do you want to do today?*
>
> **Student B:** *Let's go to the movies!*

Supply a set of small cards numbered 1 through 23. Pass the cards out in random order. Tell students not to reveal their numbers to classmates.

Practice 2: 8–10 minutes
Students should practice the exchange with several students in the classroom. They can discover what other students have written on their cards only by performing the exchange. The numbers on their cards will dictate their responses. Ask students to maintain a record of whom they talk to and how they respond. If time permits, switch cards and repeat the activity.

Evaluation 2: Observe the activity.

Application: 10–15 minutes
Ask students to complete the task described in *Words in Action #1*.

Places to Visit

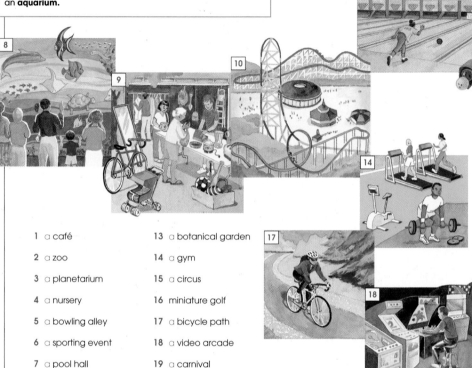

Words in Context

Try a new activity this weekend. Do you like shopping? You could go to a flea market or a **garage sale.** Do you enjoy nature? You could walk on a **hiking trail** or ride your bicycle on a **bicycle path.** Do you like animals? You could go to a **zoo** or an **aquarium.**

1	a café	13	a botanical garden
2	a zoo	14	a gym
3	a planetarium	15	a circus
4	a nursery	16	miniature golf
5	a bowling alley	17	a bicycle path
6	a sporting event	18	a video arcade
7	a pool hall	19	a carnival
8	an aquarium	20	a museum
9	a garage sale	21	a water park
10	an amusement park	22	a movie theater
11	a (hiking) trail	23	a rodeo
12	a lecture		

216

Level ★ ★

Objective: Write sentences in the simple present.

Warm-up: 15–20 minutes
Ask students to work in groups to complete the activity in *Words in Action #2*. Students should list 10 famous places for each category.

Introduction: State the objective.

Presentation 1: 15–20 minutes
Study each of the words from the word list on **pages 216 and 217** with students. After defining the words, review adjectives and then study *Word Partnerships*. Shift the focus to verbs and ask students what verb might go with the first picture. Form groups and divide the word list (items 2 to 23) among them for this activity.

Word Partnerships

a petting	zoo
a traveling	circus
a three-ring	
an outdoor	café
a sidewalk	
an internet	

Words in Action

1. What are your five favorite places to visit from this list? Compare your favorite places with your classmates'. Can you find another student with the same favorite places?

2. Work with a group. Make a list of famous:
   - zoos
   - amusement parks
   - museums

— 217 —

Warm-up: 10–15 minutes
Ask students to focus on entertainment activities. Students should think about activities that they have never done but would like to do someday. Write a few suggestions on the board and accept any reasonable answers. Individually, students should list at least three activities. Then, divide students into small groups to compare and discuss their ideas.

Introduction: State the objective.

Presentation 1: 20–30 minutes
Direct attention to the word list on **pages 216 and 217**. Make sure students understand the meaning of each item. Read *Words in Context* as a class. Pose the questions in the paragraph to students and lead a group discussion. Review question construction with students. Discuss yes/no questions and information questions. Write a few sample questions on the board using the words from the list.

Practice 1: 15–20 minutes
Ask students to write yes/no and information questions about the picture. They should write 10 questions, five of each type. Each question should include a different place from the word list.

Evaluation 1: Have students write some of their questions on the board and discuss them as a class.

Application: 15–17 minutes
Form groups and have students ask each other questions about their preferences related to activities depicted on the page spread. They can use the questions they wrote in the Practice. Ask students to retain a list of student names and their answers. Allow time for students to organize their research using a graph or grid. Schedule time for discussion.

Practice 1: 20–30 minutes
First, ask groups to think of a verb to accompany each of their assigned words. Second, have them use the verbs in sentences with their words. Students may not include the verbs *be* or *have*. Students should choose action verbs if possible.

Evaluation 1: Students should write their sentences on the board.

Application: 10–15 minutes
Ask students to write sentences about activities and places they enjoy. Students can incorporate the words from this lesson but also have them review **pages 202 through 215**. Every sentence must contain two appropriate adjectives and a verb other than *be* or *have*.

Project

If possible, supply travel brochures and atlases. Refer to the maps on **pages 172 through 175**. Divide students into groups and tell them to imagine that they are going on a three-week vacation. Ask students to choose a destination and plan a vacation by choosing places to go and things to do. Students will share their plans with the class.

Indoor Sports and Fitness

Level ★

Objective: Identify indoor sports and fitness vocabulary.

Warm-up: 8–10 minutes
Generate a conversation about how much students exercise. Explain to students that there are many forms of exercise, including some forms of housework. Discuss the fact that many experts state that exercise must be continuous for 20 minutes to be beneficial to the heart. Take a poll to determine how many minutes a week students exercise and complete a bar graph. There is a bar graph template available on the Activity Bank CD-ROM to facilitate this activity.

Introduction: State the objective.

Presentation 1: 18–20 minutes
Ask students to open their dictionaries to **pages 218 and 219.** Thoroughly present the new vocabulary and incorporate actions or pantomimes if necessary. Make sure students understand what each item means and review pronunciation. Determine what students think is the best exercise. Make a judgment as a class.

Practice 1: 8–10 minutes
Place students in groups and ask each group to make a list of the top 10 ways to get exercise. Have groups rank them 1–10 with one being the most beneficial. Remind them that they can include activities not pictured in this lesson.

Evaluation 1: Groups report to the class. Allow time to compare lists.

Presentation 2: 10–15 minutes
As a class, decide on a pantomime for items 1 and 2. Divide the rest of the words on the list among groups.

Practice 2: 8–10 minutes
Within groups, students should develop pantomimes to represent the other words on the list.

Evaluation 2: Ask students from the groups to teach the rest of the class their pantomimes or have them do the pantomimes while classmates guess what they are. Consider staging a round of charades.

Application: 10–15 minutes
In discussion groups, have students share their favorite indoor athletic activity and state why they like it.

Words in Context

Different sports and fitness activities help in different ways. **Yoga** and **martial arts** can help you relax. **Aerobics** and the **treadmill** can help you lose weight. **Push-ups** and free weights can help you become stronger.

1 martial arts	21 wrestling
2 yoga	22 a wrestler
3 basketball	23 gymnastics
4 a referee	24 a gymnast
5 a basketball court	25 weightlifting
6 a (basketball) player	26 a weightlifter
7 a basketball	27 a bench
8 ping-pong	28 a barbell
9 a ping-pong paddle	29 a dartboard
10 a ping-pong table	30 darts
11 a chin-up	31 aerobics
12 a push-up	32 a diving board
13 a sit-up	33 a diver
14 a (stationary) bike	34 a (swimming) pool
15 a treadmill	35 a locker room
16 boxing	
17 a boxer	
18 a boxing glove	
19 a boxing ring	
20 a punching bag	

Word Partnerships

sports	club
	team
	equipment
	injury
a yoga	instructor
an aerobics	class
a martial arts	

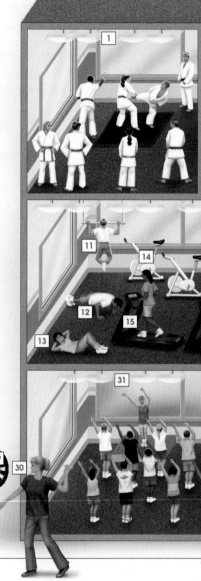

Level ★ ★

Objective: Create and discuss exercise goals.

Warm-up: 10–15 minutes
With a partner, students should complete *Words in Action #1.* Set a time limit for students to repeat this activity with other items from the list. Consider asking students who aren't performing to keep their dictionaries closed.

Introduction: State the objective.

Presentation 1: 10–15 minutes
Go over each of the words from the word list on **pages 218 and 219** with students. Develop a definition for each and review adjectives. Incorporate the adjectives from *Word Partnerships*. Remind students what *goals* are. Write some personal exercise goals on the board. Present Jerome's goal chart.

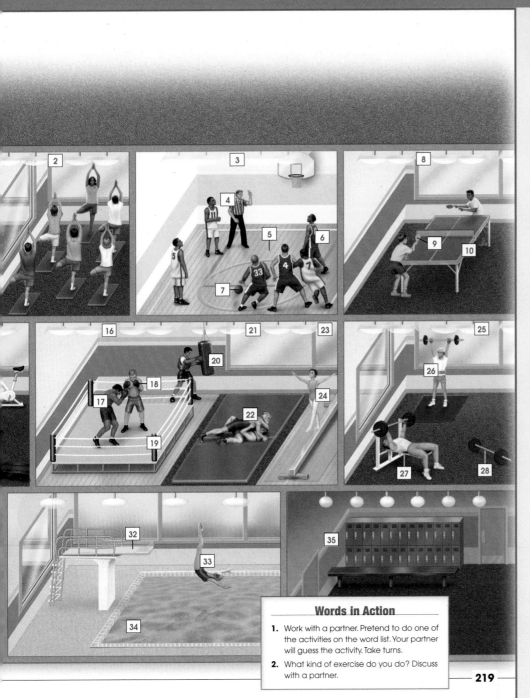

Words in Action

1. Work with a partner. Pretend to do one of the activities on the word list. Your partner will guess the activity. Take turns.

2. What kind of exercise do you do? Discuss with a partner.

Objective: Discuss and write about preferences.

Warm-up: 15–20 minutes
Ask students to form pairs for a sharing activity. Partners should discuss the questions posed in *Words in Action #2*. Encourage students to extend the discussion by including not only *what* they like but also *why* they like it.

Introduction: State the objective.

Presentation 1: 20–30 minutes
Before asking students to open their dictionaries, give them a spelling test. Read the words from the list out loud and have students spell them. Students can check their tests for accuracy as the word list on **pages 218 and 219** is formally presented. Discuss spelling patterns and practice pronunciation. Make sure students understand the meaning of each item. Read *Words in Context* as a class. Discuss how different exercises can help people in different ways. Ask students to offer input from their Warm-up discussions.

Practice 1: 10–15 minutes
Divide students into small groups to discuss what they think are the most beneficial exercises. Ask each group to select the five most beneficial exercises. All group members must agree and state why they believe each exercise is beneficial. Students should be encouraged to rely on personal experience.

Evaluation 1: Observe the activity.

Application: 15–17 minutes
Subdivide the groups into pairs. Partners should explain why they do or don't exercise and which activities they prefer. Teach students how to complete a Venn diagram. Ask students to fill in Venn diagrams about what they and their partners have in common and what they do differently. Supply copies of the Venn diagram template from the Activity Bank CD-ROM.

Day	Exercise	Minutes	Time
Mon. / Wed.	weightlifting	30	9:30 AM
Tues. / Thurs.	aerobics	30	11:30 AM
Fri.	basketball	60	10:00 AM
Sat.	martial arts	60	10:00 AM

Prepare students to discuss the chart. Pose questions such as *What does Jerome do on Wednesdays?* and *When does Jerome do aerobics?*

Practice 1: 20–30 minutes
With a partner, have students discuss Jerome's activities and write sentences about goals they might share with Jerome.

Evaluation 1: Present student sentences on the board.

Application: 10–15 minutes
Students should develop their own goal chart or schedule.

Project

Place students in groups and have them imagine they work for a local gym or fitness center. Have them create a brochure for people who have just moved to the community. The brochure should outline the sports, equipment, types of exercises, and classes the gym offers. Ask students to use as many words as possible from this lesson.

Outdoor Sports and Fitness

Level ★

Objective: Identify sports vocabulary.

Warm-up: 8–10 minutes
Write the word *team* on the board and ask students for ideas to define it. Write *teamwork* on the board. Discuss what good teamwork is. At this level, the discussion will mainly be restricted to yes/no questions. Ask if students believe it is important for everyone in a group to participate. Ask them to explain why it is or is not important. Describe different group situations and have students discuss the pros and cons of participation in each scenario.

Introduction: State the objective.

Presentation 1: 15–20 minutes
Ask students to open their dictionaries to **pages 220 and 221**. Discuss the new vocabulary and use the words in sentences. Make sure students understand what each item means and take time to review pronunciation. Students should repeat the words after they hear them. Go around the room so each student can name his or her favorite sport. Then, hold a group discussion to determine which sports are team sports. Elicit answers such as soccer, football, volleyball, and baseball. Create a pantomime for each of the sports identified in the lesson.

Practice 1: 8–10 minutes
Students should form pairs and complete the task described in *Words in Action #2.*

Evaluation 1: Observe the activity.

Presentation 2: 10–15 minutes
Start a four-column table on the board. Label the headers *sport, participant, equipment,* and *location.* Help students understand what these words mean. Fill in one example from the word list for each category. Encourage questions and discussion.

Practice 2: 8–10 minutes
Divide students into groups and have them complete the table. Table templates are available on the **Activity Bank CD-ROM.**

Evaluation 2: Complete the table on the board with student feedback.

Application: 12–15 minutes
Students should share their favorite sport from the list with a conversation group and explain why they like it.

Words in Context

Tennis is one of the most popular **sports** in the world. The rules are simple. A **player** uses a **racket** to hit a **tennis ball** over the **net**. The other player tries to hit the ball back. The first player to win four points wins the game.

1 tennis			
2 a (tennis) racket			
3 a (tennis) ball			
4 baseball	10 a volleyball	16 track	22 a uniform
5 a baseball	11 a (volleyball) net	17 a runner	23 football
6 a batter	12 golf	18 a track	24 a goalpost
7 a bat	13 a (golf) club	19 soccer	25 a (football) helmet
8 a catcher	14 a golfer	20 a fan	26 a cheerleader
9 volleyball	15 a golf course	21 a soccer field	27 a football

220

Level ★ ★

Objective: Discuss and describe outdoor sports.

Warm-up: 15–20 minutes
In groups, students should complete the task described in *Words in Action #1.*

Introduction: State the objective.

Presentation 1: 15–20 minutes
Go over each of the words from the word list on **pages 220 and 221** with

students. Make sure they clearly understand the definitions before tackling **Word Partnerships.** Discuss the following questions:

Is it a team sport, or do players compete individually?

How many players are on a team?

Is it a contact sport?

Is it a professional sport? Can players make money?

Are there positions? What are they?

Word Partnerships

a baseball	player
a soccer	
a volleyball	
a rugby	
a golf	ball
a soccer	
a rugby	
hit	the ball
throw	
catch	
kick	
a baseball	glove

Words in Action

1. Which of these sports do you like to play? Which do you like to watch? Discuss with a partner.

2. Work with a partner. One person pretends to play one of these sports. The other guesses the sport. Take turns.

221

Objective: Describe how to play an outdoor sport.

Warm-up: 15–20 minutes
Read *Words in Context* as a class and set aside time to discuss it. Go around the room and have all students say if tennis is popular in their native countries and if they can name any famous tennis players. Provide information about famous tennis players or allow time for students to use encyclopedias or the school computer lab.

Introduction: State the objective.

Presentation 1: 20–30 minutes
Formally present the word list on **pages 220 and 221.** Ask students to develop a short sentence for each word to convey its meaning through context. Focus attention back on tennis and discuss how to play tennis. Write the rules or instructions for a game of tennis on the board. Consider being specific with instructions. Encourage details. As a class, write the instructions on the board in a list format. Identify the team sports from the dictionary.

Practice 1: 10–15 minutes
Divide the class evenly, forming a group for each team sport. Assign one team sport to each group. Have group members make a list of rules or instructions on how to play their sport. Allow time for research.

Evaluation 1: Ask group representatives to write their lists on the board. Act out the instructions to determine if they would make sense to someone who has never played the sport before.

Application: 15–20 minutes
Students should write a paragraph similar to *Words in Context* for one of the sports listed on the board. Students may use notes from their group session. Review proper paragraph formation and the need to include details when describing a process. Students may choose a team sport that isn't listed in the dictionary.

Do men and women play together or separately?

Do you know any famous players?

Practice 1: 15–20 minutes
Stage an inside/outside circle activity where students form two circles. The inside circle and the outside circle have the same number of students and students face one another. Ask students to discuss the questions from the Presentation about several of the pictured sports. Then ask one circle to move two or three seats to the right so that they have new partners. Repeat the activity with a new sport. If there isn't enough room for two circles, make two lines facing one another.

Evaluation 1: Observe the activity.

Application: 15–17 minutes
With a partner, students should discuss the same questions about another familiar sport that isn't on the word list. Share any new sports that are mentioned with the rest of the class.

Project

With a group, ask students to create a new outdoor sport. Have them describe the rules and/or demonstrate how it is played. Have them consider where it will be played, how many people can play at once, what the objective is, and what equipment is needed. Schedule time for group presentations.

Level ★

Objective: Identify winter sports vocabulary.

Warm-up: 8–10 minutes
Generate a conversation about the weather and then focus attention on today's weather. Go around the room so all students can state the coldest weather and the hottest weather they remember. Show students a world map or refer to **pages 174 and 175.** Extend the conversation by identifying countries where it is cold most of the time. Ask students if it snows in their native countries, and if so, how often.

Introduction: State the objective.

Presentation 1: 18–20 minutes
Ask students to open their dictionaries to **pages 222 and 223.** Present the new vocabulary in depth and define each item. Use the words in sentences to clarify definitions. Review pronunciation by having students repeat the words. Identify places in the picture and include ones that are not necessarily labeled, such as *ski lodge, hill,* and *slope.* Create a cluster activity where the primary circle is *winter sports.* Label the secondary circles *places, equipment,* and *people.* Use the places from the previous conversation to fill in a few tertiary circles.

Practice 1: 8–10 minutes
Ask students to complete the cluster. Hand out copies of the template available on the Activity Bank CD-ROM.

Evaluation 1: Complete the cluster on the board.

Presentation 2: 8–10 minutes
Read items from the word list out loud and have students point to them in preparation for the Practice to follow. Put the words into context by using them in sentences.

Practice 2: 10–15 minutes
Tell a story using the new vocabulary. Ask students to point to the items when they hear them. Then ask students to quiz each other. One student says an item and the other student points to it. To begin, students may look at the word list, but after a set time the word lists should be covered.

Evaluation 2: Observe the activity.

Application: 10–15 minutes
Take a class poll. Ask students if they love, like, dislike, or hate cold weather and winter sports. Develop a class bar graph using the template from the Activity Bank CD-ROM.

Winter Sports

Words in Context

Skiing began in Norway in the 1700s. Early **skiers** used long wooden cross-country **skis** and wooden **ski poles.** Today there is a new kind of **winter sport** called **snowboarding. Snowboarders** don't use ski poles. They slide down the slopes with both feet on a **snowboard.**

Word Partnerships

a hockey	team
	game
	arena
	rink
a skiing	injury
	lesson

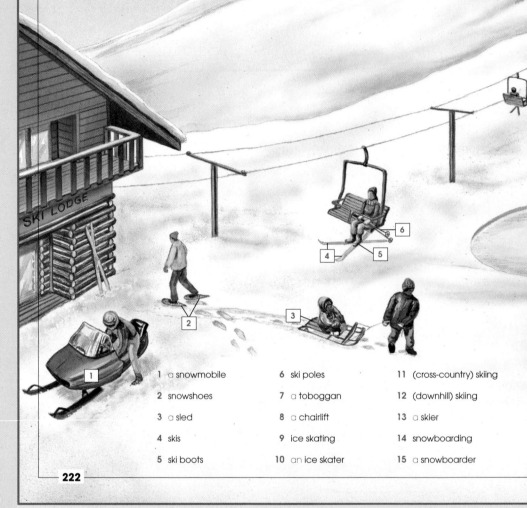

1	a snowmobile	6	ski poles	11	(cross-country) skiing
2	snowshoes	7	a toboggan	12	(downhill) skiing
3	a sled	8	a chairlift	13	a skier
4	skis	9	ice skating	14	snowboarding
5	ski boots	10	an ice skater	15	a snowboarder

222

Level ★ ★

Objective: Describe winter sports.

Warm-up: 15–20 minutes
Place students in groups and have them complete the activity described in **Words in Action #1.**

Introduction: State the objective.

Presentation 1: 15–20 minutes
Study the words and make sure students understand what each item means, including **Word Partnerships.** As a class, create a cluster. There is a cluster template available on the Activity Bank CD-ROM. Label the center circle *winter sports.* The secondary circles are specific sports. The tertiary circles are *clothing* and *equipment.* In this cluster, there is a fourth set of circles. These circles include the actual clothes and pieces of equipment. Tell students that the clothing and equipment may not be on the word list.

Warm-up: 8–10 minutes
Read *Words in Context* as a class and discuss it. Ask students if they have ever heard of snowboarding and if the sport is popular in their native countries. Extend the conversation by mentioning the Winter Olympics and see who can remember where the most recent Winter Olympic Games were held. Ask students to state if their native countries participate in the Winter Olympics.

Introduction: State the objective.

Presentation 1: 20–30 minutes
Direct attention to the word list on **pages 222 and 223**. Make sure students understand the meaning of each item. Brainstorm with students to identify verbs that could be used to describe the scene. Write the verbs in a column on the board. Have students help identify any adjectives that could be used and list these in a second column. List appropriate adverbs in a third column.

Practice 1: 20–30 minutes
Depending on class size and level, have students work in groups, in pairs, or individually to write sentences that describe the scene. Have them give names to people in the picture as they write. Ask students to imagine what some of the people in the pictures are thinking and write these ideas as well.

Evaluation 1: Ask for volunteers to read their sentences aloud or write them on the board.

Application: 30–40 minutes
Have students write a short story about something that might have happened to one of the characters they created. Explain that the short story must include a problem or conflict. If students have trouble coming up with a conflict, provide a few prompts.

16 a snowboard
17 (ice) hockey
18 a scoreboard
19 a score
20 an ice (skating) rink

21 a goal
22 a (hockey) player
23 a hockey stick
24 a (hockey) puck
25 (ice) skates

Words in Action

1. Which winter sports are the most fun? Which are the most dangerous? Discuss with your class.

2. One student names a winter sport. The other students take turns naming clothing and equipment for that sport.
   - Student A: *Hockey.*
   - Student B: *Ice skates.*
   - Student C: *A hockey stick.*

223

Let students look in other dictionary lessons for help with the cluster. Review **pages 218 through 221**. Create a master cluster on the board based on student answers. Students can reference this while completing the Practice. Prepare students to do *Words in Action #2* based on the cluster activity.

Practice 1: 15–20 minutes
Ask students to complete the activity suggested in *Words in Action #2.*

Evaluation 1: Ask for volunteers to quiz the class by describing winter sports.

Application: 15–20 minutes
Have each student describe his or her favorite winter sport and quiz partners or groups.

Project

Create a survey about winter sports and make a bar graph to show the results. Ask how much experience students have with downhill skiing, cross country skiing, snowboarding, hockey, and ice skating. Students must respond with *none, a little, a lot,* or *I am an expert.* Write the questions on the board and have each group be responsible for gathering data for one sport. Then put the results together as a class.

Level ★

Objective: Identify games, toys, and hobbies.

Warm-up: 10–15 minutes
Write *toys* and *games* on the board. Help students understand the meaning of these words by giving examples. Ask students for several examples as well. In groups, ask students to name as many games and toys as they can. Extend the activity by having students divide their lists into games adults play and games children play. Compile group answers into a master list.

Introduction: State the objective.

Presentation 1: 15–20 minutes
Ask students to open their dictionaries to **pages 224 and 225.** Read the word list out loud and ask students to repeat the words to practice pronunciation. Define the words and make sure students understand what each item means. Prepare students to complete the task described in *Words in Action #1.*

Practice 1: 10–15 minutes
Allow time for students to work individually on *Words in Action #1.* Divide students into groups to compare lists. Tell groups that they should imagine they are a family. Ask them to rank all the activities from the picture in order, from what they would most like to do as a family to what they would like to do the least.

Evaluation 1: Group representatives put their lists on the board for a class discussion.

Presentation 2: 8–10 minutes
Prepare students to play Bingo. Remind them of the rules and tell them to write eight items from the word list on a piece of paper or on the Bingo card template available on the Activity Bank CD-ROM. As an alternate activity, students can use the prewritten, prelabeled Games Bingo worksheets, which are also available on the Activity Bank CD-ROM.

Practice 2: 10–15 minutes
Call out words from the word list in a random order. Students should cross out items on their lists as they are read out loud. The first student to cross out all of his or her items is the winner. As the winner reads his or her words aloud, take the opportunity to review the definitions.

Evaluation 2: Observe the activity.

Application: 10–15 minutes
Ask students to identify three activities they would do with their own friends or families.

Games, Toys, and Hobbies

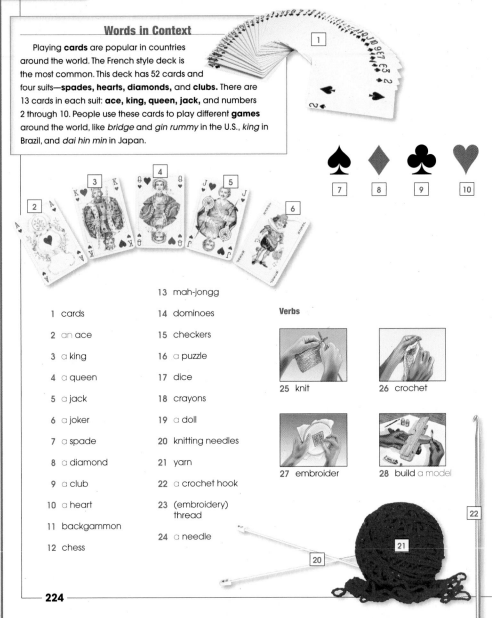

Words in Context

Playing **cards** are popular in countries around the world. The French style deck is the most common. This deck has 52 cards and four suits—**spades, hearts, diamonds,** and **clubs.** There are 13 cards in each suit: **ace, king, queen, jack,** and numbers 2 through 10. People use these cards to play different **games** around the world, like *bridge* and *gin rummy* in the U.S., *king* in Brazil, and *dai hin min* in Japan.

1 cards
2 an ace
3 a king
4 a queen
5 a jack
6 a joker
7 a spade
8 a diamond
9 a club
10 a heart
11 backgammon
12 chess
13 mah-jongg
14 dominoes
15 checkers
16 a puzzle
17 dice
18 crayons
19 a doll
20 knitting needles
21 yarn
22 a crochet hook
23 (embroidery) thread
24 a needle

Verbs

25 knit
26 crochet
27 embroider
28 build a model

Level ★ ★

Objective: Form yes/no questions.

Warm-up: 10–15 minutes
Place students in groups and assign the task from *Words in Action #2.* Make a bar graph of the results. There is a bar graph template on the Activity Bank CD-ROM to facilitate this activity.

Introduction: State the objective.

Presentation 1: 15–20 minutes
Present each of the words from the word list on **pages 224 and 225.** Review adjectives and then incorporate the terms in *Word Partnerships.* Have students identify different items from the page spread using adjectives describing shape and color. Describe several items and ask students to call out the names of the items when they recognize them. Teach students how to form yes/no questions.

Word Partnerships

a board	game
a card	
a chess	board
a checker	piece
a deck of	cards
a hand of	
play	cards
	a game
king of	hearts
nine of	spades

Words in Action

1. Make a list of your three favorite games from the list. Put the list in order, with the game you like best at the top. Share your list with a partner.

2. Take a poll to find out the favorite games of the students in your class.
   - Which is the most popular game?
   - Which is the least popular game?

Objective: Use the imperative tense.

Warm-up: 8–10 minutes
Ask students to read **Words in Context** and discuss it in groups. Bring the groups together and answer any questions that come up with the reading or group discussions. Extend the conversation by asking what kinds of card games students play in their native countries. Make a list of the games on the board and have students describe their rules or objectives.

Introduction: State the objective.

Presentation 1: 20–30 minutes
Present the word list on **pages 224 and 225**. Make sure students can use each word in a sentence that exemplifies the definition. Write instructions on how to play a familiar and simple card game. Show students how to use the imperative and how the subject in this form is assumed, but not written or spoken. Create a grammar chart on the board to study the imperative in depth. Ask students to take notes or dictation on the card game instructions. See if students can repeat the instructions back to you. Review verbs that are most effective in giving instruction.

Practice 1: 20–30 minutes
Depending on class size and level, students can work in groups, pairs, or individually. Ask students to write instructions using the model you provided. Their instructions can be for any game either from the word list or from personal experience.

Evaluation 1: Ask for volunteers to share their instructions.

Application: 30–40 minutes
Ask students to dictate their instructions to partners and then check each other's work. Students should focus on the imperative and make sure the directions are clear enough that someone who has never played the game before would be able to understand them.

Practice 1: 15–17 minutes
Explain to students how to play "20 Questions" and ask them to work in pairs. One student chooses an item and the other student asks yes/no questions until he or she can guess what the item is. After a set amount of time, students should choose toys, games, and hobbies not listed in the dictionary and challenge their partners. Model the game for students and have them practice in pairs.

Evaluation 1: Ask for volunteers to perform the game in front of the class.

Application: 20–25 minutes
Stage a class session of 20 Questions. Ask students to choose items in the classroom or the school and play the game. Encourage the use of adjectives as students progress.

Project

In groups, students should imagine they work for a new toy company. The company is creating an original board game. Have groups develop directions and diagrams to accompany the game. Ask groups to present their ideas and instructions to the class.

Level ★

Objective: Identify audio and video vocabulary.

Warm-up: 10–15 minutes
Pantomime filming a video of the class. For authenticity, consider bringing a video recorder into the classroom. Find out if any students own a video camera. Make a list of electronic items students might own. Include in the poll *a video camera, a TV, a VCR,* and *a stereo.* Ask students to choose which they would own if they were only allowed to own one.

Introduction: State the objective.

Presentation 1: 15–20 minutes
Ask students to open their dictionaries to **pages 226 and 227.** Go over the new vocabulary. Pay special attention to pronunciation. Define each item carefully and use it in a sentence. Encourage student input. Have students point to an item in the dictionary when they hear its name. Say items in a random order.

Practice 1: 10–15 minutes
Form pairs to quiz each other. Student A says an item and Student B points to it. Increase the difficulty by restricting use of the word list after a set amount of time. Repeat the activity after students reverse roles.

Evaluation 1: Observe the activity.

Presentation 2: 8–10 minutes
Explain ranking to students. Tell students that for this activity, no two items can receive the same ranking. Ask students to imagine they are a family moving to a smaller house. Due to space issues, they can't bring everything from their current home to their new home. Allow time for individual thinking and have students write down one or two items that they would definitely bring with them.

Practice 2: 10–15 minutes
Divide students into small groups to rank all the items on the list from the most important to the least important possessions to move. Each group should develop only one list and agree on the ranking.

Evaluation 2: Compare lists after groups share their rankings.

Application: 10–15 minutes
Ask students to make a list of audio and video equipment they want to buy. Ask those who are able to explain in English why they want the equipment.

Camera, Stereo, and DVD

Words in Context

Audio equipment keeps changing. Until the 1980s, most people listened to music on **records** or **tapes.** Then in 1983, **CD players** and **CDs** became available. By 1998, more people bought CDs than records. By the late 1990s, MP3 technology became popular. Now **MP3 players** are becoming one of the most popular items at electronics stores.

1 (a roll of) film	11 headphones	21 a VCR / a videocassette recorder
2 a zoom lens	12 a CD player	22 a video(cassette)
3 a camera	13 a CD / a compact disc	23 a remote control
4 a camcorder	14 a speaker	24 a DVD player
5 a tripod	15 a stereo (system)	25 a DVD
6 a plug	16 a tape / a cassette	
7 an adapter (plug)	17 a boom box	
8 a record	18 a satellite dish	
9 an MP3 player	19 a television / a TV	
10 a (personal) CD player	20 a (video) game system	

Word Partnerships

a digital	camera
a 35-millimeter	
a disposable	
shoot	(a roll of) film
develop	
turn up	the TV
turn down	the stereo

— **226** —

Level ★ ★

Objective: Ask for prices.

Warm-up: 10–15 minutes
Assign groups to complete the task in *Words in Action #1.* Discuss the results as a class.

Introduction: State the objective.

Presentation 1: 15–20 minutes
Present each of the words from the word list on **pages 226 and 227.** Define each item as a class. Lead a class discussion about *Word Partnerships.* Shift focus to the verbs (items 26–31). Use each verb in a sentence so students can understand how to use it in context. As a class, assign regular and sale prices to each of the items on the list. Review vocabulary that might be used in an electronics store. Discuss electronics stores in students' communities. Prepare students to perform this model conversation.

Verbs

26 play

27 fast forward

28 rewind

29 pause

30 stop

31 eject

Words in Action

1. Which three items on the list would you most like to get as gifts? Why? Discuss with a partner.

2. Which items on the list could help you learn English? How? Discuss with your class.

227

Student A: *Do you have anything on sale today?*

Student B: *Sure, TVs are 20% off.*

Student A: *That sounds great! What else is on sale?*

Student B: *Boom boxes are only $57. That is a savings of $10.*

Practice 1: 15–20 minutes
Form pairs and ask students to practice the conversation, substituting information from the word list and price list on the board.

Evaluation 1: Ask for volunteers to demonstrate in front of the class.

Application: 20–30 minutes
In groups, students can create an advertisement for an electronics store. Encourage students to keep the prices reasonable. Supply copies of electronics advertisements to use as a guide. Let students take on the role of customers and ask for prices.

Objective: Make purchases.

Warm-up: 8--10 minutes
Focus attention on the pictures on **pages 226 and 227** and pose the question from *Words in Action #2*. Split the class into small groups and provide time for each group to prepare a list of items they believe to be helpful. Groups should share their ideas about how and why each item on their list could help English language learners.

Introduction: State the objective.

Presentation 1: 20–30 minutes
Present the word list on **pages 226 and 227**. Read *Words in Context* and have students write sentences to explain what these words mean. Ask students to use all the words from the list. Check sentences as students work and choose each student's best sentence to read to the class. Schedule enough time for students to read their sentences to the class. Lead a group discussion about what students think different items might cost in stores. After all students agree on a price, they should list these in their dictionaries or on a separate piece of paper.

Practice 1: 20–30 minutes
In groups of four, have students write skits that contain roles for two customers and two salespeople. The setting is an electronics store. The characters should use words from the list and the prices agreed on in the Presentation. Have students include technical details about the objects in their conversations. Give examples.

Evaluation 1: Observe the activity.

Application: 30–40 minutes
Stage presentations after allowing ample time for students to practice their skits. Each group presents their skit in front of the class. Encourage questions and discussion after each skit.

Project

In groups, students should design an electronics store. Ask them to do the following:

1. Name their store.
2. Create an inventory list.
3. Develop a price list.
4. Decide where each item will be placed in relation to the front door of the store.
5. Draw a brochure for the store's grand opening sale.

Level ★

Objective: Identify holidays and celebrations.

Warm-up: 10–15 minutes
Ask if any one is having a birthday soon. Even if no one does, lead the class in singing "Happy Birthday." Write a list of birthday months and days on the board and discuss how students celebrate their birthdays. Draw a birthday cake on the board and write *happy birthday*. Have students think of words related to birthdays. Write all these vocabulary words on the board. Label the cake and candles illustrated on the board. Draw a wrapped gift, balloons, and pictures of other things related to birthdays.

Introduction: State the objective.

Presentation 1: 15–20 minutes
Ask students to open their dictionaries to **pages 228 and 229.** Read and define each of the words and have students pronounce them. Encourage questions and discussion. Write *American holidays* on the board. Give an example of a holiday that is only celebrated in the United States. Write *favorite* on the board. Help students understand its meaning and have them state their favorite holidays.

Practice 1: 10–15 minutes
Individually, students should list their favorite holidays or celebrations. After ample time, have students form groups to discuss their lists. Ask groups to spend part of the time focused on holidays students consider to be important to their cultures or nationalities.

Evaluation 1: Discuss the responses as a class. Write on the board any holidays not presented in the dictionary.

Presentation 2: 8–10 minutes
Divide the items from the word list among groups. Prepare students to do Practice 2.

Practice 2: 10–15 minutes
Have small groups convene. Ask students to describe the words from the list using actions. They must create a group pantomime for each word. Tell them that they will demonstrate for their classmates.

Evaluation 2: Stage a friendly game of charades where groups guess the words pantomimed by other groups.

Application: 8–10 minutes
Students should list any other religious, national, or personal events that they celebrate with friends or family. Compare and contrast lists and discuss how celebrations differ among countries and within regions.

Holidays and Celebrations

Words in Context

People celebrate the **New Year** in different ways around the world. In Brazil, many people have **parties.** They often go to the beach after midnight and watch **fireworks.** It is also traditional to throw **flowers** into the sea. The Chinese New Year happens between January 17 and February 19. Chinese people all over the world celebrate with **parades** and **firecrackers.**

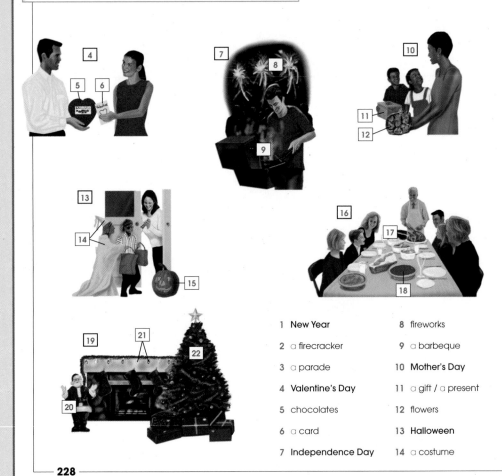

1	**New Year**	8 fireworks
2	a firecracker	9 a barbeque
3	a parade	10 **Mother's Day**
4	**Valentine's Day**	11 a gift / a present
5	chocolates	12 flowers
6	a card	13 **Halloween**
7	Independence Day	14 a costume

228

Level ★ ★

Objective: Discuss celebrations.

Warm-up: 15–18 minutes
Have small groups complete *Words in Action #1.* Discuss the results as a class.

Introduction: State the objective.

Presentation 1: 15–20 minutes
Go over each of the words from the word list on **pages 228 and 229** with students. As a class, write a sentence for each word. Discuss adjectives and focus attention on the phrases in **Word Partnerships.** Ask students for opinions about which holiday has the best food. Describe Thanksgiving in the United States. Discuss the food people customarily eat. Form groups composed of single cultures, if possible. Pose the following questions about specific holidays each group chooses:

What is the holiday?

When do you celebrate it?

Verbs

29 wrap
a present

30 light
candles

31 blow out
candles

32 open
a present

15 a jack-o-lantern

16 **Thanksgiving**

17 a turkey

18 a pumpkin pie

19 **Christmas**

20 Santa Claus

21 lights

22 a (Christmas) tree

23 a **birthday**

24 a balloon

25 a cake

26 an **anniversary**

27 a **baby shower**

28 a retirement

Word Partnerships

a birthday	party
a retirement	
a New Year's Eve	
a birthday	gift
a wedding	cake
a birthday	card
a Valentine's Day	
a Mother's Day	

Words in Action

1. Work with a group. Choose a holiday on the list. What are the different ways the people in your group celebrate this holiday? Discuss with your group.

2. Plan a birthday party for a friend.
   - What will you eat?
   - How will you decorate?
   - What gift will you give?

Who celebrates it?

How do you celebrate it?

Do you like it? Why or why not?

What food do you eat?

What time of day do you eat the meal?

Practice 1: 10–15 minutes
Students should answer these questions in complete sentences. Encourage them to incorporate adjectives.

Evaluation 1: Observe the activity.

Application: 20–30 minutes
Ask students to create new holidays individually. In describing their invented celebrations, they should answer the questions posed in the Practice. Allow time for class presentations.

Objective: Describe a favorite holiday in a paragraph.

Warm-up: 8–10 minutes
Generate a conversation involving all students. They should state their favorite holidays or celebrations and why they are favorites. Group students that made the same choices and have the groups list all the reasons this holiday or celebration ranks at the top. Groups can then present their ideas to the rest of the class.

Introduction: State the objective.

Presentation 1: 20–30 minutes
Present the word list on **pages 228 and 229**. Make sure students understand the meaning of each item and have them choose an adjective to describe each. Study *Word Partnerships* and focus attention on the adjectives. Read *Words in Context* as a class. Discuss New Year celebrations and discuss how and when different cultures celebrate it. Write one or two sample sentences describing a holiday in the dictionary picture. Consider giving this example: *On birthdays, we eat cake and blow out candles. We usually have balloons.*

Practice 1: 20–30 minutes
Ask students to write sentences describing the holidays depicted on **pages 228 and 229**. Have students write a second set of the same sentences, leaving out the words that name the celebrations. Initiate a game where other students have to fill in the blanks.

Evaluation 1: Ask for volunteers to write their sentences on the board.

Application: 30–40 minutes
Review proper paragraph structure and focus on the importance of adjectives in a description. Ask students to write a paragraph about a favorite holiday. In their paragraph, they should answer the questions *What do you do on that day?*, *When do you celebrate it?*, *Do you eat anything special?*, and *Do other countries celebrate the same holiday?* Finally, ask them to write a second paragraph about a favorite memory of this holiday with friends or family.

Project

Divide students into small groups. Read *Words in Action #2* out loud and ask students to plan the party as requested. Schedule time for groups to report to the class.

Index

Guide to Pronunciation Symbols

Vowels			Consonants		
Symbol	**Key Word**	**Pronunciation**	**Symbol**	**Key Word**	**Pronunciation**
/ɑ/	hot	/hɑt/	/b/	boy	/bɔɪ/
	far	/fɑr/	/d/	day	/deɪ/
/æ/	cat	/kæt/	/ʤ/	just	/ʤʌst/
/aɪ/	fine	/faɪn/	/f/	face	/feɪs/
/aʊ/	house	/haʊs/	/g/	get	/gɛt/
/ɛ/	bed	/bɛd/	/h/	hat	/hæt/
/eɪ/	name	/neɪm/	/k/	car	/kɑr/
/i/	need	/nid/	/l/	light	/laɪt/
/ɪ/	sit	/sɪt/	/m/	my	/maɪ/
/oʊ/	go	/goʊ/	/n/	nine	/naɪn/
/ʊ/	book	/bʊk/	/ŋ/	sing	/sɪŋ/
/u/	boot	/but/	/p/	pen	/pɛn/
/ɔ/	dog	/dɔg/	/r/	right	/raɪt/
	four	/fɔr/	/s/	see	/si/
/ɔɪ/	toy	/tɔɪ/	/t/	tea	/ti/
/ʌ/	cup	/kʌp/	/ʧ/	cheap	/ʧip/
/ɛr/	bird	/bɛrd/	/v/	vote	/voʊt/
/ə/	about	/əˈbaʊt/	/w/	west	/wɛst/
	after	/ˈæftər/	/y/	yes	/yɛs/
			/z/	zoo	/zu/
			/ð/	they	/ðeɪ/
			/θ/	think	/θɪŋk/
			/ʃ/	shoe	/ʃu/
			/ʒ/	vision	/ˈvɪʒən/

Stress				
/ˈ/	city	/ˈsɪti/	used before a syllable to show primary (main) stress

Credits

Illustrators

Denny Bond: pp. 38–39, 48–51, 90–91, 106–107, 130–131, 190–191, 202–203, 214–215 (©Denny Bond)

Higgins Bond: pp. 184–185, 212–213 (©Higgins Bond/Anita Grien)

James Edwards: pp. 9, 18–19, 34–37, 64–65, 116–117, 122–123 (©James Edwards/The Beranbaum Group)

Mike Gardner: pp. 32–33, 110–111, 145 (32–37), 146–151, 200–201, 228–229 (©Mike Gardner)

Patrick Gnan: pp. 68–69, 168–169, 178–179 (©Patrick Gnan/ IllustrationOnLine.com)

Gershom Griffith: pp. 20–21, 26–27, 100–101, 104–105, 126–127, 196 (20–25), 220–221 (©Gershom Griffith/Craven Design)

Lane Gregory: pp. 114–115 (©Lane Gregory/Gwen Walters Artist Representative)

Sharon and Joel Harris: pp. 132–133, 182–183 (©Sharon and Joel Harris/ IllustrationOnLine.com)

Phil Howe: pp. 3, 58–59, 70–71, 92–95 (©Phil Howe/IllustrationOnLine.com)

Ken Joudrey: pp. 52–53 (©Ken Joudrey/Munro Campagna)

Bob Kayganich: pp. 5, 12–13, 14 (21, 22, 31, 32), 15 (17, 18, 27, 28, 29, 30), 16 (4–6, 9–11), 17 (12–19, 24–29), 24–25, 54–55, 76–77, 96–97, 176–177, 180–181, 194 (1, 10, 11, 12), 195 (3, 5, 17, 19) (©Bob Kayganich/IllustrationOnLine.com)

Alan King: pp. 10–11, 46–47, 120–121, 142–143, 154–155, 210–211 (©Alan King/ IllustrationOnLine.com)

Barbara Kiwak: pp. 28–29, 60–61, 102–103, 108–109, 204–205 (©Barbara Kiwak/ Gwen Walters Artist Representative)

Greg LaFever: pp. 152–153, 222–224 (©Greg LaFever/Scott Hull Associates)

Mapping Specialists: pp. 44–45, 172–175 (©Mapping Specialists)

Precision Graphics: pp. 22 (24, 25), 23 (26, 27), 30–31, 42–43, 50 (10–13), 51 (14, 19), 52 (1, 2, 3, 8), 78–79, 118–119, 124–125, 134–137, 140–141, 158–159, 162 (1, 2), 164–167, 186–189, 201 (5–13), 218–219, 227 (26–31) (©Precision Graphics)

John Schreiner: pp. 80–81, 86–87 (©John Schreiner/IllustrationOnLine.com)

Dave Schweitzer: pp. 208–209 (©Dave Schweitzer/Munro Campagna)

Beryl Simon: pp. 170–171 (©Beryl Simon)

Carol Stutz: pp. 198–199, 216–217 (©Carol Stutz)

Gerad Taylor: pp. 6–7, 66–67, 72–75, 88–89, 98–99, 128–129, 192–193 (©Gerad Taylor/IllustrationOnLine)

Gary Torrisi: pp. 22–23, 138–139, 156–157 (©Gary Torrisi/Gwen Walters Artist Representative)

Meryl Treatner: pp. 56–57, 112–113 (©Meryl Treatner/Chris Tugeau)

Photos

All photographs not otherwise credited are owned by ©Thomson/ELT.

Unit One UNIT ICON CREDIT: ©Tom Grill/CORBIS; 2 all: ©Hemera Photo-Objects; 3 center: ©Hemera Photo-Objects; 4 center: ©Hemera Photo-Objects; 4 bottom: ©Royalty-Free/CORBIS; 5 all: ©Hemera Photo-Objects; 6 bottom: ©F.SCHLUSSER.PHOTOLINK/Getty; 8 bottom: ©C Squared Studios/Getty; 14 most: ©Hemera Photo-Objects; 14 (12): ©Thinkstock LLC/Index Stock Imagery, Inc.; 14 (14): ©Louis K. Meisel Gallery/CORBIS; 14 (33): ©Paul Sonders/CORBIS; 14 (34): ©Tom Brakefield/CORBIS; 15 (3): ©Dmitri Iundt/CORBIS; 15 (4): ©Randy Faris/CORBIS; 15 (5, 6, 27): ©John Coletti; 15 (15, 16): ©C Squared Studios/Getty; 15 (25): ©Melissa Goodrum; 15 (26): ©Catherine Ledner/Stone/Getty; 15 (35, 36): ©Jacque Denzier Parker/Index Stock Imagery; 15 (37, 38, 39, 40): ©Hemera Photo-Objects; 16 left: ©Scott Baxter/Getty; 16 center: ©David Buffington/Photodisc Green/Getty; 17 bottom left: ©COMSTOCK Images

Unit Two UNIT ICON CREDIT: ©Royalty-Free/CORBIS; 24 top right: ©Hemera Photo-Objects; 24 bottom left: ©David Shopper/Index Stock Imagery, Inc.

Unit Three UNIT ICON CREDIT: ©Thinkstock/Getty; 27: ©Royalty-Free/CORBIS; 29 top left: ©SW Productions/Photodisc Green/Getty; 29 top right: ©Royalty-Free/CORBIS; 29 center left: ©Jerry Koontz/Index Stock Imagery, Inc.; 29 center right: ©Zefa Visual Media-Germany/Index Stock Imagery, Inc.; 29 bottom left (small): ©Chris Carroll; 29 bottom left (big): ©Hemera Photo-Objects; 29 bottom right (small): ©Ariel Skelley/CORBIS; 29 bottom right (big): ©Royalty-Free/CORBIS

Unit Four UNIT ICON CREDIT: ©Jose Luis Pelaez, Inc./CORBIS; 40 (1): ©Ghislain & Marie David de Lossy/The Image Bank/Getty; 40 (7): ©Stewart Cohen/Index Stock Imagery, Inc.; 40 (8, 16, 18, 20): ©Hemera Photo-Objects; 40 (9): ©Michael Newman/PhotoEdit; 40 (10): ©Jerry Tobias/CORBIS; 40 (15): ©David Young-Wolff/PhotoEdit; 40 (17): ©Patrik Giardino/CORBIS; 40 (19): ©Don Romero/Index Stock Imagery, Inc.; 41 (3): ©Francisco Cruz/SuperStock; 41 (4, 11, 22): ©Hemera Photo-Objects; 41 (5): ©GeoStock/Photodisc Green/Getty; 41 (13): ©SW Productions/Index Stock Imagery, Inc.; 41 (14): ©SuperStock; 41 (21): ©Morocco Flowers/Index Stock Imagery, Inc.; 41 (23): ©Steve Prezant/CORBIS; 41 (24): ©Myrleen Ferguson Cate/PhotoEdit; 42 top: ©Shuji Kobayashi/Stone/Getty; 42 center: ©Image Source/SuperStock; 42 bottom: ©Michael Newman/PhotoEdit; 44 top left: ©Hemera Photo-Objects; 44 top right: ©Springfield Photography/Alamy; 44 bottom left: ©Peter Guttman/CORBIS; 44 bottom right: ©Hemera Photo-Objects; 45 all: ©Hemera Photo-Objects

Unit Five UNIT ICON CREDIT: ©Photodisc Collection/Getty; 54: ©Mitchell Gerber/CORBIS; 56 top right: ©Hemera Photo-Objects; 56 center left: ©Willie Holdman/Index Stock Imagery Inc.; 56 center right: ©Stewart Cohen/Taxi/Getty; 56 bottom left: ©Chris Carroll/CORBIS; 56 bottom right: ©Hemera Photo-Objects

Unit Six UNIT ICON CREDIT: ©Cydney Conger/CORBIS; 62 (1): ©Cydney Conger/CORBIS; 62 (2): ©Dean Conger/CORBIS; 62 (3): ©Bob Krist/CORBIS; 62 (4): ©Elfi Kluck/Index Stock Imagery Inc.; 62 (5): ©Vince Streano/CORBIS; 62 (6): ©Craig Lovell/CORBIS; 62 (7): ©Michael Newman/PhotoEdit; 62 (8): ©RO-MA Stock/Index Stock Imagery Inc.; 62 (9, 10): ©Hemera Photo-Objects; 62 (11): ©Massimo Listri/CORBIS; 62 (12): ©Joseph Sohm; Visions of America/CORBIS; 62 (13): ©Reinhard Eisele/CORBIS; 62 (15): ©Yvette Cardozo/Index Stock Imagery Inc.; 62 (16): ©Philip Coblentz/Brand X Pictures; 62 (17): ©Phil Cantor/SuperStock; 63 (14): ©Pawel Libera/CORBIS; 63 (18): ©Rene Sheret/Stone/Getty; 63 (19): ©Mitch Diamond/Index Stock Imagery Inc.; 63 (20): ©Anselm Spring/Image Bank/Getty; 63 (21): ©Royalty-Free/CORBIS; 63 (22): ©Joseph Sohm; ChromoSohm Inc./CORBIS; 63 (23): ©Michael S. Yamashita/CORBIS; 67: ©Hemera Photo-Objects

Unit Seven UNIT ICON CREDIT: ©Burke-Triolo Pruductions/Getty; 82–85 most: ©Hemera Photo-Objects; 82 (5): ©Photodisc Collection/Getty; 82 (11): ©Seide Preis/Getty; 82 (17): ©Royalty-Free/CORBIS; 82 (24): ©Picture Arts/CORBIS; 82 (27): ©Keith Seaman/FoodPix; 82 (33): ©Maximilian Stock, LTD/FoodPix; 83 (7): ©Photodisc Inc./Getty; 83 (28): ©Paul Poplis/FoodPix; 84 (2): ©Judd Pilossof/FoodPix; 84 (9, 18): ©Royalty-Free/CORBIS; 84 (10): ©John Coletti; 84 (20): ©Picture Arts/CORBIS; 84 (21): ©Evan Sklar/Food Pix; 84 (22): ©Cindy Jones/FoodPix; 84 (30): ©Craig Orsini/Index Stock Imagery Inc.; 85 (25): ©Picture Arts/CORBIS

Unit Eight UNIT ICON CREDIT: ©C Squared Studios/Getty; 97 bottom right: ©Hemera Photo-Objects; 112 (1, 10): Veer Incorporated; 112 (2): © Royalty-Free Division/Masterfile; 112 (3): ©Nick Koudis/Getty; 112 (4): ©Barry David Marcus/SuperStock; 112 (6): ©Jules Frazier/Getty; 112 (7): ©D. Boone/CORBIS; 112 (11): ©Stacy Gold/National Geographic/Getty; 113 (5): ©Royalty-Free/CORBIS; 113 (8): ©Veer Incorporated; 113 (9): ©Reuters/CORBIS; 113 (12): ©Francisco Rojo Alvarez/Getty

Unit Nine UNIT ICON CREDIT: ©Wes Thompson/CORBIS

Unit Ten UNIT ICON CREDIT: ©Herrmann/Starke/CORBIS; 140 top center: ©Hemera Photo-Objects; 142 all: ©Hemera Photo-Objects; 144 (1): ©Amy Etra/PhotoEdit; 144 (2, 3, 12, 14, 15): ©Photodisc Collection/Getty; 144 (4, 7, 13): ©Hemera Photo-Objects; 144 (5, 8, 10, 11): ©Hemera Photo-Objects; 144 (6): ©Siede Preis/Photodisc Green/Getty; 144 (9): ©Joe Atlas/Brand X Pictures; 145 top left: ©Stockbyte/Ablestock; 145 (16): ©Michael Newman/PhotoEdit; 145 (17, 20, 23, 26, 28): ©John Coletti; 145 (18): ©COMSTOCK Images; 145 (19, 21, 24, 25, 27): ©Hemera Photo-Objects; 145 (22): ©C Squared Studios/Photodisc Green/Getty; 145 (29, 30, 31): ©Joe Atlas/Brand X Pictures

Unit Eleven UNIT ICON CREDIT: ©PictureNet/CORBIS; 160–163 most: ©Hemera Photo-Objects; 160 (1, 4, 7, 18): ©COMSTOCK Images; 160 (3): ©C Squared Studios/Photodisc Green/Getty; 160 (9): ©Seide Preis/Photodisc Green/Getty; 160 (12): ©Photodisc Green/Getty; 161 (24, 30): ©C Squared Studios/Photodisc Green/Getty; 161 (26): ©Royalty-Free/CORBIS; 161 (32): ©Stockbyte; 162 (3): ©Seide Preis/Photodisc Green/Getty; 162 (4, 5, 28): ©John Coletti; 162 (6): ©Patrick Olear/Photo Edit; 162 (7, 14, 17): ©C Squared Studios/Photodisc Green/Getty; 162 (8): ©Jules Frazier/Getty; 162 (12): ©COMSTOCK Images; 163 (18): ©Royalty-Free/CORBIS; 163 (19, 29): ©John Coletti; 163 (20, 22, 24): ©Seide Preis/Photodisc Green/Getty; 163 (30): ©Widstock/Alamy

Unit Twelve UNIT ICON CREDIT: ©L. Clarke/CORBIS; 174: ©Digital Vision

Unit Thirteen UNIT ICON CREDIT: ©Digital Vision/Getty; 183 (25): ©Hemera Photo-Objects; 184 (1): ©Hemera Photo-Objects; 186 (7): ©Photodisc Collection/Getty; 191 (29): ©Jules Frazier/Getty

Unit Fourteen UNIT ICON CREDIT: ©Don Farrall/Getty; 194 (8, 14): ©Hemera Photo-Objects; 194 (7): ©Dennis MacDonald/PhotoEdit; 194 (7): ©Thinkstock LLC/Index Stock Imagery, Inc.; 194 (13): ©Seide Preis/Photodisc Green/Getty; 195 (18, 20, 21, 22, 27): ©Hemera Photo-Objects; 195 (15): ©Widstock/Alamy; 195 (23, 24, 25, 26): ©Seide Preis/Photodisc Green/Getty; 195 (28, 30): ©COMSTOCK Images; 195 (29): ©TRBfoto/Photodisc Green/Getty

Unit Fifteen UNIT ICON CREDIT: ©Don Farrall/Getty; 203: ©Hemera Photo-Objects; 206–207 most: ©Hemera Photo-Objects; 206 (1, 6, 22): ©Photodisc Collection/Getty; 206 (8, 18, 19): ©C Squared Studios/Photodisc Green/Getty; 207 (3, 13, 15, 16, 17, 26, 28): ©Photodisc Collection/Getty; 207 (2): ©Spencer Grant/PhotoEdit; 207 (27): ©Photodisc Green/Getty

Unit Sixteen UNIT ICON CREDIT: ©Digital Vision/Getty; 212 (1): ©Hemera Photo-Objects; 223 (25): ©Hemera Photo-Objects; 224–226 most: ©Hemera Photo-Objects; 224 (1): ©Royalty-Free/CORBIS; 224 (22): ©John Coletti; 225 (16): ©C Squared Studios/Getty; 225 (16): ©ACE STOCK LTD/Alamy; 225 (19): ©Erin Garvey/Index Stock Imagery, Inc.; 226 (1): ©C Squared Studios/Getty; 226 (3): ©COMSTOCK Images; 226 (7): ©F.Schlusser/PhotoLink/Getty; 227 most: ©COMSTOCK Images; 227 (9): ©Mediacolor's/Alamy; 227 (14, 15, 19, 21, 23): ©Hemera Photo-Objects; 227 (20): ©Judith Collins/Alamy; 227 (24, 25): ©John Coletti